Macroeconomics in Africa

Charles Harvey

Fellow of Institute of Development Studies, University of Sussex

Revised Pan-African Edition

MACMILLAN

First edition published by Heinemann Educational Books Ltd 1977
Revised Pan-African edition first published 1985
Reprinted 1989, 1990

Published by MACMILLAN EDUCATION LTD
London and Basingstoke
Associated companies and representatives in Accra, Auckland, Delhi, Dublin, Gaborone, Hamburg, Harare, Hong Kong, Kuala Lumpur, Lagos, Manzini, Melbourne, Mexico City, Nairobi, New York, Singapore, Tokyo

ISBN 0–333–40714–8

Printed in Hong Kong

British Library Cataloguing in Publication Data
Harvey, Charles, *1937–*
Macroeconomics in Africa.—Rev. Pan-African ed.
1. Macroeconomics
I. Title
339 HB171

Contents

List of Tables

List of Figures

Preface to Second Edition

When the first edition of this book was written, I had only worked in one African country, Zambia, and so only felt confident in using Zambian macroeconomic examples. Since then I have worked for three years in Botswana, for much shorter periods in Sierra Leone, Senegal, Uganda and Malawi, and visited a number of other countries for conferences and to talk to people in universities, governments and central banks. Although this clearly does not enable me to write with authority about all the English-speaking economies in Sub-Saharan Africa, I have felt rather more confident of being able to draw examples from a wider range of countries. Having used the book myself while teaching at the University in Botswana, and from the comments of others who have used it for teaching, it is also clear that the constant references to one country were irritating.

Circumstances have also changed. At the time of writing most African economies are suffering from the worst world economic recession since the Second World War. The second edition thus places rather more emphasis on the problems created by balance of payments deficits. Other changes include a much greater use of balance sheets in the chapter on money and banking, and a greater use of graphs.

Users of this second edition should not be deceived by the generalising of many statements. Phrases such as 'in most African economies' and 'usually' or 'normally' should alert the reader to check whether what is being said applies to the local economy, in current circumstances. It may not. But I remain confident that it will be easier to apply the analysis of this book to African situations than the analysis of 'Western' texts, which are based on industrial economies while purporting to be universally applicable.

October 1983

Preface to First Edition

All good macroeconomic text books are set in the context of a particular economy. It is almost impossible to discuss the measurement of national income or the workings of the monetary system, for example, without reference to particular national income figures and monetary institutions. This alone makes it difficult to teach macroeconomics in anglophone Africa using British or American textbooks. The student is forced to read and learn a great deal about the British or American economy in order to understand the text; and the teacher must spend a great deal of time explaining the differences between Western and African conditions. *Some* comparison of this sort is probably valuable, but a little goes a long way.

However, much more serious problems are created by using Western textbooks. Basically, they deal extensively with problems of little or no relevance to Africa, and discuss very little or ignore completely problems which are of very great if not fundamental importance in Africa. To some extent this is merely a matter of balance–the need is for less about industry, more about agriculture and the export sector. From an African point of view too much attention is given in Western texts to domestic profit-seeking investment as a source of fluctuations in national income, whereas in Africa export prices, foreign investment, fluctuations in agricultural supply are often more important.

To some extent, though, it is more than a matter of balance. The structure of African economies is so fundamentally different in some respects from the structure of, say, the British economy, that parts of established theory simply do not apply and may indeed be positively misleading.

For example, the emphases on the relationship between savings and investment, on liquidity preference, on the interest rate as a determinant of investment, all depend on the existence of well-developed capital markets and a variety of financial intermediaries which do not exist in African economies. There are thus a series of links, in the basic macroeconomic model of Western texts, which do not exist in African conditions.

A second example: rising demand for manufactured products would, according to Western theory, induce investment in increased production facilities. In Africa it is more likely to induce increases in imported inputs and in profits sent out of the country, if manufacturing is foreign-owned.

These criticisms are relatively easy to make. The problems lie in deciding how to handle them in a textbook. There are three rough categories.

(1) Situations where the student can usefully learn existing theory, for example how to measure national income in the modern sector, but must also learn additional material, in this example how to measure and compare subsistence income. This results in very long chapters.

(2) Situations where the basic type of analysis is useful, but must be applied to African situations which do not occur in industrialised economies and are thus not treated in Western textbooks—for example national income analysis applied to the doubling of export prices over a very short period.

(3) Situations where 'Western' theory is thoroughly inappropriate and the text must really start from scratch with a new approach, in order to avoid a major learning and teaching effort for the acquisition of misleading theories—for example investment theory. Existing theory must of course be mentioned in these cases, but preferably in a very minor way at the end, when more appropriate ideas have already been thoroughly discussed.

Clearly the last category is hardest to handle. It can be very damaging if a student starts off with the wrong set of ideas. At the same time it may be unfair to put a new approach into something called a textbook. This problem is made worse by the fact that new theories are often hard to test, because official statistics are collected to serve old-established theories. On the whole I have been slightly cautious. It is to be hoped that future texts will be able to be more adventurous as more research results become available.

The book is based on a second-year course in macroeconomics which I taught for four years at the University of Zambia. Although other African economies are mentioned in making comparisons and in using research results, the book is based to a considerable extent on the Zambian economy. It seemed much better to rethink macroeconomic theory from a relatively thorough knowledge of one economy than to try and do so from a more superficial knowledge of several. After all it was the indiscriminate application of 'English' theory to African economies, without making clear that industrialised economies are a very 'special case'[1] with their own (usually unstated) sets of assumptions, that caused all the trouble in the first place. Clearly I did not want to fall into the same trap. However, If Zambia is something of a special case in Africa, I am confident that it will be much easier to adapt the analysis of this book to the conditions of, say, Malawi or Nigeria than to adapt the analysis of a typical Western text. In short, this book is written with English-speaking African students in mind; the use of a mainly Zambian context will have reduced the analytical errors. Teachers both in Zambia and elsewhere will in any case use local and/or updated material for their own teaching.

The choice of subject matter is fairly conventional. The book covers the 'usual' macroeconomic topics except that trade cycle theory is excluded. I have assumed that students have done an elementary introductory course in economics, although the book could probably be read with only a little difficulty by a beginner. A knowledge of simple algebra and graphs is also assumed—without it no student can pretend to even a remotely serious study of the subject.[2] It has also been assumed that university economics courses go on to cover important subjects in greater depth in the third (and fourth) years—this one book cannot cover everything.

NOTES

1 The reference is to Dudley Seers, 'The Limitations of the Special Case', *Bulletin of the Oxford Institute of Economics and Statistics*, May 1973, reprinted in K. Martin and J. Knapp (eds). *The Teaching of Development Economics*, London, Frank Cass, 1967.

2 See my article 'Mathematics and the teaching of economics' in I. Livingstone *et al.* (eds), *The Teaching of Economics in Africa*, London, Chatto and Windus for Sussex University Press, 1973.

Acknowledgements for the Second Edition

Students who have used the first edition have been very helpful in providing both encouragement and constructive criticism, especially students at the University in Botswana in the late 1970s. Various reviewers and publishers' readers inspired changes in this second edition. Michael Hubbard, of the University of Botswana, provided particularly helpful suggestions, arising from a very thorough understanding of both the economic issues and the problems of teaching. Pat Lacey organised the preparation of the book for publication with great good humour, helped particularly by Sonia Hill and Sue Kirwan (formerly Sue Humphrey, who also helped with the first edition).

Acknowledgements for the First Edition

The original encouragement to write the book came from correspondence students at the University of Zambia for whom I first wrote up my lectures. Colleagues who gave tutorials in the course, especially Tom Warke, supplied valuable feedback and criticism. Robert Baker and James Fry, who have taught the course more recently, also provided helpful comments; Percy Selwyn, Alex Tweedie and Dudley Seers read some chapters with great care, and Reg Green read nearly all of it, covering the draft in blunt-pencilled, pointed comments. Christine Smith agreed to act as a student guinea-pig, in the absence of a class taking the course, and also did some work on Zambian figures for the book; her work was both helpful and encouraging. Sue Humphrey typed all of it more than once, drew most of the graphs and never looked more than slightly disapproving. Patience Nyadza typed the index quickly and efficiently. Finally, my wife, by virtually never mentioning it, enabled me to forget it when I was at home.

1 *Introduction*

1 *The difference between macroeconomics and microeconomics*

The distinction between macroeconomics and microeconomics is more than just a casual and convenient division of economics into two parts. Macroeconomics is the study of large aggregates (*makros* is the Greek word for large) such as national income, aggregate demand and supply, aggregate consumption and investment. Because these aggregates are large in relation to the national economy, a change in one aggregate tends to affect all the others.

For example, if wages rise, wage-earners will spend more. This in turn will increase the demand for goods and services, which will increase employment, profits, imports and possibly prices. As a result, tax revenue will increase and government may decide to spend more; wages may rise further as a result of increasing demand for labour or as a result of trade union activity to get higher wages to offset price rises. Meanwhile the availability of bank credit might be reduced by these changes, which in turn would prevent further changes from taking place; and increasing demand for imports and rising prices might cause the government to take some action to protect the balance of payments.

Thus in macroeconomic analysis it is important to take account of the effect of changes in one variable on all the other variables; and to take account of 'feedback', that is, that a change in one variable may eventually feed back on to that variable itself. In the example given, a change in wages affected not only a number of other macroeconomic variables, but also fed back in the form of further changes in wages.

Microeconomics, on the other hand, is the study of small individual parts of the economy (*mikros* is the Greek word for small) where it is reasonable to assume that there is no feedback. For example if there is an increase in the wages of people making shoes, the cost of shoemaking increases and the price of shoes may go up or the profits of shoe-making firms may go down, or both. But it is reasonable to assume that the increased incomes of the shoe-workers do not cause a significant increase in the demand for shoes, because the shoe-workers are a very small proportion of the total number of people who buy shoes. In addition, any increase in the price of shoes has a negligible effect on the general price level and is not likely, therefore, to cause the shoe-workers to demand further wage increases. In other words it is reasonable to assume, in studying a small, microeconomic sector of the economy, that there are no feedback effects.

Another way of putting the distinction between microeconomics and macroeconomics is to say that in microeconomics one can assume '*ceteris paribus*' (which is Latin for 'other things being equal'). This means that one analyses a small sector of the economy on the assumption that changes in that sector are too small to affect the rest of the economy. One can therefore assume all other factors unchanged (or 'equal'). In macroeconomics it is normally quite wrong to assume *ceteris paribus*—indeed the main purpose of macroeconomic analysis is to examine how 'other things' change in response to each other.

The three main macroeconomic aggregates are demand, supply, and income.[1] If total demand increases, total supply will increase or prices will increase. In either case, income rises. If income rises then people with increased incomes will try and demand more goods and services; that is, demand increases again. There is thus a continuous flow of causation:

DEMAND → SUPPLY AND PRICES → INCOME → DEMAND, etc.

Again pointing out the important difference between macro and micro, in microeconomics the same flow of causation looks like this:

DEMAND FOR SHOES → SUPPLY OF SHOES AND PRICE OF SHOES → INCOMES OF SHOE-MAKERS

but the incomes of shoe-makers do *not* significantly affect the demand for shoes, so that the chain of causation is broken and there is no feedback effect.

Deciding which is a macro and which a microeconomic variable is not always easy; furthermore there is some variation from country to country. For example, the price of any particular commodity is clearly a microeconomic variable in most countries. In African economies, one or two export commodities account for a large proportion of export earnings; and, because international trade is so important, the dominant export commodities can also account for a large proportion of national income. For example, in Zambia copper has accounted for as much as 92% of exports and 38% of national income;[2] although Zambia is something of an extreme case, in nearly all the economies covered in Table 1.1, one or two commodities are so important that anything to do with their prices or levels of output must clearly be treated as a macroeconomic event.

Table 1.1 Importance of leading export commodities, 1976–80

Country	*Leading export*	*Share of leading export in total exports (%)*	*Share of leading export in Gross National Product (%)*
Botswana	Diamonds[a]	34–61	16–40[b]
Gambia	Groundnuts	54–91	26–40
Ghana	Cocoa	54–63[c]	6–11[d]
Kenya	Coffee	21–41	3–11[b]
Lesotho	Wool & mohair[e]	26–51[c]	3[f]
Malawi	Tobacco	43–55	9–12
Mauritius	Sugar	67–85[b]	24–41[b]
Nigeria	Petroleum	90–95	21–34[c]
Sierra Leone	Diamonds[g]	43–60	8–12[b]
Sudan	Cotton	45–65	3–6[c]
Swaziland	Sugar	32–56[b]	19–41[d]
Tanzania	Coffee	27–42	3–6[b]
Uganda	Coffee	74–98[b]	4–10[c]
Zambia	Copper	83–92[b]	28–38[b]
Zimbabwe	Tobacco	11–16[h]	3–4[i]

NOTES

a Botswana's leading exports in 1976 were copper nickel matte (34% of exports) and beef (28%) with diamonds in third place (24%). The leading export was diamonds thereafter.

b 1975–79

c 1974–78

d 1973–77

e Exports of *goods* from Lesotho earn only about 10% of the cost of imports; the main source of foreign exchange is remittances from migrant workers ('net factor income from abroad' was 76% of the cost of imports and 37% of GNP in 1974).

f 1974

g These figures underestimate the importance of diamond exports in most years because large quantities of diamonds are smuggled out of the country, mainly through Liberia.

h 1978–80 (earlier figures not available)

i 1978–79.

j For similar information for other African countries see the sources quoted below. See also World Bank *Accelerated Development in Sub-Saharan Africa: An Agenda for Action* (1981), Table 10 'Principal merchandise exports' which shows Africa's main commodity exports and which country is the leading exporter in each case; and Table 14 'Exports: Commodity Concentration and Fluctuation in Values' which shows for each country the share in total exports of the three leading commodities in 1961 and 1976–78, and an index of fluctuations in export earnings in 1955–65 and 1965–79.

Sources: *International Financial Statistics, Zimbabwe Monthly Digest of Statistics.*

Similarly, in a rich country like the USA, the price of any one foodstuff is very much a microeconomic variable. Americans are mostly rich enough to enjoy a varied diet and to spend quite a small proportion of their incomes on food. In poor countries the staple food is such an important part of the total expenditure of the urban and rural poor, and such an important part of the income of the rural poor, that anything affecting its production and price is probably best treated as a macroeconomic factor. Thus the prices paid to farmers for maize, for example, and the prices paid by consumers for maize meal are macroeconomic variables in countries where maize is the staple food, both because of the impact on income and welfare, and because of the effect on wages of a change in basic food prices. Indeed, basic food prices are often determined by governments, sometimes with a subsidy to the consumer, precisely because of their great importance to the majority of the population.

2 *The circular flow of income*

The flow of money from demand to supply and prices, and back into people's pockets as income, is often called the 'circular flow of income'. Because the income being discussed is aggregate income in the whole economy, or national income, macroeconomics is often called 'national income analysis'.

There are three main 'leakages' out of the circular flow of income. The demand for goods and services is not *all* satisfied by production within the economy–some demand is met by imports. Buying imports increases the incomes of foreigners. In a small economy, like any of those in Africa, the amount of income created for foreigners by an increase in imports is highly unlikely to cause a noticeable increase in the demand for a country's exports. Even in the case of Nigeria, whose economy is relatively large by African standards, a *doubling* of imports would add only 0.8% to world trade: this would not add significantly to the demand for Nigerian exports. The next largest importer among the countries of Table 1.1 accounts for just over 0.1% of world trade. In other words, there are negligible feedback effects from an increase in imports in an African economy, so that imports create a *leakage* out of the circular flow of income. For most countries in fact it is true that their demand for imports is so small in relation to world trade that it is reasonable to assume *ceteris paribus*, or no feedback effects from an increase in imports. Only in the case of Britain in the nineteenth century, when two-thirds of international trade was British, or the USA in the twentieth century (and perhaps Japan in the last part of the twentieth century), would it be necessary to investigate the feedback effects on the demand for exports, of an increase in imports. The flow of causation now looks like this:

```
           ↗ DOMESTIC SUPPLY  ↘
DEMAND  →  DOMESTIC PRICES   →  INCOME  →  DEMAND, etc.
           ↘ IMPORTS ■
```

The second main leakage arises because not all increases in income result immediately in increased spending. Savings also increase. If people whose incomes increase bury money in the ground, or keep it under the bed, or deposit money in a bank or a building society or the Post Office, then demand remains unaffected by the amount of money that is saved, *provided that* the savings institutions do not immediately lend the money, for spending by someone else. If, say, the bank in which savings are deposited lends the money to people to buy cars, to businesses to buy new equipment and to the government to spend more than it has received in taxes, then the savings leakage from the circular flow of income is offset by a new injection into demand caused by spending out of borrowed money. But there is not a direct connection between the amount of savings, on the one hand, and the amount of spending financed by lending, on the other hand: savings, therefore, are a leakage out of the circular flow of income, and lending by banks and other financial institutions is an injection into the circular flow. In addition, some savings may be invested directly by the saver, for example a business may retain some profits, for investment in new buildings and equipment. The flow of causation now looks like this:

```
                                LENDING↘
           ↗ DOMESTIC SUPPLY ↘          ↗ DEMAND  →  etc.
DEMAND  →  PRICES ──────────→  INCOME
           ↘ IMPORTS ■                  ↘ SAVINGS ■
```

The third main leakage is taxation. If income increases, people usually find themselves paying more tax. In Africa, income tax is paid by only a small proportion of people. But other forms of taxes on income, such as the Personal Levy in Zambia and Local Government Tax in Botswana are levied on all wage earners; and many wage earners also pay compulsory contributions into various forms of provident fund. The latter are not strictly a tax, because contributions are returnable to contributors at a later date; but the macroeconomic effect is the same, because contributions are compulsory and cannot therefore be spent, and because this leakage increases as income increases.

Companies also pay increased tax if their profits increase. In addition to taxes on income, the government receives more revenue from increased spending. Cigarettes and alcoholic drinks are taxed, so that if, as is very likely, people spend part of increases in income on cigarettes and beer, some of the money leaks out of the circular flow of income to the government, rather than increasing the incomes of bar-owners and the people who make cigarettes and brew beer. A wide range of imported goods is also taxed, so that money spent on imports, especially luxury imports like big cars which carry exceptionally high tax rates, causes a flow of income to the government as well as to foreign manufacturers.

Now obviously if government promptly spends every increase in its revenue from taxes then tax is not really a leakage from the circular flow of income. In practice, the connection between tax receipts and spending by government is not very close *in the short term*. The government's spending plans cannot usually be changed quickly in response to changes in tax receipts–civil servants' salaries, for example, which are a large part of government spending, are normally only changed as a result of a fairly lengthy review procedure, and the number of civil servants employed changes fairly slowly too. Spending on development projects may tend to increase as tax revenue rises, and decrease as tax revenue falls, but again not in the short term because it takes some time to start or stop the spending of money on development projects. In the long term, tax revenue is a very important determinant of government spending, although even in the long term there are other determining factors, such as aid receipts, government borrowing and creation of money.[3]

Allowing for the existence of government alters the flow of causation to look like this:

GOVERNMENT SPENDING (↓ DEMAND)
INVESTMENT FROM SAVINGS (↘ DEMAND)
↗ DOMESTIC SUPPLY ↘ LENDING (↘ DEMAND)
DEMAND → DOMESTIC PRICES → INCOME → DEMAND → etc.
↘ IMPORTS ■   INCOME → SAVINGS ■
↘ TAXATION (on goods) ■   INCOME → TAXATION ■ (on income)

Government spending is shown as an independent factor affecting demand, to indicate that it is not directly affected in the short term by changes in tax revenue, and that it can increase quite independently of tax revenue, through government borrowing for example.

The final addition to demand comes from exports. Historically, exports have been the most important source of monetary demand in African economies, and still are in some countries. Furthermore, fluctuations in export demand are very important in determining what happens in African economies, because so much of economic activity is dependent on the foreign exchange earned by exports and the taxes paid by exporters. A great deal of export fluctuation is outside the control of the African countries themselves, because export prices–of such things as coffee, copper, tobacco, cotton, sugar, even diamonds and petroleum–are determined by world markets or by other outside forces.[4] This is in sharp contrast to countries which export manufactured goods, where domestic events, for example rising costs, affect the demand for exports via changes in export prices. The final version of the circular flow of income now looks like this:

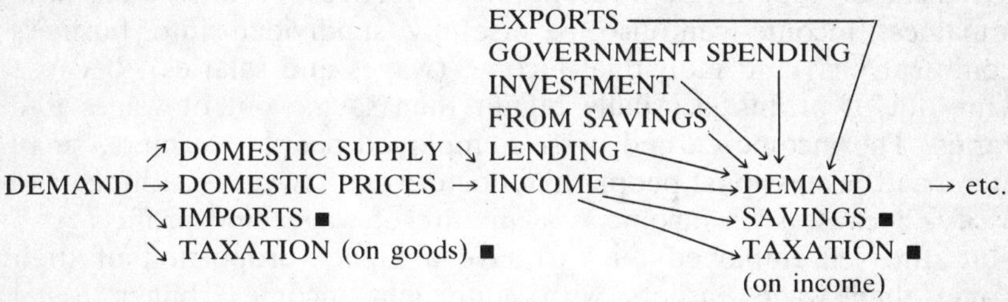

3 *The main macroeconomic aggregates*

The above formulation yields most of the main components of demand and supply. Demand is made up of:

- i Consumer demand (consumption–that is, the demand for food, clothing and other day-to-day necessities by individuals, paid for mainly out of income)
- ii Investment demand–that is, the demand for long-lasting goods such as buildings and machinery, roads and dams, paid for mainly out of savings and borrowing
- iii Government demand–that is, spending by government in providing services such as defence and education, paid for mainly out of taxes
- iv Export demand–that is, in Africa, the demand for export commodities such as tobacco and cotton by foreign buyers.

Supply is split into only two main components, namely:

- a Domestic (home) production
- b Imports.

The subdivisions of demand are used because the factors influencing consumption, investment, government spending and export demand are clearly very different. The subdivisions of supply are used because domestic production generates domestic income, whereas imports generate income for foreigners. Clearly the two types of supply have quite different feedback effects.

Further subdivisions of demand and supply are frequently used: for example, small farmers and urban wage earners tend to have different consumption habits, so it is sometimes useful to treat them separately.

Investment can usefully be subdivided into investment by individuals (mainly in housing) and investment by firms (mainly in productive buildings and machinery). Firms can be subdivided further into large and small, or locally owned and foreign-owned, as for example in chapter 7, where the investment behaviour of different types of firm is discussed. For the moment, however, the analysis will be mainly confined to the four main subdivisions of demand and the two of supply.

Because of the different economic objectives of individuals and companies, income can also be usefully subdivided into business income (profits) and individual income (wages and salaries), because saving out of profits is usually higher than saving out of wages and salaries. The income earned by self-employed people–farmers, small traders and professional people like doctors and lawyers–is difficult to classify, because such income is a mixture of wages and profits. As a result, the self-employed tend to save a higher proportion of their income than wage earners with equivalent incomes, but a lower proportion than is saved out of large-scale business profits.

The subdivisions of demand, supply and income, and the variables which may be of particular interest in any particular African economy such as the prices of the staple food and the main export commodity, are not the only important macroeconomic variables. From the diagrams of the circular flow of income it is clear, for example, that anything affecting the general level of prices must also be important–such as wages (and therefore trade unions and the labour market) and the prices charged by the foreign producers who supply imports. In addition, African economies still produce only a small range of goods, so that any source of foreign exchange is important in determining the level of income, including not only export earnings, but also inflows of money from foreign borrowing, aid and foreign investment, and the outflows that result. And all the factors affecting the amount of spending out of money borrowed from within the economy, such as interest rates and the supply of credit, must also be studied.

4 *Aggregates and large numbers–an advantage of macroeconomics*

One further point should be made about working with economic aggregates. An aggregate such as consumption is made up of the consumption spending of a very large number of individuals. It is likely therefore that the sort of random factors which can affect micro-economic decisions will cancel out. For example, the spending of an individual will be the result not only of his income, savings and borrowing ability, but also of special factors such as the birth of a child, the death of a relative, the prospect of losing his job. These special factors would make it very difficult to forecast an individual's spending in any particular year. But when the spending of large numbers of people is aggregated, most of these special factors cancel out. One man spends more because of a funeral, another spends less because he is ill. Furthermore, deaths, births, marriages, illnesses all tend to be much the same from year to year unless some 'macroevent' occurs, universal enough to affect large numbers of people, such as a drought or an epidemic. It is thus probable that changes in aggregates can be analysed without having to pay attention to random personal events. The tendency for random events to offset each other if the numbers involved are very large is sometimes called the 'law of large numbers'.

Another advantage of macroeconomics is that while any particular individual may be able to get credit from his friends, not everyone can do this, since someone must be doing the lending. In fact such private lending and borrowing must by definition cancel out over the community as a whole, so that spending out of borrowed funds can be analysed in terms of changes in the total amount of institutional credit, from domestic banks and other financial institutions, and from international lenders, while ignoring interpersonal loans.

Similarly, while an individual farmer can always increase his holding of land, and an individual employer can get more skilled labour, all farmers and all employers cannot get more land and more skilled labour at the same time unless there is an unused supply of these resources.

Not all macroeconomic aggregates are subject to the so-called law of large numbers, however. Investment, especially in a small economy, is made up of a relatively small number of large projects. This is especially true of many government investments, which are undertaken by government partly because they are so large, as for instance large hydroelectric schemes like Kafue in Zambia and Volta in Ghana, and the Tanzam railway. A great deal of private sector investment is also undertaken in large, discrete amounts, by a small number of companies—particularly large-scale mining developments, but also a great deal of investment in manufacturing. In trying to explain such investments it is thus very necessary to take account of factors which are special to a particular investment decision, such as the granting of an exclusive mining or manufacturing license, or the granting of tariff protection for a particular product, as well as general macroeconomic factors such as the rate of growth of income or the availability and cost of bank credit.

Government's current expenditures, and to a lesser extent capital expenditures, show characteristics of both sorts. The total is made up of a large number of relatively small amounts, and changes are the result both of large numbers of individual decisions, and of general economic factors such as the growth of the economy. So government spending can be analysed to *some* extent in the same way as economic aggregates like consumption and imports. But at the same time a single decision, for example to raise civil servants' salaries or to build the infrastructure for a big new mine, can have a significant effect (even at times a dominant effect) on the figures for total government spending.

5 *Conclusion*

The absolutely vital thing to grasp from this chapter is the way that changes in aggregate demand and supply cannot be analysed without taking account of feedback. Most fundamentally, feedback occurs through changes in income. The detailed *way* in which feedback occurs depends on the ability of the home economy to increase its output in competition with imports, on how much prices rise, on the tax system, and so on. Each of the key macroeconomic variables will be discussed in detail in subsequent chapters, but students will find those chapters easier to follow if they think of all the implications of a statement such as: 'Every price rise is an increase in someone's income.'

This book is mostly about the modern or monetised sector of the economy. In Africa, large numbers of people remain in the subsistence sector, that is, they produce mainly for their own consumption and consume mainly what they themselves produce. Such activity is not part of the circular flow of *money* income which has been described in this chapter. However it is important to remember that although subsistence production is very little affected *directly* by changes in the macroeconomy, there is some indirect influence. Production for own consumption and investment normally uses few if any purchased inputs, and by definition the output is not sold. But relatively few farmers have no monetary dealings at all: and as regards their subsistence activities they *do* have alternatives. They can produce a cash crop for the market and buy some or all of their basic food supply; or they can seek employment locally with other farmers or in non-agricultural work. Even more important in Africa, they can migrate to towns to find work, when paid work is available or a chance of finding paid work seems likely to be available. In some countries, most importantly Lesotho, but also including Botswana, Swaziland, Mozambique and Malawi, many people migrate to South Africa to find work. Clearly, therefore, events in the modern or monetised sector of the economy have crucial indirect effects on the incomes of subsistence farmers and their families, in the form of alternative sources of income and in the amount of a household's total time that is devoted to subsistence production.

NOTES

1 Changes in demand, supply and income tend to affect the availability of bank credit, as already mentioned. For the time being it is assumed that such monetary effects can be ignored; they are explained in chapters 8 and 9.

2 This is a deliberately vague statement: the next chapter goes into the definition of national income in greater detail, and discusses just how to measure the contribution of a major export commodity whose international price varies sharply.

3 How banks and governments create money is explained in chapter 8.

4 The diamond price is largely controlled by a private mining company (De Beers); the petroleum price is determined partly by market forces and partly by the members of OPEC (the Organisation of Petroleum Exporting Countries) in which its African members have some influence, but not a controlling influence.

2 *Measuring National Income*

1 Introduction

If two people live in similar sorts of houses in the same town, earn their living by going out to work, spend their incomes in similar sorts of ways in the same group of shops, have roughly equal access to the same range of publicly provided services like health care, education for their children and the protection of the law, then it is reasonable to compare their economic wellbeing by comparing their money incomes or the spending of their money incomes. If two people live totally different lives, one of them being an urban wage earner, another a small farmer living in a village, producing mainly for his own consumption and using money irregularly and for only a minor part of his needs, then it is not really very reasonable to compare their economic wellbeing by means of monetary measures, even with adequate data.

The majority of people in Africa still live in villages and depend, for satisfying their basic needs, on consumption of their own production—although the use of money is increasing. Yet figures are published claiming to show, in money terms, the incomes of small farmers, and these figures are added to other forms of income in order to reach a figure for national income. National income figures are used to compare the economic achievements of different nations, and of nations over time. There is tremendous pressure on governments to produce national income figures, and if governments do not produce the figures other private people and organisations do; the figures are then used for all sorts of purposes whether or not they are published with suitable warnings about their unreliability and lack of comparability. It is very important therefore to know how national income estimates are compiled, how accurate are the component parts of the total, and just what it is that a figure for national income, even if based on accurate facts, really does measure.

The distinction between estimate and fact is very important. Some parts of the national income statistics can reasonably be said to be fact. For example, statistics relating to large-scale production of minerals for export, such as those for chrome in Zimbabwe, diamonds in Botswana or copper in Zambia, tend to be reliable because provided by a small number of large, well-organised companies; furthermore, some of these minerals (although not all) are sold at well-publicised prices in international markets. Other parts, however, are based on partial information like surveys, from which only estimates of the whole can be deduced. Or they are based on complete but unreliable information: for example foreign payments are recorded by large numbers of bank clerks who may not fully understand the categories used by the statisticians and who have relatively little motive to provide an accurate breakdown of the figures; or accurate figures are available of exports marketed through official agencies, but a significant part of total exports are smuggled into neighbouring countries and so are not recorded. Because all national accounts are combinations of facts (of varying degrees of reliability), estimates and guesses, the total should always be described as an estimate.

The whole process of measuring national income was developed in industrialised economies, so the concepts and techniques are better suited to measuring income in the modern than in the rural sector of African economies. Even in the modern sector, though, and in its relations with the rural sector, some problems arise. The first priority then is to show how national income is estimated in a modern economy, or sector of an economy, and then to discuss how these methods are applied elsewhere.

2 *Measuring Gross Domestic Product in the modern sector: the product method*

'National income' is the term normally used in conversation to mean the total of goods and services produced in a year in a particular country. A more precise term is 'Gross Domestic Product' or GDP. GDP can be measured in three different ways, by adding up production, income or expenditure.

In adding up the *production* of each sector of the economy it is most important to avoid double-counting. Products which are bought by other producers ('intermediate' products) would be double-counted if the total sales of all producers were added together. So the concept of 'value added' is used. Each producer buys certain inputs and adds value to them before selling his production. For example, a shoe manufacturer buys leather, rubber and shoelaces which he manufactures into shoes. His value added is the value of the shoes minus the cost of what he buys from other producers. A very simple account for a shoe firm might be as in Table 2.1.

Table 2.1 Receipts and payments of a shoe manufacturer

Payments	*$'000*	*Receipts*	*$'000*
Purchase of leather	35	Sale of shoes	100
Purchase of rubber	5		
Purchase of shoelaces	5		
Rent	5		
Wages and salaries	35		
Gross Profit	15		
	100		100

The value added in this case is the value of sales less the cost of intermediate goods. If the cost of leather, rubber and shoelaces is not deducted from the value of sales then the production of the leather tannery, the rubber processing firm and the shoelaces produced by a textile firm, would be counted twice. If any of these intermediate inputs has been imported it is obviously important not to count them as part of national product. Furthermore, if part of the profit is sent abroad to foreign shareholders then it is of no value to the local economy.[1] In underdeveloped countries it is quite common for a foreign-owned company to be set up to assemble imported components; in such cases the sales may be very high, but the local value added and thus the benefit to the country may be very small. For example, new motor car assembly plants in Africa use mainly imported components, so that the value added locally consists almost entirely of the value of the labour used in assembling the imported components, plus profit. The long-term value of such projects depends greatly on whether the factory stimulates local production of motor car components.

Value added in the case illustrated by Table 2.1 is total sales ($100 000)[2] minus purchases of intermediate goods ($45 000), which is $55 000 (assuming the firm is locally owned and the profits are not sent abroad).

The concept of value added leads directly to the concept of income. Value added in this example is made up of payments to land (rent $5000), labour (wages and salaries $35 000) and capital (profit $15 000). Land, labour and capital are the three classical factors of production. Payments to these factors are rent, wages and salaries, and profits, which are the three types of income. From this you should be able to see why total output is equal to total income. The value added by each business is the contribution of that business to total output, and *also* consists of incomes which are payments to the factors of production.[3]

A problem arises if the firm produces some shoes which, at the end of the year, it has not yet sold. Perhaps demand for the firm's shoes has fallen off; or perhaps the firm expects a big upsurge in demand quite soon, and wants to be able to supply it quickly, before its rivals. Whatever the reason, an addition to stocks is treated as an addition to output—above all, the shoes are there, and having been produced during the year are part of that year's total output.[4] As far as value added is concerned the addition to stocks is treated as though the firm had sold the shoes to itself. Suppose then that the shoe firm had added to stocks of finished shoes by $20 000, in addition to sales of $100 000. The account would then be as in Table 2.2.

You will notice that gross profit has gone up, although actual cash sales are unchanged; that is, the calculation of profit assumes that an addition to stocks is as good as a sale. It is not, of course. If the stock eventually proves unsaleable, the firm would find that it had in fact made no profit. There is a moral to this, which is to beware of buying a business whose profits are represented by additions to stocks rather than by cash. The actual valuation of stocks and work in progress is obviously difficult, cautious firms tending to value them at cost, that is allowing nothing for the firm's profit margin, even if this understates their true value.

Table 2.2 Receipts and payments of a shoe manufacturer (including unsold stock)

Payments	*$'000*	*Receipts*	*$'000*
Purchase of leather	42	Sales of shoes	100
Purchase of rubber	6	Addition to stocks	
Purchase of shoelaces	6	of finished shoes	20
Rent	5		
Wages and salaries	42		
Gross profit	19		
	120		120

Gross profit is put down in the accounts as a 'payment'. It is, in a way, since conceptually profit is considered as a payment to owners of the business, that is, as a payment to capital as a factor of production. The other reason for showing profit as a payment is that there is an accounting convention that both sides of an account must add up to the same figure. Profit is described in the accounts as 'gross' profit because nothing has been deducted from the accounts for the depreciation of capital goods–buildings and long-lasting machinery.

Because capital goods are those which last a long time it is normal business practice to account for them over their estimated useful life. That is, gross profit is reduced each year by an estimated amount, called depreciation, which is that year's share of the cost of capital goods used up in production. Because it is only an estimate, influenced by many factors and estimated differently from firm to firm, national accounts are normally calculated gross of depreciation.[5] That is why the word 'Gross' is included in GDP. An estimate for depreciation of capital assets for the country as a whole is then subtracted from the GDP to arrive at *Net* Domestic Product.

The basic components of GDP are thus the amounts of value added by each sector of industry. This method of calculating GDP has the additional advantage of indicating the relative size of each sector's contribution to GDP, and changes in relative size over time. 'Industry' in this context means not only manufacturing industry, but mining, construction, transport, agriculture, telephone and Post Office services, the services provided by retail and wholesale traders, electricity and water services, insurance, banking, and so on. The provision of services is as much a part of production as the production of physical commodities. The value added by a retailer, for example, is the total of sales less the cost of buying his stock and less the cost of other inputs bought from other sectors of industry such as electricity. In the case of the one-man business, value added consists of rent (if any) plus the profits of the business–these profits being of course the income of the trader. Many people misunderstand the service provided by traders, seeing them simply as people who make an easy profit out of their less fortunate fellows. But by keeping stocks of goods available in convenient places and at convenient times, and by selling goods in conveniently small quantities ('breaking bulk') traders perform a service as essential as the original production of the goods by farmers, miners and manufacturers.

The official figures for GDP in Britain and Kenya in a recent year are given in Table 2.3. GDP is broken down by sector: each figure shows the value added in that industry. For example, the value added in the construction industry in Kenya in 1978 was K£91 million, and in Britain in the same year was £8494 million. The percentage shares of different industries in total production are, as one would expect, very different in the developed economy of Britain and the developing economy of Kenya: most noticeably, manufacturing has a much bigger share of GDP in Britain, even though Kenya has, by African standards, a relatively large manufacturing sector.

Table 2.3 GDP at current prices by economic sector: Kenya and Britain 1978

	Kenya		*Britain*	
	K£ mn	*%*	*UK £ mn*	*%*
Agriculture, forestry, fishing	664	36	3716	3
Mining and quarrying	4	–	4439	3
Manufacturing	246	13	40048	28
Electricity, gas and water	37	2	4737	3
Construction	91	5	8494	6
Wholesale and retail trade	198	11	15099	11
Restaurants and hotels	41	2		
Transport, communications, storage	93	5	11798	8
Owner-occupied dwellings	118	6	5352	4
Finance, other real estate, business services	96	5	14827	10
Public administration and defence	83	4	10464	7
Public services including health and education	175	9	9674	7
Other services	47	3	18645	13
less imputed bank service charge[a]	– 37	– 2	– 6098	– 4
GDP at current producers' value[b]	1856[c]	100	141195[c]	100

NOTES

a Banks derive very little of their income by "selling" their services; most of their income derives from the difference between what they pay in interest on deposits and what they receive in interest from lending money and holding other assets such as Treasury Bills. So an imaginary service charge is imputed, that is it is assumed that banks (and other financial intermediaries) receive a service charge equal to the difference between interest received and interest paid. Because it is not possible to allocate this imputed charge among all the other sectors, it is all charged to a "dummy sector" and each of the other sectors' contribution to GDP is slightly too large.

b Shares of GDP by sector are shown at "producers" values, that is in terms of the money actually received by producers. Market prices, the prices paid by purchasers include indirect taxes such as sales taxes and import duties—see Section 6 for further explanation.

c In 1978, on average K£1 = UK £1.348 at official rates of exchange; see section 11 for the dangers of making international comparisons of GDP using official rates of exchange.

Source: *United Nations Yearbook of National Income Statistics*, 1979

3 *Measuring GDP in the modern sector: the income method*

As already explained, value added is precisely equal to the various forms of income. It is thus possible to calculate GDP by adding up income, rather than by adding up production. The main sources of income are:

wages and salaries
profits
self-employment income
rent.

The profits of government-owned companies, like electricity companies and railways, are sometimes called 'surpluses'—presumably because of a general political attitude to nationalised industries. Firms are usually nationalised by left-of-centre governments who have a certain dislike of the profit motive, so that if nationalised firms continue to make profits it may be tactful to call them surpluses.

In the *UN Yearbook* only two types of income are distinguished: see Table 2.4. In that table, operating surplus includes rent, imputed income from owner-occupied property (see section 7 below), self-employment income and the profits of companies (gross of depreciation).

Table 2.4 *GDP by type of income: Kenya and Britain 1978*

	Kenya		*Britain*	
	K £ mn	%	*UK £ mn*	%
Wages and salaries	718	39	98423	70
Operating surplus	1138	61	42772	30
	1856	100	141195	100

NOTE:
Operating surplus includes depreciation, and rural household consumption of own products.

Source: as Table 2.3

Self-employment income is presumably included in 'operating surplus' on the grounds that the self-employed are running their own businesses. Their incomes are therefore the 'profits' of these businesses and so are included in 'operating surplus'. That may be quite a good way of describing the one-man trading business which is providing essentially the same service as the large trading company with hundreds of employees. But it is stretching the definition to include 'rural household consumption of own products' which is mainly the subsistence income of small-scale farmers whose lives are not 'business-like' at all.

4 Measuring GDP in the modern sector: the expenditure method

Since every sale of goods or services involves both a seller and a buyer, it should be obvious that GDP can also be calculated by adding together all forms of spending in the economy—*provided that* purchases of intermediate goods and services are excluded. Intermediate purchases are the goods and services bought by businesses and included in production. It is necessary to exclude intermediate purchases in calculating national expenditure in order to avoid double-counting. In exactly the same way, value added has to be used rather than gross sales when calculating national output. So there are two main components of national expenditure: consumption and investment.

Personal consumption consists of people buying goods and services for their personal use: food, clothing, furniture, bus trips, haircuts, etc. Although some of these things may not be used up (consumed) immediately, all purchases by individuals are counted as consumption, except houses which are treated as investment. The other item in consumption is government current spending.

Investment includes spending by businesses and governments on items such as buildings and machinery, the development of new mines and the improvement of land, which are not immediately used up in production. The amount of investment goods estimated to have been used up in production is called consumption of fixed capital, or depreciation, and can be deducted to give Net Domestic Product (or Expenditure). As has already been explained, estimates of depreciation contain a great deal of guesswork.

As when calculating value added, additions to stocks must be included, since it is assumed that businesses buy additions to stocks from themselves. The point is that an addition to stocks of goods is a form of production which is not immediately consumed, and is thus a second form of investment. In the simplest case, a subsistence farmer who produces more than he consumes, and stores the surplus, is investing for the future. In the modern sector as well, some part of investment usually consists of an addition to stocks. This item can be negative: in Africa a net fall in stocks occurs, for example, when exports have been prevented by transport failure (which causes a net increase in stocks) and are subsequently sold, when the transport situation improves, or when drought creates the need to consume food stocks. In developed countries, industrial firms reduce their stocks of raw materials when they expect raw material prices to fall in the future, or because high interest rates have increased the financial cost of holding stocks.

In order to distinguish between these two types of investment the first is called 'Gross Fixed Capital Formation' in the national income accounts, the second is called 'Net Change in Stocks'. In fact Gross Fixed Capital Formation is not all 'fixed' in the literal sense, since it includes, for example, investment in earth-moving equipment by construction firms, and in lorries for shifting ore by mining companies.

The other form of investment which must be included is the difference between exports and imports. If, as is sometimes the case during a period of high export prices, a country's exports are greater than its imports, then the 'export surplus' is a form of investment in foreign assets. A country receives foreign exchange for its exports, and has to use foreign exchange to pay for its imports (since foreign suppliers do not want to be paid in the local currency of an African country). If exports are greater than imports then, ignoring the complication of other items of the balance of payments at this stage, foreign exchange reserves will rise or foreign borrowing can be repaid. Either way, net foreign assets increase. This is a form of investment: foreign assets can be used to buy imports in future years, just as a farmer's accumulation of food not needed for immediate consumption is an investment in stocks which can be consumed in the future. Naturally, investment abroad can, like the net change in stocks, be negative as well as positive.

Table 2.5 GDP by categories of expenditure: Kenya and Britain 1978

	Kenya		*Britain*	
	K £ mn	%	*UK £ mn*	%
Private consumption	1341	63	95391	59
Government consumption	407	19	32736	20
Total consumption	1748	82	128127	79
Gross fixed capital formation	509	24	29205	18
Net change in stocks	89	4	1541	1
Net export of goods and services	– 221	– 10	2381	2
Total investment	377	18	33127	21
Total expenditure on GDP	2125	100	161254	100

Source: as Table 2.3.

Now Table 2.5 shows total expenditure on GDP to be different from GDP as calculated earlier by the product and income methods—yet all three methods should give the same result. The reason for the difference is that when consumers buy cigarettes or beer, for example, the market prices includes a large amount of tax, which ends up with the government. The producer only receives the amount *net* of tax (that is, after payment of tax to the government); out of this he is able to pay the factors of production, namely wages and profits. Table 2.5 therefore shows expenditure at market prices whereas Tables 2.3 and 2.4 showed GDP at 'factor cost'. This distinction is further discussed in Section 6.

5 *Subsistence farming*

Subsistence output is, by definition, not bought and sold. It creates two problems therefore for the national income statistician, the first conceptual and the second practial.

The *conceptual* problem concerns what should and what should not be included in the national income accounts, of the many activities undertaken by a household for its own consumption, and at what prices. Thus it is not at all clear whether estimates of subsistence output should include the value of gathering fuel, fetching water, converting maize into maize meal and then into cooked food, and of building huts, fences and cattle kraals. It is even harder to decide what value to put on the output from these activities when the output is very seldom (if ever) sold for cash.

The *practical* problem is that it is extremely difficult to get information about subsistence activities. The production of goods and services that are not bought and sold does not result in accounting records which can be used by a national income statistician. Furthermore, there are large numbers of small, scattered farms; roads to such farms are very bad or non-existent; and the farmers are often illiterate and naturally keep no records; so that survey work is difficult, expensive and frequently unreliable. Subsistence output is thus quite different from the marketed output of export crops which usually passes through the hands of marketing boards and for which records are readily available (except where smuggling is widespread).

In trying to value subsistence output the statisticians use the fiction that the farmer produces something (output), buys it from himself (expenditure) and receives income as a result (income). In principle, if the amount and value of output are known then expenditure and income are also known. But even in the case of, say, maize production where prices are known, a problem remains. Because the farmer consumes his own product there are no transport and distribution costs–transport and distribution services are not needed. In recording *output*, therefore, it is correct to value maize at the 'farm gate' price, that is, the price paid to a commercial farmer if his maize were to be collected from his farm. The price is of course lower than the price of maize at a centralised market, and both are lower than the price of maize as sold by traders.[6] In addition the manufacturing process of converting maize to maize meal is commercialised in towns, and the costs and profits of millers are incorporated in the price paid for maize meal by urban consumers. If, therefore, one wishes to compare the *welfare* of urban consumers and subsistence farmers, by valuing their consumption of basic foodstuffs, then clearly the correct price to use is the urban price of maize meal. In other words, one would have to impute to subsistence output some sort of value added by non-existent transport and distribution services, and the 'manufacturing' activities of the farmer's wife in converting maize into meal.

The almost invariable practice of national income statisticians in Africa is to value output of foodcrops only, and to value them at prices which make *output* figures comparable, that is, to use farm gate prices. While this is a perfectly sound procedure if primary interest is in agricultural output, it is wholly inadequate in comparing the *welfare* of rural and urban people. Yet this is what is implied by taking subsistence output, dividing it by the population dependent on subsistence farming and then comparing this derived figure of subsistence income per head with the urban wage income per head of the urban population. Clearly like is not being compared with like, and the result is absurd.

In trying to make sensible use of published estimates of subsistence output, it is absolutely essential, therefore, to be clear as to what it is that has been measured. Thus if most estimates of subsistence output are in fact estimates of the output of the main food crops, and if the estimates are good ones, then they can be quite useful in providing information on, say, changes in the amount of food grown and eaten by subsistence farmers. But such estimates are not only useless but thoroughly misleading if used to compare the incomes of subsistence farmers with the incomes of urban dwellers. The town dweller has to pay cash for his housing, fuel, lighting, transport to and from work, beer, entertainment, water and for all sorts of public services via local taxes. The subsistence farming family provides most of these services for itself.

It would in theory be possible to record the fact that the subsistence farmer enjoys home-brewed beer, shelter, fuel and so on, but it is not even theoretically possible to put a value on most of these goods and services. It is true that even in the most isolated village most goods and services are exchanged occasionally for cash, but the price implied by such a transaction cannot necessarily be taken as typical, precisely because cash transactions themselves are not typical. Services performed for others in a village form part of a whole network of rights and obligations, the time scale of which can be as long as a man's lifetime. The money that changes hands on any particular occasion may thus represent all sorts of considerations additional to the actual service performed at that time. For example, one man may help a neighbour build his hut for nothing, because that neighbour lent him some cattle for last season's ploughing; another man could be paid an exceptionally large amount for the same service because the neighbour hopes to obtain a favour in the future. Where cash transactions are the norm, as in towns where most people perform specialised jobs for cash, and buy everything they need for cash, prices reflect more truly what goods and services are worth to the buyer, and the impersonal nature of *most* transactions excludes other considerations. Of course, even in town traders give discounts to friends and family, friends lend money interest-free, whereas banks and hire purchase companies charge interest; but in the urban market economy, impersonal or 'arm's length' transactions are the rule rather than the exception.[7]

Again, even in the monetised, market-dominated sectors of an African economy there are some services which some people perform for themselves while others pay to have them done. For example one man may paint his own house, another may pay a professional decorator. The service performed by the do-it-yourself householder almost certainly is left out of the GDP estimates, while the output of the professional decorator should be, and probably is, included. But by and large the bulk of output in the market sectors is included in the official estimates of GDP. Value added by mining companies, by supermarket chains, by steelworks and by hotels is recordable and is recorded. And value added by the big organisations is very large compared with the anomalies and omissions. None of this is true in the subsistence sector.

In practice, most estimates of subsistence output in Africa are very shaky indeed. No account is taken of the different prices needed to measure output on the one hand and income (or welfare) on the other, even for the main subsistence foods; and very little attempt is made to include other items of subsistence output.

In Zambia, for example, the subsistence output estimate was for many years totally useless. It was based on very out-of-date estimates, for only a few districts, of the *dietary* habits and needs of the rural population. It was then assumed that the farmers grew (and caught in the case of fish) these requirements. This 'estimate' was then updated by almost equally shaky estimates of the growth in population. What this process therefore did was to *assume* answers to many of the questions that ought to have been asked. It did not tell us whether in fact farmers succeeded in supplying themselves and their families with the food they needed, nor did it tell us anything about variations from year to year or changes in the trend of production over time. The figures were thus useless for assessing or preparing government policy, or indeed for anything else.

At first sight it might appear that the error was unimportant in Zambia's case, since subsistence farming output was shown as K109 mn in 1978 which was only about 7% of GDP. This means that even a 100% error in estimating subsistence output would only have produced a 6% error in estimating GDP. But the estimate of subsistence output affected the largest and probably the poorest group in the population, [8] and was used for many purposes. In other African countries, subsistence output is much more important both in terms of population and in relation to GDP.

In addition to variations in the importance of subsistence farming, different countries use different 'production boundaries'. Items that are within the production boundary are those that are included in estimates of GDP, and the production boundary varies much more in estimates of subsistence output than in estimates for other sectors of the economy. For example hut-building, fuel-gathering, the 'manufacturing' services of wives, are treated as being inside the production boundary in some countries, outside it in others. Furthermore, different countries use different ways of measuring the items that *are* included.[9]

Given the extremely difficult problems, both conceptual and practical, in estimating subsistence output, there is real doubt as to whether it is worthwhile at all. Van Arkadie and Frank, for example, seem to conclude that all measures are worthless. Certainly the variations between countries make it quite as invalid to use the published statistics to make comparisons of rural standards of living in different countries as it is to use estimates of subsistence output for making welfare comparisons between rural and urban people.

Even if quite good estimates of food crop production by small farmers were available, and these estimates were used purely to estimate change over time within the same rural communities, there would remain considerable conceptual problems in using the figures. Some of these problems are common to both monetary and non-monetary sectors of the economy, but they tend to be more fundamental in the villages.

Firstly, national income accounting puts no value on leisure. If people become more productive and are able to produce the same quantity of goods in less time, they are better off provided that they put a positive value on leisure; but this is not recorded in national income. The growth of welfare in industrialised economies tends to be under-recorded because of this factor, since working hours have been gradually reduced over time. In the village economy, on the other hand, the growth of output, perhaps of new crops for export, may be at the expense of leisure, so that the growth of welfare is exaggerated by the statistics. This is especially important when leisure is used for maintaining vital kinship and other relationships, vital because of the risks involved in small-scale, low-technology farming, and the need for help with tasks like hut-building and harvesting.

Secondly, national income accounting tends to take no account of the gradual movement of transactions into the market economy. Again, this occurs in the urban industrialised world, as people use rising incomes to pay for services previously performed within the household and thus not recorded in the statistics. But the change is a more basic one in rural Africa, since village life is moving from a situation in which a large proportion of 'economic' activity is excluded from GDP estimates, towards one in which most goods and services will be exchanged for cash, and will therefore tend increasingly to be included in GDP estimates. It is thus probable that the growth of income in the villages will be exaggerated by official statistics as commercialisation of village life proceeds.

Thirdly, there is a much greater interconnection between rural and urban life than has been suggested so far. Just as the conventions of national income accounting are ill-suited to a situation in which more than half of the male labour force works in another country (as in Lesotho) or in which a big proportion of the highly skilled are temporary residents (as in Botswana), they are also ill-suited to making sense of the *internal* patterns of migration.

In many parts of Africa, village populations are dominated for most of the year by women, children and old men. Most of the men of working age are absent in the towns, working or seeking work. These men send money to their families and bring money and goods with them when they return, temporarily or permanently, to their villages. In addition, people from the villages visit relatives in town, or send children to visit, in order to enjoy access to urban amenities. In Botswana, admittedly something of an extreme case, many households have two or more dwelling places: in a modern town, in a large traditional village, at 'the lands' (where crops are grown) and at a cattle post.[10]

As a result of this internal, and in some countries external, migration, rural households have become less capable of deriving their livelihoods from agriculture, depending to an increasing degree on transfers of money from absent relatives, non-agricultural employment and beer-brewing. Thus crops and livestock yielded only 11% of total income for the poorest tenth of a sample of households in Botswana (and only 16% of a group ranging from the 15th to the 50th percentile).[11] Another study showed that among small-scale Zambian farmers, whose farming was intended mainly for their own consumption, between 35% and 48% of cash income came from non-agricultural employment.[12] Small farmers do sell some of their output because they aim to produce a surplus in a normal year as an insurance against bad years.[13]

Such survey studies as the two referred to above tell us far more about small-scale farmers than the official figures have ever done, even though surveys are inevitably limited in their coverage. Even surveys, though, tend to emphasize averages, and averages conceal not only variations about the average, but also the extreme vulnerability of poor rural households. Farming is risky in all countries and at all levels, but it is riskier for poorer farmers, using unsophisticated techniques. It is riskiest of all where men have migrated in search of work:

> The fate of the farm family in which the father is absent . . . is at best insecure and at worst disastrous. . . . It is even more vulnerable to natural disasters than most other families precisely because those who would normally be most adept at securing assistance, either from official sources or more likely from kin groups, are not on the spot. . . . A rise in school fees, a reduction in the fertility of the land, the unforeseen need to make major improvements on the farm, and perhaps most of all, the sudden drying up of remittances as the migrant either loses his job or decides to start a new family in town—any of these can upset the delicate equilibrium of the family and, without substantial support from the kin group, can lead to almost total destitution.[14]

Even survey figures for household or per capita income do *not* of course include all forms of imputed income, and such items as are included are valued at the farm gate price. They include nothing for the manufacturing services of housewives, nor for transport and distribution which would normally have to be paid for by the urban consumer. In other words, even when a very detailed survey is carried out (and the UNZALPI survey for example was very detailed indeed, involving daily visits to each farm in the sample, over a period of two years) so that the facts are known as well as it is possible to know them, it is still not possible to compare rural and urban welfare.

Apart from the pricing problem and the impossibility of putting any value on the general pleasantness of living in town or country, even the most elaborate surveys leave out such welfare items as water and recreation (except beer). It would thus be absolutely incorrect to say that the average family in a rural sample was living at the same standard as an urban family with a cash income of the same amount.

Clearly an urban family would need much more than this, but how much more it is impossible to say.

6 *Factor cost and market prices*

In the modern sectors of an African economy, almost everyone works at something fairly specialised, receives cash income as a result, and then buys the goods and services wanted, out of that cash income. It is therefore reasonable to estimate the output of goods and services on the assumption that prices roughly reflect the value that people place on them. Increases in the amounts of goods and services produced will be reflected in statistics of purchases and sales, scarcity will be reflected in prices, and so on. There are however some exceptions, even in the modern sectors of an African economy.

In the first place some goods and services are taxed, and others subsidised. For example cigarettes and beer are usually taxed, maize meal may be subsidised. There are thus two ways of valuing such goods: at the market price, the price actually paid by the buyer, including the tax or minus the subsidy; or at the 'factor cost' of production, that is the amount which goes to the various factors of production in wages, rent and profit, but not including taxes or subsidies. There are, then, two ways of measuring GDP: 'GDP at market prices' and 'GDP at factor cost'. The relation between the two is:

GDP at factor cost = GDP at market prices
minus indirect taxes
plus subsidies.

Thus if the government levies a tax on bottled beer, the market price paid by the consumer includes the tax; the price received by the producer excludes the tax, so that the cash available for distribution to the factors of production, the factor cost of production which is necessary in order for production to take place, is the market price minus the tax. Similarly, if the government subsidises the cost of fertiliser to farmers, then the market price paid by farmers is less, by the amount of the subsidy, than the amount of money received by the producer and available for paying the 'factor costs' of production, including profit (if any).

In most African countries subsidies are very little used, Zambia being the only anglophone country where subsidies amount to more than 10% of indirect taxes. Mauritius, Zimbabwe and Tanzania are the only others with significant spending on subsidies. Some of the items that have been subsidised at one time or another are maize meal, fertiliser, milk in low-income housing areas and exports of tobacco.

Many indirect forms of subsidy exist, such as providing parastatal firms with low-interest government loans or allowing such firms to run at a loss; only direct subsidies to goods or services are recorded in calculating GDP.

Indirect taxes, on the other hand, are widely used in Africa. In most countries they amount to between 10% and 15% of GDP (20% in Lesotho); only in Botswana (9%), Malawi (7%) and Nigeria (1%) are indirect taxes less than 10% of GDP. Nigeria is presumably able to neglect this source of revenue because of the large revenues from oil.

7 *Imputed income in the modern sector*

Another problem in calculating GDP is that even in the monetised modern sector of the economy, not all services are bought and sold. The most important examples are housing and housewives' services. People who own their own houses do not pay rent, although they derive the same service from housing as people who live in rented housing. The statisticians therefore *impute* income to owner-occupiers, that is they assume that a man living in his own house receives an income equivalent to the rent he would have to pay if he did not own the house, and that this income is then spent on buying housing services from himself. The recorded output of housing services is thus increased by an imputed amount.[15]

Housewives' services are on the other hand ignored by the statisticians, mainly on the grounds that it is too difficult to value them and too difficult to discover the quantity produced. In practice, even the domestic service which *is* paid for in cash is almost certainly underestimated by the statisticians. In many countries in Africa, the employment figures leave out domestic servants altogether, or else include only the roughest of estimates. This is an example of a type of employment in which statistics are extremely difficult to obtain. Another example would be self-employed car-washers and vegetable sellers. Conceptually there is no difficulty since their production is equal to the value of their services as paid for by their customers, less any purchased inputs, but the difficulty lies in obtaining the facts about their activities.

8 *Government services*

The final 'sector' of the economy to be included is government. It has been argued from time to time that many government services, such as defence and the maintenance of law and order, are really intermediate products which are necessary in order for economic activity to take place. There is some virtue in this point of view, but it is extremely difficult in practice to distinguish between government services which ought to be classified as intermediate products and government services which are final products to be enjoyed by the public like any other product. For example education is partly a necessary input into economic activity, since much modern sector production depends on educated manpower, and partly a service to be enjoyed by the participants in the same way as some of the services provided by private businessmen, for example cinema shows or football matches. In principle, some private sector services and commodities, such as transport to work and working clothes, could also be treated as intermediate products.

In practice all government services are treated as part of national product. They are valued at *cost* even though this means that the methods of valuation in government and non-government sectors are different. Government services provided free or at cost contain no element of profit in their valuation as do private sector goods and services. This is inevitable because there is normally no way of estimating what the value of government services would be if they were produced and sold by private businessmen for profit.

Provided the range of services supplied by government stays the same then GDP estimates will remain roughly comparable from one year to the next; but if sectors of the economy move into or out of the government sector then comparison over time will become invalid as the method of valuation changes. For the same reason, comparison of GDP between countries with differing proportions of production in the government sector will suffer from the same problem of differing methods of valuation.

Including all government services in GDP means assuming that all such services are valued by the community, particularly if GDP estimates are used as a measure of the wealth and welfare of peoples. For example if defence expenditure increases, people may or may not feel better off, depending on how seriously they view the problem of the nation's security. Yet excluding government spending from GDP would not necessarily improve matters, since even defence services have some value to everyone, and other services like health and education are of obvious and immediate value to most people.

It should be clear, though, from this discussion of government services that the *composition* of GDP, as well as its actual size, is very important; and that changes in the composition of GDP may be as important as changes in its size. For example, if a country goes to war local factories will start to produce war materials, imports will be of tanks and fighter aircraft instead of motor cars and passenger airliners.

The people will be heavily taxed to pay for war spending while at the same time fewer consumer goods will be available because production and imports have been switched to guns and tanks. Because GDP includes government services valued at cost, it is possible that GDP will appear the same in wartime as in peacetime. GDP may even appear higher in wartime as unemployed people are employed as soldiers. But to deduce from this that the people are in some sense better off is clearly misleading, since the composition of GDP as between government spending on defence and the provision of other goods and services has changed so drastically.

9 Domestic Product, National Product and the income of foreigners

The total of value added for all sectors of the economy, plus the total of government services valued at cost, is equal to Gross *Domestic* Product. Domestic is the word used to describe production within a country's borders. But in African countries, a great deal of the value added by domestic industry is transferred abroad. The main reason is that a large part of African industry is either wholly or partly owned by foreigners, who therefore own all or part of the profits. Normally, part of these foreign-owned profits, which are an important part of the value added of domestic industry, is transferred to their owners in the form of dividends paid abroad.[16] African governments have been active in trying to reduce the size of this problem, by taking over foreign-owned industry, by forcing foreign-owned firms to sell part of their shares to local people or local institutions, or by going into partnership with foreign firms right from the beginning. To the extent that such action really makes use of local resources–local savings, local skills and local labour–it must reduce the outflow of profits.

But new forms of ownership, however ingenious, cannot remove the great shortage of resources that faces all African countries; the result is that domestic value added flows out of Africa in other ways, for example as payments on the management contracts that have often to be used even when local ownership is more than 50%, or as interest on the foreign loans used to buy a share in a business. There has, of course, been a great deal of scope for reducing the level of profits paid abroad where these were unnecessarily high, higher that is than the level needed to keep the firm in operation, well managed and willing to expand when appropriate; and agreements have been renegotiated and tax regimes altered to this effect, especially for mining companies. The fact remains that so long as African countries have to use foreign resources–of capital, management, access to markets, skills, technology, etc.—part of the value of local production will tend to be paid abroad, because otherwise access to those resources would dry up very quickly.

The outflow of foreign dividends, less any inflow of money because of foreign investment by African residents (mainly interest on the government's foreign exchange reserves invested in foreign financial markets) is known as 'net income paid abroad'. It is subtracted from GDP to arrive at Gross *National* Product, or GNP. The idea, then, is that GNP represents that part of domestic production which generates income for local people and can be spent for their welfare. In Africa, GNP is normally *less* than GDP, because of the widespread foreign ownership of African assets. In developed countries, GNP is frequently *greater* than GDP, because such economies enjoy net income *from* abroad, as the result of past investment in mines, factories and plantations in the rest of the world.

As should be clear by now, though, this adjustment is not large enough. African countries do not only make use of foreign investors,

Table 2.6 Importance of private remittances out of selected African countries in 1979

	Private unrequited transfers (SDR mn)	*GNP estimates (SDR mn)*[b]	*Transfers as % of GNP*
Botswana	10.4	450	2.3
Ethiopia	3.0	3110	0.1
Gambia	1.5	120	1.3
Ghana	4.8	3500	0.1
Kenya	21.6	4500	0.5
Malawi[a]	5.0	610	0.8
Mauritius	4.3	650	0.7
Nigeria	277.0	42800	0.6
Seychelles	1.6	40	4.0
Sierra Leone	1.4	660	0.2
Swaziland	3.5	250	1.4
Tanzania	18.8	3620	0.5
Uganda	14.3	2870	0.5
Zambia	88.0	2170	4.1
Zimbabwe	44.4	2580	1.7

NOTES
a 1976
b The weakness of international comparisons of GNP is discussed below, section 11; GNP estimates are used here as a way of indicating the relative importance of private remittances.

Source: United Nations *Balance of Payments Statistics Yearbook*, 1981 and World Bank *Acelerated Development in Sub-Saharan Africa: an agenda for action*, 1981.

they make use of other foreign resources which also have to be paid for in one way or another. The most obvious case concerns foreign skilled labour. Expatriates are still widely used in Africa, and these people, as temporary residents, send a significant proportion of their incomes out of the country. The calculation of GNP takes account of profits sent abroad (less any profits received) but takes no account of expatriate remissions. This is because GNP is defined as the income available to residents of the country, a definition derived from use in developed countries at a time when 'resident' was normally not sufficiently different from 'national' to make very much difference.

Although these sums of money are at the command of residents, they are really very similar in principle to profits sent out of the country, that is, payments for the use of foreign resources: physical resources and know-how in the case of profits, human resources in the case of expatriate savings and other remittances. Clearly this problem is not permanent, since expatriates will eventually nearly all be replaced by Africans; but it remains substantial some twenty years after independence.

As can be seen from Table 2.6, only a handful of countries continue to suffer outflows of more than 1% of GNP in private transfers abroad; 10 or more years ago the percentages would have been much higher. In 1970 the outflow of private remittances from Zambia was 10% of GNP, for example. It is also likely that in many countries the actual outflows are larger than those officially recorded, because exchange control restrictions have created incentives to get money out of Africa by all sorts of illegal methods.

The deduction of net income paid abroad (basically profits of foreign-owned companies leaving the country) is not a sufficient adjustment to GDP. In recognition of this point, the new system of national accounts adopted internationally through the United Nations in 1970 (the 'New SNA') took account of the problem of expatriate remittances by creating a new concept 'National Disposable Income'. This is arrived at as shown in Table 2.7.

Table 2.7 National disposable income

GDP at market prices
less profits paid abroad (net)
= Gross National Product
less 'Private unrequited transfers (net)'
less 'Consumption of fixed capital' (Depreciation)
= 'National Disposable Income'

It would be rather clearer if the new concept was known as 'Net National Disposable Income' since it is in fact net of depreciation of fixed capital. Nevertheless it is undoubtedly a better concept than the old one of GNP which only took account of foreign ownership of capital.

If national income statistics were only used by professional economists with a close knowledge of the African economy being discussed, who could be expected to know the peculiarities of the system, then these points would be of little importance. But the statistics are used much more widely–by politicians to make political points, and by international agencies to decide which countries get various forms of aid. The older concept of GNP continues to be used. For example, the International Development Agency is the 'soft loan' member of the World Bank group; that is, the IDA lends at very low interest rates and with very long periods of repayment to countries with GNP per head of less than US$625. Countries with a higher GNP per head must borrow at the much higher rates and shorter repayment periods of the World Bank. In these sorts of circumstances the definition of national income is of more than technical statistical interest. It is perfectly possible for a country with GNP per head of more than US$625 in 1978 dollars to have a GNP *per citizen* below that figure.

The Government of Botswana has actually performed this calculation, by *adding* to GDP the income earned by Botswana citizens working abroad (mainly migrant mine and farm workers in South Africa) and *subtracting* from GDP the income earned by non-citizens in Botswana, profits and wages, net of course of any taxes paid since tax payments to the government by non-citizens are available for spending on the welfare of citizens.

In Botswana, therefore, the estimates show that income accruing to citizens is only just over 80% of GDP per head, and is expected to fall slightly in the medium term. The point here is that estimates of national income per head are not just empty statistical calculations; they are used for official purposes, of which IDA lending is only one example. Equally, this is only one reason why international comparisons of GNP can be misleading; others are dealt with in section 11 of this chapter.

It is interesting to compare the statistical treatment of the well-paid expatriates in Africa with that of the low-paid migrant labourers who go to work in South Africa, from countries such as Botswana, Lesotho, Mozambique and Malawi (a small number used to go from Zambia but this was stopped after independence). These men leave their homes and families to work mainly on South African mines and farms. The typical contract for such migrants is for a year to eighteen months, not so very different from the typical two-year expatriate contract (which

Table 2.8 Estimated income accruing to citizens of Botswana as a percentage of GDP

	Percentage of GDP at market prices			
		1978/79		*1984/85*
GDP at market prices		100,0		100,0
+ citizens' wage income from abroad	7,4		3,3	
+ net interest from abroad	1,1		4,6	
− non-citizens' share of gross operating surplus, net of taxes	16,7		18,4	
− non-citizens' share of wages, net of taxes	9,9		8,9	
= net inflow of income		− 18,8		− 19,4
Income accruing to citizens of Botswana as a percentage of GDP		81,2		80,6

Source: *Botswana National Development Plan 1979–85.*

can work out at 21 months if leave is taken out of the two years). Yet the African migrant labourers are treated as residents of their home country since both their consumption (abroad) and their remittances are added to GNP. The difference perhaps is that migrant African labourers normally leave their families at home; but as Africa's expatriates frequently have children at boarding school outside the country and a substantial proportion of African migrants are single men seeking to save enough money to buy some cattle and to pay bride-money, the differences in family circumstances have some (if not many) similarities. The more general point here is again that the GNP definitions originated in industrialised countries, and have been awkwardly adapted to African conditions, sometimes to the practical disadvantage of African countries.

10 Changing prices

In the first part of this chapter, the figures for national income, whether calculated by product, income or expenditure method, were all in 'current prices'–this means that the statistics use the prices actually paid at the time. The trouble with this concept is that if prices change significantly over time then national income figures will reflect changes in prices as well as 'real' changes. 'Real income' in this context means the goods that a man can buy, as opposed to his 'money income'.

Since the Second World War prices in all countries have tended to rise continuously. Nearly everyone is aware therefore that his real income, his economic welfare as represented by the goods and services he is able to buy, has gone up less fast than his money income. A man whose income is twice as large as it was is *not* able to buy twice as much of everything. Furthermore, prices have tended to rise faster and faster over time: in Sub-Saharan Africa prices rose on average at more than 10% a year in the 1970s, compared with an average of only 2.8% a year in the 1960s. It has become a great deal more important, therefore, to adjust economic data for the effect of price rises if the data are not to be very misleading.

The national income statistics attempt to allow for changing prices by calculating GNP at 'fixed prices'. This means estimating GNP in, say, 1980 at the prices prevailing in 1975. In principle, this should show how much real or physical output has increased, and therefore the amount by which the nation as a whole has more goods and services at its disposal.

Although prices of different goods and services have a tendency to change in the same direction at the same time, obviously they do not all move together, nor do they change by the same amounts. It is necessary therefore to calculate *average* price increases. The best-known of these averages is the 'consumer price index' which attempts to average the change in the prices of the consumption goods and services bought by the average citizen. There are many other price indices—for wholesale prices, building materials, commodity prices, etc.—but they all attempt to solve the same problem, namely how to express the *average* price rise for a group of items.

Even if all the components of national income have been suitably 'deflated' to give a series free of the effects of inflation, there remains one problem peculiar to countries like those in Africa. If the price of an important export commodity goes up, such as oil in Nigeria or cocoa in Ghana, the current value of export production goes up, even if physical output in barrels of oil or tonnes of cocoa does not. It is quite possible, in fact, for the *value* of output to increase at the same time as the *volume* of output goes down. In such circumstances there is no absolutely correct way of showing what has happened in 'real terms'.

On the one hand, real income goes up if export prices go up faster than import prices. If this happens, the country is able to buy more imports with the foreign exchange earned by selling exports, and 'real income' has risen therefore (this effect is known as an improvement in the terms of trade).

On the other hand, if the volume of production, or 'output at constant prices', has not risen, then it may also be correct to show this in the statistics.

The point is that 'real GDP' means two rather different things: it is useful to measure the actual quantities of output, because this shows whether an economy has produced more (more tonnes of copper or bags of maize or barrels of oil). With prices rising as fast as in the 1970s and 1980s it is clearly very important to have statistics which show changes in the volume of physical production, because the value of output is so much affected by inflation. It is also useful, though, to know whether a country, and therefore the people of that country, are better off as a result of their efforts. Information as to whether an increased volume of production results in people being better or worse off is vitally important.

Industrialised countries have a very diversified export trade, made up mainly of manufactured goods whose relative prices do not change very much. As a result, the terms of trade effect on 'real GDP' is not nearly so important. The terms of trade of a country such as France or Germany *do* change, but the changes are relatively small. The average price of France's exports never doubles or halves in relation to the average price of France's imports. Such enormous changes can and do occur in African economies: for example, between 1975 and 1977 Ghana's cocoa production fell by 40%, but the value of cocoa exports rose by 23% because of a rapid rise in the price of cocoa on world markets. Over the same period Ghana's total exports rose by 25%, because cocoa contributed nearly 60% of Ghana's exports at that time. There is no major industrial country with a single commodity so dominant in exports.

Most African countries have one or two commodities dominant in their export trade, as shown in Table 1.1. It is essential, therefore, in using statistics of 'real GDP' or 'real GNP' to note whether or not the estimates have been adjusted for changes in the terms of trade.

11 Making international comparisons of national income

Estimates of national income are, or should be, well known to be very inaccurate. Many forms of income are only guessed at; many are left out. Prices often do not reflect economic welfare. In particular, the incomes of small farmers and their families are very seriously underestimated and are not comparable with urban incomes. Yet the majority of the population is often in this rural category. Even in the most urbanised African countries, more than 60% of the population was still rural in 1980, and in Uganda, Tanzania, Lesotho, Kenya and Malawi the figure was 85% or more.

In spite of their well-known drawbacks, national income figures, usually divided by population estimates (which may be almost as shaky as income estimates), are widely used. Nearly every book on the economic development of underdeveloped countries quotes the United Nations figures for per capita income of poor and rich countries, and invites the reader to compare them. The typical table looks like this:

Table 2.9 Per capita GNP of selected countries in 1975 (at current market prices, in US dollars)

USA	6265	Columbia	508
Japan	3856	Zambia	421
Britain	3664	Tanzania	159
Portugal	1482	Ethiopia	91
Chile	625		

Source: UN, *Statistical Yearbook*, 1978, Table 193

The notes at the end of the table in the UN *Statistical Yearbook* actually say 'The estimates. . .are designed to facilitate international comparisons of economic activity.' The UN is only trying to offer a useful service by gathering into one volume all the national income figures provided by the various governments. The fact is, however, that the figures as published, and so often quoted, are quite meaningless. What they appear to say is that the average level of income in Ethiopia is the same as could be bought in the USA for $91. This is wholly absurd. An annual income of $91 in the USA would mean quite simply–starvation. A person with $91 to spend in a year would be quite unable to buy enough food to stay alive, quite apart from clothing, housing, fuel for cooking and keeping warm in the winter, etc.

The comparison between rich and poor countries is basically absurd for the same reason that comparisons between urban and rural income is almost impossible–namely that the town-dweller has to buy many things that the country-dweller enjoys for nothing or provides for himself. Such things are either left out of national income accounting, or grossly undervalued in terms of a welfare comparison. In addition, the price level in low-income areas is usually lower than in high-income areas. These two points have been discussed already.

These are further reasons why international comparison can be very misleading. Figures are converted to dollars at official exchange rates, but the latter seldom reflect at all accurately the purchasing power of currencies. For example, from the end of 1978 to the end of 1980 the Ghanaian currency (the cedi) had the same official exchange rate against the US dollar (US$0.3636 = one cedi). During those two years prices in Ghana rose 138%. During the same period, Liberian prices rose only 27% while the Liberian dollar was exactly equal to a US dollar. So the different rates of inflation were *not* reflected in the official exchange rates used to 'convert' estimates of GNP into US dollars.

People in different countries have different consumption habits and priorities. As a result, even countries at a roughly similar stage of development cannot be accurately compared. The French put a higher priority on good food and wine than on housing; the Americans prefer hygiene to good food; large numbers of Indians do not eat beef or drink alcohol for religious reasons, so their perceived needs are different from other peoples'. These factors make welfare comparisons impossible.

Different climates have a big impact. In cold countries whole industries are devoted to providing warm houses, warm clothing, sunny foreign holidays, heated swimming pools. All of this activity counts as production and is thus included in GNP. In hot countries warmth comes free but nobody adds an extra amount to GNP to allow for this.

The contribution of public services to welfare is enormous but difficult to value. For example it can be quite cheap to lay on fresh drinking water in a shanty town. The increase in government spending is thus quite small and will show up as a small increase in GNP and GNP per head. But the increase in welfare, in improved health, in a reduction of the back-breaking labour of fetching water, in the sheer pleasure of drinking and washing in clean water, is immeasurable. Similarly, it can be quite cheap to remove some diseases, thus greatly improving people's prospect of a healthy life.

Averages for income per head conceal the distribution of income. If the rich get richer but the poor remain as poor as ever, *average* income goes up but it is difficult to believe that the nation is better off. Before independence in countries like Kenya and Zambia the white population was as well if not better off than the average for industrialised countries like Britain, but the *per capita* national income figures showed a much lower figure and concealed the fact that Africans were mostly very poor and were denied access to education, to land, indeed to most of the things enjoyed by the whites. The same is still true of South Africa and Namibia.

Finally, income figures take no account of insecurity. If people frequently lose their jobs, or if they even *think* they are likely to lose their jobs, then they are worse off than people in steady employment at the same average income. That is why relatively secure jobs in the civil service, and in large stable institutions like banks, are greatly prized when unemployment is very bad. Similarly farmers, especially

Table 2.10 Structure of GDP in some African economies (percentages)

		Agriculture	*Mining*	*Manufacturing*	*Trade*	*Government*	*Other Services*
Botswana	(1978)	20.2	15.8	6.9	20.3	14.8	22.0
Ethiopia	(1976)	48.4	0.2	8.8	9.0	7.1	26.5
Ghana	(1976)	51.3	1.4	13.3	13.3	7.3	13.4
Kenya	(1978)	35.8	0.2	13.2	12.9	13.9	24.0
Liberia	(1977)	16.1	22.8	8.8	11.1	11.5	29.7
Malawi	(1973)	52.2	0.1	10.0	12.5	5.9	19.3
Mauritius	(1976)	19.7	0.3	22.2	12.9	12.1	32.8
Nigeria	(1977)	23.4	24.7	4.9	21.4	6.9	18.7
Seychelles	(1977)	15.7	—	5.5	21.4	17.5	39.9
Sierra Leone	(1977)	39.1	9.7	7.8	13.2	6.5	23.7
Swaziland	(1973)	31.1	4.7	25.6	11.3	8.2	19.1
Tanzania	(1978)	50.9	0.4	9.1	12.2	—	27.4 —
Uganda	(1976)	56.4	0.2	5.9	8.1	13.0	16.4
Zambia	(1978)	10.2	33.5	10.2	7.7	12.3	26.1
Zimbabwe	(1977)	16.6	7.3	22.0	11.8	9.9	32.4

NOTES
Agriculture includes forestry and fishing. Mining includes quarrying (very small in all cases). Trade includes hotels and restaurants (small in most cases, but half the total in Seychelles). Other includes construction, finance, transport and communications, electricity and water and social and community services.

Sources: UN *Yearbook of National Income Statistics*.

small farmers in tropical countries, are constantly threatened by uncertain rains, diseases that attack cattle and crops, fire, locusts and marauding elephants. That is why they tend to save more (proportionate to their income) than urban workers.

A World Bank research project has attempted to re-estimate real GDP for a number of countries, using the actual purchasing power of local currencies rather than conversions at official exchange rates. As one would expect, the real GDP of developing countries turned out to be much larger than shown by normal methods of estimation. In 1973, Kenya (the only African country in the World Bank sample) had real GDP equal to 0.36% of GDP in the USA, not 0.18% as shown by official statistics. GDP per head was 6.12% rather than 3.97% of US GDP per head.[17]

12 *Comparing the structure of output between countries*

Table 2.10 shows the relative contribution of the main economic sectors to GDP in several African countries in the late 1970s.

Although the table does give a broad picture of the breakdown of these countries' economies, the student should note the following points:

(i) The larger is the contribution of agriculture, the more unreliable is the total (and the relative contributions of the other sectors) because agriculture is so difficult to measure.

(ii) Because the bulk of the population is rural in all these countries, the figures give a very inaccurate picture of their output, income and welfare.

(iii) On the other hand, the figures are relatively reliable for the modern sectors of the economies.

(iv) Definitions of sectors are a bit arbitrary. For example the processing of copper ore in Zambia is treated as mining rather than manufacturing, whereas the slaughter of cattle and subsequent export of chilled deboned beef is treated as manufacturing rather than agriculture in Botswana.

(v) The figures are shown at market prices and so exaggerate the contribution of heavily taxed sectors.

(vi) The proportion of GDP contributed by sectors producing for export tends to vary with export prices. For example, the proportion of GDP contributed by agriculture in Ghana is higher when the cocoa price is high so that the proportions contributed by all other sectors are necessarily smaller.

13 Conclusion

Perhaps it is just as well that income levels (as measured conventionally) do not measure welfare. The prospect of *all* the countries of the world attaining similar levels of income to those of the industrialised, rich countries is extremely remote. It may be quite simply impossible because there are not enough resources, especially of raw materials.

It is not entirely the fault of the statisticians that national income figures are wrongly used. The figures were asked for in the first place by economists and by governments who had been influenced by economists. There is now a growing realisation that other indicators of development are of equal if not greater importance. Seers has suggested three main indicators: the absolute necessities of life (food, clothing, shelter), a way of earning one's own living so as not to be dependent on others (a job, a farm or a business), and a reasonable level of equality of income. A country cannot claim to be better off if absolute poverty, unemployment and inequality have not been reduced.[18]

Others have added long lists of 'social indicators' measuring life expectancy, child mortality, availability of education and health services, prevalence of various diseases, and so on. This is definitely a desirable trend. Ideally, national income statistics should be used only by professional economists and statisticians who fully understand their limitations and their uses. They *are* useful, particularly in the modern sectors of the economy and when used in relation to output rather than welfare; but the trouble is that it seems impossible to impose such restrictions.

NOTES

1 See section 9 of this chapter for a discussion of foreign-owned income.

2 Always look carefully at any statistical table to see what the units are—in this case thousands of dollars.

3 It is assumed here that rent is paid to an individual. If it is paid to a property company, for example, then it becomes an intermediate payment for the shoe factory, and part of the gross 'sales' of the property company.

4 Changes in the amount of 'work-in-progress', that is in the amount of goods actually in the middle of being processed, are treated in the same way as additions to stocks of finished goods, since they too are part of production.

5 Recent changes in national income accounting recommended by the United Nations include the estimation of depreciation on government assets such as schools and hospitals.

6 The general tendency to underestimate the income of poor countries and poor areas, because these areas have lower price levels, which in turn is caused by the structure of transport costs, is dealt with at length in Dan Usher, *The Price Level*

and the Meaning of National Income Statistics, Oxford University Press, 1968, especially chapter 1.

7 For an account of village life and the difficulty of applying economic concepts and national accounting principles to it, see Phyllis Deane, *Colonial Social Accounting*, Cambridge University Press, 1953, chapter IX.

8 'Affected' because many farmers who are dependent mainly on subsistence output also have other sources of income. 'Probably' the poorest because some shanty-town dwellers may be as badly or worse off than small farmers.

9 See B. Van Arkadie and C. Frank, *Economic Accounting and Development Planning*, Nairobi, Oxford University Press, 1966, chapter XII, for several examples of these variations from East and Central Africa.

10 See chapter 7 of Christopher Colclough and Stephen McCarthy *The Political Economy of Botswana: a study of growth and distribution*, Oxford University Press, 1980.

11 See Republic of Botswana, *The Rural Income Distribution Survey in Botswana 1974/75*, Gaborone, 1976.

12 The two figures refer to samples from the districts of Mumbwa and Katete, Universities of Nottingham and Zambia Agricultural Labour Productivity Investigation (UNZALPI) Report No. 3, pp. 147, 149, Nottingham and Lusaka, 1970.

13 See W.M. Allan, *The African Husbandman*, London, Oliver and Boyd, 1967, for further description of the 'normal surplus' and its effect on the amount of maize sold by small farmers from year to year.

14 Charles Elliott, *Patterns of Poverty in the Third World: a study of social and economic stratification*, New York, Praeger, 1975, p. 99.

15 The fact that many people in Africa live in heavily subsidised housing is in fact usually ignored by the statisticians because the subsidy is 'hidden', for example by charging rents based on historic cost. The statisticians should really increase the recorded output by the amount of the subsidy.

16 Dividends are that part of profit paid out to shareholders, who are the owners of a business. There are 'exchange controls' which lay down rules about how much much of foreign-owned profits may be sent out of the country: see chapter 8.

17 Irving B. Kravis *et al.*, *International Comparisons of Real Product and Purchasing Power*, World Bank, 1978.

18 Dudley Seers, 'What are we trying to measure?', *Journal of Development Studies*, April 1973.

3 *Excess Demand and Spare Capacity*

1 The link between national income concepts and aggregate demand, supply and income

There is a clear link between the concepts of aggregate demand, supply and income of chapter 1, on the one hand, and the national accounting concepts of expenditure, output and income of chapter 2, on the other.

Demand is not exactly the same as expenditure, but the two are very similar. Both can be broken down into the same categories for analysis: the main categories are government demand and spending, and demand and spending for investment, consumption and exports. Demand is not always expressed as actual spending because the goods and services are not always available, or because buyers cannot get credit even though they may be creditworthy. Thus demand may be greater than expenditure. In general, it is not possible for demand to be less than expenditure, since if goods and services are actually bought, demand must have been at least as great as expenditures. The one exception to this is that producers may be unable to sell all of their output, so that stocks may accumulate involuntarily. Since increases in stocks are assumed to be 'bought' by firms from themselves, then in this case 'spending' can be greater than demand.

The supply of goods and services is the same as output (or product). There are two exceptions. Firstly, goods can be supplied from accumulated stocks which were produced in some previous period. In such a case supply would be greater than current production. In this case, however, supply would be the same as output as defined for national income purposes, since that definition includes changes in stocks. Secondly, supply also includes imports–it is possible for a country to import more than it exports and to pay for the difference out of accumulated savings of foreign exchange, or by borrowing from foreign countries. Imports cannot normally be paid for in local currency, so that if imports are greater than exports, payments have to be made out of the earnings of past production (that is, an earlier excess of exports over imports) or out of future production, when part of future inflows of foreign exchange will have to be used to pay the debt service on foreign loans.[1]

The two concepts of income are very close. Income accrues in the form of profits, wages and salaries and self-employment income (including income from farming), some of which is re-spent within the country and some of which is sent out of the country in the form of dividends to foreign owners of local business, interest on loans and expatriates' savings. The important factors concerning income are thus who gets it (which should reveal something of how it is likely to be disposed of), and whether the income is available to be spent within the country or not.[2]

2 *Excess demand*

If demand is greater than supply, there are various ways in which the economy can react. Demand could exceed supply for many reasons—for example as a result of a high wage increase granted by the government, or a big increase in the price of an export crop which is passed on to farmers, or as a result of a big foreign loan which is spent on building new schools or railways or roads. Alternatively, excess demand may occur because of sudden reductions in supply, for example because of a poor harvest or problems with international transport routes, such as can occur in land-locked countries whose transit countries experience civil war or other problems.

The possible reactions to excess demand are categorised below. Basically the supply of goods for sale can be increased in four main ways—by increasing output, reducing accumulated stocks, increasing imports, reducing exports. In addition demand can be frustrated or prices can rise. These are not alternatives since all six possibilities can occur simultaneously or in any number of combinations. The discussion of these possibilities that follows is by no means a comprehensive one: most of them are discussed at much greater length in later chapters.

The intention at this point is to give a rapid overview which should help in understanding the rest of the book.

(1) *A reduction in accumulated stocks of raw materials, work-in-progress and finished products*. Sometimes businesses carry stocks precisely in order to be able to meet sudden increases in demand. In much of Africa, sellers or users of imported goods need to keep large stocks because of being so far from most of their foreign suppliers. Not only does it take a long time between ordering increased supplies and the arrival of the goods, but the length of the time-lag can vary

sharply. The certainty of occasional poor harvests, because of Africa's unreliable climate and farmers being poorly equipped to cope with variations in the weather, leads both individual farmers and governments to hold stocks of basic foods, especially grain. Because grain is relatively expensive to transport, especially overland, storage costs are usually less than the additional cost of imports of such foods as maize and rice. However, there is clearly a limit to meeting excess demand by running down stocks. If demand continues at the new higher level then some other reaction is bound to occur. In practice, moreover, the normal reaction to a period of rising aggregate demand is for there to be an overall increase in stocks throughout the economy. In general, the bigger the national income the bigger the level of stocks should be. Thus although stocks can be run down to meet excess demand in the short run, this process is limited in the long run not only by the fact that stocks must eventually be exhausted, but also by the tendency for producers to try and restore their stocks and even to build them up to higher levels than before.

(2) *An increase in production*. For an increase in production to occur, there must be unemployed resources which can be used in combination. Thus manufactured output can be increased if there is labour available with the right skills and in the right place, if there are machines available with unused capacity and if other inputs (fuel, raw materials, services, transport) can also be increased. Most commonly this situation exists if factories have dismissed workers in some recent period of time, because of a lack of demand for their products. In such circumstances labour with the right skills is probably available locally, since the workers should be able to return to their old jobs. They might of course have found other jobs, or returned to their villages, in which case output would not be able to increase so quickly or easily. In the case of agricultural output, production of most goods cannot be increased in the short term, that is in less time than it takes to grow a crop. The commonest time-lag is thus a year, but many agricultural goods take even longer, for example an increase in the breeding and rearing of beef cattle, or the seven years it takes to get a cocoa crop from the time of planting. Furthermore, these are minimum time-lags, since they assume that farmers have the capacity to increase output: unused land or ability to raise productivity, and access to all the necessary goods and services used in production such as labour, seed, fertiliser, water, marketing and so on.

(3) *An increase in imports*. Even if there is no spare capacity within the economy, there is usually spare capacity somewhere in the world, so that increased demand can usually be met by importing. Nevertheless, there are various other reasons why imports may not increase in response to an increase in aggregate demand: the country may not be

able to pay for additional imports; imports may be controlled by bureaucratic means; international transport routes may not have spare capacity. Most African countries have introduced and maintain strict import licensing precisely because of a lack of foreign exchange to pay for imports that would otherwise be demanded. There have been other reasons for introducing import controls, for example to control where imports come from and to protect local producers of import-substitutes, but one effect of controls has been to slow down the growth in total imports.[3]

(4) *Diversion of exports to the home market.* For example, 95% of Zambia's exports are copper, and because the copper fabrication plant only absorbs a tiny proportion of production, excess demand in Zambia cannot really be absorbed by diverting exports to the home market. In other African countries much the same applies: Ghanaians consume little cocoa, Ugandans little coffee compared with the amounts exported. In principle, however, excess demand could be met in this way. For example rising demand for maize means less available for export, and the same applies to some other agricultural products which are exported and bought locally. Some countries export surplus supplies of electricity, for example Mozambique from Cabora Bassa; as home demand for electricity rises, the amount available for export will be reduced. If African countries develop their *manufacturing* sectors to the point where exports of manufactured goods become significant, then there will be a possibility of meeting excess demand by diverting manufactured exports to the home market. Clearly this can only happen if manufacturers have no spare capacity to meet excess home demand by increasing output, and if manufacturers are prepared to deny their overseas customers in favour of customers at home.

(5) *Demand may be frustrated.* If goods and services are not available then demand, whether from consumers, government, businesses or the overseas buyers of exports, may simply not be expressed as actual expenditure. Africa's recent history provides many examples of this. On the one hand, very rapid increases in aggregate demand after independence, or as a result of a boom in export earnings, have created shortages of many key goods and services. For example, some intended government spending could not take place because many civil service posts were unfilled and many civil servants, both African and expatriate, were new to their jobs. Some consumer demand has also been frustrated, when local production and imports have been unable for one reason or another to increase fast enough. On the other hand, most African countries have sooner or later experienced shortages of foreign exchange, which in turn has resulted in imported goods not being available. In extreme cases, some goods have been rationed by governments, as with petrol in Zambia after Rhodesian UDI in 1965.

Frustrated demand may either be postponed, in which case expenditure will be higher at some later date (than it would have been otherwise), or it may never take place. For example, motorists who did not use their cars so much as they wanted to during petrol rationing could not make up for it afterwards–weekend trips not taken have gone forever. Similarly, a government post not filled means a salary not paid, and unless the government hires two people to clear the backlog of work, that money does not get spent later. Permanently frustrated spending is clearly more effective in coping with excess demand, but even delays can serve a very useful purpose since the capacity of the economy may have increased by the time the money comes to be spent.

(6) *Rising prices*. If supply, from home or abroad, cannot be increased and if demand cannot be contained by rationing or the simple non-availability of goods and services, then prices will be driven up by excess demand. This has happened in African countries, as in the rest of the world, in recent years. There have undoubtedly been other reasons why prices have risen, but excess demand has contributed to inflation in spite of price control measures.

3 Excess supply

An imbalance between supply and demand can also mean that demand is less than supply. This can cause reductions in output and imports, an involuntary build-up of stocks or more goods available for export (provided that there is a market abroad for goods not wanted at home). Cuts in government spending, for example, usually cause a fall in construction work (because such cuts tend to be more severe on development spending than on civil servants providing current government services) and a fall in imports. Stocks, on the other hand, often fall in such circumstances, suggesting that the desire to reduce stocks in the face of falling demand can be greater than any involuntary build-up of unsold output.

Clearly there is no mirror image of frustrated demand–if demand is less than supply all demand can probably be met (some types of demand may still be frustrated, but in aggregate this will not be so) and there is normally no equivalent way in which excess supply can be absorbed. However if a period of excess supply follows quickly after a period when a lot of demand was frustrated, then it is possible that for a while producers will be able to maintain production, by meeting a backlog of orders accumulated during the earlier boom period.

In principle, prices may fall in a period when demand is less than supply–the analysis of markets suggests that this should be so. But prices in the modern world are notoriously 'sticky downwards'. By this is meant that while prices are quick to rise in response to excess demand, they do not usually fall in the reverse situation. There are many reasons for this: for example government guarantees some important prices such as the prices paid to farmers for agricultural goods; and manufacturers and traders are often very reluctant to reduce prices, because they fear the damaging effects of competitive price-cutting and are doubtful about whether demand for their products will increase as a result of lower prices. Most important, wage earners resist very strongly any attempt to cut wages, especially in those sectors with strong trade unions. The result of successful resistance to wage cuts is that the cost of labour to employers does not fall in a situation of excess supply, and this makes it harder for employers to reduce the prices of their products.

Import prices are independent of the balance or imbalance of supply and demand in African economies; excess supply *may* reduce the rate of increase of prices for *locally* produced goods and services, but import prices are unaffected, so that prices are very unlikely to fall overall. A reduction in the rate of inflation may be a very significant achievement, but it is different from an actual fall in prices, especially in its feedback effects.

4 *Feedback effects*

Increases in output and rising prices clearly increase the incomes of producers. In both cases the value of sales increases, incomes therefore increase and unless the whole of the increase in incomes is saved, or taxed and not spent by the government, then spending will increase further. Increases in output and rises in prices are not in any sense a solution therefore to a situation of excess demand, since increases in income will feed back into aggregate demand. Since it is normal for some part of increases in income not to be spent (or to be spent on imports with minimal feedback effects) each successive feedback will be smaller than the previous one, suggesting that some sort of balance or equilibrium between supply and demand might eventually be reached–if no new event occurred to prevent that possibility in the meantime. The conditions under which equilibrium might be reached, and how much output and prices might rise in achieving it, will be discussed at greater length in subsequent chapters. For the moment, the essential point is that disequilibrium can lead to further disequilibrium as a result of feedback–responses to excess demand which increase incomes must lead to further increases in demand.

If additional goods are put up for sale out of accumulated stocks, then in principle no new income is created. The production of stocks is theoretically assumed to generate income; selling off the stocks, therefore, yields no new income, and thus has no feedback effects. This process does mean, however, that firms exchange physical assets (accumulated stocks) for cash. It is not possible to 'spend' stocks, although a firm can borrow, using stocks as security. It is possible to spend cash. Firms might therefore increase their spending if they had been unable to borrow for some reason. Firms' reaction to a reduction in stocks also depends on why they built up stocks in the first place. If the stocks were involuntarily accumulated for lack of demand, then no further action need be expected. But firms might react by trying to rebuild stocks to their former level, or even to a new higher level in keeping with a higher level of demand. In these circumstances, a secondary reaction would be increases in output with the attendant feedback effects.

An increase in imports creates income for foreigners, who are not likely to spend that income in any particular African country. As explained in chapter 1, only in a very large country is there likely to be any feedback effect. As the number of industrialised countries grows it is unlikely that any one country will again dominate world trade as Britain and the USA once did, so that any individual country will be able to ignore the feedback effects of increasing its imports. Of course some local income increases if imports increase; traders selling imported goods do very well. In Africa a large range of goods is still imported because of the low level of industrialisation, so that most traders sell some imported goods and some sell nothing else. Again, traders' income is technically local output and so should be analysed as such, but it should be remembered that some local income is directly dependent on the level of imports.

The frustration of demand clearly has no impact on income. If money is not spent, then no income is received. If demand is postponed, then increased spending at some time in the future will have an effect on income at that time, but the immediate effect of the frustration of demand is quite simply that the circular flow of income is stopped to the extent that spending does not take place. Perhaps this explains the attraction of bureaucratic attempts to frustrate demand. A government trying to control a situation of excess demand faces the problem that some of the possibilities create further income and thus further demand, whilst increases in supply from imports and export diversion both damage the balance of trade and so create problems of their own. Rationing, which is a bureaucratic way of frustrating demand, may then seem the only solution. But bureaucracy has its own cost since extra civil servants have to be paid, or existing ones diverted from other duties; and rationing is politically unpopular and may lead to the development of uncontrolled illegal (or 'black') markets. In addition, the frustration of demand does not provide a channel for the unspent income. It may be saved, but in Africa that may mean an increase in the sending of savings abroad if it is expatriate demand that has been frustrated, and that too damages the balance of payments; or it may mean that people spend their incomes on unrationed goods and services, creating different problems.

5 *Equilibrium and disequilibrium*

Situations of excess demand and excess supply are forms of disequilibrium, by definition. An economy is described as being 'in equilibrium' if aggregate demand equals aggregate supply. That is, equilibrium exists if the demand for goods and services of consumers, government, businesses and export customers is equal to domestic output and imports. This concept of equilibrium is a 'static' or short-term one, since it excludes long-term changes in the production capacity of the economy. In contrast, a 'dynamic' equilibrium in a growing economy is one in which long-term growth in supply is matched over time by long-term growth in demand.

Most of this book is concerned with short-term equilibrium and disequilibrium. This is not because the long-term growth and development of an economy are not important. On the contrary, long-term solutions to the problems of poverty and backwardness are of absolutely fundamental importance and occupy a great deal of the attention of all the governments in Africa and elsewhere in the developing world.

Short-term problems remain however, and have to be understood in order to be tackled. As a working definition of the difference between short term and long term, short term will be taken as a period within which the capacity of the economy to produce goods and services can be assumed to be unchanged. This means assuming that although investment may be taking place, the increased output made possible by investment is not yet available, and that the capacity of the work force, although growing in the long term through growth in population and through better education and training, is unchanged. Some of these assumptions will be relaxed at times, since it is not possible to dissociate short-term from long-term problems. The reaction of an economy to a short-term disequilibrium will almost invariably have an important influence on its long-term development.

A great deal of macroeconomic analysis consists of examining the effects of disequilibrium in an economy. For example, in African economies the effects on the economy of changes in the production of exports, and of changes in the price of exports, are of great importance. A convenient way of analysing these effects is to assume that the economy is initially in equilibrium, with aggregate demand and supply equal to each other, and then to examine how much the various macroeconomic aggregates will change as a result of, say, a change in an export price, and to try and determine what their new levels will be if and when a new equilibrium is reached.

Because of the feedback effects, of changes in output for example, it is clear that equilibrium will not be immediately restored by the reaction of the economy to a situation of disequilibrium. However, in a situation of excess demand, further increases in demand via increases in income are usually smaller with each round of the circular flow of income. Taking an increase in aggregate demand caused by, say, an increase in government spending, the income of consumers and businesses will increase as a result. But not all of these increases in income will be spent. Some will be taxed, some will be saved, and some of the spending will be on imports, which does not create new domestic income. In short, leakages from the circular flow of income gradually reduce the size of successive rounds of spending. Eventually, therefore, it is possible that a new equilibrium could be reached, at a higher overall level of economic activity and of national income, provided that no new injections into the circular flow of income occur in the meantime. Emphasis on comparing the hypothetical equilibrium values of national income before and after a state of disequilibrium is why macroeconomics is often called 'national income analysis'.

6 *Equilibrium expressed in terms of saving and investment*

Saving is defined as that part of income that is not spent on current goods and services. In other words, saving is income minus consumption. Investment is defined as spending which is not for current consumption but for future consumption or to increase the capacity to produce in the future. In other words investment is total spending minus consumption.

Since total spending has been defined in such a way that it is equal to total income, both being equal to GNP, it follows that saving equals investment. Both are equal to that part of national income which is not consumed (that is, not used up during the current period and so available in some way for the future).

It may help to make this clear if the relationship is expressed in symbols. If

Y = income (GNP) = output available for consumption or investment

C = consumption by individuals
I = investment (fixed domestic investment plus increase in stocks)
G = government current spending on goods and services
X = exports
M = imports

then because total supply equals total spending

$$Y + M = C + I + G + X$$

or as it is more frequently written

$$Y = C + I + G + X - M$$

Now savings consist of that part of income which is not consumed, so

$$S\text{(savings)} = Y - C - G$$

Since Y (domestic output) is the same as income, and consumption consists of consumption by individuals plus collective consumption by government, it follows that

$$S = Y - C - G = I + X - M$$

But the difference between exports and imports ($X - M$) is a form of investment. If the country exports more than it imports then foreign exchange reserves will rise, or foreign loans can be repaid. Either way, net foreign assets increase, which is a form of investment. Like all forms of investment, it will allow greater future consumption than would otherwise have been possible—because of the existence of additional foreign reserves, or because loans no longer have to be repaid.

In other words saving equals investment, if 'investment' includes investment abroad.

Although saving and investment are by definition equal after the event (or '*post hoc*' which means 'after this event' in Latin) the intentions of savers and investors before the event (*ex ante* in Latin) may not be equal. The reason is that some saving is *not* done by the same people who make investment decisions. Individuals save out of their incomes, and put money in a box under the bed, or deposit money in a bank or building society. Investment is *mainly* undertaken by government and by businesses, in pursuit of their various interests, and both government and businesses are normally net *borrowers* of money. To some extent the saving and investment decision is the same: businesses retain profits rather than distributing them to shareholders *in order to* invest; and government runs a current surplus of revenue over current spending *in order to* finance its capital spending. Individuals also save in order to invest in housing, but the normal practice in private house buying, as in capital spending by businesses and government, is for investment to be partly (or even mainly) financed by borrowing.

Now if saving is a result of decisions by one group and investment is the result of decisions by another group, there is no reason to suppose that savings plans and investment plans will be equal, even though the two groups overlap a bit. If savers plan to save more than investors plan to spend, total demand, which consists of consumption demand plus investment demand, will be less than income and thus less than output. This amounts to a situation of excess supply.

Similarly in the reverse situation, if investors plan to spend more than savers plan to save, investment demand will be more than the resources released by saving (or non-consumption), which amounts to a situation of excess demand. It is thus possible to express equilibrium and disequilibrium in terms of savings and investment rather than in terms of aggregate demand and supply.

The supposed advantage of focusing on savings and investment is that this also focuses attention on financial markets and financial institutions. The main way in which money not spent by consumers is made available to investors is through 'financial intermediaries'. Thus if a saver puts money in the Post Office Savings Bank, that is a loan to the government. Savings deposited in a commercial bank may be lent to business borrowers, or to the government by purchase of government stocks and bills.

But not all investment is financed out of borrowing, as has been explained; and investors are not the only borrowers. A significant proportion of consumption is also financed by borrowing, especially the purchase of 'consumer durables' (long-lasting items such as cars and refrigerators). This form of credit, known as consumer credit, is of greater importance in rich countries where production and sale of consumer durables is a greater proportion of economic activity than in Africa. But it is of growing importance in Africa. Furthermore, some African governments (for example, Malawi) have at times borrowed to finance *current* expenditure; while other governments, for example Zambia in the late 1960s and Botswana in the late 1970s, have several times had an annual surplus of tax revenue over both current and capital spending, which means that in those years investment by government (a large proportion of total investment) was financed without any net borrowing at all.

It seems, therefore, that there is no great advantage in paying here as much attention to the savings-investment relationship as is done in other textbooks. The important things for the student to know are firstly, that

actual (or *post hoc*) saving = actual (or *post hoc*) investment.

This statement is simply true by definition. Secondly, the student should know that

> planned (or *ex ante*) saving is *not* necessarily equal to planned (or *ex ante* investment

because plans are made by different (but overlapping) groups of people. As far as the equilibrium of the economy as a whole is concerned, it is much more useful to concentrate on the relation between aggregate demand (which could be described as planned spending) and aggregate supply, since all the factors affecting equilibrium are then included.

7 *Spare capacity and 'unemployment'*

If an increase in demand is to be met by increased domestic output there must obviously be some sort of spare production capacity in the economy. More specifically, unused resources must be available in the right combinations and the right places so that production can increase in response to the increased demand. Thus it is not sufficient to have unemployed labour in the country if that labour is in the wrong place, has the wrong skills or has no capital goods with which to work.

In industrialised countries the scarcest resource is nearly always labour. Spare capacity is thus usually referred to as unemployment, meaning unemployment of people. A situation of full utilisation of capacity (that is, a situation where no further increase in output is possible) is normally called 'full employment', since as output increases labour becomes scarce while there is still an adequate amount of capital available.

In Africa the scarcest resources are skilled labour, foreign exchange for imports and physical capital.[4] Thus the expansion of most African economies after the achievement of independence was greatly hindered by shortages of skilled labour and the inadequate inheritance of such things as roads, housing and production capacity in every sector of industry. Meanwhile shortages of skilled labour were bound to be prolonged by the lack of schools and other training institutions. Some skilled labour can be imported, but this tends to be extremely expensive in both direct salary costs and in indirect costs such as the provision of housing and other facilities. Physical capital is also expensive and has to be built up slowly over the years.

The emphasis on the level of unemployment as the key indicator of capacity to increase output in an industrialised economy dates from the 1930s when the 'great depression' caused millions of workers to lose their jobs. In an industrialised economy, workers depend on jobs for their living. They no longer have any link with the rural sector, which is much too small anyway to absorb a significant number of unemployed urban workers. In Zambia, by contrast, the copper miners thrown out of work by the great depression simply returned to their villages. Many had not even brought their families to town, and there was enough land for all.

The sort of unemployment which occurred in industrial economies in the 1930s, where factories are closed for lack of demand for their products, is sometimes called 'demand deficiency' unemployment. It is also called 'Keynesian' unemployment because the English economist Keynes is credited with finding the solution–namely to stimulate demand. If somehow demand can be increased, labour can return to work at very short notice and output can quickly increase. That may seem very obvious, but at the beginning of the great depression governments reacted to falling demand and growing unemployment by *reducing* their spending, which made things worse.

The existence of unemployment in Africa is an important social and political problem, but very little of it has been caused by lack of demand. On the contrary, the urgency of development needs has tended to push African economies into situations of excess demand rather than the opposite. Cutbacks in government spending do occur from time to time, and these cutbacks cause unemployment, especially in the construction industry, but also in other sectors of the economy. It is always very important therefore for aggregate demand to be maintained at a level which employs as many people as possible, so that there is no *unnecessary* unemployment. The scarce resources of skilled labour and capital should be used as fully as possible.

'As fully as possible' suggests that other considerations may be important. This is so. Most importantly, high levels of demand lead to a high demand for imports. So long as African countries have an adequate supply of foreign exchange, whether from growing export volume or prices, or from inflows of foreign aid and foreign loans, imports can be increased and paid for; but falling export prices, for example, may mean having to reduce demand even at the risk of throwing men out of work. Another important consideration is inflation, since a high level of demand may cause prices to rise faster than is desired.

If unemployment in Africa is only marginally caused by lack of demand, what does cause it? Before describing the main cause, some relatively unimportant forms of unemployment should be dealt with first. In all countries there is a small proportion of the work force that is basically *unemployable*. Some people are unemployable because of physical or mental limitations or because they are simply 'work-shy'. In addition, some people are unemployed because they are in the process of changing their jobs. Provided their next job is fairly certain such people are not really a problem. Unemployment statistics in industrialised economies usually try and identify this group in a rough and ready way by distinguishing between those who have been unemployed for a short time, for example less than six weeks, and those who have been unemployed for longer. Temporary unemployment is called *frictional*.

More serious as a social and political problem is so-called *structural* unemployment, which consists of people thrown out of work because their industry is in decline and their skills are becoming obsolete. This is a serious problem in the older industrialised countries. Britain, for example, has serious structural unemployment in mining, shipbuilding and textile industries which are declining because substitutes have been found (oil for coal, cheaper or more efficient overseas labour in shipbuilding and textiles) or because other nations have overtaken Britain and can compete by making a cheaper product (Japan in shipbuilding, Hong Kong in textiles). Structural unemployment is often associated with *regional* unemployment, so that workers have not only to learn new skills but to move to new areas, or the government is faced with trying to persuade new industries to go to the declining areas.

The development of industry in Africa is too recent for much of this type of structural unemployment to exist. There are a few abandoned mines, long since worked out or rendered unprofitable by changing relative prices; and some tourist areas have lost custom, usually for political reasons (for example Livingstone and the Victoria Falls during the period of the war in Zimbabwe, and Uganda during the periods before and after the fall of Amin). There is a sense, however, in which it would be possible to describe Africa's main form of unemployment as structural. People whose rural skills are of no use in the modern sector of the economy are seeking work in towns, where there is a shortage of people with industrial skills and advanced education but a surplus of job-seekers who are unskilled in the modern sense and have little or no education. The problem is made much worse by one of the effects of increased availability of education. The number of relatively unskilled primary school leavers is much greater than the number of unskilled jobs being created each year; a large proportion of those with a primary education seek urban jobs, because they are not willing to farm in rural areas even where spare land exists. Even in those countries where secondary school leavers and university graduates can still get jobs, there is every reason to expect, from African manpower forecasts and from experience of developing countries in other parts of the world, that unemployment will soon shift up the educational scale where it has not done so already.

The African employment problem is thus 'structural' in very different ways from the meaning of that word in industrial countries. African countries are investing heavily in education and training; at the same time many of the ablest rural inhabitants are leaving their villages and farms to seek employment in the towns. Not only do the most enterprising tend to be the ones who leave, but the education system has the effect of selecting the ablest children and funnelling them up through the educational system. The farther up they go, the less likely are they to return to their villages, and to agriculture as a way of making a living. The more efficient are the selection methods at each state of education, the more efficiently does education remove the ablest, in an intellectual sense, from the rural areas.[5]

The problems of urban-rural migration and unemployed school-leavers cannot be tackled here.[6] Clearly some sort of two-pronged attack, involving the creation of better opportunities to make a living in rural areas and the creation of more jobs for the relatively unskilled, is necessary. Equally clearly the problem has little to do with short-term equilibrium and disequilibrium in aggregate demand and supply. The latter remains important, but can only have a relatively small effect on unemployment.

One further type of unemployment should be mentioned—*disguised* unemployment. This refers to workers who are not actually unemployed but whose usefulness in their work is so low that production would fall by very little if they ceased work. In the extreme case, disguised unemployment is defined as a situation in which workers have zero marginal productivity. The situation is supposed to arise in agriculture where there is a severe shortage of land so that there are more workers than are needed to maintain production; or in the urban sector where employers hire more workers than they need, because of very low wages and widespread unemployment. It can also occur in the urban informal sector, where large numbers of people compete for a limited market, for example selling oranges or washing cars: removing people from this type of activity does not result in any reduction in output. It is unlikely that there is significant disguised unemployment in rural Africa: in much of Africa land is not scarce, and research has shown that migration of household members in search of employment does reduce rural output. It is possible that some urban employers do hire more workers than they need, but it is unlikely that there is a significant amount of disguised urban unemployment in most African countries because of the cost, especially in those countries where urban wages are not particularly low.[7] In Kenya, on the other hand, the government actually tried to compel all employers to increase their labour force by ten per cent regardless of their labour needs. To the extent that this move was successful there must have been some disguised unemployment as a result.

8 *Output and employment*

Short-term fluctuations in the volume of non-agricultural output are normally reflected in employment. If the short term is defined as a period during which the stock of capital does not change, which must mean that skills and productivity cannot change either, then output changes can only occur by using more or less labour. Normally this will be reflected in the number of people employed. However, those in jobs may work longer or shorter hours, so that instead of an increase in employment there is an increase in overtime; and instead of a reduction in employment there is a reduction in overtime and an increase in short-time working—for example the four-day week. Output in agriculture can vary because of variations in the weather, or because of crop and animal diseases; variations in planned output, for example as shown in acreage planted, are more likely to be reflected in employment in a similar way to changes in non-agricultural output, although published statistics are less likely to pick up the employment changes in agriculture because of the more widespread use of family labour.

Employment may not respond to changes in output because of the practice of 'labour hoarding'. Employers may prefer to retain (or 'hoard') their workers rather than dismiss them when output falls, because they expect the fall in output to be temporary. In this situation it is often more efficient to keep the labour force together than to dismiss workers who may not be available when demand and output recover.

Governments in Africa may also put political pressure on employers to maintain employment. Such political pressure is greater in parastatal industry, where governments have a more direct influence on employment policy, through ownership and participation on the board of directors. But less direct political pressure can also be effective: employers need to avoid governments' disapproval because of their many contacts with government departments on other issues, such as work permits, import licences and government contracts.

Labour hoarding is more likely to occur the greater is the skill level of the workers involved, for both economic and political reasons. The more skilled the workers, the more difficult it can be to replace them when output needs to be increased to former levels, because of the greater scarcity of skilled labour in Africa. Skilled workers are also more likely to be able to bring political pressure on a government, whether through a trade union or by other means. So mining companies tend to maintain their labour force when output falls, whereas employment in construction falls quite quickly when output falls because of the greater use of unskilled labour and the lower level of unionisation and political organisation of workers in the construction industry.

NOTES

1 Note that 'foreign earnings' can include such things as the remittances of migrant workers abroad and grants of aid, as well as sale abroad of goods and services.

2 The conventional distinction is between domestic income and national income. But as explained in chapter 2, this distinction would only deduct from domestic income money accruing to overseas residents—mainly shareholders in businesses in Africa. Money sent out of the country by short-term expatriate residents in Africa is sent out *in order to* be spent abroad, and should not really count as domestic income.

3 It is not possible to distinguish between the effects of higher prices and controls on the volume of imports into African economies. However, there is no doubt that the rate of growth of imports in Sub-Saharan Africa slowed down by more than the slowdown in the rate of growth of GDP, when the 1970s are compared with the 1960s.

Average annual growth rates

	1960–70		*1970–79*	
	GDP	*Imports*	*GDP*	*Imports*
Low-income semi-arid	+2.3	+4.8	+2.2	+5.5
Low-income other	+3.9	+6.2	+1.7	−0.5
Middle-income oil importers	+4.5	+6.6	+3.1	+2.3
Middle-income oil exporters	+3.4	+1.6	+4.6	+3.3
Sub-Saharan Africa	+3.9	+6.0	+2.9	+3.3

Source: *Accelerated Development in Sub-Saharan Africa: an agenda for action*, World Bank, 1981, Appendix Tables 2 and 7.

4 Physical capital means machinery, lorries, trains, buildings, roads, etc.

5 There are some exceptions to this, in that some of the most successful urban people have invested in large-scale agricultural production, out of savings or bank borrowing or both, for example in cattle in Botswana and in tobacco estates in Malawi. However, this can hardly be said to be a significant reversal of rural-urban migration, even if one of its better aspects may be to create more rural sector jobs.

6 It should not be assumed from the above paragraphs that investment in education by African governments is a mistaken policy. There is a body of research which shows that investment in education is highly profitable, and that investment in primary education is the most profitable of all.

Social returns to education in Africa

Education level	*Rate of return (per cent)*
Primary	29
Secondary	17
Higher	12

Source: George Psacharapoulos, 'Returns to education: an updated international comparison' in Timothy King (ed.) 'Education and Income', World Bank Staff Working Paper No. 402, 1980, quoted in World Bank, *Accelerated Development in Sub-Saharan Africa: an agenda for action*, 1981, Table 6.1.

7 But see the last section of this chapter on labour hoarding, which could be described as a form of short-term disguised unemployment.

4 *The Consumption Function*

1 Definition of consumption

The economic meaning of consumption is the using-up of economic resources so that they are not available in the future. From the point of view of the individual, consumption is that part of income that is spent on 'consumer goods'—the remainder of income being defined as savings. It is actually possible for the individual to have consumption greater than income, by spending past savings or borrowing, in which case the individual has 'dissaved' or had 'negative savings'.

From the point of view of the national economy, consumption includes current spending by government; and saving by the nation as a whole includes not only saving by individuals out of their incomes, but also saving by government. Government saving occurs if current government revenue from taxation and other sources is greater than current government spending. Government saving, like private saving, can be negative, if the government runs a current deficit and has to borrow to pay for its current spending.

Business income, or profits, is technically part of the private income of the individuals who own the business. Nevertheless a business is described as 'saving' if it retains part of its profits rather than distributing them as personal incomes to owners. Some of the distributed income may also be saved, but this is usually described as being part of private saving.

Commercial farms are a form of business. Commercial farmers can consume or save their cash incomes in the same way as other businessmen. Subsistence production of, say, maize can either be consumed or 'saved' in the form of accumulating stocks. Subsistence production of investment goods, such as the clearing of land or the building up of cattle herds, is a form of income which is by definition saved and invested simultaneously.

These definitions give rise to a number of problems. For example, a great deal of spending by individuals is on goods which are not immediately 'consumed'. The most obvious of such goods are the large, expensive, long-lasting items like cars, refrigerators and furniture, known as consumer durables. Precisely because these items have a fairly long life they can very often be obtained on credit by means of loans or hire purchase arrangements. Nevertheless they are defined as consumption, as are more obviously consumable items like tins of food which are bought and stored in the home without being consumed at once. The only item of private spending which is *not* treated as consumption is the purchase of a house.

This definition of consumer spending by individuals means that the purchase of an item like a car for private use is treated as consumption, but when it is bought by a business it is investment. The importance of consumer durables is, however, relatively minor in poor countries; and demand for consumer durables has less immediate effect on the domestic output of poor countries since the poorer the country the more likely are consumer durables to be imported. Even those items which are manufactured locally are mainly assembled from imported parts so that the local value added is small.

2 *Importance of consumption*

Of the four main components of demand–private consumption, investment, government current spending and exports–private consumption is normally the biggest. This can be seen in Table 4.1, which shows the relative importance of the components of demand in a few African countries. The exception is Zambia, where the copper industry is so large in relation to the rest of the economy, that export demand is sometimes as large as, or larger than demand from private consumers. In all African economies, the share of private consumption in total demand is partly a function of export prices: when export prices go up, so does the share of exports in total demand, so that the share of consumption goes down. Again, Zambia is the extreme case: between 1974 and 1979 private consumption's share of total demand varied between 25% and 34%, with export's share varying between 23% and 36%, usually in the opposite direction. But there were sharp variations elsewhere, too, for example in Sierra Leone where private consumption's share of total demand varied from 58% to 65% over the same period.

Remembering what was said in chapter 2 about the undervaluation of subsistence output and consumption, because they are valued at farm gate rather than urban retail prices and because some subsistence activities are completely omitted from official statistics, the share of private consumption should really be even higher, especially in those

Table 4.1 Components of final demand: selected countries (1979) (percentages)

	Kenya	*Nigeria*	*Sierra Leone*	*Tanzania*	*Zambia*
Private consumption	47	48	65	60	33
Government consumption	14	9	5	12	19
Total consumption	61	57	70	72	52
Gross fixed capital formation	15	24	11	16	13
Increase in stocks	4	—	1	1	2
Export of goods and services	20	19	18	11	33
Total supply (GDP plus imports)	100	100	100	100	100

NOTES
(1) Figures for Nigeria are for 1978
(2) Figures for Sierra Leone show too low a percentage for exports because a large but varying proportion of diamond exports are smuggled and not recorded in official figures; consequently percentages for other categories of demand are too high.

Source: *International Financial Statistics*

countries, such as Tanzania, where subsistence activities are relatively important.

Whatever the detailed statistical arguments, it should be clear that the determinants of private consumption are crucially important to understanding how the macroeconomy functions, and in particular, how much of a change in income is spent by consumers since this determines the size of the feedback effect of any change in spending. This is discussed in the next section.

3 *The determinants of changes in private consumption*

It is obvious that over any length of time, consumption by individuals must be determined principally by their income. To a much lesser extent, some people are able to spend on consumption out of past savings or by borrowing. The main problem to be examined here, though, is the effect on consumption of *changes* in income, and other short-term changes in the economy. Since private consumption is a very large component of total demand it is also a very large part of the feedback from changes in demand. Thus the important thing to investigate is the short-term *change* in consumption that occurs as a

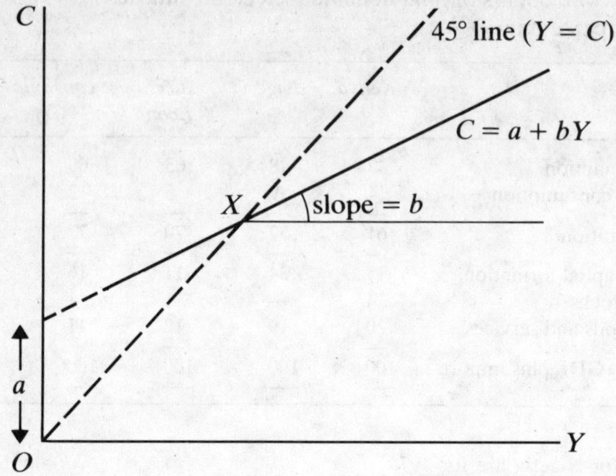

Figure 4.1 Consumption function $C = a + bY$

result of a *change* in income. This is called the 'marginal propensity to consume' or the 'mpc'. Basically it describes the feedback effect via consumption of a change in income:[1]

$$\text{mpc} = \frac{\Delta C}{\Delta Y}$$

if C = private consumption,
Y = income.

On the other hand, the 'average propensity to consume' or the 'apc' is the proportion of total income that is consumed:

$$\text{apc} = \frac{C}{Y}$$

These are simply definitions. There is a *theory* which says that consumption is related in a particular way to income, thus

$$C = a + bY$$

where a and b are positive *constants*. What this theory is suggesting is that consumption increases or decreases with income in a particular way, namely that consumption is determined by income according to a linear formula. Some consumption, represented by a, is independent of changes in income; the remainder varies with income in such a way that b is in fact the marginal propensity to consume (see below for an algebraic demonstration of this). This theory is attributed to the English economist Keynes, and is called the Keynesian consumption theory (or consumption function). On a graph it looks like Figure 4.1. The theory of $C = a + bY$ implies several things about consumption, including:

(1) consumption is greater as income is greater, and less as income is less;

(2) if income changes from Y to Y^1, then the new level of consumption will be

$$C^1 = a + bY^1$$

compared to

$$C = a + bY$$

Subtracting one equation from the other gives

$$C^1 - C = b(Y^1 - Y)$$

or

$$\Delta C = b\Delta Y$$

or

$$\Delta C/\Delta Y = \text{mpc} = b$$

The theory thus implies that the marginal propensity to consume is a constant, b.

(3) the average propensity to consume, $\frac{C}{Y}$, is

$$\frac{C}{Y} = \frac{a}{Y} + b$$

so that the apc gets *smaller* as income increases. This is the same as saying that the average propensity to save gets *bigger* as income increases. In other words, the richer people get the more they save.

(4) if income is very low, consumption will equal income, so that no saving takes place at all. This is shown in the figure by the point X where the line $C = a + bY$ cuts the dotted line $Y = C$ (the line at 45° from the origin, 0). If income is even lower than at the point X, then consumption is greater than income, saving is negative and so is investment. This can happen to a subsistence farmer, for example, if he has a poor crop and survives by eating stocks of food accumulated in a previous period. In such a situation the farmer is dissaving and disinvesting. It can happen to a nation if net investment is negative, that is, if depreciation of the nation's capital is greater than gross investment; in these circumstances saving is also negative.

The Keynesian consumption theory seems quite plausible. But so did the consumption theory in use before Keynes wrote his *General Theory* in 1936.[2] This earlier theory, now known as 'classical theory', suggested that saving was mainly determined by the rate of interest offered to savers. If the rate of interest on bank savings accounts and other investments was high, then people would save more and of course a low rate of interest would reduce the incentive to save and so cause an increase in consumption. This theory therefore put the emphasis on saving, suggesting that people first decide how much to save, the remainder of the income being available for consumption. Keynesian theory puts the primary emphasis on consumption.

The only way to decide which theory is correct is to examine the facts. Before doing so, however, it is worth pointing out that the classical theory as described above does not take full account of the possible effect of changes in the rate of interest paid on savings. If the rate of interest *rises*, people's savings will be worth more in the future so that the need to save is reduced, and people may save *less*. In practice, research has failed to find any significant connection between interest rates on the one hand, and the division of income between savings and consumption on the other hand. No research has been done on this question in Africa, perhaps because the monetary authorities have mostly chosen to make very few changes in nominal interest rates,[3] but there is no apparent reason for thinking that such research would yield results any different from the research done in other countries.

There may, on the contrary, be some reason for thinking that interest rates are even less likely to influence the amount of savings in Africa than elsewhere. In African countries, rural people save large amounts of money in the form of banknotes: the motive for saving is the extreme uncertainty of rural income, the reason for saving in banknotes is that most rural people are too far from a financial institution for a savings account to be convenient. Thus the Bank of Botswana *Annual Report 1976* (p. 13) estimated rural note holdings in Botswana to be three and a half times as large as urban note holdings, and commented on peoples' reluctance to open bank accounts, even when they had to go to a bank to change their notes when a new currency was issued. This is evidence of a significant volume of cash saving completely outside the world of savings institutions and interest rates.[4]

Some evidence of the relationship between income and consumption in Africa is available from household budget surveys. One of the main reasons for carrying out such surveys is to provide weights for consumer price indices. However, the same sources can also be used to identify the changing proportion of income consumed by households at different levels of income. The results of one such survey are shown in Figure 4.2. A very similar picture emerges from similar surveys in other countries.[5]

The points representing the two lowest income brackets should

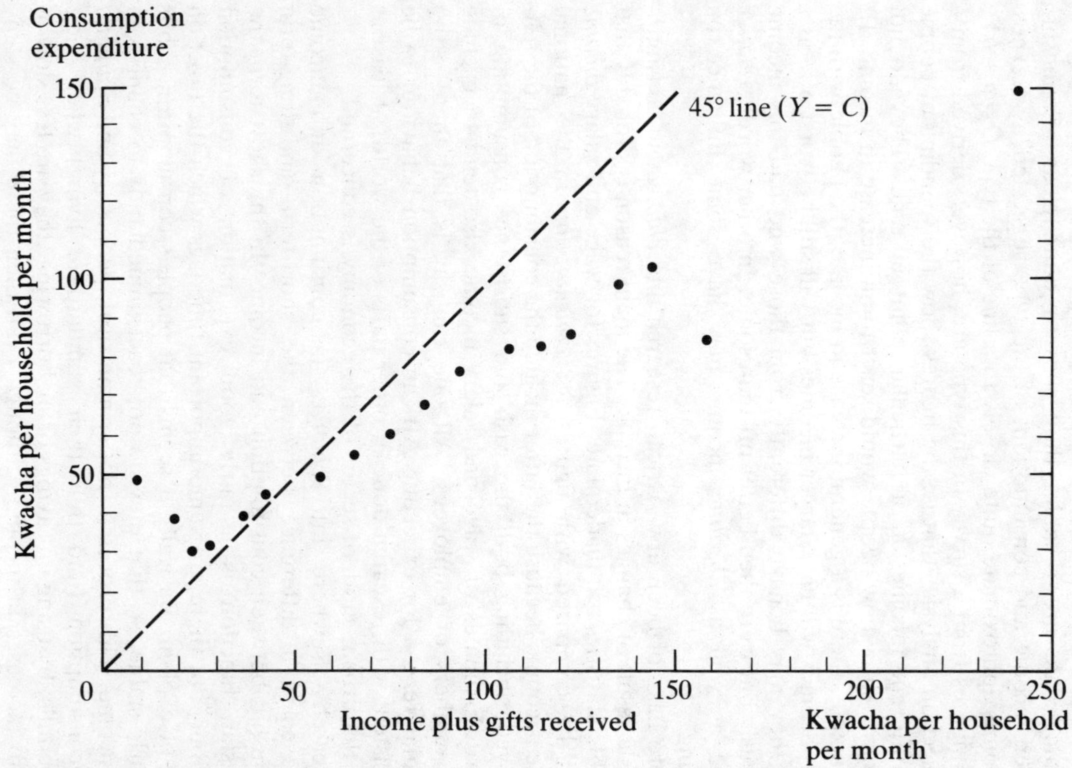

Figure 4.2 Cross-sectional figures for consumption and income of urban households in Zambia
Source: *Some important tables of Urban Budget Survey: 1966–68*, Lusaka, CSO, 1973

probably be ignored, since expenditure is shown to be much higher than total receipts including loans and that is not possible. There must have been some errors of measurement, presumably in underestimating receipts, since 269 households with an average membership of five persons could not have survived on total receipts, including receipts of goods as well as of cash, of just over K10 per month. Assuming the remaining data are reliable, they show a quite clear relationship between income and consumption, of the type suggested by Keynes. The points approximate quite closely to a line of the type $C = a + bY$.

The figures from a survey of this type are, however, derived from a cross-section analysis–that is, the figures show the spending of people with different incomes at a particular point in time. They do not necessarily show how people would react to an increase in income. If, for example, there is a general increase in income, the people with the lowest incomes will have larger incomes but will still be worst off–as a result they may behave differently from those who had this income previously but were then better off than some. In other words, *relative* income as well as *absolute* income may have some influence on spending.

There has not been any African research into *changes* in consumption as a result of changes in income. The main reason is probably that available statistics are inadequate. Figures for wage and salary *income* cannot be compared with figures for *consumption* in the national income accounts because the latter include the consumption of the self-employed, including both the cash and subsistence consumption of farmers. Estimates of wage and salary income also tend to exclude large numbers of employees. All one can say is that there is no particular reason for expecting African consumption behaviour to be inconsistent with research done in other parts of the world, at least as far as the urban, modern sector of the economy is concerned.

Research elsewhere into *changes* in consumption and income has revealed a difference between the short-term and long-term relationship between consumption and income. In the short term the Keynesian function is a fairly good explanation of consumption behaviour, but there are some important time-lags which the function does not explain. Basically it seems that people's consumption habits are fairly stable, so that they do not react immediately to changes in their income. This process is not symmetrical: people try and *maintain* their consumption (and thus their standard of living) when their income falls, by using up savings or by borrowing; they are less slow to react to increases in income, although even then there may be some time-lag so that savings increase for a while as people adjust to new income levels.

Various theories have been put forward to explain these variations on the simple Keynesian consumption function. The 'permanent income' hypothesis suggests that people consume according to what they estimate their income is likely to be in the long term, or permanently. Short-term variations of income away from these expectations are therefore ignored as far as possible. An alternative theory is that consumption depends on the 'previous peak' income; that is, people adjust their spending to the highest that their income has ever been. If income increases above its previous peak level, consumption increases accordingly; if income falls below its previous peak level, consumption does not fall, or does not fall to the level it had reached when income was previously at that point.

Both the permanent-income hypothesis and the previous-peak theory have received quite strong confirmation from American data. Clearly they are theories whose main relevance is for growing, industrialised economies where changes in incomes are marginal, that is, relatively small in relation to total income. One would not necessarily expect them to apply to the predominantly agricultural economies of Africa. In fact American research has discovered that farmers have significantly different savings habits from the rest of the population—they save more at all levels of income. This factor makes only a small difference in industrialised economies because farmers are a small proportion of the population (less than 10% in America).

In Africa, however, it is very important. Furthermore, the most likely reasons why farmers save more than urban workers at similar income levels are, firstly that they face greater uncertainty and so need savings against natural disasters and price variations ('precautionary' savings); and secondly, that they are both businessmen and ordinary consumers at one and the same time which means their incomes have some of the characteristics of business incomes—saving is usually much higher out of profits than out of wages and salaries. Clearly the first of these factors, uncertainty, is much greater for African than for American farmers. Against this, African farmers generally have much lower incomes so that their *ability* to save is less.

Estimates of the savings of African rural households are rare, because of the extreme difficulty of measuring income and consumption in the African rural context. Thus the otherwise very detailed and thorough Rural Income Distribution Survey in Botswana had to admit that

> Additional cash savings were *estimated* as an increasing fraction of the residual income, as the income increased, by a model which was very subjective. The consumption of the richest households has been calculated according to the model, but no reliance can be placed on these particular figures. . . median consumption is surprisingly low, it may indicate that the model used has over-estimated household savings among lower income households.[6]

However, rural survey data from Zambia from the same period as the urban budget survey from which Figure 4.2 is derived, do appear to show very clearly what one would expect, namely that poor rural households save a much higher proportion of income than poor urban households, even allowing for urban prices being higher than rural prices; this is shown in Table 4.2.

Table 4.2 Monthly savings of rural and urban low-income households

	Income per head K	*Savings per head K*	*Savings as % of income*
Rural households	3·37	1·02	30
Urban Budget Survey households	12·08	0·97	8

Sources: Universities of Nottingham and Zambia Agricultural Labour Productivity Investigation (UNZALPI) Report No. 3, Tables 1/9 to 1/12, pp. 147–50 as corrected by Report No. 5; p. 111; and as for Figure 4.2.

Research into the *long-term* relationship between consumption and income reveals a rather different picture. This should be clear from Figure 4.1. If an economy has been growing over time, then income at some time in the past must have been so low that it was actually less than the point on the graph where income equals consumption. But this would mean that total consumption was greater than total income at that time. Clearly that was not so, since the economy could not have grown over time with negative savings. So the short-term consumption function $C = a + bY$ *cannot* also represent the long-term function.

The explanation is partly given by the previous peak income theory already discussed. It is also partly explained by the concept of relative poverty. People are influenced in their consumption spending not only by the absolute level of their income, but by the incomes of the other people in their society. As average incomes rise, therefore, what was once an adequate income, out of which people could save, becomes an inadequate income out of which people are unable to save because of the higher consumption standards set by a richer society. This is sometimes called the demonstration effect.

In the less developed countries there is a particular type of demonstration effect arising out of contact with people from richer countries. This *international* demonstration effect, particularly strong in Africa where there is a large expatriate labour force, but also transmitted by means of films and magazines, pushes up consumption. In addition,

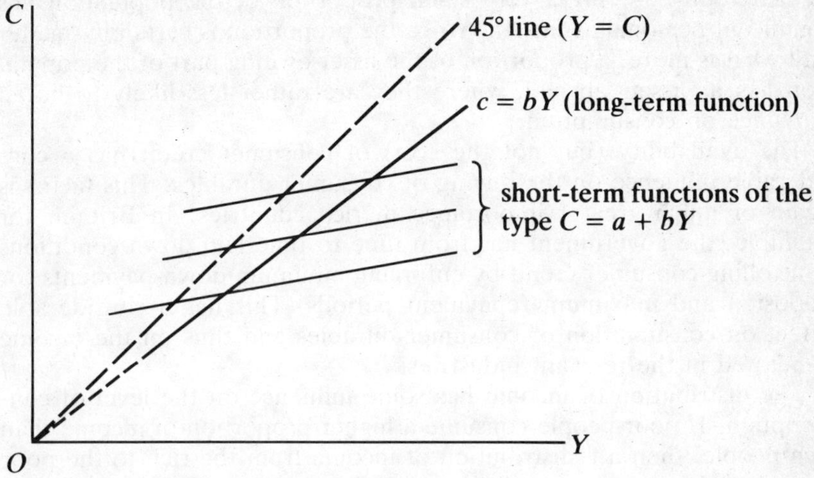

Figure 4.3 Short-term and long-term consumption functions

localisation of jobs previously performed by expatriates leaves behind their previous salary structure, or some modification of it, and also their housing. The infrastructure created for the highly paid expatriates does not disappear when they are replaced, and this creates upward pressures on consumption.

For whatever reason, it appears from research in industrialised economies that over the long term, decades rather than years, consumption is *proportional* to income; the long-term consumption function is thus of the form $C = bY$. If the short-term consumption function is of the form $C = a + bY$, then it must shift upwards on the graph as economic growth pushes up people's incomes. This is illustrated in Figure 4.3.

4 *Other factors affecting consumption*

The possession of assets makes additional consumption possible. 'Liquid' assets, that is cash or assets that can be turned quickly and easily into cash, probably have a greater influence on spending; but even illiquid assets like housing can be used to increase spending because they make borrowing easier, and because the possession of assets reduces the need to save. However, this factor is almost certainly very small in Africa. No research has been done on it, but even in rich countries only a very small proportion of the population has significant personal assets. In Africa the proportion is certainly smaller and what is more, a proportion of the asset-owning part of the population has its assets abroad, where they are rather less likely to be an influence on consumption.

The availability (but not the cost) of consumer credit has a considerable influence on the buying of consumer durables. This factor is again of much greater importance in rich countries. In Britain, for example, the government has from time to time laid down conditions controlling consumer credit by enforcing minimum down-payments (or deposits) and maximum repayment periods. This has a considerable effect on consumption of consumer durables and thus on the income generated in the relevant industries.

The distribution of income has some influence on the level of consumption. If poor people consume a higher proportion of income than rich people, then a redistribution of income from the rich to the poor should lead to an increase in consumption. It is rare, however, that a major change in income distribution occurs over a short period, so that this factor is unlikely to have much effect on the analysis of short-term changes in the economy. Similarly, the migration of rural people to town is likely to result in consumption being higher than it would otherwise have been, if urban workers consume more at each level of income than farmers. The situation is complicated in Africa by the fact that many migrants to towns retain strong rural connections, oscillating between town and village themselves, investing quite heavily in rural production (for example in cattle in Botswana, in tobacco in Malawi, in cocoa in Ghana) and sending remittances to family members still in the rural areas. Rural-urban migration may only rather gradually increase people's propensity to consume as they become permanently urbanised, and even then only among those with access to modern sector incomes (because of their greater security). Again, it is unlikely that rural-urban migration could have much effect on the analysis of short-term economic changes.

A final influence on consumption which has received a great deal of attention in economic writing is the 'real-balance effect', also known as the 'Pigou effect' after the English economist who first discussed it. If prices rise, the real value of money balances is reduced: other things being equal this will reduce consumption since people's liquid assets have fallen. Conversely, if prices fall, the real value of money balances increases, increasing consumption. The argument also applies to assets other than money balances whose value is fixed in money terms. For the same reasons that assets, liquid or otherwise, have a very small influence on consumption, the real balance effect is also small. Those with substantial money balances are in any case precisely those who are least likely to allow their standard of living to fall as a result of rising prices.

5 *The impact of the consumption function $C = a + bY$*

Despite the reservations and complications already discussed, a consumption function of the type $C = a + bY$ is quite a good first approximation to consumption behaviour in the short term. The function expresses two very important ideas: firstly that income is the main influence on consumption, secondly that there is a marginal propensity to consume which expresses the amount of a *change* in income that gets spent and thus creates further changes in income. The marginal propensity to consume is thus a measure of the amount of *feedback* from a change in demand.[7]

Suppose that there is an increase in investment, for example the building of a factory or the construction of a road. The spending of money for investment will create income for those who work on the project and for those who supply inputs to the project in the form of cement, bricks, machinery, etc. Those who receive additional income will spend it according to their marginal propensity to consume and so create yet more income. The total rise in income will therefore be greater than the original increase in investment spending. Clearly the total rise in income will depend on how much income is created by each successive round of spending–in other words the total rise in income will depend on the marginal propensity to consume out of an addition to income. By assuming that consumption is given by the formula $C = a + bY$ it is possible to calculate very simply the total rise in income that could occur from a change in demand.

Assume that there is no government and no foreign trade, so that demand is made up of consumption and investment demand only. This assumption is made here purely in order to make it easier to understand the working of a simple model: clearly it is unrealistic, but as will be seen in subsequent chapters, introducing government spending, taxation and foreign trade into the model makes it rather more complicated but does not alter the basic principle of the model as explained here.

Assume also that the economy is temporarily in equilibrium so that aggregate demand and supply are equal, and both are equal to income. This can be expressed thus:

$$Y = C + I = \text{demand} \qquad \text{(i)}$$

The only other assumption needed is that

$$C = a + bY \tag{ii}$$

If the value of C in equation (ii) is substituted in equation (i) then

$$Y = a + bY + I$$

or
$$Y - bY = a + I$$

or
$$Y(1 - b) = a + I$$

or
$$Y = \frac{a + I}{1 - b} \tag{iii}$$

What equation (iii) expresses is that at each level of investment spending there is a value of income (Y) at which the economy will be in equilibrium. In other words, at each level of investment spending there is a level of income which will be just the right amount for *savings* out of that income to be equal to investment demand.

Now suppose that for some 'exogenous' reason, that is some reason not explained by this simple model of the economy, investment demand increases from I to I^1. This will create new income, some of which will be spent. If investment demand were to continue at the new level, I^1, then a new equilibrium level of income, Y^1, would eventually be reached; at this new income level, savings out of income would also have risen to the new investment level. The new equilibrium level of income would be given by the formula in equation (iii) so that:

$$Y^1 = \frac{a + I^1}{1 - b} \tag{iv}$$

Subtracting equation (iii) from equation (iv) gives the *difference* between the two equilibrium levels of income, thus:

$$Y^1 - Y = \left(\frac{a + I^1}{1 - b}\right) - \left(\frac{a + I}{1 - b}\right)$$

or
$$Y^1 - Y = \frac{a + I^1 - a - I}{1 - b}$$

or
$$Y^1 - Y = \frac{I^1 - I}{1 - b}$$

or
$$Y^1 - Y = (I^1 - I)\left(\frac{1}{1 - b}\right) \tag{v}$$

Equation (v) expresses the fact that the change in income caused by a change in investment demand is a *multiple* of the change in investment demand. The multiple is $1/(1 - b)$, and is thus determined entirely by the marginal propensity to consume. An alternative way of expressing equation (v) is

$$\Delta Y = k\ \Delta I \tag{vi}$$

where ΔY is the change in income caused by a change in investment ΔI, and k is the 'multiplier'. Another way of defining the multiplier is to say that where a change in demand causes a change in income, then the multiplier is the ratio of the change in income to the change in demand that caused it–algebraically $k = \Delta Y/\Delta I$.

It is also possible to express the multiplier in terms of the marginal propensity to save. If people spend four fifths of their income, say, then by definition they save the other fifth. In other words the marginal propensity to save, s, is equal to $1 - b$. So

$$k = \frac{1}{1-b} = \frac{1}{s}$$

In reality, the value of the multiplier is not simply determined by the marginal propensity to consume and save. It is also affected by other leakages from the circular flow of income, most notably by tax rates and by the amount of spending on imports. These complications will be dealt with in later chapters, but, as has been said already, the *method* of finding a formula for the multiplier remains essentially the same.

6 *Another way of deriving the multiplier formula*

There is another way of deriving the formula for the multiplier which uses slightly more difficult algebra, but which often helps students to understand the process better.

Suppose as before that investment increases by an amount ΔI. This will create new income. Some of this income will be spent. The actual amount spent is $b\ \Delta I$, since that is the meaning of b, the mpc. For example if the marginal propensity to consume out of an increase in income is $\frac{2}{3}$, then $\frac{2}{3}$ of ΔI will be spent on consumption.

The spending of $b\ \Delta I$ will create new income of that amount. Some of this new income will in turn be spent, namely $b(b\ \Delta I)$ will be spent. This creates new income of $b^2\ \Delta I$. Of the new income $b^2\ \Delta I$, $b(b^2\ \Delta I)$ will be spent, creating new income of $b^3\ \Delta I$. This process continues indefinitely. As a result the total increase in income, ΔY, is

$$\begin{aligned} Y &= I + bI + b^2I + b^3I + \dots \\ &= I(1 + b + b^2 + b^3 + \dots) \qquad \text{(vii)} \end{aligned}$$

Of course each successive addition to income is smaller than the previous one, since *some* of each increase in income is saved and so does not create new income. It so happens that there is a formula for the sum of an infinite series of the type $(1 + b + b^2 + b^3 + \dots)$ where b

is less than 1. The formula is $1/(1-b)$. The proof is as follows.

Multiply out the expression

$$\begin{aligned}&(1-b)(1+b+b^2+\ldots+b^n)\\&=1+b+b^2+b^3+\ldots+b^n\\&\quad-b-b^2-b^3-\ldots-b^n-b^{n+1}\\&=1-b^{n+1}\end{aligned}$$

Rewriting,

$$(1+b+b^2+\ldots+b^n)=\frac{1-b^{n+1}}{1-b}$$

Now suppose n becomes infinitely large, then b^{n+1} tends to zero, because b is less than 1, and the formula becomes

$$1+b+b^2+b^3+\ldots=\frac{1}{1-b}$$

Equation (vi) for the change in income caused by a change in investment demand then becomes

$$\Delta Y=\Delta I\frac{1}{1-b}$$

or

$$\Delta Y=k\,\Delta I \qquad \text{(viii)}$$

This equation (viii) is exactly the same as equation (vi)–as indeed it should be since both methods, if correct, must give the same answer.

7 *The multiplier expressed graphically*

In Figure 4.1 a consumption line was shown of the type $C=a+bY$. At this stage, assuming no government and no foreign trade, the only other form of expenditure is investment, and it has been assumed that investment is not affected by the other variables in the model. It starts at an initial level I, and then shifts upwards to I^1 and remains at that new level. In Figure 4.4, then, the total expenditure line, $C+I$, is a line parallel to and above the consumption line in Figure 4.1; the vertical distance between the consumption line and the total expenditure line is I, the (constant level of investment spending).

Equilibrium in Figure 4.4 is represented by the point A, where total expenditure $(C+I)$ is equal to income and output (Y), or where the $C+I$ line cuts the 45° line (the locus of all points of equality between spending and income). Equilibrium income is shown by OB.

Now consider an increase in investment from I to I^1. This will shift the total expenditure line upwards by an amount $I^1-I=\Delta I$, as shown

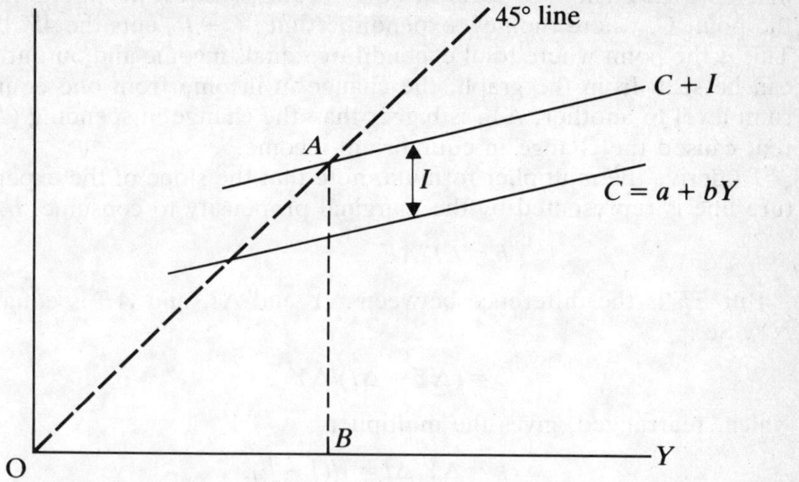

Figure 4.4 Equilibrium between total expenditure and income and output

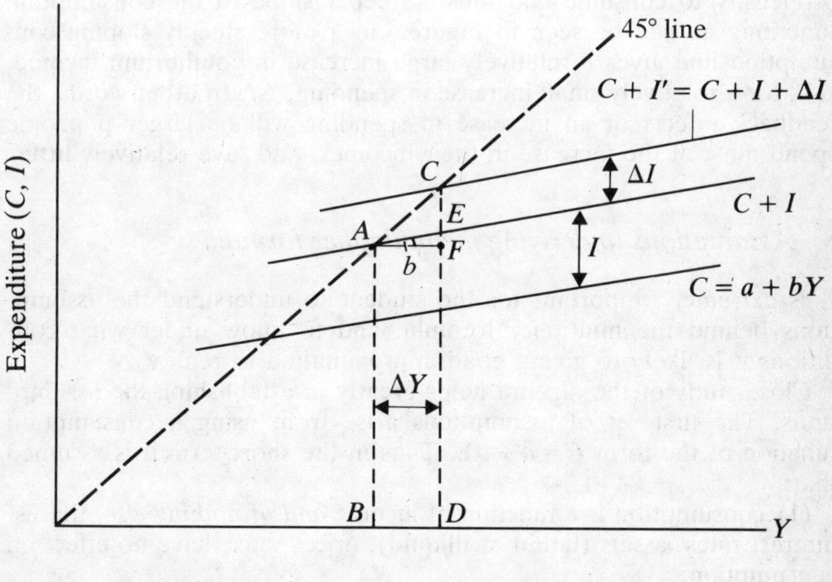

Figure 4.5 Effect of a change in spending on equilibrium income

in Figure 4.5. The new level of equilibrium is shown in Figure 4.5 at the point C, where the new expenditure line, $C + I^1$, cuts the 45° line. This is the point where total expenditure equals income and output. As can be seen from the graph, the change in income from one equilibrium level to another, ΔY, is bigger than the change in spending (ΔI), that caused the change in equilibrium income.

To derive the multiplier formula, note that the slope of the expenditure line is represented by the marginal propensity to consume, b, or

$$b = EF/AF$$

But EF is the difference between ΔY and ΔI, and AF is equal to ΔY. So

$$b = (\Delta Y - \Delta I)/\Delta Y$$

which, rearranged, gives the multiplier

$$k = \Delta Y/\Delta I = 1/(1 - b).$$

It is worth noting that the consumption line in Figure 4.5 has been drawn with a relatively gentle slope, that is, the marginal propensity to consume is relatively small. This means that the feedback effects of an increase in investment spending are relatively small, giving a small multiplier effect on income.

In Figure 4.6, the same lines are drawn, but with a bigger marginal propensity to consume and thus a steeper slope to the consumption function. As can be seen in Figure 4.6, a more steeply sloping consumption line gives a relatively large increase in equilibrium income, ΔY, for a relatively small increase in spending, ΔI. In other words, the feedback effects of an increase in spending will be larger if people spend most of the increase in their incomes, and save relatively little.

8 *Assumptions underlying the multiplier formula*

It is extremely important for the student to understand the assumptions behind the multiplier formula, and to know under what conditions it is likely to give a good approximation to reality.

Close study of the algebra helps greatly in establishing the assumptions. The first set of assumptions arise from using a consumption function of the form $C = a + bY$. Thus in the short term it is assumed that:

(1) consumption is a function of income *and of nothing else*, that is, interest rates, assets (liquid or illiquid), prices, etc., have no effect on consumption;

(2) consumption is a *linear* function of income.

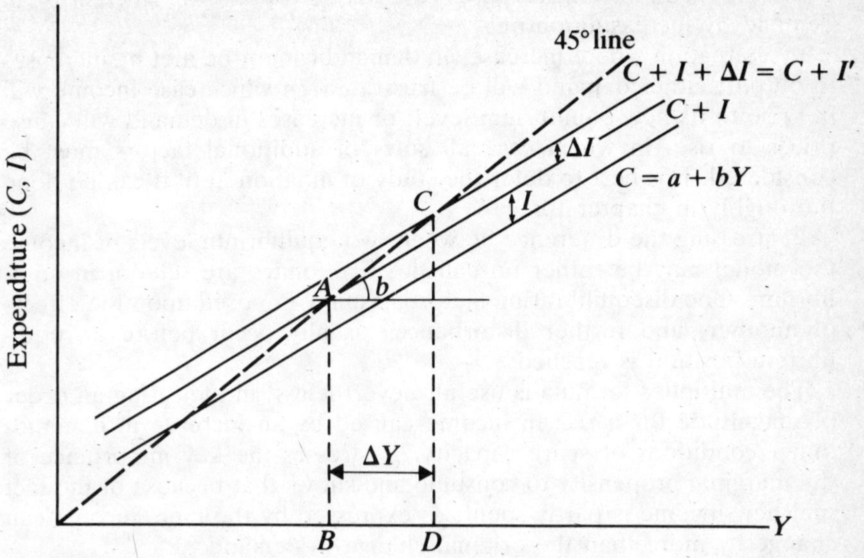

Figure 4.6 Effect of a change in spending on equilibrium income with a steeply sloping consumption line

The second set of assumptions arises from the simple algebra used to derive the formula for the multiplier. Thus when equation (iii) is subtracted from equation (iv) it is necessary to assume that:

(3) a and b are constants (this is essentially the same as assuming that the consumption function is linear);

(4) investment remains at its new level I^1 until the new equilibrium level of income is reached–in other words it is assumed that investment demand is not affected by changes in the level of income.

The last set of assumptions is not apparent from the formula, and will probably not become fully clear until later chapters have been read. Nevertheless, the student should note at this stage that nothing has been said about the effect of changes in investment and income on money and credit, nor of the effect of the changes on prices, nor, since the economy has been assumed to have no government or foreign trade, of the effect on the budget and the balance of payments. It is necessary to assume, therefore, that:

(5) no monetary restraint prevents income from rising as indicated by the formula.

It is probably also *wise* to assume that:

(6) the economy has spare capacity to meet the increases in demand by increasing output.

In a situation where increases in demand cannot be met by increases in output, either demand will be frustrated, in which case income will *not* rise to its new equilibrium level; or increases in demand will cause prices to rise, in which case all sorts of additional factors must be considered. It is best to defer the study of inflation until it can be done thoroughly in chapter 10.

In stressing the difference between two equilibrium levels of income the model may be rather unrealistic. Economies are seldom in equilibrium. One disequilibrating factor is usually imposed upon the effects of another, and further disturbances usually occur before an equilibrium position is reached.

The multiplier formula is useful, nevertheless, in indicating an order of magnitude for a rise in income caused by an increase in demand, under conditions of spare capacity. It stresses the key importance of the marginal propensity to consume and shows that because of the fact that new income is partly spent, as expressed by the mpc, income can change by more than the original change in demand.

The analysis is equally useful for indicating the size of a fall in income that may result from a *fall* in demand when the economy has *not* been experiencing rapid inflation—under inflationary conditions other factors must be considered.

NOTES

1 For those who have done no calculus, 'ΔC' is simply a short way of writing 'a small change in C'; and ΔY means a small change in Y. Δ is a Greek capital D, and is written 'delta'.

2 J.M. Keynes, *The General Theory of Employment, Interest and Money*, London, Macmillan, 1936.

3 In Malawi, for example, there were only two changes in Bank Rate in the years 1968 to 1978, from 5½% to 6% in 1970 and from 6% to 7% in 1976. Zambia's Bank Rate remained at 5% throughout the same period. Similar policy was followed in other African countries. There is some indication that since about 1978 a more active interest rate policy has been pursued in a number of countries, Malawi for example making changes in both 1979 and 1980.

4 Theoretically, the cost of holding savings in the form of non-interest-bearing cash increases as interest rates increase, because of the income forgone. There is no evidence that interest rates do have such an effect in rural Africa; other factors, including those mentioned in the text, dominate.

5 See, for example, Tanzania, Bureau of Statistics, *1969 Household Budget Survey*, Vol. 1, *Income and Consumption*, 1972.

6 Republic of Botswana, Central Statistics Office, *The Rural Income Distribution Survey in Botswana 1974/75*, (Gaborone, 1976, p. 105).

7 *Any* consumption function of the form $C = f(Y)$, that is, where consumption is a function of (determined by) income, implies by definition a marginal propensity to consume. In calculus terms mpc $= dC/dY = f^1(Y)$.

5 *Government Expenditure*

1 Definition

In the national accounts, government consumption expenditure is defined to include spending by local authorities as well as by the central government, on the provision of services. In Africa, local sources of revenue are relatively small so that local authorities rely fairly heavily on grants from the central government. Spending by the central government is thus a good indicator for total consumption spending by government even though the two are not the same. This is important since central government spending figures tend to be easily and quickly available, and, at the time of the annual budget, estimates of central government spending are published for the year ahead. Statistics based on the national income definition are published some two or three years after the event.

The national accounting definition of government consumption spending excludes 'transfer payments'. These include the payment of pensions, and subsidies to parastatal organisations. The reason for this distinction is that such transfer payments are not direct purchases of services and so should not be counted as part of the national income. They are not the same as payments to teachers for example, which directly create a service forming part of national output. Transfer payments do not actually purchase a service and so do not create any output. From the point of view of this chapter, however, the question is whether transfer payments create demand. Payments to people create demand indirectly, as they are spent by their recipients, but this demand is less than the transfer payment by the amount of any saving. Subsidies, for example subsidies on the price of maize, are paid to farmers who spend this income less any savings. In any case, pensions are a fairly small part of government expenditure, and with some exceptions so are subsidies, so that the error in treating statistics for government current spending as if they are identical with government consumption expenditure is small enough to be ignored for the discussion in this chapter.

2 Growth

Government spending in Africa since the ending of the colonial period has grown very fast. On the one hand colonial neglect of almost every category of government activity meant that newly independent African countries had an enormous backlog of necessary spending that needed immediate attention. On the other hand, independence opened up some new sources of finance for many countries, including aid, new sources of tax revenue, the borrowing of money from domestic banking systems and, in some cases, the capture of flows of money that had previously been paid abroad.

The very rapid growth of government spending can be seen in Table 5.1. The table also shows that overall there was a slowing down in rates of growth in the 1970s, suggesting that the upsurge of government spending could not be sustained as external economic circumstances became more hostile. However, several countries increased government consumption even faster in the 1970s, including Nigeria (rapid increase in income from oil), Botswana (increased revenue from mining and a new customs union agreement) and Malawi (growth in agricultural exports).

Table 5.1 Average annual growth rates of public and private consumption in Africa compared, for 1960–70 and 1970–79 (percentages)

	Public consumption		*Private consumption*	
	1960–70	*1970–79*	*1960–70*	*1970–79*
Low-income countries	4.7	4.5	4.1	3.2
Middle-income oil importers	6.7	9.4	3.9	4.3
Middle-income oil exporters	8.8	6.8	2.6	4.6
Sub-Saharan Africa	6.0	5.8	4.0	3.3

Source: World Bank, *Accelerated development in Sub-Saharan Africa: an agenda for action*, 1981, Appendix Table 4.

The differences between public and private consumption growth rates shown in Table 5.1 are highly significant when sustained over a period as long as twenty years. The rates shown meant that public consumption tripled, whereas private consumption only doubled, from 1960 to 1979.

Average growth rates conceal large variations. Different African countries have had very different experiences: for example Ghana had to cut back so severely in the 1970s that public consumption actually fell slightly on average, and other countries facing economic difficulties also had rates of growth lower than the rate of increase of population, implying a fall in the availability of public services per head. In contrast, some countries including those already mentioned above, had high and rising rates of increase of public consumption.

There were also sharp variations in the progress of government spending from year to year. Furthermore, budget estimates of government spending have frequently been very different from what the governments actually spent. Budget estimates indicate what a government plans to spend. Sometimes the estimates are underspent, as occurred in Botswana in the mid-1970s and in Zambia in the mid-1960s for example. More commonly, budget estimates are overspent, and the government has either to present supplementary estimates during the budget year or in some other way authorise (before or after the event) the spending of more money than was originally planned.

3 *The control of government spending*

Governments do control their own spending. Governments have the power to decide on a new education policy, say, and to authorise the spending of tax receipts, grants of aid or borrowed money on the necessary school buildings, teachers' housing, teachers' salaries and necessary equipment like exercise books and chalk. But spending programmes, once they have begun, tend to acquire a life of their own. Governments are subject to political pressures from various sources to maintain and increase their spending, or at any rate not to cut it. It is also very noticeable that the capital spending of governments is much more volatile than their current spending, and furthermore that governments seem more able to implement cuts in capital spending than to implement cuts in current spending.[1] Why is this?

In the first place, a large part of government recurrent expenditure is on wages and salaries, and a further part is on the means to enable government employees to get on with their jobs: offices, desks, transport, telephones, electricity and the like. Governments are normally extremely reluctant to dismiss civil servants, so that salaries continue to be paid. Even among daily paid workers, government policy may be to maintain employment.

Secondly, past and current *capital* spending creates a need for *current* spending to make use of the new capital. Schools and hospitals, once they have been built, must be manned and equipped if they are not to be wasted. Only in an extreme crisis will a government allow buildings and equipment to lie empty and idle once they have been built and paid for.

The third point is that governments, as well as guaranteeing civil servants security in their jobs, make other commitments which, once entered into, may involve much greater expenditure than was originally intended, or even imagined. For example, a guaranteed producer price for maize or tobacco costs the government more if the rains are favourable and the crop is good, and a failed maize crop may be even more expensive if the government then has to import maize expensively and sell at a low guaranteed price to consumers. Governments also have commitments to parastatal corporations: if the national airline makes a loss or the agricultural lending body finds that farmers are not repaying their loans, governments may have to make up the deficits in order to keep the institutions in operation.

A fourth point is that some expenditure is dictated by external circumstances. The most obvious category is defence: wars or other disturbances in neighbouring countries force governments to increase their spending on national defence, as occurred in Botswana and Tanzania, for example, in the late 1970s, because of the war in Zimbabwe and the situation in Uganda. Military expenditure remained constant as a proportion of GNP in Africa as a whole, but this figure is dominated by Nigeria whose huge military expenditures in 1968 had fallen (as a percentage of GNP) ten years later. A majority of the remaining Sub-Saharan African nations increased their military expenditures relative to GNP over the same period.[2] Other examples of expenditures dictated by external circumstances are the costs to land-locked countries of rerouting external trade when transit routes are disrupted, and the cost of coping with refugees from neighbouring states.

A fifth point is that African governments have taken on rapidly increasing responsibilities, and therefore rapid increases in the duties of civil servants, at the same time as there have been severe shortages of skilled manpower such as accountants and experienced high-level administrators. As a result control over public expenditure has been less than complete. Many items of expenditure have been greater than provided for in budgets and nothing has been done about it, in spite of such expenditure being technically illegal.

In the most general sense the government of the day commits itself, politically and sometimes legally as well, to do certain things: to maintain law and order, to defend the country from external threat, to cram as many students into existing schools and as many sick people into existing hospitals as the buildings can hold, to maintain embassies abroad, to provide cars for cabinet ministers and to do innumerable other things. If they cost more than estimated then in normal times the government will foot the bill, either by introducing supplementary estimates, or simply by 'illegally' overspending the money provided for in a budget.

As already noted, it is easier to reduce capital spending than current spending. The main reason is that capital spending is less continuous. In any particular year a number of projects will be ending so that annual spending can be reduced if new projects are not started. Another way of reducing capital spending is by spreading projects over a longer period so that spending in any particular year is reduced. Neither of these methods is as easy as it sounds. Many large projects cost vary little in their early stages, while engineering studies are conducted, tenders invited and contractors appointed. Starting them later may therefore save very little actual spending in the short term. Spreading a project over a longer period may lead to inefficiency; and if the project is integrated with others, a late finish may cause huge problems. For example, a new road to serve a new mine *must* be ready for when the mine needs it.

The widespread tendency for spending cuts to be implemented more readily in the capital budget contributes to overspending overall. Governments frequently announce spending cuts in both current and capital budgets, but tend only to achieve them in the capital budget.

The next most vulnerable area is non-salary recurrent spending. When times are really hard, public employees have to make do with fewer cars, less paper, less petrol and with poorly maintained buildings and offices. Eventually this leads to great inefficiency: school inspectors cannot leave their offices to inspect schools, university libraries cancel their journal subscriptions and cannot buy new books, clinics run out of drugs early in the financial year. But it seems to be a widespread characteristic of governments that even in the most severe financial crisis such extreme inefficiency is preferred to the sacking of any civil servants.[3]

The fact that government spending tends to have a life of its own and frequently turns out to be more than planned by the government is fairly well known. Less obvious is the fact that very rapid *increases* in government spending may also prove impossible to implement. The main reason is that physical resources are not always available. Just as it may be difficult to dismiss civil servants, so it may be difficult to hire new ones quickly, especially where there is a severe shortage of skilled manpower.

Underspending by governments usually occurs when a government finds that the money available to it increases very suddenly by large amounts. This can happen, for example, when export prices rise rapidly, or when a major new mine or industry comes into production, or when a government discovers a major new source of overseas finance. The desire to increase spending rapidly, as expressed in budget estimates, combined with a limited capacity to do so, can and does sometimes lead to underspending. The point is that the efficient spending of increased revenues requires real resources: administrative manpower to decide on how to spend the money, negotiate contracts and monitor performance, skilled labour to manage and implement new projects and activities, and physical availability of inputs and infrastructure. Some of the resources that are in short supply can be imported, for example construction capacity or skilled manpower, but even these importable resources can only be obtained with some delay. That is why rapidly expanding government sectors typically have large numbers of unfilled vacancies. In Nigeria, for example, actual development spending has consistently been less than planned. 'Such shortfalls or "slippages" have been...attributable much less to shortage of finance than to lack of sufficient executive capacity.' By the time of the Third Plan, published in 1975, this had been recognised, and two sets of figures were given, of 'nominal' planned spending (Naira 43.3 billion) and 'effective' planned spending (Naira 26.5 billion). Actuals for the first two years were 70% of the nominal plan and 113% of the effective plan, although 'probably the correct interpretation of these results is not that slippages were less than expected but that inflation was faster than expected.'[4]

The capacity of African governments to make effective use of increases in the money available for spending, has increased enormously in the twenty or so years since the end of the colonial period. Furthermore, most governments have recently suffered from much lower availability of financial resources than could be used effectively. As a result, underspending of budget estimates is likely to be less frequent than it has been in the past. It should also be noted that two types of spending can be increased very quickly indeed: salaries can be increased by executive decision, so that government spending on salaries can increase more or less instantaneously by this means (in contrast to the difficulty of quickly increasing this category of spending by hiring more people); and certain imported weapons, such as jet aircraft and guided missiles, can be bought very quickly and are so expensive that by this means government spending on defence can rise very fast (in contrast to the difficulty of increasing defence spending by hiring, training and housing more soldiers).[5] Both these categories of spending, salaries and defence, can be large enough, as a proportion of total spending, for changes in them to affect total spending significantly.

4 *Government spending and tax revenue*

Clearly the amount of revenue received by government from taxation could have some influence on the level of government spending.

Taxation is not the only source of finance for government–some revenue accrues from government's trading activities, government can borrow both domestically and from abroad, some finance is received in the form of aid and government has the power to create money by 'borrowing' from its central bank (see chapter 8). But tax revenue is the most important source of finance.

Indeed, the amount of tax revenue available is often treated *politically* as the best indicator of the correct level of government spending. In its extreme form, this point of view holds that the budget should always be balanced, with expenditure equal to current revenue. This very old-fashioned view has now been replaced because of a better understanding of the needs of the economy. Basically, the level of government spending should be decided by two main factors: the capacity of the economy, that is, the potential level of internal supply; and the external position, that is, a combination of the physical ability to supply imports and the financial ability to pay for them.

In periods when foreign exchange is freely available to pay for imports, from whatever source, the size of the government's spending programme should really be decided by the internal capacity of the economy, and, for land-locked countries, the capacity of external transit routes to handle imports efficiently. A large increase in the available foreign exchange can arise from several different sources. For example, in Nigeria in the 1970s the development of oil production was accompanied by rapidly increasing oil prices, providing a double source of increased foreign exchange earnings; in Ghana in the early 1960s and in Zaire in the early 1970s easy access to suppliers' credits[6] and eurodollar loans[7], respectively, rapidly increased the money available to the two governments; in Botswana in the 1970s a combination of a new Southern African Customs Union Agreement, good rainfall for cattle-raising plus access to high beef prices in the EEC, and the development of new copper-nickel and diamond mines, caused very rapid increases in foreign exchange availability.

In each of these cases, then, the government at the time enjoyed rapidly increasing revenues. However, the internal capacity of the economy to spend the money was not affected by such external events as high export prices, or easy access to foreign credit. The spending of such money requires matching domestic resources, including not only such things as construction capacity and manpower with the right skills, but also transport capacity to get goods into the country initially and distributed within the country, and the administrative capacity to choose projects wisely and see that they are properly administered. In other words, the availability of money does not remove any of the other non-financial constraints which exist and prevent rapid development. A well-documented example of trying to do too much too quickly, and therefore failing to control selection of projects, was in Ghana in the period 1960–65. Because of major design faults a cocoa-processing complex included silos useless for storing cocoa and a chocolate factory which could operate only at a heavy loss. An integrated textile mill was supplied with faulty looms which could only operate at less than half capacity with expensive expatriate management. A steel mill was not capable of handling the planned throughput of scrap, and its management was on a fixed fee basis, independent of performance. A shoe factory proved incapable of using local leather and was so late in coming into production that styles had changed and rival factories had started. Three canning factories had a much larger capacity than could be supplied by local pineapples, mangoes and tomatoes, and the planned output of the mango cannery was twice that of world trade at the time. Much blame attaches to foreign contractors and machinery suppliers who promoted these projects, but it was also true that Ghana's capacity to consider projects properly was not adequate at the time.[8]

In contrast, increases in tax revenue from domestic sources should, in principle, make additional government spending possible. If people are paying more to the government in taxation, then they have less money available for consumption. This should release resources to satisfy the demand created by additional government spending. For example, if the tax on cigarettes is increased, consumers will pay more for cigarettes and have less to spend on other things. Or they will buy fewer cigarettes. Either way aggregate demand is reduced so that an increase in demand via government spending should be possible without creating excess demand.[9]

To some extent the same argument can be used of domestic borrowing (provided that it is not from the central bank, as is explained in chapter 8). If money that would have been saved by consumers, and spent on private sector investment by one means or another, is instead lent to government, then government can increase its spending without creating excess demand. The point, in both cases, is that government can safely increase its spending *provided that* private sector spending has been reduced. In some circumstances tax revenue is quite a good indicator of what governments can safely spend, for example when tax revenues change largely because of changes in personal income tax or sales taxation. But in African economies, as already pointed out, there are many circumstances in which an increase in tax revenue can occur *entirely* as a result of an increase in export prices, for example. The increase in export prices does not reduce the spending of anyone within the country and so does not normally make it possible for government spending to increase. If, however, government spending has been held down because of a foreign exchange shortage, to the point where the domestic economy has spare capacity, then an increase in 'external' tax revenue, or in funds from external borrowing, can be spent without creating excess demand.

This latter type of situation has in fact become much more common since the oil price rise of 1974 pushed most oil-importing developing countries into balance of payments deficit. Part of the response to that crisis has been to restrict domestic demand in order to reduce imports; in addition, recession in the developed economies, especially after the second oil price rise in 1978, reduced the demand for African exports and therefore worsened still further the balance of payments of most African countries. As a result it has been quite a common situation in African economies for factories to be producing at less than half their capacity because of the shortage of foreign exchange for imported inputs, for farmers to be unable to get as much imported fertiliser or spare parts for machinery as they could use productively and for other sectors to be unable to operate at their full capacity. Clearly, in such situations, there is no domestic capacity constraint on additional government spending so that any increase in external sources of revenue can be spent without creating excess demand, provided that the foreign exchange shortage, for example of spare parts, has not actually *destroyed* domestic capacity to produce.

What about the reverse situation? If government revenue *falls* because of some purely external event (a fall in export prices or a fall in the availability of foreign loans) should a government necessarily reduce its spending? Clearly, a reduction in the money available to government because of such external events does not reduce the capacity of the domestic economy, since the number of roads, machines, skilled labourers, railway wagons, power stations, etc., is unaffected. So government spending can continue as before without creating excess demand for domestic resources. However, the decreased inflows of foreign exchange will reduce the country's foreign exchange reserves in such a situation, so that government spending can only be sustained so long as the foreign exchange reserves are large enough to finance the fall in foreign exchange inflows, or if private spending on imports is also reduced. Few African countries are in such a fortunate position. It has happened, though, that export prices have fallen, in a situation where the fall can reasonably be expected to be temporary and foreign exchange reserves have been adequate, so that the government has felt able to maintain its spending while allowing the foreign exchange reserves to fall. The problem with such a policy is that there is normally no way of knowing whether a fall in foreign exchange inflows is indeed temporary. If it is not, then an adjustment, including an adjustment in government spending, is necessary.[10]

In Africa, this distinction between changes in tax revenue as a result of external events, and changes in tax revenue which affect private domestic spending, is absolutely crucial. It can be quite wrong to look at the forecasts of tax revenue to see how large an increase in government spending is justified, without also specifying the source of the increases in revenue. Equally, a forecast fall in tax revenue need not mean that government spending need be reduced, since it does not necessarily reduce the amount of goods and services that can be supplied to the government by the domestic economy. So the government can maintain (or continue to increase at the same rate) its spending *provided that* enough foreign exchange is available.

There is a very important distinction, of course, between the limits that domestic production capacity and foreign exchange availability place on government spending, and what governments actually try to do. Furthermore, since the government is not always able to control the rate of growth of its own spending, actual spending may not in any case reflect the government's own intentions, particularly in the short term. In the long term, governments increase their capacity to spend growing revenues, and are forced to reduce their spending in the face of falling revenues. From the point of view of building up a short-run model of the economy, though, there is no obvious equation for G, government spending. Certainly it is not a simple function of tax revenue.[11]

5 *The impact of changes in government spending*

A change in government spending is a change in aggregate demand and therefore has feedback or multiplier effects. These effects are precisely similar to those of a change in investment demand, as described in the last chapter. However, when government is introduced into a model of the economy, it is obviously necessary to investigate how taxation affects the model. If government spends more money, then under most systems of taxation some of it will come back to the government in the form of income tax and taxes on the goods that people buy out of their increased incomes. About the only tax that is *not* affected by changing incomes is the poll tax—for example as was levied in many African countries during the colonial period. Basically then, tax receipts are a function of income. As a first approximation, tax receipts can be assumed to be a linear function of income, so that a tax function would be of the form

$$T = \bar{t} + tY \tag{1}$$

where T = total tax revenue
Y = income
and $\bar{t}$ and t are constants.

Equation 1 should really be defined assuming constant export prices, because tax changes resulting from changing export prices vary according to the structure of the export industry in each country. For example, higher diamond prices result in higher government revenue in Botswana, some of it received almost at once, some with a delay because dividends on the Botswana government's 50% share in diamond mining are paid after the end of the mining company's financial year. In Sierra Leone, in contrast, a large proportion of diamond production is smuggled out through Liberia and so escapes export taxation, and the resulting income probably escapes income tax as well. Only the spending of the increased income from higher diamond prices, to the extent it occurs on taxed goods, would generate additional government revenue. For the time being it is reasonable to assume that tax revenue is dependent on income as shown in equation 1, bearing in mind that this assumes constant export prices. The effects of changing export prices on the economy will be discussed in the next chapter.

What the tax function expresses is that tax revenue depends on income only. Furthermore, if income changes from Y to Y^1 then tax revenue will be

$$T^1 = \bar{t} + tY^1 \qquad (2)$$

Subtracting equation (1) from equation (2) gives

$$T^1 - T = t(Y^1 - Y)$$

or

$$t = \frac{(T^1 - T)}{(Y^1 - Y)}$$

Therefore t is the ratio of a change in tax revenue to a change in income; in other words

t = the marginal propensity for tax receipts to change in response to a change in income.

In common language, t could be called the marginal tax rate—*not* in the personal sense of the marginal tax rate paid by an individual on an increase in his income, but in the national, macroeconomic, sense of the marginal tax rate for the economy as a whole always assuming constant export prices.

In some economies the amount of tax that is independent of income ($\bar{t}$ in the equation) may be fairly small—mainly taxes on capital such as death duties (on the wealth of people who have died) and poll taxes where they exist. In Africa, taxation of exports is largely independent of changes in income *in the short term*. Clearly, export taxation depends not only on export prices but also on the volume of exports and on production costs, which can change substantially over time. But in the present context, namely the short-term effects of a change in government spending, export taxation is indeed unaffected. In Africa, therefore, the term t can be very large, but independent of other variables in the model. It is not, in the long term, constant–but in analysing the effects of a change in government spending on the economy it is reasonable to assume revenue from exports as constant in the absence of knowledge to the contrary. In any case, even if export revenues *do* change there is often very little further impact on the domestic economy in the short term, as will be explained in the next chapter.

The simple model of the economy, with government spending and taxation included, is now

$$Y = C + G + I \qquad \text{(i)}$$

$$C = a + b(Y - tY)$$
$$= a + bY(1 - t) \qquad \text{(ii)}$$

The consumption function has been modified on the assumption that consumption is a function of disposable income, that is income after the payment of domestic taxes (for simplicity at this stage the difference between direct and indirect taxes is ignored). Consumption has been assumed to be unaffected by the level of $\bar{t}$.

No equation has been added for G. In a situation where government spending has been very severely restrained to protect the balance of payments, it may be possible to take the brakes off very fast–a lot of spending plans will already be in existence and ready to go. But even in these particular circumstances the response will be to a change in the balance of payments prospects, that is to a rise in export prices and therefore in export tax revenue, which is exogenous to the model. So it seems best to assume G as constant in the short term, or as determined by exogenous factors. Both amount to the same thing in terms of the model, namely that G is not a function of any of the other variables in the model.

Substituting for equation (ii) in equation (i) gives

$$Y = a + bY(1 - t) + G + I$$

or
$$Y(1 - b + bt) = a + G + I$$

or
$$Y = \frac{a + G + I}{1 - b + bt} \qquad \text{(iii)}$$

A change in government spending, from G to G^1, would eventually lead to a new level of income Y^1

$$Y^1 = \frac{a + G^1 + I}{1 - b + bt} \qquad \text{(iv)}$$

Subtract equation (iii) from equation (iv) to get the *change* in income resulting from a change in G, and

$$Y^1 - Y = \frac{G^1 - G}{1 - b + bt}$$

or

$$Y^1 - Y = (G^1 - G)\frac{1}{1 - b + bt} \qquad \text{(v)}$$

In other words the modified multiplier formula is

$$k = \frac{1}{1 - b + bt}$$

There is an additional positive term (bt) on the bottom line, indicating that this multiplier is smaller than the formula derived in the last chapter ($k = 1/1 - b$). The economic explanation is that taxation is an additional leakage from the circular flow of income. If demand increases, income will increase but some of this income accrues to the government in the form of taxation. If the government does not respend this income, but adds to its reserves or repays borrowing (and those repaid do not spend the money), then income will not increase by as much as it would have done in the absence of taxation. Each successive round of spending is smaller because some income and some spending accrues to government and is not respent at once.

The larger is t, the marginal tax rate, the smaller is the multiplier. In other words, fluctuations in income are dampened or reduced by the existence of taxes responsive to income and spending, and are further reduced the higher is the marginal tax rate. The economy is thus stabilised by the existence of a large government sector requiring high rates of tax. This stabilising factor is not as powerful as it might be in Africa because so few people pay income tax. Changes in disposable incomes of those who do not pay income tax are *not* reduced by tax. On the other hand taxation is heavy on such goods as beer and cigarettes which are bought by all income groups; and a wide range of imported goods subject to customs duties are bought by all but the poorest, so that changes in income (and therefore in spending) *are* reflected in tax receipts.

6 *Assumptions behind the multiplier analysis*

In analysing the effects of a change in government spending, a number of assumptions have been made. Some are the same as described at the end of the last chapter: consumption is a linear function of income, investment remains unaffected as income changes. To these must be added two more: government spending is unaffected by changes in receipts from taxation, taxation is a linear function of income and of nothing else. Finally, nothing has been said about the budget surplus or deficit. If government spending changes and as a result tax receipts also change, then the balance between the two will also change. For the time being it is necessary to assume that the changing budget position is financed in such a way that there are no further feedback effects on income and spending. Thus an increase in the deficit is assumed *not* to be financed by increased borrowing from the public, or if this does take place such borrowing is assumed not to reduce private sector spending (consumption or investment). Similarly, it is necessary to assume that an increased surplus is not used to repay earlier government borrowing from the private sector, or that such repayment is not then respent.

As before, the analysis is best suited to a situation in which changes in demand are reflected mainly in changes in output, since some of the assumptions are particularly unrealistic under inflationary conditions. When prices are fairly stable it does give some idea of how the economy reacts to changes in demand, with necessary emphasis on the marginal propensity to consume, and the marginal tax rate (in the macroeconomic sense).

In this chapter emphasis has been placed on control of government spending by the government itself, other determinants (if any) of government spending and what it *ought* to be from the point of view of the management of aggregate demand. The differences between current and capital spending have therefore been ignored except in so far as *control* of total capital spending may be easier than control of total current spending. Capital spending is, however, a part of investment and capital spending decisions by government have some common features with private investment decisions. Discussion of this aspect of government spending is postponed to the chapter on investment.

NOTES

1 An example of this was when the Zambian government tried to reduce its spending in 1972 because of a fall in copper export prices, as shown below.

	Actual 1971	*Estimate 1972*	*Actual 1972*
Current spending	315	266 (−49)	325 (+10)
Capital spending	157	145 (−12)	146 (−11)
Total	472	411 (−61)	471 (−1)

Source: Government of Zambia, Financial Reports and Estimates of Revenue and Expenditure.

As can be seen from the numbers, the Zambian government tried to reduce both current and capital spending, but current spending actually rose slightly, whereas capital spending was indeed cut very much as planned.

2 World Bank *Accelerated Development in Sub-Saharan Africa: an agenda for action*, 1981, Appendix Table 43.

3 Governments do impose freezes on the creation of new civil service posts and the filling of vacancies. Although this eventually reduces the number of government employees, it does so slowly and inefficiently, since in bad times fewer people quit their jobs voluntarily, and vacancies do not occur in the jobs that would be eliminated first in a planned reduction of employment.

4 From Anthony Kirk-Greene and Douglas Rimmer, *Nigeria since 1970: a political and economic outline* (London, Hodder and Stoughton, 1981), pp. 142–144. The quotations are from p. 143.

5 Capacity to make effective use of advanced weapons systems can lag behind the purchase of military hardware, because of the training period and reluctance to use mercenaries, but the point stands that actual purchase of weapons can, barring political obstacles, be very rapid.

6 'Suppliers' credits' are a form of finance for imports of capital goods. The foreign supplier of, say, machinery for a new factory offers to supply the goods on credit, so that the buyer does not have to pay for the goods immediately. Such credit is of course tied to purchase of the particular goods being offered by the foreign supplier and is not available for any other purpose.

7 'Eurodollar loans' are loans made by banks accepting large deposits mostly in dollars but also in other currencies, outside the countries of origin of the currencies concerned. Thus it is possible to make a deposit in US dollars with a bank in, say, London, and such moneys can then be lent to, among others, the governments of developing countries. The interest rate is determined by market forces, and the borrower has to pay whatever the short-term interest rate on eurodollar deposits happens to be, plus a margin, so that the cost of a loan varies during the life of that loan. A large number of African countries have borrowed from the eurodollar market.

8 Andrzej Krassowski *Development and the Debt Trap: economic planning and external borrowing in Ghana* (Croom Helm for ODI, London 1974), pp. 84 to 88. Another example: 'It is unfortunately true that slippages in any sector or project can be counteracted by waste, especially where funds are ample. Rate of disbursement may be pushed up in face of real constraints on execution, with the result that expenditure targets are more nearly met but value for money is not obtained. The macroeconomic reflection of this behaviour is inflation, the rate of which clearly accelerated in Nigeria with the discontinuity in the scale of development spending...in 1975...the fundamental cause was the attempts of the Nigerian governments to buy more than the economy was capable of supplying, given its inflexible productive structure, shortages of technical skills and executive capacity, and limited physical ability to import and distribute foreign products', Kirk-Greene and Rimmer, *op.cit.*, pp. 145–6.

9 Not all the productive resources released by a reduction in cigarette-making are of much use to a government, for example machinery or skills which are specific to cigarette manufacture. But the demand for some more generally useful resources is reduced, for example managers capable of managing other activities, transport, electricity, etc.

10 In practice, prudent governments allow for both possibilities by cutting back to some extent and thus preventing the foreign exchange reserves from falling by the full amount of a reduction in foreign exchange inflows.

11 It is an interesting exercise to compare the figures for tax revenue and expenditure over a period of years, both forecast and actual, and, in the case of tax revenue,

with and without the changes caused by export price changes, to see whether there is a consistent relationship. In cases where this has been done, changes in government spending have indeed been shown to be independent of changes in tax revenue.

6 *Exports and Imports*

1 Definitions

Exports are goods and services that earn foreign exchange. Imports are goods and services that have to be paid for in foreign exchange. Exports and imports of *goods* are called visible trade. Thus the sale abroad of coffee, cocoa, copper, manufactured goods such as textiles or beer, and of any other physical object comes under the category of visible exports. Similarly, imports of food, fuel, machinery, cars and tractors, whisky and fertiliser, count as visible imports.

Buyers of African exports pay for them with foreign currency, either the currency of the buyer if that is acceptable, or one of the international currencies. The main international currency is the US dollar, but the currencies of other major industrialised countries, such as the British pound, the German Deutschmark and the Japanese yen, are also acceptable because they can be easily and freely converted into each other or into US dollars.

In nearly all cases, the foreign exchange received for exports must be sold by the exporter to the exporting country's central bank. The exporter then has domestic currency, which can be used to pay wages and other local costs.

Importers must almost always pay for imports in foreign currency, because foreign suppliers of imports are almost never willing to be paid in the domestic currency of the African importer. With few exceptions, African governments do not allow their own citizens or institutions to hold foreign currency, so importers must use domestic currency to buy, through their commercial banks, foreign currency from the central bank. This procedure nearly always applies even to exporters who also need to import; that is, exporters may not use their foreign exchange earnings to pay for any imports they need, but must sell their export earnings to the central bank and apply with everyone else for foreign exchange to pay for imports.

It is also possible to earn foreign exchange by selling services to foreigners. For example, foreign tourists or business people visting an African country have to change their foreign currency into local currency to pay for hotels, taxi rides, restaurant meals, safaris and souvenirs. The African country is thereby selling services to foreigners for foreign exchange, and this activity is categorised as the selling of invisible exports.[1] The most important invisible exports earnings in African countries are from tourism, the remittances of migrant workers (the 'service' being exported in this case is that of labour) and earnings of interest on the central bank's holdings of foreign exchange reserves (the 'service' available to foreigners being use of the country's savings of foreign exchange).

Earnings from transport are also important for transit countries, because land-locked countries have to pay for the use of rail and road systems to move their exports and imports. This was an exceptionally important source of foreign exchange earnings to Mozambique in the past, and probably will be again in the future.

Similarly, any service which must be paid for in foreign exchange is classified as an invisible import. Invisible imports include such items as payments for foreign shipping services on visible trade, interest payments on foreign borrowing, the payment of dividends by foreign-owned companies to their shareholders abroad and payments for foreign travel.

It may seem paradoxical, if not absurd, to describe a foreign tourist stepping off a plane at the international airport as an 'invisible' export, but earning foreign currency by selling services to tourists is just as valuable to an African economy as the earning of the same number of dollars by selling copper or coffee on international markets.[2] The way to distinguish between invisible imports and exports is to concentrate on the flows of money. Invisible exports are like visible exports in that both result in the *receipt* of foreign exchange, whereas invisible imports and visible imports both require *payments* of foreign exchange.

Most African countries would have large deficits on invisibles were it not for transfers. The main reasons for this are: foreign ownership and management of African mines, factories, banks and, in some countries, farms; the fact that few African countries own shipping lines and so must 'import' the transport costs of their foreign trade; and the high and increasing cost of foreign loans. Kenya is an exception because of a highly developed tourist industry. Positive net transfers result mainly from grants of aid and, in some cases, from migrant workers' remittances. The exceptions are Nigeria, which no longer receives grants of aid because of its oil wealth, and Zambia, where the size of expatriate remittances offsets inflows of grant aid. The increase in the price of oil in 1978, on top of earlier increases from which African countries had not recovered, was the main reason why Nigeria was the only country in Table 6.1 with a current account surplus in 1980.

Table 6.1 Visible and invisible trade, 1980 (US $ millions)

	Visible exports	*Visible imports*	*Visible trade balance*	*Invisible exports*	*Invisible imports*	*Net transfers*[b]	*Invisible trade balance*	*Current account balance*
Botswana	553	592	− 39	167	286	+ 129	+ 10	− 29
Gambia[a]	54	95	− 41	24	41	+ 16	− 1	− 42
Ghana	1159	1075	+ 84	122	369	+ 69	− 178	− 94
Kenya	1243	2397	− 1154	770	740	+ 138	+ 168	− 986
Malawi	294	341	− 47	71	229	+ 68	− 90	− 137
Mauritius	431	512	− 81	153	194	+ 19	− 22	− 103
Nigeria	23422	15948	+ 7474	1977	5958	− 578	− 4559	+ 2915
Sierra Leone	214	386	− 172	56	119	+ 53	− 10	− 182
Sudan	689	1127	− 438	341	324	+ 226	+ 243	− 195
Swaziland	363	351	+ 12	28	159	+ 51	− 80	− 68
Tanzania	530	1067	− 537	179	319	+ 128	− 12	− 549
Uganda	319	322	− 3	15	115	+ 86	− 14	− 17
Zambia	1251	1136	+ 115	122	657	− 172	− 707	− 592

NOTES
a 1979.
b Net transfers include 'private unrequited transfers' (mainly immigrant worker and expatriate remittances) and 'government unrequited transfers' (mainly grants of aid).

Source: *International Financial Statistics*

2 *Determinants of export prices and their effects on income*

Overwhelmingly, African exports are of primary products whose prices are determined by forces outside the control of the producing countries. The prices of African export commodities are mostly determined by world market forces, that is, by the supply and demand for the product in world commodity markets. Even where a commodity is sold on long-term contract, as is the case for most of Zambia's copper for example, the contract does not specify a fixed price but one that varies with market prices on the London Metal Exchange.

There are some exceptions to this dependence on world market prices: diamond prices are maintained at fixed levels for extended periods by De Beers, who have an effective monopoly in gem diamonds (although price changes when they do occur are very much affected by the supply and demand for diamonds)[3]; nickel prices were for a long time fixed by the world's leading producer, International Nickel Company of Canada, but this control broke down in the late 1970s; some beef is sold to the European Economic Community (the EEC) at prices maintained by the EEC well above world market levels, although the amount sold in this way is limited to a quota for the main African beef exporters[4]; and similarly the EEC guarantees a price for the sugar exports of some African countries.[5] Even in these cases of guaranteed, or partially guaranteed prices, however, the prices actually received by African countries for their exports are not within the immediate control of any one country. The main possible exceptions are the price of oil, over which Nigeria exercises some control through membership of the Organisation of Petroleum Exporting Countries,[6] and the price of cloves (over which Tanzania has considerable influence because Zanzibar is the main world producer).

There are other commodities whose prices could possibly be manipulated by African producers, acting alone or together with fellow producers in Africa or elsewhere. However, the great need for export revenue in the short term has nearly always meant that the whole of current production available is sold on the world market for what it will fetch by individual countries, while attempts by groups of countries to restrict output in order to maintain or raise prices have never lasted for very long. There was one attempt, by private copper mining companies, to hold prices *down*, in order to discourage users of copper from switching to substitute products such as aluminium, but this too was short-lived.[7]

African exporters are, then, almost exclusively price-takers in export markets. In other words, export price changes have to be accepted as beyond the control of African governments. The *structure* of each export industry, however, which is to some extent within the control of governments, at least in the long-term, determines the effects that export price changes have on each economy. By structure is meant:

— *ownership*, in order to trace the flow of income from exporting
— *taxation*, in order to identify that part of export price changes that goes to governments
— *marketing arrangements* (for agricultural products) in order to establish how much of an export price change reaches farmers
— *debts and profitability*, in order to discover whether an increase, say, in export prices will be reflected in increased profit or in repayment of past debt and reduction of losses.

There is, in fact, no substitute for a thorough knowledge of the structure of each export industry, in order to be able to analyse the impact of export price changes. Some examples which bring out the main points are discussed below, but there are usually some details unique to each case.

Ownership is crucial, both whether the export industry is owned by local African interests or by foreigners, and whether by corporations or by individuals. For example, mining companies in Africa have been, and to a lesser extent still are, owned by foreigners. After-tax income flows abroad therefore, unless successfully reinvested in the industry or prevented from being paid to foreign owners by exchange or other controls. Thus the diamond export industry in Botswana is 50% owned by foreigners and 50% owned by the Botswana government. Increases in diamond prices, to the extent that they accrue to the diamond mining company and are paid out eventually as dividends to the *foreign* shareholders, have no further impact on the Botswana economy. The same analysis applies to that part of the Sierra Leone diamond export industry which is in the hands of a foreign-owned mining company. In contrast, a large part of Sierra Leone diamond exporting is done on a small scale by local people who sell either to the Government Diamond Office in Sierra Leone (if the price is high enough) or to private buyers across the border in Liberia (if the price there, net of transport and smuggling costs, is higher). In either case, higher diamond prices pass directly to producers who, being local people, spend their incomes within the country with all the usual multiplier effects.[8]

Taxation of exports is clearly a key determinant of how much of an export price change reaches producers and how much affects government revenue. Some mining companies have had marginal tax rates above 70%, for example the Zambian copper mines and Botswana's diamonds (if the effect of the government's shareholdings is included).

In such cases, the greater part of an export price change is reflected in government revenue, with very little effect on government spending in the short term if the arguments of the previous chapter are correct. Only the relatively small part of a price change that affects after-tax income is reflected in exporters' income and therefore in spending (where the mine is locally owned). The feedback effects are small, therefore. In the two examples cited, of Zambian copper and Botswana's diamonds, the local economy is almost completely insulated in the short term from export price changes, except insofar as the government reacts quickly to changes in its own income and increases or decreases its spending. The same analysis can be used for the oil industry in Nigeria: changes in export prices affect only the income of foreign shareholders and governments, and thus only affect the rest of the economy via government spending.[9] In contrast, tobacco estates in Malawi and Zimbabwe receive any change in export prices directly by means of local tobacco auctions. Any change in income thus affects local income and spending directly, with the usual multiplier effects. There is no tobacco export duty, so the full impact of price changes is felt on producer incomes; to the extent that those incomes are subject to corporate or personal income tax, the multiplier effect is reduced.

Marketing of export crops in Africa is more often than not in the hands of government-owned institutions: the Cocoa Marketing Board in Ghana, the Agricultural Development and Marketing Corporation (ADMARC) in Malawi, and so on. These marketing organisations usually have a monopoly of exporting over some or all crops.[10] To the extent that such a monopoly is successfully maintained, it is possible to insulate producers from fluctuations in world market prices for the relevant exports, and this is frequently done. The marketing board pays a constant price to farmers and export price fluctuations are reflected in the profit or loss of the marketing board rather than in farmers' incomes. In such circumstances, the full implications of export price fluctuations depend on what happens to marketing board surpluses, and when. For example, the Botswana Meat Commission (the BMC), which has an effective monopoly of beef exports from Botswana, is not allowed by its own rules to run more than a fairly limited surplus or deficit; it also reviews the prices paid for live cattle every three months. As a result, changes in international beef prices feed through quite quickly to cattle farmers, with very little interference by the BMC.[11] ADMARC on the other hand ran large surpluses for many years, with buying prices to farmers maintained constant over long periods. The feedback effects of export price changes for Malawian smallholders occurred, therefore, via the disposition of ADMARC surpluses.[12]

Debt and profitability of export industries or marketing boards, can, in some instances, be the main factor determining the effect of export price changes. If, say, a mining company has been unprofitable because of low metal prices, and has covered its losses by borrowing abroad, then an upward movement in metal prices may simply result in some of the foreign debt being repaid. If metal prices fall even further, then the mining company may simply borrow more from abroad–if it can. In both cases, the short-term effect on the rest of the economy is negligible. Only in the long term does the amount of foreign debt repaid, or the amount of additional foreign borrowing, affect when the mine again becomes profitable and is able to pay taxes and distribute dividends. Both the copper-nickel mine in Botswana and (to a lesser extent) the copper mines in Zambia were in just this situation in the late 1970s and early 1980s.[13] Similarly, if a marketing board has been running at a loss it is unlikely to be able to pass on to farmers any increase in export prices until its losses have been converted into profits, its accumulated debt repaid and, in some cases, some financial reserves acquired.

To sum up, the short-term impact of export price changes depends on *whose* income is changed as a result: government, mining company, marketing board or farmer. The secondary impact of export price changes then depends on what the income recipient is likely to do as a result of a change in income. Each student of an African economy must know, therefore, the structure of the major export industries in the country, and the likely propensities to spend of those people or institutions which receive income from exporting. This is not as difficult as it may seem: the exports of most African economies are dominated by a relatively small number of industries, whose essential characteristics can quickly be discovered. Marginal propensities to spend in the short run are also quite easy to approximate: individuals spend according to their marginal propensity to consume; governments (it has been argued) maintain their spending despite short term fluctuations in tax revenue unless their spending has previously been severely constrained; foreign-owned mining companies either change their investment plans or alter their dividends to foreign shareholders;[14] locally-owned mining companies face the same choice between investment and distribution of profit, but distribution to local owners has further feedback effects (unless it is to government as owner) whereas distribution to foreign owners does not; marketing boards either alter their payments to farmers or alter the investment of their surplus or repay debt.

There is a further important effect of export price changes, because of the overall change in the availability of foreign exchange. In a world without marketing boards or governments or foreign mining companies, exports would simply be produced by individuals. Changed export prices would alter exporter's incomes, and therefore their spending. The change in spending would alter the demand for imports and the system would be self-adjusting. In the modern world, however, various institutions intervene in this process, because they can continue to demand imports even when their income is falling. They may also fail to increase their demand, including demand for imports, when their income is rising. Thus governments, as is well known, do not dismiss civil servants or teachers or the army when export prices fall. Income, and therefore spending on imports is maintained. If *incomes* do not change as a result of export price fluctuations then *either* the foreign exchange reserves fluctuate, *or*, because the foreign exchange reserves may not be large enough, governments try to limit imports by imposing controls. Nearly every African government has implemented import licensing controls, and exchange controls on the purchase and sale of foreign exchange. Some controls, though, are much more severe than others. The main purposes of such controls are firstly to reduce the *overall level* of foreign exchange payments to levels that can be afforded, and secondly to change the *composition* of imports by allowing priority imports and foreign payments, while not allowing other imports and foreign payments. At the same time exchange controls usually require that exporters sell their foreign exchange earnings for local currency, and that residents do not hold foreign currency. In this way the authorities try to allocate the available foreign exchange according to official priorities.[15]

Just as a fall in important export prices may induce a government to introduce or tighten controls, so a rise in export prices may enable a government to relax controls. Many African countries have experienced situations of extreme foreign exchange shortage, forcing their governments to ration foreign exchange severely. The result has been shops empty of imported goods, factories running at a small fraction of capacity for lack of imported inputs, vehicles not being used for lack of spare parts, clinics without drugs, buildings not being maintained, etc. In such circumstances, a rise in export prices can have a dramatic effect in getting an economy moving again–provided the increase in foreign exchange inflows does not all have to be used to pay off previously accumulated debt.[16] The detailed impact of a relaxation of controls depends on the priorities of the controlling authorities, who can in principle choose, for example, whether to allow more imports of consumer goods (very little feedback effects) or of industrial inputs (much larger feedback effect because it enables factories to rehire workers and resume production). Whether changes in foreign exchange inflows are *in fact* allocated according to government priorities depends on how effective the controls are in practice.

3 Determinants of export volumes and their effects on income

Most African export industries produce almost entirely for the export market, with only a small proportion of output for the domestic market. Thus almost all of Ghana's cocoa, or Kenya's coffee or Malawi's tobacco is exported, with relatively minor amounts being consumed at home. Indeed in many African countries commodities have been exported, processed abroad, and then re-imported in their processed form. For example, Nigeria's oil-refining capacity was for many years inadequate to supply Nigeria's own demand for petrol and other refined petroleum products, so that Nigeria was exporting crude petroleum and importing petrol, etc. However, by 1981, her refining capacity was roughly large enough to supply the Nigerian market.[17]

Even in Nigeria, though, only about 10% or so of oil production is used within the country. This means that a large fluctuation in home demand creates only a very small fluctuation in total demand for oil. Thus a 10% increase in home demand, if it were met from oil that would otherwise have been exported, would cause only a 1% fall in the volume of exports. In other words, fluctuations in domestic income, whether from changes in consumption or government spending or investment, have a negligible effect on the volume of exports both in Nigeria and in other African countries. Similarly, the overall level of inflation, itself affected by the level of domestic demand, has a relatively small effect on the volume of exports. Mining companies normally maintain production, in the short run, even when it is unprofitable, either because they expect that profitability will return quite quickly, or because governments insist that they maintain production in order to maintain export earnings and employment.[18] Farmers also maintain their export production, in the short run, more or less regardless of domestic economic conditions. In both cases, rising domestic costs, not matched by rising producer prices, will eventually affect export production: mining companies will lose interest in the investment necessary to expand or even to maintain production; and farmers will tend to move into other crops if they appear more profitable. Similarly, low levels of domestic demand may, in the long run, have pushed some farmers away from producing for the domestic market and into export production; low domestic demand may also, by holding down domestic costs, have some long-term positive effect on mining exports.

It is possible that the level of domestic demand may one day have a greater short-term effect on exports from African economies, especially as industrial exports become more important. For example, if half the output of a factory is exported and half sold on the home market, then a rise in home demand would reduce the output available for export—if the factory had no spare capacity and if the management was willing to neglect export markets in order to supply the home market. If, on the other hand, such a factory had spare capacity then supplies to the home market could be increased without affecting the flow of output to export markets. Such circumstances are at the moment rare in Africa. Most export industries produce, as has been noted, almost entirely for export, and most industry has been set up to supply domestic markets. A limited amount of manufactured goods are exported from a few African countries, including Kenya and Zimbabwe for example, but overwhelmingly exports are still dominated by primary commodities.

The income generated by exporting is thus, like the income generated by government spending, yet another exogenous variable in the model, independent, that is, of the other variables. Exports do vary enormously. As we have seen, prices are extremely volatile for most export commodities, but they are nearly all outside the control or influence of the exporting countries. Export volume also varies in the short term, but again not in ways that are systematically related to the other main macroeconomic variables: the weather affects production of agricultural exports, as does disease; strikes and accidents affect mining output; transport problems affect exports, particularly in land-locked countries; and the availability of foreign exchange for inputs to production, itself a function of export prices among other things, may also affect export production, even though exporters often receive priority in the allocation of foreign exchange for obvious reasons.[19]

Variations in export volume, however, are a great deal more likely to have a direct impact in the short term on the rest of the economy. There are various ways in which African economies may be insulated from short-term fluctuations in export *prices*, but changes in export *volume* (unless entirely the result of changes in stocks) require changes in *output*. And changes in output normally involve changes in purchases from the rest of the economy as well as changes in producer incomes. For example, it may be possible for a marketing board to prevent export price fluctuations from reaching farmers, but if the farmers produce more, and sell it to the marketing board for export, farmers' incomes rise accordingly. Similarly, fluctuations in mining export prices may be reflected mainly in mining company dividends paid abroad and in government revenue, with little short-term impact on the local economy; but changes in mining output usually involve changes in payments to local factors of production such as labour, electricity, transport, etc. In the past, some export industries in Africa have been 'export enclaves', that is they have used almost entirely imported inputs, including imported skilled labour, and so have had very little connection with the domestic economy. But export enclaves are never entirely isolated from the local economy, even if only because they all employ some unskilled labour, and over time the connections increase.[20]

It is fairly certain, then, that changes in export volume have short-term feedback effects, via producer incomes. Before proceeding to a formal analysis of these effects, though, it is necessary to examine the determinants of imports. Payments for imports are a major leakage out of the circular flow of income and it would obviously be misleading to analyse exports without at the same time analysing imports.

4 *The determinants of imports*

In the absence of government controls and physical constraints, the level of imports is mainly determined by the level of demand in the economy. The more income people have, the more imports they will buy. Furthermore, locally produced goods nearly all have an 'import content', that is, some imports are used in their production. Part of any increase in spending leaks out of the circular flow of income and creates income for foreigners. In Africa, this leakage tends to be very large because African economies are so underdeveloped. With only a relatively small range of goods and services being produced locally, African economies rely on imports for most manufactured goods, for nearly all the machinery used in industry, and for a wide range of foodstuffs even including at times some basic foods. Furthermore, most locally manufactured goods have a high import content.

Some invisible imports (imports of services) are closely related to visible imports of goods. Thus foreign payments for freight, insurance and banking charges normally vary in the same way as payments for imported goods. In addition, demand for foreign travel varies with domestic income in much the same way as demand for other imports; and payments of dividends to foreign owners of capital normally depend on company profits, which in turn are part of domestic income. However, payment of interest on foreign loans may vary with foreign interest rates, which are not connected with local income, as well as with the volume of such loans which is at least partly dependent on local income. Similarly, expatriate and other remittances are also only rather loosely connected with short-run changes in income.

Broadly speaking, however, most import payments, visible and invisible, almost certainly depend more on local income than on anything else, *provided that* import licensing, exchange controls, transport problems or other constraints do not seriously intervene to prevent *demand* for imports from being expressed in *actual* imports. This proposition is illustrated in Figure 6.1, which shows that in Malawi, which

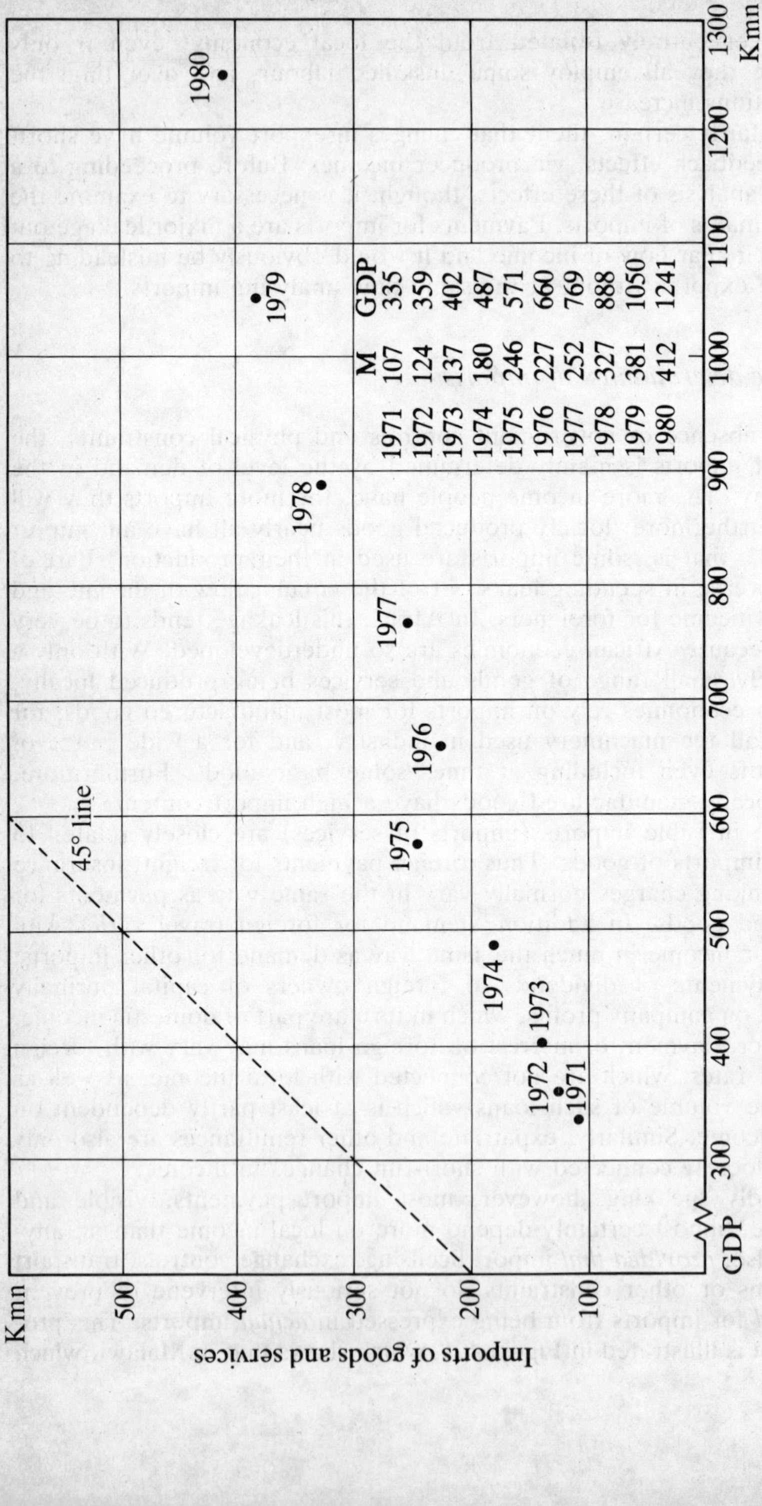

	M	GDP
1971	107	335
1972	124	359
1973	137	402
1974	180	487
1975	246	571
1976	227	660
1977	252	769
1978	327	888
1979	381	1050
1980	412	1241

Figure 6.1 Imports and GDP, Malawi, 1971–80
Source: *International Financial Statistics*

had comparatively few controls affecting imports during this period, imports and GDP were indeed closely related. It is worth noting that, in the one year (1976) when spending on imports fell despite a rise in GDP, there was a fall in stocks in contrast to rises in all the other years covered. This suggests that demand for imported goods may temporarily have been met by running down stocks.

Table 6.2 Average propensities to import in some African countries 1970 and 1980 (percentages)

	1970	*1980*		*1970*	*1980*
Botswana	63	65	Nigeria	17	33
Ethiopia	24	18	Seychelles	66	82
Gambia	46	87	Sierra Leone	30	32
Ghana	24	12	Swaziland	75	60
Kenya	30	41	Tanzania	28	27
Lesotho	47	76	Uganda	19	5
Liberia	42	53	Zambia	37	37
Malawi	35	33	Zimbabwe	25	26
Mauritius	49	63			

NOTES
(1) The source used defines imports to include payments for invisibles such as insurance and freight but excludes net income paid abroad, that is, payment for the use of capital. See IFS for detailed definitions. Figures for imports of goods only used for the Gambia and Zimbabwe.
(2) Under the 1970 column figures for Botswana are for 1968/69, Seychelles 1972.
(3) Under the 1980 column, other years are: 1979 Sierra Leone, Zambia, Zimbabwe; 1978 Mauritius, Nigeria, Uganda; 1977 Ghana, Swaziland; 1976 Seychelles; 1974 Lesotho.

Source: *International Financial Statistics* (IFS), National Accounts Tables.

The figures in Table 6.2 not only show the degree of openness of each economy, but are closely connected with the absolute size of each economy. The smaller the economy, the more likely is it that a high proportion of goods must be imported; thus some of the highest ratios are for the countries with the smallest populations (Seychelles, Swaziland, the Gambia, Botswana, Lesotho). Only where countries have economies and populations of the same orders of magnitude is it possible to make relatively unbiased comparisons (See Table 2.6 for relative magnitudes of GNP). The figures do suggest, therefore, that Zambia and Kenya have more open, or import-dependent, economies than Ethiopia and Tanzania.

Taking two particular years for comparison can give a false impression since one or both years may not be representative of a trend. However, it is clear enough that Nigeria, for example, has been able to increase imports much faster than GDP because of its oil wealth. Also worth noting is that some of the countries which have tried to industrialise aggressively (Kenya, Mauritius) have become more rather than less import-dependent, probably because of the high import content of their new industrial products. The fall in the ratios of Ghana and Uganda are more the product of absolute shortages of foreign exchange to pay for imports than a measure of success in import substitution.

Returning to the short-term determinants of imports, in the absence of controls or with controls unchanged in their impact, the main short-term determinant of the level of imports is the level of income in the economy, giving an import function of the type

$$M = \bar{m} + mY$$

Where M = imports

$\bar{m}$ = that part of imports unaffected by income

m = marginal propensity to import (or, more precisely, the marginal propensity for imports to change as a result of a change of income).

This function only holds, however, if export prices are assumed unchanged or if Y is defined to exclude the effect of changes in the export prices. The function is also more likely to represent import behaviour where there is some spare capacity in the economy; as aggregate demand approaches aggregate supply, even these goods which *are* produced locally become scarce and additions to demand for those goods have to be imported. This will tend to raise m, the marginal propensity to import. In the same circumstances, domestic prices will tend to rise, making imports seem relatively cheap, again putting upward pressure on the marginal propensity to import.

5 *The impact of changes in the volume of exports*

This section deals with the multiplier effects of changes in exports. It turns out that these are quite similar to the multiplier effects of changes in government spending. The formula becomes a little more complicated than the one derived in the last chapter, because of the introduction of an import function. This also makes the model much more realistic, since propensities to import can be very high in Africa, as was shown in Table 6.2.

Before deriving the formula, though, it is important to discuss the way in which changes in export volume feed back into the economy. In general if exporters produce more, then their incomes rise, they spend part of their incomes, save part, and pay part to the government in the form of tax. Some of the spending is on imports, which creates income for foreigners and can be assumed to have no further feedback effects; the remainder creates local income and a further round of feedback effects occurs.

It is possible, though, that the process is not always so straightforward. Just as an increase in export *prices* may not feed into domestic incomes that are likely to be spent (as described in section 2 above), so it is also possible, though less likely, that changes in volume may not feed into personal incomes for spending. For example, mining company output can vary because of problems in obtaining inputs (coal, electricity, chemicals) or in getting rid of output (transport, markets), or in producing output (mining accidents). In such circumstances, mining companies may retain their workforce and continue paying them, so that a part of income does not fall when output falls. Similarly, wage income does not always rise when output recovers. The main impact of volume changes would then be on mining profits and taxation rather than on personal incomes, and the feedback effects would probably be very small: it is quite likely that neither mining companies nor governments would change their spending because of income changes caused by temporary changes in mining output.

Changes in agricultural export volume, on the other hand, are normally reflected in farmers' incomes. So a good rainy season, with resulting high output, would be reflected in higher income for farmers (unless there was a downward price movement) and the consequent feedback or multiplier effects. It is also quite possible, of course, that mining output changes *are* reflected in income changes for workers; and that mining-company spending on other inputs (other than labour, that is), will normally fluctuate with output and so have the normal feedback effects.

For the remainder of this section it will be assumed that changes in export volume are fully reflected in export producers' income. The analysis also applies to changes in export price that are fully passed on to producers. The student should remember that before applying the analysis to a particular African economy, it is essential to know how export industries are actually structured, so that the analysis can be qualified in whatever way is necessary.

In order to derive a formula for the feedback effects of a change in exports, ΔX, which is fully reflected in exporters' income, we have the following equations.

$$Y = C + I + G + X - M \qquad \text{(i)}$$
$$C = a + bY(1 - t) \qquad \text{(ii)}$$
$$M = \bar{m} + mY \qquad \text{(iii)}$$

Substituting for M and C in equation (i)

$$Y = a + bY(1 - t) + I + G + X - \bar{m} - mY$$

So $$Y = \frac{a + I + G + X - \bar{m}}{1 - b(1 - t) + m}$$

Using the same algebraic method as before, this means that the modified multiplier for a change in investment or exports or government spending is

$$k = \frac{1}{1 - b(1 - t) + m} \qquad \text{(iv)}$$

Since this new expression has $+m$ on the bottom line it is smaller than the expression derived in the last chapter

$$k = \frac{1}{1 - b(1 - t)}$$

The new expression, equation (iv), is smaller because an additional leakage has been introduced: some spending is on imports, so each successive round of spending out of increased income is less by the marginal propensity to import.

For example, an increase in exports, ΔX, will create new income of that amount. The marginal propensity for this new income to be spent and create new income will depend on the marginal propensity to consume (b) out of income remaining after marginal tax $(1 - t)$ and after deducting the amount spent on imports. So the income created by the new spending, ΔX, is

$$(b(1 - t) - m)\Delta X \qquad \text{(v)}$$

This new income will be spent, taxed, etc. creating new income

$$(b(1 - t) - m)^2 \Delta X \text{ and so on.}$$

By the same algebra as used in chapter 4, the final increase in income will then be as follows:

For simplicity, write $c = b(1 - t) - m$, so

$$\Delta Y = \Delta X + c\Delta X + c^2\Delta X + \ldots$$
$$= \Delta X \frac{1}{1 - c} = \Delta X \frac{1}{1 - b(-1t) + m}$$

This gives the same multiplier as in equation (iv); as in chapter 4 it is simply an alternative way of deriving the expression for the multiplier, k. The algebra, and therefore the multiplier, is exactly the same for a change in investment spending, ΔI, or for a change in government spending, ΔG. Each such change either increases or decreases peoples' incomes, with the same multiplier effects.

Now that both taxation and imports have been introduced into the model, the formula for the multiplier takes account of all the leakages in the circular flow of income first discussed in chapter 1. In a 'typical' African economy (if there is such a thing) the multiplier is quite small. Most people have low incomes, and so tend to have high marginal propensities to consume; most people pay relatively little tax, so that disposable (after tax) income is a high proportion of gross income. Both these effects tend to produce a high multiplier: for example, if $b = 0.9$ and $t = 0.1$ then the multiplier, ignoring the marginal propensity to import, would be

$$k = \frac{1}{1 - b(1-t)} = \frac{1}{1 - 0.9(1 - 0.1)} = \frac{1}{0.19} = 5.3$$

But of course the role of imports in Africa is large. Taking marginal propensities to import to be the same as average propensities (which they may not be, but the assumption is probably sound enough to give the right order of magnitude) and using the 1980 figures from Table 6.2, the multiplier becomes

$$k = \frac{1}{1 - b(1-t) + m} = \frac{1}{0.19 + m}$$

and this gives multipliers of 1.3 for Swaziland, 1.7 for Kenya, 1.9 for Nigeria, and so on.[21] In other words high marginal propensities to import sharply reduce the multiplier effects of a change in spending–by governments, investors or exporters (or consumers, for that matter, but consumers' habits change slowly so that it is normally assumed that consumers *react* to a change in other forms of spending rather than *initiate* a change in spending out of a constant level of income).

The student is once more reminded of the assumptions made in deriving this multiplier formula:

— the consumption and import functions are linear, implying that the marginal propensities to consume and import are constant
— investment, government spending and export demand are all exogenous, implying that they are unaffected by changes in income
— the changes in the budget and balance of payments surplus or

deficit, which occur as income changes, in no way affect spending or income

These assumptions are only approximations to reality. Much more complicated models can be built, using more elaborate functions to describe consumer behaviour, for example, and subdividing the main macroeconomic variables in order to approximate the behaviour of different groups more closely. Some qualifications and alternatives have already been discussed. The likely determinants of investment, so far assumed constant, and the impact on money and credit of changes in the budget and balance of payments positions, will be discussed in the next three chapters.

One last reminder: the multiplier formula derived in this chapter is more likely to be a useful approximation in a situation where the main impact of a change in spending is on output rather than on the rate of increase of prices. Economic behaviour, and therefore the functions used in a macroeconomic model, is likely to be different (and less predictable) as inflation occurs and changes in intensity. Inflation, or rather the successful control of inflation without doing too much economic damage, remains one of the major unsolved economic problems. The main theories of inflation, and some of the policies that have been tried in order to control inflation, are taken up in chapter 10, after the discussion of investment and money; but the reader is warned that the discussion raises more questions than it provides answers.

6 *Conclusion*

African economies remain surprisingly insulated from the *short-run* impact of changes in export prices. Foreign ownership of export industries (sugar, palm oil and tea plantations, for example, as well as mines), rates of export taxation ranging as high as 75% or so on marginal profits, the use of parastatal marketing boards to intervene between agricultural exporters and price changes in export markets— all these structural factors tend to prevent changes in export prices from reaching ordinary consumers who are likely to change their spending quickly.

In the *long run*, African economies remain extremely vulnerable to export prices, which are almost wholly outside their control. Dependence on imports remains high, and in some countries has even increased over time. Furthermore foreign exchange reserves and access to credit are seldom adequate to maintain imports for consumption and investment, except in the very short term. In general, changes in export volume have a much greater direct impact on the other sectors of African economies than changes in export prices. *Any* change in export earnings may eventually have an impact on macroeconomic policy, by making it possible to import more or forcing a country to import less; this might be called an indirect effect. But changes in export volume also have direct effects, on farmers' incomes, on employment (although not always) and on purchases from other sectors (export enclaves having little contact with the rest of the economy are diminishing in importance).

NOTES

1 Strictly speaking, the sale of goods in local shops to visiting foreigners should be treated as a form of visible export, but it is not usually possibly statistically to identify such transactions separately, so all the local expenditure of foreign visitors, measured by the amount of foreign money they change into local money, is counted in the statistics as sales of services, and thus as invisible exports. The resulting misclassification is probably very small.

2 All export industries, whether mining or tourism or agriculture, have to buy imports. In order to compare their contributions to the foreign exchange position of the country, foreign exchange payments should be subtracted from gross earnings of foreign exchange to arrive at the *net* position.

3 In 1981, however, a slump in the demand for the larger gem diamonds led to De Beers forcing producing countries to stockpile a large proportion (by value) of diamond production. Thus although *price* was maintained, the *volume* of export sales was reduced. See, for example, Bank of Botswana, *Annual Report*, 1981, p. 1.

4 Botswana and Kenya. Furthermore, although Botswana and Kenya receive a high price for beef exports up to the amount allowed by their EEC quotas, the dumping of surplus EEC beef in other markets tends to drive down the world market price of beef and even to exclude other exporters, as happened to Botswana exports of beef to Angola in 1982.

5 Sugar exports are sold at market prices, but the EEC will buy, at an agreed price, any sugar that cannot be sold above that agreed price, up to agreed quantities. The African countries involved are Kenya, Madagascar, Malawi, Mauritius, Congo, Swaziland, Tanzania and Uganda. This agreement, part of the Second Lomé Convention between the EEC and 58 countries of the African, Caribbean and Pacific (ACP) regions, is especially important to Mauritius whose quota is over 80% of 1976 exports, and for whom sugar is the country's dominant export. *The Courier: Africa-Caribbean-Pacific*, *European Community* No. 58, Special Issue, Nov. 1979 'ACP-EEC Convention of Lomé II'.

6 The crucial element of Nigeria's influence on oil prices is whether Saudi Arabia is prepared to alter its own output in order to affect the price received by Nigeria. Although OPEC is often described as a cartel, in the 1970s it did not act as a cartel in the sense of allocating output quotas among its members. Saudi Arabia, and to a much smaller extent other 'surplus' producers who have larger oil revenues than they can immediately spend and large cash reserves, can afford to reduce output to raise oil prices. Most other OPEC producers, including especially Nigeria and Indonesia because of their large populations and consequent large development spending needs, are normally very unwilling to reduce export volumes. Nigeria's influence over Saudi Arabia has to compete with other Saudi Arabian objectives, so that although Saudia Arabia has indeed sometimes acted so as to move the oil price in the direction desired by Nigeria, Saudi Arabia has sometimes done the exact

opposite. In the 1980s, OPEC began to act like a cartel, by allocating export quotas to members.

7 The world market price rose so high above the 'producer price' being maintained by the largest copper-exporting companies that inevitably the system broke down—in April 1966 the world price of copper was $550 per long ton compared with a producer price of $336 per long ton. See my chapter 'Tax reform in the mining industry' in Mark Bostock and Charles Harvey (eds), *Economic Independence and Zambian Copper* (New York, Praeger, 1972, p. 134).

8 In both cases, small-scale diamond producers receive a price net of trading profits and export taxes, so that some of the gain from higher diamond prices in world markets accrues to middlemen and the governments of Sierra Leone or Liberia or both. Competition between buyers exists and tends to keep traders' profits down; similarly competition between the two governments tends to keep export taxes down.

9 Export price changes also affect the ability of banks to lend money—this point is discussed at length in chapter 8.

10 In the case of ADMARC the monopoly is only over smallholder exports, not estate exports. In the case of the Cocoa Marketing Board, the monopoly is not complete because of the possibility of smuggling cocoa out through neighbouring Togo.

11 See Botswana Meat Commission Annual Reports. Nearly all of the change in payments to cattle farmers is reflected in cattle farmer incomes because of the failure of the Botswana Government to impose income tax on the bulk of cattle farmers' taxable income. There is a small tax on BMC turnover. See Derek J. Hudson, 'The taxation of income from cattle farming' in Charles Harvey (ed) *Papers on the Economy of Botswana* (Heinemann, London, 1981, pp. 66–83).

12 See ADMARC Annual Reports for disposition of surpluses—roughly half has gone into estate agriculture, the other half is invested widely in other sectors of the economy.

13 The Zambian copper mines also borrowed from the Bank of Zambia. The short-term effect is again insignificant.

14 The incentives for foreign mining companies to invest or distribute their profits is discussed in chapter 7. Such companies may also repay debts, as noted above.

15 Surprisingly little has been published on exchange controls in Africa. A major study of Zambian exchange controls concluded that the overall outflow of foreign exchange could only be affected temporarily by exchange controls, and at high cost in administrative resources and loss of confidence by the private sector. Robert Liebenthal, 'What can exchange controls achieve? Some suggestions based on Zambian experience 1965–73' (IDS Discussion Paper No. 130, Institute of Development Studies, Sussex, 1978). See also J.N. Bhagwati *Anatomy and Consequences of Exchange Control Regimes*, (National Bureau of Economic Research, 1978).

16 In the 1970s and 1980s Zambia, for example, took longer and longer to pay for imports, which is a form of short-term borrowing. The 'import payment arrears' reached 36 months at times; in other words suppliers of goods and services to Zambia were having to wait up to 36 months to be paid. When the copper price rose in 1979, for example (90% or more of Zambia's exports are of copper) some of the addition to foreign exchange inflows had to be used to reduce the arrears, which fell by $187 million. A similar thing happened in Ghana in the same year, when part of a rise in export proceeds was used to reduce payments arrears by $75 million. *International Financial Statistics*, Zambia and Ghana pages.

17 Nigerian consumers were actually victims of the worldwide oil shortage in 1974. Anthony Kirk-Greene and Douglas Rimmer *Nigeria Since 1970: a political and economic outline* (Hodder and Stoughton, London, 1981, p. 89).

18 Governments may even be prepared to provide financial support for mining companies to keep them exporting, even when they are foreign-owned: both the Botswana and Zambian governments have done this, for example, because of low nickel and copper prices.

19 Export instability is not necessarily a serious problem. If export proceeds fluctuate *above* the level necessary to pay for all the imports that can be effectively used, then the only impact is on the country's foreign exchange reserves. In general, no doubt, large but fluctuating export proceeds are preferable to low but stable ones. This may be why MacBean found no correlation between export instability and low growth. Alisdair I. MacBean *Export Instability and Economic Development* (Allen and Unwin, London, 1966).

20 For example, payments by the Zambian copper mining industry to other industrial sectors of the Zambian economy grew from K41 million in 1956/7 to K178 million in 1969. Over the same period, wage payments to Africans increased from K13 million to K56 million. For 1956/7 see Table 2.4 in Robert E. Baldwin *Economic Development and Export Growth: a study of Northern Rhodesia 1920–1960* (University of California Press, Berkeley, 1966); for 1969 see *National Accounts and Input-output Tables 1969* (Central Statistics Office, Lusaka).

21 These numbers are purely illustrative and should not be used for the countries mentioned. Marginal propensities to consume and marginal propensities for tax revenues to change may be quite different from those arbitrarily assumed in the text. A marginal tax propensity of 0.2 rather than 0.1 would reduce the multiplier for Kenya, for example, from 1.7 to 1.4.

7 *Investment*

1 *Definition*

Investment occurs when current output is not immediately consumed, but instead makes more consumption possible in the future. So investment in the macroeconomic sense is spending on factories and machinery, the development of new mines, increases in herds of cattle, the building of roads, the building up of the national stock of maize, the building up of foreign exchange reserves and so on.

Investment in people, through education and health services and improved nutrition, is not treated statistically as investment. Only that part of educational spending which goes on long-lasting equipment and buildings is treated as investment. There is thus a somewhat artificial distinction between current and capital spending on such services from the point of view of the long-term development of the country. This chapter, however, is concerned only with the short-term determinants of macroeconomic investment spending as conventionally defined.

In common speech the word investment has other meanings. It is used to mean the purchase, by an individual or by an institution, of a second-hand asset. For example, a transport company might buy some second-hand buses in order to supply additional transport services, or an individual might put some of his savings into existing urban property for letting; in both these cases there would be no new investment overall because the purchase in one part of the system is offset by a sale in another. Only a purchase of something second-hand, for example machinery, *from abroad* is investment in the macroeconomic sense. The word investment is also used in common speech to mean the purchase of a financial asset, as, for example, investing in a savings bank or a building society. Although this is investment to the individual concerned, in that it enables him to increase his future consumption, it is not national investment since one person's financial purchase is a form of lending offset by another person's borrowing. The only financial transaction that is a macroeconomic investment is the using of a balance of payments surplus to buy foreign financial assets.

Strictly speaking, not all investment results in more consumption in the future. Some investment fails to lead to greater future output. Furthermore, even if greater output does result from an investment the increased resources may be further invested, putting off any increase in consumption still further in the future. A more generalised definition, therefore is that investment is spending which is intended to create a future flow of income which may in turn be either invested or consumed. This chapter is concerned with the determinants of investment spending rather than with its longer-term results.

In looking at the theory of investment it is gross investment that is important. Gross investment is actual spending on investment. Net investent is gross investment minus depreciation. However, it is gross investment spending that has a short-term macroeconomic impact, so that there is some justification for studying it in the first instance.

Gross investment consists of three parts. The main and most important part is Gross Fixed Capital Formation, which consists of investment in buildings, machinery, land clearance, drilling of boreholes, fencing, roads, railways, sinking of mine shafts—in other words the creation of long-lasting productive assets.[1] Most of the remainder of this chapter will be about determinants of Gross Fixed Capital Formation. It is simply noted here that investment in the macroeconomic sense can also be in two other forms: net increase in stocks and net investment abroad, both of which represent current output not consumed immediately, and therefore available for increased consumption in the future.

2 *Investment as a source of fluctuations*

In more industrialised economies, private sector investment is the element of demand most likely to fluctuate. For this reason investment theory plays a particularly key role in the explanation of national income fluctuations. While investment fluctuations are also important in Africa, other sources of income fluctuation can sometimes be just as, if not more, important.

There are a number of reasons for concentrating on investment as a source of macroeconomic fluctuations in industrial economies. The population in Western Europe, Japan and North America is overwhelmingly urban and dependent on wages or pensions. There are relatively few farmers and self-employed people; and the high income of this group enables its members to maintain their consumption even when their incomes fluctuate, out of savings or credit. Even the unemployed are paid by governments so that the income of a person thrown out of work does not fall to zero, enabling some consumption spending to be maintained. As a result, consumption spending in industrial economies tends to be fairly stable.

In contrast, investment spending in industrial economies is largely dependent on expectations of future profit, on the availability of finance, and on the capacity utilisation of the existing stock of capital. Imagine a factory which uses ten machines to produce its product, each machine having a useful life of five years. If demand for the factory's product is steady, and all the machines are in use, then the management will replace two machines each year. A fall of 10% in demand would cause replacement demand to fall from two machines to one, a fall of 50%. An increase in demand of 10% would cause demand for new machines to increase from two to three, a rise of 50%, if there was no spare capacity; a rise in demand following a period of recession when some machines were idle, would not induce any additional investment in machines.

Fluctuations in investment demand are not determined as simply as suggested in this example: for example the scrapping of old machines can be postponed, and existing machines can be worked more intensively. But the point remains, that investment spending is potentially much more volatile in industrial economies than is consumption spending, simply because of the long-lasting economic life of investment goods. In addition, a change in expectations about the future level of demand, perhaps quite unconnected with the existing level of demand, could induce quite large changes in the demand for new machines, as could the availability of finance to pay for the desired level of investment.

Many of the same arguments apply to investment spending in Africa, although, as will be explained later in the chapter, there are several important additional causes of changes in investment spending. The point here, though, is that there are other equally important sources of macroeconomic fluctuations in Africa, notably export prices, the weather and wages policy. The large changes in export prices that can occur, and their possible impact on income and spending, have already been discussed. With the majority of people living in rural areas and dependent on the weather for their incomes to a greater extent even than farmers in developed countries,[2] drought or excessive rain can create large variations in income and spending. The dominance of many African governments as an employer, and their indirect influence on private sector wages, means that changes in official wage policy can sometimes have larger effects than changes in investment: for example, a series of wage awards in the private and public sectors in 1967 in Zambia caused consumption to increase by two and a half times as much as investment in that year.[3]

3 Theories of investment

In industrial economies, two main theories of investment have been dominant: that investment depends on the rate of interest and that investment depends on the current level of income (or the rate of change of income).

Both of these theories are based on some assumptions about businessmen's motives and the economic circumstances in which they invest. Most fundamentally of all, businessmen are assumed to invest in the expectation of making a profit. For example, a businessman will build a factory because he expects to be able to sell the factory's product for more than the costs of production; this future flow of profits must be enough to 'justify' the original cost of the investment. The truly logical way of making such a calculation is explained at length in a later section. It is enough at this point to grasp the basic idea.

Imagine a businessman thinking of building a shoe factory. He must estimate the demand for the shoes he will be manufacturing; he must estimate the cost of making the shoes, including the cost of buying raw materials, of labour, of power, etc.; he must find the finance, from his own savings, those of his relatives, from a bank, etc.; he must also pay for the finance, by paying interest, by promising a share of future profits, or (conceptually at least) by forgoing the interest he could have earned by investing his money elsewhere; he must also take into account the cost of the factory itself. He will also make some adjustment to his calculations to allow for the many uncertainties and thus the risk of being wrong. Either he will 'discount' (that is, reduce) his profit estimates to allow for risk, or he will only invest if his profit estimates are very high.

Within this general framework, investment theories have concentrated on just a few variables. Thus the theory that investment depends on the rate of interest requires that the cost of finance is the key variable, all other costs, all revenue estimates, the availability of finance, etc., being assumed unimportant.

The theory that investment depends on current income, or the rate of change of income, is really a theory about revenue expectations and the availability of funds. On the one hand, high or rising income is assumed to create expectations of high or rising income in the future and thus of profitable investment opportunities. This assumes, therefore, that one of the things that businessmen worry most about is their prospects of selling their product; and that recent trends in income are a good guide to those prospects. On the other hand, high or rising income is assumed to create high profits out of which investment can be partially or wholly financed. In addition, high profits make it easy to borrow (although it does not follow that banks, for example, have funds to lend even if they are willing to lend; see chapter 8).

Both of these theories are discussed in greater detail in later sections of this chapter[4] since they continue to dominate economic textbooks. But in African countries, only some types of investor fulfil the underlying assumptions of these theories. These assumptions include:

(1) that investors expect to sell mainly on the home market, so that their sales estimates depend on what is expected to happen to home demand;

(2) that investors are primarily interested in making a profit out of future production from their investment, and spending that profit on consumption or further investment within the domestic economy;

(3) that when profitable investment opportunities exist, there are investors with adequate access to finance, know-how, inputs, markets for outputs, and knowledge of the opportunities;

(4) that investment takes place within the general framework of the market and of existing government rules and regulations;

(5) that investment is financed out of local savings, so that the local interest rate represents the cost of finance. Several important categories of investor in Africa do not fit these assumptions, for example: interest rate represents the cost of finance.

Several important categories of investor in Africa do not fit these assumptions, for example:

(i) most exporters (of minerals and agricultural products) sell almost entirely to overseas markets, where demand is independent of local economic conditions;

(ii) foreign investors are frequently more interested in getting their profits out of the country than in local investment opportunities, however profitable; are more interested in making a profit out of selling machines or intermediate inputs (produced abroad) than in using them for profitable local production;[5] and are more interested in protecting or increasing their share of the import market than in the amount or profitability of local production;

(iii) parastatal firms can run at a loss financed by the government, and borrow money for investment from the government, both of which allow them to ignore profitability (as normally defined) when deciding to invest;

(iv) large-scale investors, especially large-scale foreign investors, often obtain changes in the existing framework of government rules and regulations *as a condition for* undertaking an investment;

(v) significant proportions of investment are financed out of foreign funds, so that if interest rates are a determinant of investment (and they may not be) it is *foreign* interest rates not local ones that matter.

(vi) small-scale farmers and other small-scale businessmen tend to have poor information about investment opportunities in the market economy, poor access to credit, know-how, markets, inputs, etc., because of physical remoteness, illiteracy, poor communications, etc; furthermore, small-scale farmers investing in order to increase production for their own consumption, that is, 'subsistence' investors, are relatively little affected by conditions in the market economy; in particular, individual investment in housing is constrained by problems of legal rights to land as well as by lack of access to credit and other inputs.

In short, it would be quite wrong to assume that all types of investor in African countries are similar and make investments for the same reasons. As a minimum one should distinguish between:

Those who plan to produce for export, those who plan to produce for the domestic market and those who plan to produce for their own consumption.

Those whose primary source of profit is from the supply of imports and those whose primary source of profit is from local value added.

Those who can be assumed to have access to finance, know-how, markets, management, etc., and those who cannot take advantage of profitable investment opportunities because of lack of such access.

Large-scale investors who can get concessions from government and small-scale investors who cannot.

Those with access to both foreign and local finance, and those with access only to local finance.

Further subdivisions are also necessary at times, especially in the case of foreign investors, as will be seen in the following sections.

4 *New foreign investors: 'market-protectors'*

The most important type of new foreign investor[6] is the firm seeking to protect or increase its share of the domestic market, previously supplied by overseas production in the form of imports. Such a firm is not therefore new to the country in the sense of having no previous experience of it. On the contrary it has been supplying the market for some time, typically progressing from using a local agent to setting up its own distribution facilities (this may already involve a form of investment, although not in manufacturing).

Most foreign firms regard African countries as risky and unprofitable areas for investment. African governments are regarded as unstable, likely to nationalise foreign firms without 'adequate' compensation, likely to impose discriminatory taxes on foreign firms or to impose restrictions on the remission of profits. Furthermore, African national markets are typically small so that local manufacture will not benefit from the cost-saving advantage of large-scale production (economies of scale).

As a result, a foreign firm with a share of the import market will normally prefer to continue to manufacture in its own country and export the product to Africa. It will only decide to manufacture in an African country *either* if it is threatened with losing its share of the import market *or* if local 'manufacture' offers an opportunity of greatly increasing its share of the import market, preferably by performing some relatively minor activity which continues to depend heavily on imports.[7]

Threat of market loss comes either from government putting heavy tariffs on imports or from a rival supplier of imports investing in local manufacture and seeking tariff protection against imports of competing products. This latter strategy is of course the way in which firms seek to increase their share of the market. But even when such an investment is decided upon, the investor will try and minimise his risks by investing as little of his own money as possible, and by transferring as little as possible of the manufacturing process to the African country.

> Accordingly, they spent their time looking for ways to reduce the exposure of the company's capital to a situation they conceived to be risky and uncertain. For example, they looked for assurances of repatriation of capital, and they negotiated for higher customs protection and guarantees against devaluation. They further investigated various means to reduce the size of the dollar investment. A search for loans in local currency and negotiations aimed at reducing the percentage of local value added by production in the proposed factory were two important factors in this respect.[8]

Thus it is quite usual for a 'factory' to be set up which does little more than assemble and package imported inputs. The inputs are now treated as 'intermediate products' and come in free of import duties, while rival products continue to carry duty as 'finished products'. The investor will usually attempt to secure from government a higher tariff on competing imports[9] in order to protect what is now a local 'industry'. This enables him to charge a higher price than before and, so he hopes, to capture a bigger share of the market. A few rather low-skill jobs are created for local people; some expensive assembly and packaging machinery is imported; maintenance of the machinery and management of the operation requires highly paid expatriates to be employed, meanwhile the consumer pays in the form of higher prices, and reduced choice of product if rival products are no longer available.

A further problem for the African government is that the firm is now in a position to manipulate the price of its intermediate product supplies. If local tax rates are increased or exchange controls imposed on profit remission, then by raising intermediate product prices the firm can make higher profits at home and lower profits in Africa. This process is an example of 'transfer pricing' and effectively avoids local taxes and exchange controls.[10]

In practice, firms often succeed in taking advantage of tax holidays and guarantees of profit remission (or succeed in bargaining for them at the time of the investment). Yet these additional advantages are largely irrelevent to the original investment decision, if the main reason for investing is to get maintained or increased sales of intermediate products and so increase profits in the country of origin.

This description of a typical 'market-protecting' investment does not mean that there is no potential gain from it for African economies. Tough requirements on training and localisation of the labour force, on the increasing use of local rather then imported inputs, and taxes on concealed forms of profit remission, can increase the local gains. The most difficult form of control is over transfer pricing because it is often so difficult to find out what prices ought to be. However, many products which are traded between associated companies are also traded at 'arm's length', and methods exist for establishing other prices so that it *is* possible (although difficult) to control transfer pricing to some extent.

An alternative strategy is part-ownership by government. This has advantages and dangers for both sides. The main advantage for government is increased control of a type not obtainable from 'external' methods of control such as taxation and exchange control; ideally part-ownership should enable government interests to be cared for by means of increased knowledge of the running of the business. Part-ownership, whether majority or minority, does not necessarily give control, however[11], and requires the government to put up some of the cost of the investment; in addition, part-ownership may cause the government to believe that everything necessary for control has been done, and so to relax other controls which may still be very necessary. Many private firms do not at first like the idea of being in partnership with the government, but often find that it interferes very little with existing management practices and can have considerable advantages in the form of political acceptability and the additional privileges of being a parastatal—mainly protection in various forms from competition but also such benefits as access to government finance.

Where a government insists on all major new industrial investments being in partnership with the state, it may be that the availability of government money becomes an important determinant of new foreign investment. This would mean that export prices, ease of borrowing from foreign banks, and other sources of government finance, would have an important influence on industrial investment. State participation in major new industrial investments may also affect the type of investment that is undertaken, perhaps taking more account of social needs, using local raw materials, etc. However, African policy is ambiguous, requiring parastatal businesses to 'show a greater consideration for social benefit than would normally apply to privately owned companies. They...must operate in a business-like manner ....'[12]

Another way of looking at this question of state participation is to note that putting money directly into industrial investment may be a better way of 'spending' state money than by offering tax concessions and having generous rules on the remission of profits. Concessions may not even attract any additional investors (those that do invest would have invested anyway in order to protect their markets); meanwhile they lose the country a lot of money from the profits of existing investors.[13]

This discussion has not produced a theory which would succeed in predicting the amount of market-protecting investment. It is not a sufficient condition for investment that the local market should have grown by enough to justify a local plant, since import suppliers prefer to continue to supply from abroad unless their market is threatened (by government or by a rival supplier). Indeed Kilby has shown that in Nigeria there was typically no local manufacture for many years after the market had grown big enough to justify such an investment; then within a very short period several factories would be set up by rival firms, each determined to prevent the others from capturing the whole market even though this meant that huge amounts of excess capacity were created.[14] It might be thought that excess capacity would lead firms to seek export markets; but small scale of production and newness lead to high costs and anyway many foreign investors prohibit exports that might threaten their other markets supplied from their countries of origin.[15] Also, industrial investments in Africa tend to be in the same products, which reduces the possibility of intra-African trade.[16]

The discussion does suggest that market-protecting investment will take place as a result of threat; but what causes the timing of the threat, or how much investment it will induce, is not apparent. Profitability is not relevant, since it is determined by the concessions obtained from government, especially on tariffs and the degree of monopoly. Even if firms do not succeed in obtaining sufficient concessions from government to guarantee local profitability, the investment may still take place because of the profits to be obtained from supplying inputs (possibly at favourable transfer prices) or in the hope of obtaining concessions at a later date.

5 *New foreign investors: 'non-market-protectors'*

In the previous section, two reasons for foreign investment were identified, namely protection of or increase in a firm's share of the local market by setting up local production facilities. The question to ask in this section is what other reasons an investor might have for risking his money in remote and underdeveloped African countries, of which the investor has no previous experience, and which are apparently (to the investor) highly unstable politically. It is an unfortunate fact that only bad news about Africa appears in most foreign newspapers and that bad news about one African country tends to create a bad impression about others, to those who have no first-hand experience of the countries involved.

The 'classic' answer to this question, that is, the answer given in a lot of academic writing and implied by the sort of concessions frequently offered to foreign investors, is that investors will appear, attracted by the size of the market and comforted as to the security of their profits (and being allowed to remit them out of the country) by the promises of governments and the speeches of presidents, ministers and ambassadors. But with the possible exception of Nigeria, African economies offer very small local markets, the policies of governments towards foreign investors have frequently been changed and an enormous number of regulations—on work permits, local borrowing, licensing, immigration, building, etc.—make the starting-up of a new business difficult and therefore expensive. In any case, the most obvious candidates for the tax concessions and other inducements, offered by governments to foreign investors, are precisely the market protectors of the last section. They already supply the market from abroad and so have several advantages over complete newcomers to the local scene. It is difficult, therefore, to see what sort of investor could possibly be interested in such a remote and apparently risky investment.

In his investigation of foreign investors in Nigeria, Kilby found only one 'classic' investor. He divided what he called the non-market-protectors into five types.[17]

(a) The 'classic' investor, attracted by the size of the Nigerian market, looking for a profitable investment opportunity.
(b) Individual investors (including crooks) seeking the backing of government agencies on favourable terms.
(c) Manufacturers trying to sell redundant machines.
(d) Machinery manufacturers seeking a profit by selling their machinery.
(e) Machinery merchants seeking a profit by selling other people's machinery.

Only the first type did not require Nigerian public capital—all of the remainder were not prepared to back the investment entirely with their own money. In the case of the machinery merchants their contribution was typically very small indeed.

The most important point about types (2) to (5) is therefore that they expect somebody else to put up the money and take the risks; and in the case of types (3), (4) and (5) the firms had little or no interest in successful *production* since their profit came from selling machinery. The profit from selling machinery accrues to the so-called investor before the factory even begins production; and it accrues to the foreign supplier in his own country, so the profit does not depend on future profitable production, nor on permission to transfer future profits out of the African country.

Redundant machines are not necessarily 'wrong' for countries in Africa; indeed second-hand machinery may be cheaper and more suitable to local conditions if, for example, it is easier to maintain and uses more labour than more modern machinery. In buying second-hand machinery it is important to ask why it is being sold. If it is worn out, or if it is being replaced by more efficient machinery which would also be more efficient in Africa—then it is almost certainly poor value. If it is available because a firm has gone bankrupt, or if it is being replaced by a machine less suitable to African conditions, then buying second-hand may be a sound policy. Nevertheless, there remain considerable difficulties in using second-hand machinery successfully.[18]

The worst form of investment for Nigeria was by machinery merchants. None of the firms ran profitably and so they required subsidies out of public funds. They absorbed over £30mn of public investment money. The reasons for failure were that investments were made for political rather than economic reasons, machines were often of the wrong sort and badly matched with each other, and the quality of the management was poor. Most fundamentally, the machinery merchants had no interest in successful production, not even for the sake of the reputation of the machines since they were selling other people's machines. The UNCTAD study quoted above found a similar situation in Ethiopia, where the risks were taken by the Ethiopian government and eleven out of a sample of twelve firms made losses.[19]

Management is very important. Buying a complete factory and then trying to hire management on the international market is seldom successful. On the other hand a firm investing in order to manufacture its own product (usually a market-protector) with foreign personnel supplied from its own operations elsewhere, clearly has a real interest in successful production and a much better chance of achieving it because of the people it can use and the technical back-up of its worldwide operations. Such a firm also has an interest in the reputation of its product. On the other hand such firms have greater opportunities for transfer pricing.

For all types of non-market-protectors (as for market-protectors) profitability depends very heavily on government decisions. The most important government decision is usually on the level of tariff protection, but others include price control over both inputs and outputs and the degree of monopoly or competition permitted. In any case, profitability is not a sufficient condition for investment, since even the existence of an opportunity to make profits is not certain to induce investment if potential investors consider the situation to be too risky. Even if a government is correct in believing that its own country is politically stable and a low-risk area for foreign investment, it may be unable to persuade foreign firms that that is the case. Nor is profitability a necessary condition for investment since profit may be made out of selling machines, selling intermediate products or buying output rather than out of local production.[20]

One type of non-market-protecting investment remains to be discussed, namely investment in producing raw materials for export – this is so important that it is dealt with in a separate section.

6 *Investment in mining*

Mining investment is a special case. It is both extremely risky and, potentially, extremely profitable. Mining companies thus need large amounts of finance to carry the risks of prospecting and the cost of developing mines, often in places without any previous modern development. Mineral ore bodies are seldom located conveniently near to existing railways, towns, water supplies, skilled workmen, etc. At the same time the very large profits that can be made encourage such investment.

There are thus two obvious determinants of mining investment. One is the expected future price of the mineral (for which the present price may be a guide); the other is anything which reduces the risk of prospecting and then developing a mine, or which reduces the risk of not being able to make a profit once a mine has been developed. Taking price expectations first, there are unfortunately a number of reasons why the current price is not a very good guide to investment.

Some mining investments are so obviously profitable that they take place regardless of expectations as to the future price of the mineral. Secondly, international mining companies are in a good position to use international sources of finance and so are not necessarily dependent on a high current price to generate investment funds.

Thirdly, political expectations affect profit expectations. Fourthly, it takes a long time to develop a new mine (typically, five years) so that once begun, investment is likely to continue despite price fluctuations, unless price expectations fall so low that it seems worthwhile to cancel an investment when it is half-developed.

Yet another reason why mining investment may take place independently of short-term price movements is that the need to secure a regular supply of the metal may be more important than making a profit from mining. Thus Japan, having industrialised later than Western Europe and North America and having a very rapid rate of growth in the 1960s, actually invested in copper mining in Zaire, then Congo (Kinshasa), when the political risks were very high, certainly high enough to prevent any other sort of foreign investment. Japan was unable to buy enough copper through the London Metal Exchange (LME) because relatively little copper is actually sold through the LME. Zambia's copper, for example, is sold at prices based on the LME prices, but most of it is sold on long-term supply contracts to particular customers. The only way, therefore, for Japan to secure increased supplies of copper was to invest in mining with the promise of long-term supply contracts.

Despite all the above arguments that investment can be independent of prices and price expectations, they obviously have some influence. It has been argued that there is in fact an investment cycle. High prices induce investment; after a time-lag for the development of the new mining capacity, additional supplies bring the price down; investment is then neglected and a new shortage develops, driving prices up again. Furthermore, the sort of world shortage of the metal that induced Japanese investment in Zaire in the 1960s, normally coincides with high prices and therefore with high profits out of which to finance investment.

The point, as far as any individual country is concerned, is that other considerations are frequently more important, even if this investment cycle explains investment world-wide. In modern Zambia, for example, non-price factors have been dominant[21]; and before independence some at least of the periods of heavy investment can also be explained by non-price factors: for example, the granting of exclusive prospecting licences in the 1920s, and the setting of a thirty-six year limit on the BSA Company's enjoyment of the mineral royalty in 1950.[22] The first of these was a risk-reducing factor.

Another aspect of mining investment is that it has to be relatively long-term in nature. Prospecting takes time; the development of a new mine, once an ore body has been identified, takes an average of something like five years, as already mentioned; the life of a mine is seldom less than ten years, often more than twenty. Furthermore, there is no question in mining of a minor investment in assembly and packaging; mining requires a massive investment in fixed capital (very fixed in the case of the mine itself; the investor cannot remove a hole in the ground).

Mining can also create a very large investment compared with any single industrial investment. Manufacturing investment tends to be limited by the size of the local market, at least initially, whereas the size of a mining investment is determined more by the size of the mineral deposit and can be very large in relation to the local economy. Size and relative permanence create both strengths and weaknesses in the bargaining relationship between governments and mining companies.[23] Most important, both sides know that ultimately they have to reach agreement on how the mining industry is to be run and owned. In other sectors of the economy there are examples of foreign firms closing down their operations or being closed down by the government, rather than reaching agreement.

Finally, mining, and also foreign investment in agricultural raw materials for export, create a conflict between the investor and local interests in the development of further processing. The foreign investor who has refining plant with spare capacity in some other country will be unwilling to invest in refining capacity in the country where the mine or plantation is. The local government must then use what bargaining power it has to increase the proportion of value added locally. This is the counterpart of the problem of increasing the proportion of value added locally by import-substituting firms.

7 *Foreign investment: expansion of existing investment*

Foreign investors with an existing investment in the country (provided that they have an interest in production) are affected by some of the same factors as locally-owned businesses. Thus some (gross) investment is necessary in order to maintain a business as depreciation occurs, and most businesses try to expand with the market. On the other hand foreign-owned business may have additional or alternative objectives not shared by locally-owned firms; for example:

(a) To get profits out of the country.
(b) To maximise the purchase of intermediate inputs from associated companies (also a way of getting profits out).
(c) To invest in areas not reserved by law for local citizens (or expected to be reserved by law in the future).

As a result, the reaction of the foreign-owned businesses to a profitable investment opportunity could be quite different from that of a locally-owned business—namely to get profits (and capital too, where possible) out of the country rather than to invest in expanded capacity. Similarly, a foreign firm with a profitable opportunity to increase the proportion of value added locally, by extending the local production process, would not necessarily do so, but might prefer to continue importing as much as possible from the parent company. Thirdly, African governments have been reserving an increasing number of business opportunities for their own citizens; non-citizens must react to or avoid these new laws and may also try to anticipate the way such laws are likely to develop in the future.

The nature of investment may well also be affected by whether investors are foreign or local. Basically, the foreign investor is less sure of having a long-term future in the country—that is why he is often more interested in profit abroad than profit locally—and so prefers investment in short-term projects. As a result, the foreign investor may avoid investments with a long-term pay-off, even when that pay-off is very high. A fairly minor example is the way foreign investors prefer to rent office accommodation and executive houses, rather than buying, even when rents are very high. Local institutions, faced with the same relative costs tend to buy (or build) because they do have a long-term future in the country.

Not all types of foreign investor have the same opportunities for pursuing their particular objectives. Thus the long-term resident foreigners to be found in many parts of Africa (Asians, Southern Africans and sundry Europeans in Zambia; Italians, Greeks and Lebanese in Ethiopia, etc.) are less likely to be buying intermediate inputs from associated companies than branches of multinational companies and other companies with non-resident ownership. For the same reason, resident foreigners find it more difficult to get money out of the country—transfer-pricing by collusion with suppliers is more difficult to organise than transfer-pricing within the same group of companies.

It is not possible to say what type of foreign investor has the shorter time-horizon. Resident expatriates may wish to get their money out, but some of them may believe in a long-term future for themselves in the country and some may have nowhere to go—or prefer the risk of staying to the risk of going. Foreign companies with non-resident ownership might appear to have long-term prospects: many have been encouraged to invest by the government and they can survive (as corporate bodies) the complete localisation of personnel, for example.

But foreign firms may have a short-term view of their likely profitable life in an African country, because government policies may change, because of the risk of expropriation, etc. Where they are essentially in the business of selling management expertise or some other form of technology their exclusive knowledge may be short-lived as local people acquire it. In the extreme cases of those foreign investors who are not interested in production, having made their profit out of selling machinery before production starts, it is unlikely that an expanding market will induce investment—most of such firms run at a loss anyway.[24]

Attitudes to investment in Africa probably change over time. Thus in Zambia immediately after independence, some of the locally resident foreign businessmen left as fast as they could, despite the enormously profitable opportunities created by the post-independence boom. Of those that now remain presumably most are relatively confident of the short-term to medium-term prospects. Their attitudes are fairly sensitive to government policy changes, however, not only as regards Zambianisation of various sectors of the economy but also in such matters as how they are treated in the queues for credit, import licences, etc.

Similarly, the attitudes of companies owned by non-residents are adversely affected by such events as takeovers and changes in government; but over time investor confidence tends to recover as investors discover they can survive and make profits. For example, in South Africa, normally regarded as the safest haven for foreign investment in Africa, investor confidence was badly shaken by the changes taking place in the rest of Africa in the late 1950s, and by Sharpeville, so that there were large net outflows of investment finance in the years 1959-65; a net inflow recurred in 1966. After the Soweto uprising in 1976 there was again a net outflow of direct investment, although on a relatively smaller scale, presumably because investors had become less apprehensive about such events; the outflow ended in 1980.

Summarising this section, then, it would seem that foreign investors with an existing stake in the country, whether resident or non-resident, may respond to profitable opportunities in much the same way as domestically-owned businesses. But although a profitable opportunity is a necessary condition for the expansion of a foreign-owned business, it is not a sufficient condition since the business may have alternative objectives to that of making profits on local production. Secondly, a foreign-owned business may be unwilling to commit itself to a project whose profitability will only be realised over a relatively long period whereas locally-owned businesses (especially parastatals) are more likely to be able to take a longer view.

Where a parastatal is in partnership with foreigners, investment behaviour depends on who is the dominant partner, how the contracts were written, whose money is invested in expansion. Clearly the motive for government participation is precisely to change foreign investor behaviour in the direction of local interests, but in practice this objective is not automatically achieved simply by participation. On the one hand, government participation should give foreign investors greater security, better access to government services (import licenses, credit) and other government-allocated benefits (tariff protection, monopoly). On the other hand, state participation reduces foreign investors' freedom of manoeuvre, and may create an increased obligation to fall in with government policy (price control, recognition of unions, local purchasing of inputs). The relationship between the partners is essentially a bargaining one, whose outcome depends on their relative strengths and weaknesses and is therefore difficult to predict.

8 *Locally-owned investment*

In the previous sections of this chapter, foreign investment was discussed on the implicit assumption that there was a domestic counterpart with which it could be compared. It is important to ask, for African countries, whether there is really a significant class of domestic businesses which is comparable to the class of foreign businesses—in being capable of using modern technology (and having access to it), in having access to bank credit, to urban (and overseas) markets, etc.

Generally speaking, in most African countries there is a small but rapidly growing group of citizens owning and running 'modern' businesses in such sectors as farming, transport, retailing, etc. but large-scale industry and mining are still dominated by foreign investors, increasingly in partnership with the government; and the purely capitalist, purely domestic sector is still mainly made up of businesses which do not have very good access to technology, bank credit, markets, etc.

This means that investment opportunities may not be taken up, when local investors do not have the means, and foreign investors do not regard the opportunities as profitable enough to allow for the risks as they perceive them. This would suggest that government could induce investment either by providing technical assistance to local investors, or by reducing the risks as perceived by foreign investors. The policy of trying to induce foreign investment has already been discussed; trying to help local investors is just as difficult—for all sorts of fairly obvious reasons. It is very hard indeed for the small-scale local business to change its whole nature so that it begins to use modern technology and large-scale modern manufacturing methods.

Makers of buckets from corrugated iron sheet in the corner of some local market are not easily transformed into metal-processing manufacturers employing hundreds, using precision machine tools and a production line. It is much more likely in fact that they will be put out of business by imports or by the local assembly (or last-stage manufacture) of imported inputs by a foreign investor. The competing foreign investor also has the advantage of being able to advertise his product and its alleged superiority, even though the locally-produced product may be more suitable for local people and their needs. In fact the small-scale local business is often discriminated against by government policy. Restrictive licensing of taxis, retail stores, hawkers, etc., reduces opportunities. Legal requirements regarding land use, building regulations, etc., have the same effect and also make it difficult to get credit. There are many other examples.

Small-scale agriculture is really only an example of locally-owned and operated business. The constraints are particularly severe, because of remoteness, lack of information and know-how, etc. Farmers do, however, respond to profitable opportunities when these constraints are not operative or when they are overcome by a sufficiently well-organised and efficiently delivered package of services. For example, the opportunity provided by the growth of copper mining and urban demand for food in the 1930s produced a very rapid response from Zambian farmers in the products which they already knew how to produce: maize and beef.[25] New technologies have been successfully adopted in Africa, for instance in cotton-growing and poultry-farming, as a result of a combination of attractive prices and well-organised programmes. As with other forms of business, though, apparently attractive investment opportunities may not be taken up because local farmers do not have the means and because those who do have the means are not interested (because the profit will be spread over too long a period or because they are simply more interested in getting their money out of the country).

What this discussion amounts to therefore is that a period of rising income, which creates all sorts of profitable investment opportunities, and of freely available investment funds (whether from high profits or bank credit being available), will not have a uniform effect on every sector of the economy. Where local people already have the means to take up investment opportunities, investment is likely to occur. Where local people are not able to invest and foreigners are unwilling, investment will not take place and either imports will increase or goods and services will simply not be provided. Meanwhile, high foreign-owned profits will be remitted abroad, legally or illegally.

There is also a class of locally-owned investment which cannot really be compared directly with foreign investment, namely investment in the 'traditional' as opposed to the 'modern' sector of the economy. Mostly this sector consists of small-scale farming, but it also includes other types of small-scale business using relatively simple technology and relatively few modern sector inputs. Such investment is undertaken when it is a more profitable use of labour and other resources then their alternative uses, and it is as important as modern sector investment for future development. That may seem rather an obvious point to make, but it is worth stressing because farmers who choose to build up their cattle herds instead of selling them, or who choose to clear new land or build new houses instead of working for wages, are often accused of behaving irrationally. On the contrary, it can safely be assumed that people make the best use of their time and other resources that they can, given the information available to them and their need to survive (it is no use maximising profit over five years if you cannot feed your family in year two).

Relatively little is known about traditional sector investment, for much the same reasons that relatively little is known about subsistence income. For example, the build-up of cattle herds in Botswana, an important form of investment in that country, has to be calculated by use of a quite elaborate model, precisely because direct information is not available.[26] However, it should be noted that some investment in the traditional sector has the effect of *withdrawing* expenditure from the modern sector of the economy in the short term. For example, a decision to build up a cattle herd instead of exporting some cattle for cash would reduce the amount of expenditure in the economy if it can be assumed that some income from cattle sales would have been spent. Similarly, a decision to work on land-clearing or house-building instead of working for cash wages would have the same short-term effect. Such investment decisions therefore have exactly the opposite effect of decisions to invest by spending cash, which create money income with accompanying multiplier effects.

9 *The calculation of expected profit*

Some investment is determined mainly by expectations of profit rather than by government decisions. Of course all investment decisions are affected by broad government policy—on taxation, the cost of such government-supplied inputs as electricity, coal and railway transport, and many other policies. But these policies tend to apply to all firms indiscriminately. It is reasonable to assume these various policies unchanged while examining the impact of purely economic variables on investment, provided that the investment decision does not depend on a change or concession in government policy peculiar to that investment decision. For example, if an investment decision depends on the granting of a protective tariff or a change in a government-controlled price then 'pure' economic factors cannot be considered independently of government decisions.

An investment decision made on the assumption of unchanged

government policy (or simply allowing for the general possibility of favourable or unfavourable changes) will normally be based on expectations of profits; that is, the difference between expected revenue and expected cost. Even some of those investment decisions dependent on a particular goernment decision can be included in the framework since investors can be assumed to calculate the effect on the expected returns of the government action.

Suppose, for example, a transport operator is planning to buy another lorry. In principle he or she should estimate its useful life, what he can sell it for at the end of its useful life, how much revenue it will earn and the running costs. The timing of each cost and each receipt is also of great importance. This is because an expense now of K100 costs the investor more than an expense of K100 in a year's time. If the money has to be borrowed then interest must be paid on an immediate payment; if the investor has cash, then spending it now means he cannot put the money in a bank or building society to earn interest. In either case, the spending of cash now costs more than the spending of cash later.

The same argument applies to the receipt of revenue now, which is worth more to the investor now than the receipt of revenue at a later date. Receipt of cash now enables the investor to reduce his borrowing and pay less interest, or to put more money into a financial institution and receive more interest.

The variation in value of costs and receipts according to their timing is especially important in investments with a long 'gestation' period, that is, a long time from when costs start to when receipts start. Hydro-electric schemes are a good example of an investment with a long gestation period: building a dam and installing hydroelectric machinery can take years, during which expenses are high, while no revenue is received until the project is complete. If money has been borrowed to build the dam, interest must be paid during the construction period; if investors put in their savings to finance the scheme, they must forgo alternative earnings on their savings until the scheme begins to earn a profit.

In principle, an investor expecting to sell a product for \$100 should not mind whether he receives \$100 now or \$100 $(1+r)$ in a year's time, if r is the annual rate of interest obtainable on savings. If he receives \$100 now he can put it in a savings account so that in one year it will be worth $\$100 + r \times \$100$, or \$100 $(1+r)$.

Another way of expressing this is to say that the 'present value' of $\$100(1+r)$ receivable one year in the future is \$100. By the same process \$100 becomes $\$100(1+r)^2$ in two years' time if it remains invested in a savings bank. So the present value of $\$100(1+r)^2$ receivable two years in the future is \$100.

Generalising this into a formula, the present value of a sum $x(1+r)^n$, receivable n years' time in the future, is x. Writing

$$x(1+r)^n = y$$

then the present value of y, receivable n years in the future is x. But

$$x = \frac{y}{(1+r)^n}$$

In other words, a sum y receivable n years in the future is worth less in present terms, and the lesser amount is given by this formula.

Similarly, if a cost of \$100 can be put off for a year, the investor should not mind if it costs \$100 $(1+r)$ in a year's time since he can earn $r \times$ \$100 in interest on the cash, or save that amount in borrowing costs.[27] So the present value of a cost of \$100$(1+r)$ in a year's time is \$100. Generalising as before, a cost of y in n year's time has a present-day value of x, where

$$x = \frac{y}{(1+r)^n}$$

If the investor, whether a private investor or the government, does not make such calculations, then there is no way of distinguishing between investments where costs are immediate or postponed to a later date, or between investments with early or delayed receipts. The process of calculating the present value of future costs and receipts is called 'discounting to present value', and the interest rate used is sometimes called the 'discount rate'.

The estimated present value of an investment is the difference between the present value of estimated benefits and the present value of estimated costs. The 'rate of return' on an investment is the interest rate which would have to be used to reduce the present value to zero. The example of a lorry should help to make this clear.

Suppose the lorry has a life of three years (quite generous for some parts of Africa) costs \$3000, and is expected to have costs and revenue as shown in Table 7.1.

The present value of the flow of payments and receipts, discounted at 10% is

$$\text{Present value} = -3000 + \frac{1300}{1+0.1} + \frac{1200}{(1+0.1)^2} + \frac{1100}{(1+0.1)}$$
$$= -3000 + 1182 + 992 + 826 = 0$$

In other words the expected rate of return on this investment is 10%. Although the total of net receipts is \$600 greater than the

Table 7.1 Investment in a lorry

	Start of year 1	*End of year 1*	*End of year 2*	*End of year 3*
Purchase of lorry	3000	—	—	—
Running costs	—	1200	1300	1400
Receipts	—	2500	2500	2500
	– 3000	+ 1300	+ 1200	+ 1100

NOTE
Assumption is that all running costs and receipts are met simultaneously at year-end. This makes little difference to the calculation. It would occur if the lorry was leased to a subcontractor who simply paid over the net revenue at the end of each year. It is also assumed that the lorry has a scrap value of nothing at the end of three years.

original investment of $3000, these receipts are expected in the future while the $3000 must be paid at once.

Another way of putting it is to say that if the investor had to borrow $3000 and pay 10% on the loan, he would end up with exactly nothing —no profit, no loss—at the end of three years. This can be seen from Table 7.2.

Table 7.2 Investment in a lorry borrowing at 10%

	Start of year 1	*End of year 1*	*End of year 2*	*End of year 3*
Net revenue (from Table 7.1)	– 3000	+ 1300	+ 1200	+ 1100
Interest due on borrowing	—	– 300	– 200	– 100
Balance outstanding	– 3000	– 2000	– 1000	—

NOTE
Assumption is that all interest is paid in one payment at year end, on the borrowing outstanding at the beginning of each year.

Yet another way of putting it is to say that if the investor had cash, he would be just as well off investing in a savings account yielding 10% as investing in the lorry. It is assumed that interest on the savings account is reinvested, and that net receipts from operating the lorry are also reinvested at 10%. This can be seen in Table 7.3.

In real life, most investors would prefer a safe 10% in a savings account to the very risky business of running a lorry for the same prospective rate of return. These figures, though, oversimplify the

Table 7.3 Investment in a lorry or a 10% savings account

	Start of year 1	*End of year 1*	*End of year 2*	*End of year 3*
Savings account:				
amount invested	3000	3300	3630	3993
interest received	—	300	330	363
Lorry:				
receipts	—	1300	4200	1100
interest	—	—	130	263
Cumulative total	—	1300	2630	3993

decision. The amounts of net revenue from running the lorry are only estimates. If, for example, the investor guesses that the earnings shown are the *minimum* he can expect, and that there is a good chance of much higher earnings, he may well prefer to gamble on buying the lorry.

The discussion in this section has been about the private investor who takes existing prices as beyond his control and seeks to make a profit within that framework. But in small, underdeveloped African economies, in which governments have interfered in many ways with the price mechanism, prices do not necessarily indicate to investors what would be to the greatest benefit of the country as a whole. It is thus open to government to try and alter the prices used by private investors–by subsidies, taxes and direct price control. For its own investments the government can use 'shadow prices'–these are the prices which government thinks reflect more accurately the 'social' costs and benefits of its investments. For example, if high wages make it unprofitable to employ a lot of labour, yet unemployment exists, then government could use a lower, shadow wage rate in calculating the social return on an investment. Once shadow prices have been established by government planners, the calculation of the rate of return proceeds in the same way. Of course if the government business then makes a loss, because it must operate in a world of real prices, then the loss must be made up from other revenue sources. There is not space here to go into the whole area of social cost benefit analysis, but the student should be aware of the possibility.

10 Investment and interest rates

Another investment theory, which deserves only limited attention, is that investment depends on 'the' rate of interest.[28] The reasoning is roughly that because there is an expected rate of return on an investment, which logically investors should calculate, then if that expected rate of return is greater than the cost of borrowed money (or than the rate obtainable on the best alternative use for the funds) the investment should be undertaken. In the example of investment in a lorry, if the rate of interest were less than 10% the investment would be profitable.

This theory focuses attention on the financial process by which savings reach investors and are spent. This process is indeed important —it will be given a great deal of attention in the chapter on money. But the *cost* of money to investors is no more important than any other cost, such as the cost of labour or of capital equipment. Indeed there are a number of reasons why the cost of money may be considerably *less* important than other costs.

The rate of interest has been treated so extensively partly because of the logical neatness of comparing rates of return with rates of interest; and partly because of the attractions of a macroeconomic model in which the rate of interest provides an equilibrating mechanism between savings and investment. As explained in chapter 3, it is rather misleading to concentrate on savings and investment rather than on aggregate demand and supply; and savings are *not* in any case determined by the rate of interest. Because investment theory in basic textbooks still gives great attention to this idea, some space must be given to the reasons why it has little relevance in developed economies and even less relevance in underdeveloped ones.

Interest rates have the smaller influence on costs (and so on profitability) the shorter is the life of the investment. This is easily shown by arithmetical examples; it is necessarily true that present value is affected more by the interest rate the greater the number of years involved, since present value is derived by dividing by $(1 + r)^n$, where n is the number of years in the future. Clearly the larger is n, the greater is the influence of $(1 + r)^n$ on present value. Another way of expressing the same idea is to note that the shorter the life of an investment the greater is the depreciation charge as a proportion of costs and, therefore, the smaller are other costs as a proportion of costs, including borrowing costs.

There are a number of reasons why investors assume a short life for investments, shorter perhaps than is indicated by the physical life of machinery and buildings. Technical change and changing consumer tastes shorten the life of investments; political uncertainties, especially strong in underdeveloped countries, reduce investors' time horizons; foreign investors discount especially heavily for political risk. The foreign investor is also more likely to be using foreign funds, in which case any influence of an interest rate on the investment decision is of a foreign interest rate.

Another way of expressing the importance of uncertainty is to note that investors expect a very high rate of return in order to allow for risk. Thus if investors expect a 30% return on investment and the interest rate is, say, 8% then even quite large variations in the interest rate will be very unlikely to affect the investment decision.

Investment takes place not only out of borrowed funds but out of retained profits, the investor's own savings and the savings of close relatives and friends. Although there is a theoretical opportunity cost to using one's own funds, it may be ignored since it is not a cost that has to be met by making a cash payment. Furthermore, the interest on funds lent is usually less than that on funds borrowed and so has less influence. Some investors are unwilling or unable to borrow, so that borrowing costs are irrelevant to them.

A great deal of investment in Africa is undertaken by people on their own account, using their own labour and therefore independent (or nearly independent) of the financial system. Such investments include the building of huts, the building up of herds of cattle, self-help urban housing, the clearing of new land, and so on. In such investments the rate of interest is so remote that it is clearly absurd to consider it.

The monopoly or tariff-protected position of many investors in Africa would enable them to pass on any increase in interest costs, in the form of higher prices; or to compensate by paying higher transfer prices, licence fees, etc., to foreign associate companies.

As has already been argued, very long-term investments are more influenced by interest rates than are short-term investments. Easily the most important example is housing. Housing investment is also peculiar in that the returns from housing are often very much more certain than the returns from other forms of investment. The reasons are that in most countries there is a gross shortage of housing, especially in towns; the shortage is usually so great in relation to the rate of building of new houses that excess demand is certain to exist for the foreseeable future; housing is such a basic need that demand for it is certain to continue. As a result the 'risk premium' in housing is very low, so that the expected rate of return does not need to be as much greater than the cost of borrowing (assuming the funds to be borrowed) as in other more risky investments. For these reasons it is argued that of all types of investment housing must surely be most influenced by interest rates. But precisely because housing is necessary, and because there is never enough of it, demand is very inelastic (that is, unaffected by price changes) so that higher costs can very easily be passed on in higher prices. So housing investment is not much more likely to be affected by interest rates than any other sort of investment. In any case, in many parts of Africa, most modern sector housing is provided by employers or by public authorities, so that interest rates are of minor (if any) importance.

The above arguments are just arguments. It remains to be seen whether there is, in practice, a statistical connection between rates of interest and rates of investment in Africa. In order to do this, it is first necessary to establish which interest rates are relevant, and which categories of investment are thought to be influenced by those rates. For example, government investment in infrastructure such as roads or schools is financed partly out of taxation, partly out of foreign borrowing and partly out of borrowing by the government from local sources at local interest rates. But even the quite small influence of local interest rates on the cost of finance may have no influence at all on investment decisions: governments do not always calculate a theoretical rate of return on their own investments for comparison with the cost of borrowing. In the parastatal sector, some finance comes from the government itself, some from abroad and some from domestic sources such as commercial banks; the interest rate charged by governments on their lending to the parastatal sector does not always move in line with other interest rates. Most African governments also have specialised lending institutions for providing credit to small-scale farmers and businessmen, and development banks for lending long-term to a wide variety of borrowers; the rates of interest charged by these institutions do not always change when other rates change, so that commercial bank lending rates do not always represent the cost of credit to the private sector. Meanwhile, commercial banks in Africa have a bias, for which they have often been criticised, towards providing only short-term credit for such things as imports and the holding of stocks of raw materials awaiting processing; if commercial bankers provide little credit for longer-term investments then the cost of commercial bank credit is not very relevant to longer-term investment decisions.

A final and important complication concerns the impact of inflation on the cost of borrowing. The amount of money borrowed by an investor is fixed in money terms. The real cost of borrowing is reduced, therefore, by inflation because the real value of $100 paid back in 1980 is a lot less than the real value of $100 borrowed 10 years earlier in 1970. Borrowers are of course aware of this; but for any particular borrower it is necessary that the price of what he or she produces goes up with the price of everything else in order for the real cost of borrowing to be less than the *nominal* rate of interest. Thus a borrower faced with having to pay, say interest of 15% a year on a loan, at a time when prices are rising at 12% a year, could argue that the real rate of interest is only 3%: interest will be $15 a year on every $100 borrowed, but the real cost of paying back $100 in a year's time will be reduced by 12% because of inflation. But if the price of what the borrower produces, whether it is maize or taxi rides or shoe repairs, does not go up as fast as 12% a year, the borrower might have to pay a high rate of interest out of profits which have not kept pace with inflation. In other words, a high nominal interest rate is a certain cost to the borrower, inflation is uncertain in its effects on the borrower's profits. So it is not at all clear what expected rate of inflation should be subtracted from nominal interest rates to arrive at a 'real' interest rate which would be relevant to investment decisions. Certainly, there are no published statistics on investors' expectations concerning future rates of inflation and how they would be likely to affect the investors' own business operations.

As it happens, *nominal* interest rates have tended to be constant over long periods of time in a majority of anglophone African countries, and to move by relatively small amounts when they do move. Only in the late 1970s and early 1980s was there some evidence of larger changes in nominal rates. For example the official discount rate in Nigeria never moved outside the range from 3.5% to 5% during the period from 1962 to 1978; In Zambia the same rate was constant at 5% from 1967 to 1975 and stayed within the range 4.5% to 6.5% from 1966 to 1980; in Mauritius the rate stayed between 6% and 7.5% from 1967–77 and was constant at 6% for seven years during that period; and in Malawi the rate stayed between 5.5% and 7% from 1968–78, and was constant at 6% for six years during that time.[29] Investment in all these countries varied by large amounts during these periods of very stable rates, so that nominal interest rates are of no use at all in explaining changes in the amount of investment spending.

Rates of inflation have varied, of course, so that price expectations and therefore the real interest rates applicable to investment decisions must also have varied.

An attempt is made in Figure 7.1 to compare *real* interest rates with the real level of investment spending in Ghana. If there was really a negative correlation between the two variables, then all the points in figure 7.1 would be grouped around a line sloping downwards from left to right, so that high real interest rates would be associated with low levels of investment spending, and vice versa. It is fairly clear from the figure that no such relationship existed over the sixteen years. To be sure, certain years (for example 1961 to 1964) appear to fit with such a relationship; but other years (for example 1968 to 1972) seem to fit the exactly opposite sort of relationship; and yet others (1974 to 1976) seem to show no relationship at all between real interest rates and real levels of investment. It is also important to note, as already explained, that the 'real interest rate' used in the figure is only a proxy for what investors *expected* the real cost of borrowed money to be; any number of other factors *could* have influenced expectations.

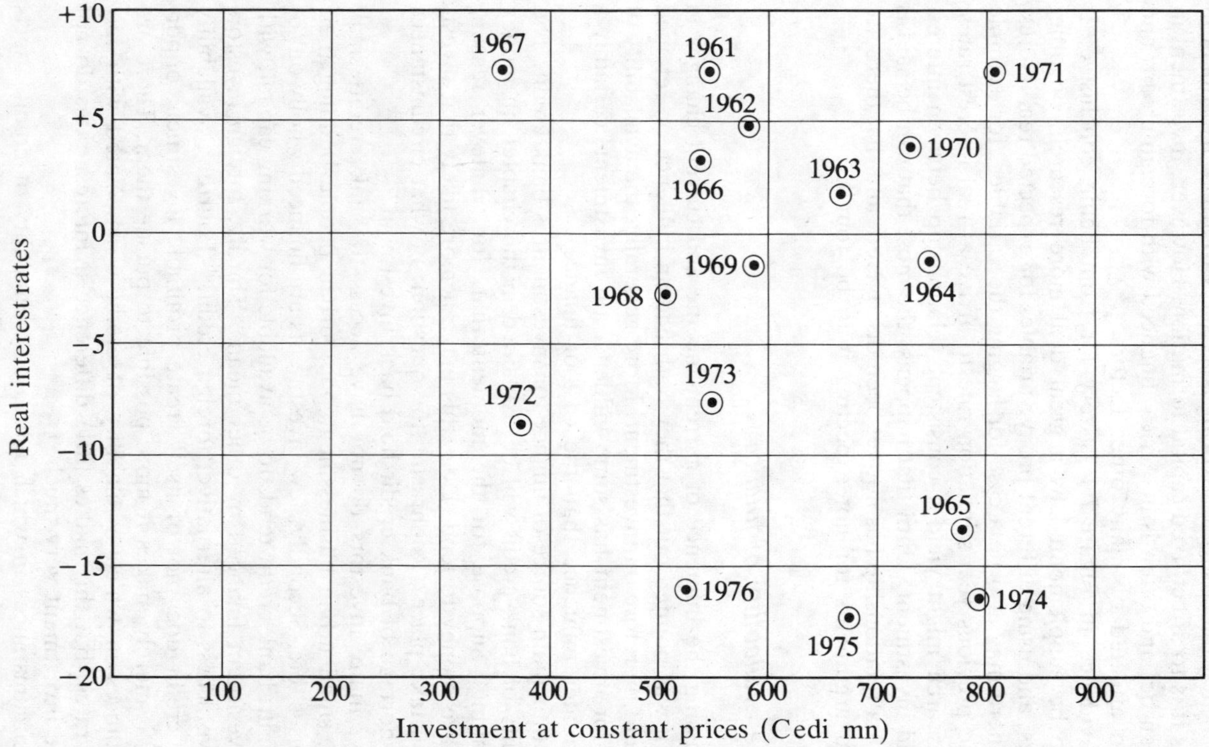

Figure 7.1 Real interest rates and investment in constant prices in Ghana, 1961–76
Sources: Gross Fixed Capital Formation plus change in stocks from *International Financial Statistics*. Interest rates (official discount rate plus four percentage points) from same source: GDP deflator (to represent inflation) from UN *Year book of National Income Statistics*.

It should also be noted that changes in stocks have been *included* in investment. In practice, stocks usually are financed out of borrowed money, so that the cost of borrowing is as likely to affect investment in stocks as it is to affect fixed capital formation. However, investment in stocks can be, and often is in Africa, financed with foreign credit, and it is also affected by many other factors.

The evidence in Figure 7.1 is very far from being conclusive. It needs to be supplemented by a great deal more research, on other countries, and using different proxy variables for expected real interest rates. There may also be a case for lagging the variables, for example using the previous year's inflation rate to arrive at real interest rates. Such research might yield a consistent relationship between interest rates and investment. Until that happens, the most that can be said is that such a relationship has not yet been discovered, and that there are powerful arguments for not expecting it to be found.

11 *The availability of finance*

In discussing the influence of current income and current changes in income it was pointed out that they both had an influence on retained profits and therefore on investment. More generally, the availability of finance for investment has some influence on investment, certainly a much greater influence than the cost of finance.

The other main source of finance for investment is bank credit. The availability of bank credit will be explained in the chapter on money and banking. Suppose for the moment that, for whatever reason, banks have money to lend. Does this make it more likely that investment will take place? Rephrasing the question: in what circumstances does a shortage of bank credit hold back investment?

Firstly, many investors do not have access to bank credit–small farmers, small urban businessmen, poor urban people building their own houses, etc. Secondly, few investments are financed wholly out of bank credit; bank credit tends to be available for working capital, with fixed investment financed by other means. Thirdly, foreign investors may have access to alternative, foreign credit.[30] Fourthly, availability of bank credit does not of itself create profitable investment opportunities, it merely makes it more possible to pursue them. There are circumstances in which availability of credit is associated with low interest rates, but this makes little difference if interest rates do not influence investment very much.

The circumstances in which increased availability of credit affects investment are these: an unsatisfied demand for credit, from people to whom the banks will lend, for the sort of investment normally financed by banks such as building up stocks and working capital, or improvements with a quick pay-off period. For example, the building up of stocks in large-scale retail and wholesale trading, or improvements to large-scale commercial farms which lead to rapid increase in output, are the sort of investments most likely to be held up by lack of credit.

Putting it another way, bank lending in Africa developed in order to finance international trade. The banks were (and still are in some African countries) foreign-owned and lent to the foreign-owned trading concerns that handled the import-export trade. To a very considerable extent bank credit is still used in Africa to finance imports (and exports in some countries). Changes in the aggregate of bank lending have more impact on imports than on anything else. Secondly, bank lending makes possible the greater use of existing investments, by providing working capital for stocks and work-in-progress. To the extent that imports and working capital are used to increase stocks then bank credit is used for investment. Thirdly, only to a relatively minor extent is bank credit used for fixed capital formation.

The unwillingness of commercial banks in Africa to lend for longer-term investment[31] has led to various attempts to provide long-term finance through government-sponsored institutions. All African countries now have one or more government-sponsored financial institutions whose main function is to provide long-term finance. Often a secondary objective is to lend to those perceived as being wrongly excluded from access to credit from the commercial banks, for example small-scale as opposed to large-scale, farmers and businesses, or citizens as opposed to foreigners and foreign-controlled businesses. Some publicly-owned development banks also participate in the ownership of businesses previously 100% owned by foreigners, and act as partners with foreigners in new businesses. The government itself is also a major source of long-term finance, lending on a large scale in many African countries, mostly to its own parastatal companies, and for housing finance. Other sources of long-term credit include building societies (mainly for private housing), provident funds and insurance companies.

All of those sources of finance are likely to be more plentiful at times of high and rising national income. Investment will probably increase at such times therefore, not only because investment demand is likely to be high, as already argued, but also because finance is likely to be more freely available. The final impact of the availability of finance on the level of investment will depend on whether an increase in investment demand is larger or smaller than any increase in available credit.

Some governments and some parastatal institutions (usually with a government guarantee) are able to borrow abroad, mainly from commercial banks operating in the euro-currency markets, but also from other sources. The ability to borrow abroad depends on how creditworthy the country appears at the time to foreign lenders. Clearly, though, foreign finance is a way of having more investment than would otherwise be possible, especially when investment would otherwise be constrained by a shortage of foreign exchange.

Generally speaking, the availability of finance is a necessary but not a sufficient condition for increases in investment spending. Lack of finance, whether local or foreign, can prevent investment. Availability of finance makes increased investment spending possible; but other factors may prevent it, such as lack of profitable investment opportunities, lack of matching inputs, or, in the case where only local finance is available, lack of foreign exchange. As with government spending, therefore, an increase in export prices or some other increase in foreign exchange availability, may make possible an increase in investment.

12 Conclusion

This long chapter has reached very few conclusions. Africa's investors vary so much in their motives, their access to information about investment opportunities, their access to technical know-how and their access to different types of finance that a general theory of investment behaviour is not likely to be found. The only common thread running through the discussion has been that the current level of income affects both investment opportunities and investment funds for most types of investor. Even then one must make major exceptions. Most agricultural investment depends heavily on government-controlled prices; new foreign investment depends heavily on government action of several sorts; investment in export production depends on expectations about externally-determined export prices.

In short, it would be odd if more than a tenuous relationship between income, or changes in income, and investment could be traced. Unfortunately, official investment statistics are available for sectors of the economy rather than for the categories of investor used in this chapter, so that much research remains to be done on their usefulness.

Appendix: Capital stock adjustment and accelerator principles

The factor most likely to increase the return on investment is high and rising aggregate demand. This enables lorries to earn money for more hours per day and factories to run nearer capacity, so that returns on investment increase. Unfortunately there is no obvious way of guessing what businessmen's expectations are. It has been suggested that the current level of income is a good guide. If income is high, profits will be high, giving both an incentive to invest and some of the means of investing, since retained profits are an important source of investment funds. If income is low the reverse will be true. This hypothesis assumes, however, that businessmen use the present level of income as a guide to future levels of income (and thus demand for their products). It also assumes that businessmen do not have any spare capacity–a situation which is quite likely at high levels of income, but not necessarily true.

A more elaborate hypothesis, taking into account the possible existence of spare capacity, is that investment varies positively with income in the previous period (there being a time-lag as investors react to income levels) and negatively with the existing capital stock. This is called the 'capital stock adjustment principle' and can be expressed thus:

$$I_1 = aY_{(t-1)} - bK_t$$

where *I* is investment, *Y* is income, *K* is the capital stock, *a* and *b* are positive constants, and the subscripts *t*, $t-1$ refer to time periods.[32]

A special case of the capital stock adjustment principle is where $b = 1$. Then

$$I_t = aY_{(t-1)} - K_t$$

and

$$I_{(t-1)} = aY_{(t-2)} - K_{(t-1)}$$

Subtracting the second equation from the first gives

$$I_t - I_{(t-1)} = a(Y_{(t-1)} - Y_{(t-2)}) - (K_t - K_t - 1)$$

But

$$K_t - K_{(t-1)} = I_{(t-1)},$$

since the change in the stock of capital is investment. So

$$I_t = a(Y_{(t-1)} - Y_{(t-2)})$$

Investment, according to this hypothesis, is determined by the rate of change of income in the previous period. This theory is known as the 'accelerator principle' since a rising income would generate rising investment which, through the multiplier, would generate yet higher income.

Because businessmen's expectations are determined by other things besides current income and the existing capital stock, neither theory is particularly useful in explaining investment. In Africa, where an increasing amount of manufacturing and other commercial investment is being undertaken as a result either of government initiative or in sectors where foreign investors are predominant, these theories could at best only explain part of investment. Nevertheless, since businessmen are not better at foreseeing the future than economic theorists are, it is quite useful to remember that high and rising income is quite likely to generate a high and rising desire to invest.[33]

NOTES

1 A minor complication is that not all 'Gross Fixed Capital Formation' is actually 'fixed' in the sense of being immovable. Investment in lorries or dumper trucks or earth-moving machinery also counts as Gross Fixed Capital Formation. Such investment is 'fixed' in the sense of being in the form of specific physical assets, in contrast to investment in, for example foreign bank deposits which can easily be switched to alternative assets.

2 The higher the level of technical development, the less dependent are farmers on variations in the weather, or indeed on crop disease and other hazards, so that poor farmers in developing countries are more exposed to risk than the relatively rich and advanced farmers of developed countries.

3 Zambian national accounts and input-output tables.

4 See Appendix for investment and changes in income: see Section 10 for investment and the rate of interest.

5 Foreign investors may also be more interested in a secure supply of the output of an investment than in its profitability—see below, section 6.

6 'New' here means an investor new to the country, i.e. making a first investment in an African country. Mining is discussed in section 6.

7 An interesting exception concerned the setting up of a brewery in Botswana by a large German brewing company. This action should have captured the Botswana beer market, but that market was so small that it amounted to only 0.35% of the company's sales. It seems probable that the real objective was to establish a protected base for gaining a share of the much larger South African market. See my chapter 'Foreign Investment in Manufacturing: the case of Botswana's brewery' in Charles Harvey (ed.) *Papers on the Economy of Botswana* (London, Heinemann, 1981, pp. 209–19).

8 Y. Aharoni, *The Foreign Investment Decision Process*, Harvard University Press, 1966, referring to a particular foreign investment decision by an American firm.

9 Or even the total exclusion of competing imports, in the extreme case.

10 Other ways of getting money out are through licensing agreements, management agreements, interest on loans from the parent company, all of which count as 'costs' and so reduce profits in Africa and increase profits in the country of origin. Transfer pricing can also occur through the under-pricing of exports to an associated company. For some gross examples of both, see UNCTAD, *Major Issues arising from the Transfer of Technology: a case study of Ethiopia*, UN, 1974, pp. 57–9. On control of transfer pricing see the papers in Part 3 of Robin Murray (editor) *Multinationals beyond the Market: intrafirm trade and the control of transfer pricing* (Brighton, Harvester Press, 1981, pp. 147–324).

11 This is further discussed in chapter 11, section 8.

12 The quotation is from ZIMCO, Chairman's Statement, Lusaka, 1970. It is typical of a particular type of official policy statement, which pretends that mutually exclusive objectives can be reconciled simply by stating them one after the other.

13 See A. Young, *Industrial Diversification in Zambia*, London, Praeger, 1973, pp. 198–204, for a more extended discussion of this point in the Zambian context.

14 See Peter Kilby, *Industrialisation in an Open Economy: Nigeria 1945–66*, Cambridge University Press, 1969, Chapter 3, especially Table 16, p. 54.

15 See C.V. Vaitsos *Intercountry Income Distribution and Transnational Enterprises* (Oxford University Press, 1974, pp. 54–9). Vaitsos found, in four Latin American countries, that 81% of contracts for the supply of foreign technology to domestic firms prohibited all exports and 86% had some restrictive clause on exports.

16 For example, by 1971 Zambia was already producing more than 70 of the 75 or so products which had been imported from Rhodesia to a value of K200,000 or more in 1964.

17 Kilby, *op.cit.*, p. 75. As Kilby's book was about industrialisation he omitted investment in raw materials–this is discussed separately in section 6 below.

18 For a successful example see Kilby, *op.cit.*, pp. 76–7; for an unsuccessful example see C. Cooper and R. Kaplinsky, *Secondhand Equipment in a Developing Country: jute processing in Kenya*, ILO, 1973, which also has a discussion of the general principles underlying the use of second-hand equipment in developing countries.

19 UNCTAD, *op.cit.*, pp. 48–9.

20 One should also note here that a profitable investment opportunity is not sufficient to induce investment by domestic investors, even though they may regard the situation as less risky and are not usually so concerned to expatriate their profits. Domestic investors suffer rather from not having the know-how, especially if they must compete with imports.

21 For example the tax system inhibited investment before 1970 and encouraged it afterwards; and the expectation of government takeover inhibited investment before 1970 whereas the agreement of terms for government participation encouraged investment afterwards. See Mark Bostock and Charles Harvey (eds), *Economic Independence and Zambian Copper* (London, Praeger, 1972, chapter 7).

22 Bostock and Harvey (eds), *op.cit.*, pp. 56–61 (chapter by A. Drysdall) and pp. 42–6 (chapter by P. Slinn).

23 See, for example, the section called 'Bargaining powers' in J. Potter's essay 'The 51% nationalisation of the Zambian copper mines', in M. Faber and J. Potter, *Towards Economic Independence*, Cambridge University Press, 1971, pp. 103–8.

24 Some never even start producing. One company whose plant was established in Ethiopia in 1968 was still not operating four years later (UNCTAD, *op.cit.* p. 49). See also Andrzej Krassowski *Development and the debt trap: economic planning and external borrowing in Ghana* (London, Croom Helm, 1974, pp. 72–89): for example 'Because of major design faults the silos were useless for storing cocoa. . .(they) still stand, fully paid and useless' (pp. 86–87).

25 See R.E. Baldwin, *Economic Development and Export Growth*, University of California Press 1966, pp. 146–59.

26 Ray Weedon and Odd Ystgaard 'Railways, immigrants, mining and cattle: problems of measurement in Botswana's national income accounts' in Charles Harvey (ed.) *Papers on the Economy of Botswana* (London, Heinemann, 1981, pp. 242–6 and pp. 250–51).

27 This statement ignores the fact that the interest paid on borrowing is always higher than can be obtained on putting savings on deposit in a financial institution. An investor with cash in hand should therefore use a lower rate of interest in calculating present value than an investor who has to borrow.

28 'The' rate of interest does not exist, as there are many rates of interest. It is arguable though that any particular investor can reasonably use one rate, or at most the weighted average of his borrowing rates and the rate he could otherwise get on his own funds.

29 Figures from *International Financial Statistics* and central banks. Official discount rates are not the same as the cost of commercial bank or other credit, but in the

countries mentioned commercial bank lending rates move closely with official discount rates. Not all borrowers from commercial banks pay the same interest rate, but the premium over 'prime lending rate' (the rate paid by the banks' most creditworthy customers) tends to be the same for the same customer over time. There are no statistics at all on any variations in the actual rates paid by commercial bank customers. Other banks, such as agricultural development banks, tend to vary their lending rates even less than the commercial banks. Insofar as investors finance their spending from their own profits and savings, the relevant interest rates are those obtainable on bank deposits, since that is the main alternative use for investors' money in Africa (assuming that savings are not allowed to be deposited in other countries and that this rule is enforceable); movements in bank deposit rates have generally been the same as movements in official discount rates, with only rare exceptions. For one example of an attempt to influence investment by altering the structure of interest rates see my article 'Botswana's monetary independence–real or imagined?', *IDS Bulletin*, Vol. 11, September 1980.

30 But foreign investors frequently prefer to use local borrowing rather than committing their own money; the availability of local credit may therefore encourage some types of foreign investment.

31 The reasons for their unwillingness are discussed in the chapters on money and banking.

32 See R.C.O. Matthews, *The Trade Cycle*, Cambridge University Press, 1959, chapter 3.

33 The accelerator theory has received far too much attention from economic theorists because it leads to an attractively neat theory of investment (or business) cycles; see Matthews, *op.cit.*, especially chapter 2.

8 *Money*

1 *Definition*

The definition of money is very simple: it is anything that people will accept as money. In the modern world there are only two sorts of money: bank notes and coin on the one hand, bank deposits on the other. These modern forms of money have great advantages over some of the items that have been used for money in the past—for example cowrie shells, copper rings, cows, cigarettes—because modern forms of money are more easily divisible, more easily stored and more precisely comparable. These qualities are needed for money's use as a medium of exchange, a store of value and a unit of account or measurement.

No type of money is perfect. Although national bank notes and coin are acceptable everywhere in Africa, they are quite expensive for the banks to shift around the country and notes can be burnt or eaten by ants. Notes and coin are also inconvenient for very large payments. Bank deposits are safer but much less convenient. Not everyone will accept a cheque in payment, banks are often not open when cash (in the form of notes and coin) is needed and in some parts of Africa there are very few banks. As a result, those who have bank accounts try and keep a convenient amount of notes and coin in their pockets with the remainder of their money safely in a bank account.

If bank cheques are not always acceptable, for example by shops, then it might seem that bank deposits do not fit the definition of money—that it be widely acceptable as money. The point is that the person to whom a cheque is offered in payment is not always sure that the payer has enough money on his bank account to 'honour' (or pay) the cheque. If the cheque has a bank guarantee on it or if the payee (the person receiving the cheque) *knows* that there is enough money to pay the cheque then there is no reason why he should not accept it. The point is, therefore, that even though cheques are not money, bank deposits are. In general, large payments, payments involving companies and governments, tend to be by cheque; small payments, especially those between individuals, tend to be by notes and coins.

One minor problem remains: there are two sorts of bank deposit. *Demand* deposits can be withdrawn 'on demand' and can be used for payments by cheque. Holdings of demand deposits are often called 'current accounts'. Normally no interest is paid on current accounts. It is also possible to deposit money in banks on *time* or *savings* accounts, which earn interest. These deposits cannot be used for making payments, nor can they be converted into cash immediately–normally withdrawals of cash can only be made of a limited sum or after a specified period of time. Strictly speaking, therefore, time and savings deposits are not money.

Nevertheless, it is sometimes useful to count time and savings deposits as money because *in practice* it is so easy to transfer them to a demand deposit account. Various other types of 'near money', that is forms of investment that can quickly and easily be converted into money, can be included in calculations of the total money supply if it seems helpful to do so. For most of this chapter the definition used will be that the money supply equals currency outside the banks plus demand deposits at banks.[1]

2 *The creation of money*

The absolutely vital point about bank deposits as money is that banks can create more of them. Bank deposits are thus quite different from other types of money like cows, copper rings and cowrie shells. Bank deposits are just figures on a sheet of paper, with no intrinsic value, and more of them can be created simply by the process of granting credit. Few people understand how this can happen, so it is necessary to explain in considerable detail.

Suppose a man (the buyer) wishes to buy a second-hand car, costing K2000 for which he has no money.[2] Suppose also that he is lucky enough to be able to get credit from his bank–Bank B. He then writes a cheque for K2000 even though he has no money on his bank account. He gives the cheque to the car dealer (the seller), who accepts it in payment for the car because he knows that the buyer's bank will honour it. The car dealer pays the cheque into *his* account at Bank S, where his account rises by the amount of the cheque.

Bank S then sends the cheque to Bank B for payment, since Bank B owes Bank S the amount of the cheque. Payment is made between banks by means of their accounts at the *central* bank. Commercial banks all have accounts at the central bank, and settle debts between themselves by authorising transfers from one account to another. Bank B then debits the car buyer's account, creating an overdraft,[3] since he has nothing on his account.

If the buyer and the seller both happen to have accounts at the same bank, then the process is much simpler: the bank debits the car buyer's account, creating an overdraft (or negative balance) and credits the car dealer's account. That is all.

From the point of view of the money supply, the result is the same. Bank deposits have gone up by the amount of the cheque, so the money supply has increased by that amount. Bank advances to the public have also increased: and if the two people banked at different banks, there has been a transfer from one commercial bank account at the central bank to another. The creation of new money is at the same time the creation of new spending power. A new car has been bought out of borrowing, not out of income; and the new money created, namely the addition to the car dealer's bank account, can in turn be spent.

In practice a bank does not go round to other banks each time a cheque drawn on another bank is paid in to the credit of one of its customers. What happens is that each bank collects together all the cheques paid into the accounts of its customers, and sorts out those drawn on other banks; at the end of the day it takes them to some agreed place used as a 'clearing house' and exchanges them with the other banks for cheques paid in by *their* customers, drawn on itself. Any differences in the totals (which are usually small in relation to the total sums on the cheques) are settled by an adjustment of the banks' accounts at the central bank.[4] It may help in understanding this process to present the changes in bank balance sheets which result from these transactions. Many students find it difficult to interpret banks' balance sheets at first, but it really is very important to try and do so.

Banks have 'liabilities', by which is meant the money that they *owe*, mainly to their depositors. People do not normally speak in terms of *lending* money to a bank, but that is exactly what they do when they deposit money in a bank. Banks also have 'assets', that is they lend or invest the money deposited with them, by lending to their customers—mainly businesses but also individuals—by lending to the government in the form of investments in Treasury Bills and government stock (for definitions see the appendices to this chapter) and by holding a relatively small amount of cash and demand deposits at the central bank. The *changes* in bank balance sheets that result from one person borrowing money and using it to buy a car are shown below.

What these numbers demonstrate is that if a bank grants an overdraft to a customer then the money supply goes up. The commercial banking system as a whole can create money simply by giving credit, which results in a rise in overdrafts (bank lending to the public) and a rise in deposits. The people who are granted credit use it by writing cheques and handing them over to people from whom they are buying

Bank B

Liabilities	*K*	*Assets*	*K*
Deposits of customers	no change	Loans to customers	+ 2000[a]
Other liabilities	no change	Current a/c at central bank	– 2000[b]
		Other assets	no change
Total liabilities	no change	Total assets	no change

Notes: a loan to car buyer b payment to Bank S.

Bank S

Liabilities	*K*	*Assets*	*K*
Deposits of customers	+ 2000[a]	Loans to customers	no change
Other liabilities	no change	Current a/c at central bank	+ 2000[b]
		Other assets	no change
Total liabilties	+ 2000	Total assets	+ 2000

Notes: a cheque paid in by car dealer b payment by Bank B.

Central Bank

Liabilities	*K*	*Assets*	*K*
Account of Bank B	– 2000		
Account of Bank S	+ 2000	no change	
Total liabilities	no change		

goods; these sellers then deposit the cheques in *their* bank accounts, thus causing a rise in deposits. This new money can of course be spent.

Bank money is simply a series of entries in bank ledgers showing how much money has been deposited at the banks by each of their customers. It is unique in that it can be created by the banks themselves. The banking sector is therefore not just another sector of the economy, like the manufacturing sector or the transport sector. It has this unique property, that bank deposits are accepted as money. Because banks can create new bank deposits simply by granting credit, they can create money. They cannot, however, create new money in unlimited amounts. The various factors which limit the creation of new money by banks are explained below.

3 *Limits on the creation of new bank deposits*

Although, as already described, commercial banks can create money by lending to their customers, they are constrained by the fact that customers *may* want to have some of their funds in the form of currency,[5] rather than keeping it all on deposit in banks. For example, the car dealer, who pays into his bank a cheque received from selling a new car, may draw out some of this new money in notes and coin in order to pay his employees or to spend on his own needs. Some of the new money will be spent in paying for new cars ordered from the manufacturer, or in paying such things as his electricity bill. Such payments, being made by cheque, merely result in transfers from one bank deposit to another, so that the money remains as bank deposits.

In general, as the level of bank deposits rises, so does the amount of money held by the public in the form of notes and coin. Even when the demand for notes and coin is not rising, banks must keep some notes and coin available for their customers. But banks know, from long experience, that they do *not* need to keep 100% of demand deposits available in notes and coin, since it is very unlikely that all their customers will want to draw out all their money at once. So banks try and keep a *proportion* of demand deposits, which they are liable to repay to their customers on demand, in the form of 'cash' (notes and coin) and in the form of their accounts at the central bank. Just as people can convert their bank deposits on current account into notes and coin, so commercial banks can draw on *their* bank accounts at the central bank for more notes and coin. If the *central* bank needs more notes, to supply the demands of its commercial bank customers, it simply orders more from the printers (and more coins from the coin manufacturers or Mint).[6]

Over the years, banks discovered how much cash they needed to keep handy in order to meet withdrawals by customers. In England, where banking first developed in its modern form, it became customary to regard 8% as a safe 'cash ratio'. The cash ratio is the proportion of demand deposits held by banks in the form of notes and coin and money deposited at the central bank.

Some African countries copied this figure when their own central banks were established: for example, when the Bank of Zambia was created in 1965 it was made compulsory for commercial banks to hold 8% of demand deposits in the form of bank deposits at the Bank of Zambia.[7] This requirement, that a minimum percentage of deposits in commercial banks be held in cash form, is also intended to protect the public against the possibility of not being able to withdraw their money. In a modern banking system, cash ratios are probably no longer necessary for this purpose, either in practice, or as a symbol of bank prudence. Cash ratios have simply become a useful way of controlling the banking system. Clearly banks need *some* cash, but usually not as much as the formal requirement; the public is protected partly by cash requirements, but more by the willingness of central banks to lend money to commercial banks if they run short of cash. Provided a bank is basically sound in that its lending has not been foolish and it has enough shareholders' capital and reserves to meet any conceivable level of bad debts, then public confidence is maintained, and the central bank does not ever have to become 'lender of last resort'— precisely because it is known that it would do so if necessary.

Now the process of money creation by banks, as described in the previous section, did *not* result in the creation of any new 'bankers' cash', that is, commercial bank deposits at the central bank. There was a *transfer* from the account of Bank B (the car-buyer's bank) to the account of Bank S (the car-seller's bank), but no change in the total of bankers' cash.[8] If both the car-buyer and the car-dealer banked at the same bank, there was similarly *no* increase in commercial bank deposits at the central bank. On the contrary the granting of credit and the creation of additional bank deposits is likely to lead to an increase in the public's holdings of notes and coin. So as advances increase the banks are likely to have to draw down their balances at the central bank in order to supply their customers with more notes and coin. In addition, as advances increase, some of the new expenditure will be spent on imports. If this results in a *net* increase in demand for foreign exchange to make foreign payments, that is if there is no offsetting increase in receipts of foreign exchange, then banks will have to run down their accounts at the central bank in order to buy foreign exchange from the central bank, so that their customers can pay for the additional imports.[9]

As a result, banks will only be able to grant more credit and create more money when they have more cash than is needed to meet the required cash ratio. In practice banks normally need not only enough spare cash to make new loans and meet any loss of cash to the public or to imports that may result, but also enough spare cash to give them a bit in hand in case of unexpected changes in their cash position.

It is not as uncommon as one might expect for banks in Africa to have a considerable amount of spare cash. Such a situation arises most frequently as a result of high prices for a country's exports, or a period of slow or zero growth in the domestic economy during which there is little growth in demand for bank credit, or both.

In such conditions, banks can create new credit and new money without worrying about their cash ratios. It is nevertheless important to ask why commercial banks would choose to have spare cash for quite long periods.[10] In general, banks prefer to invest money and earn interest on it, rather than leave it on an account at the central bank where it earns nothing. In fact the most profitable way of using money deposited with the banks is for them to lend it to customers.

Commercial banks do not, however, lend money if they do not expect to be repaid. So even when they have cash in excess of their reserve requirements they may not expand their lending. *Either* there may be a shortage of creditworthy customers, *or* their normal borrowers may be unwilling to borrow because of poor economic conditions. In short, banks will only expand their lending if people whom the banks regard as creditworthy are demanding credit and if the banks' reserve position makes additional lending possible. In general, an expanding economy creates a rising demand for credit as firms require more working capital to finance increased output; in a stagnant or declining economy firms do not want to borrow and banks do not want to lend. An expanding economy also creates profit opportunities, and increases the profits of existing activities. So an expanding economy not only increases the demand for credit but makes that demand more likely to be successful with the banks. In contrast, even very respectable businesses may not succeed in getting more credit at a time of falling demand and falling profits.

The existence of spare cash in commercial banks is not enough, therefore, to ensure an expansion of bank lending. On the other hand, a lack of spare cash really does *prevent* banks from increasing their lending, unless they can obtain additional cash from somewhere. If one bank has no spare cash and wishes to make additional loans, it may be able to obtain the necessary funds by bidding deposits away from other banks, or by borrowing from them directly. So the necessary condition for banks not being able to increase their lending is that the banks *as a group* have no spare cash. Another possibility is that banks could obtain funds from abroad; in particular, many banks in Africa are still partly or wholly owned subsidiaries of international banks, so there is a possibility that funds could be obtained from overseas head offices.

Basically, the international banks do not like lending, except for very short periods, to their branches and subsidiaries in particular countries. They did not like doing so even in the 1950s when the colonial system in Africa was still intact and there was thus little or no risk of nationalisation, expropriation or currency devaluation. All of these risks have now increased, so that it seems likely, and this likelihood is supported by the evidence, that international banks are not likely to lend to their overseas branches or affiliates for more than short periods.

It seems therefore as though the level of commercial bank deposits at the central bank, and the ratio that this must be to total deposits, are in fact of key importance in determining the banks' ability to expand the money supply. If the banks have easy access to cash overseas, which they can quickly add to their local cash balances, then they can expand credit and the money supply if there is a demand for credit from suitable borrowers. If, on the other hand, the commercial banks have no spare cash at overseas head offices, or are overdrawn, then the local cash position becomes the key factor in controlling monetary expansion.[11] The fact that bank head offices may be willing to lend to overseas affiliates for short periods may prevent the local cash ratio from having an immediate restraining effect; but the unwillingness of head offices to lend for long periods means that shortage of 'local' bankers' cash will eventually force the banks to reduce their lending.

Banks also hold 'liquid assets' consisting mainly of Treasury Bills, government stock and other marketable assets.[12] These assets are less profitable to commercial banks than lending to their customers, but can be sold for cash. Any commercial bank that is short of bankers' cash can therefore sell some liquid assets *provided that* it has some liquid assets to spare and can find a buyer. The point is that commercial banks have normally to maintain a certain ratio of liquid assets to deposits, a 'liquidity ratio' as well as a cash ratio.

In order to expand lending, therefore, commercial banks need to have not only spare bankers' cash, but spare liquid assets as well. As deposits rise, the required amount of liquid assets, normally expressed as a percentage of deposits, also rises. If the banks do not have any liquid assets to spare, some of their spare cash must be used to buy more.

In practice, most commercial banks in Africa try and keep more liquid assets than is required by liquidity ratios. If their actual liquidity ratios fall below the target level (of the officially required ratio plus a safety margin) they try to push them up again, even though there is no legal necessity to do so.

This spare margin of liquid assets protects the banks from having to make very abrupt changes in their lending policy. As will be explained in the next section, bank liquidity is subject to very sudden changes in Africa, mainly because of external economic forces. It would be very damaging to longer-term economic development if the commercial banks had to make very sudden changes in lending policy in response to sudden changes in the price of exports, for example.

In the 1960s and early 1970s, cash and liquidity ratios were very seldom changed in Africa. More recently, though, with the much more violent changes in the international environment and in particular the severe balance of payments problems of nearly all African economies, changes have become more frequent. Although there are other ways for governments, usually working through their central banks, to control bank lending (see section 9 below), the ultimate constraint is the availability of spare cash. Bankers need cash to maintain cash ratios, and to buy liquid assets,[13] so the next step is to establish what determines the level of bankers' cash, and how changes take place.

4 *Changes in bankers' cash*

In theory it is possible for the central bank to exercise complete control over 'bankers' cash' (commercial bank balances at the central bank) and thus over commercial banks' ability to expand the money supply. In practice, events outside the control of the central bank cause changes in bankers' cash, and the central bank is left with the urgent task of trying to ensure that the monetary consequences are not too damaging to the economy.

There are three *main* ways in which bankers' cash can alter: deficits or surpluses on the balance of international payments; deficits or surpluses on the government budget; purchases or sales of government debt by the central bank. Firstly, it is essential to understand how these three events affect bankers' cash; then it should be possible to understand how the monetary system affects the economy and how the central bank tries to exercise control.

(a) *Changes in the balance of payments*

Consider, for an African country, an increase in the price of exports or an increase in the volume of exports, or a fall in the volume of imports, or the purchase of a local firm by a foreign investor. All of these events can occur quite suddenly; all of them cause a sudden increase in the country's holdings of foreign exchange (over what they would otherwise have been). The mechanism is essentially the same in all the examples, so consider for simplicity the purchase of a local firm by a foreign investor, since that is a purely financial transaction without income multiplier effects.

The foreign investor has foreign exchange, for example US dollars. The owner of the local firm must have Naira. The buyer tells his bank in America to transfer dollars to the American branch of (say) Barclays Bank, for the credit of the owner of the local firm. The dollars are then sold to the central bank (since all foreign exchange owned by local people must be sold to the central bank). Barclays' account with the central bank is then credited with the equivalent local currency, and the seller's account at Barclays is credited with the same amount. As a result of these transactions, therefore, the money supply (in the form of bank deposits) has gone up, the foreign exchange reserves have gone up and, most importantly from the monetary point of view, bankers' balances at the central bank have also gone up.

Changes in the balance sheets of Barclays Bank in the African country, and of the central bank, are shown below, assuming the purchase price is 100 000 units of local currency, this time called Naira (the currency of Nigeria).

Barclays Bank (in the African country)

Liabilities	*Naira*	*Assets*	*Naira*
Deposits of customers	+ 100 000	Current a/c at the central bank	+ 100 000
Other liabilities	no change	Other assets	no change
Total liabilities	+ 100 000	Total assets	+ 100 000

Central bank (in the African country)

Liabilities	*Naira*	*Assets*	*Naira*
Account of Barclays Bank	+ 100 000	Foreign exchange reserves	+ 100 000
Other liabilities	no change	Other assets	no change
Total liabilities	+ 100 000	Total assets	+ 100 000

It is clear that Barclays Bank must now have more cash than it needs to meet the cash reserve requirements. The deposits of its customers have gone up by 100 000, and only a relatively small percentage of this will be required to be held as a cash reserve. Actual holdings of cash, meanwhile, have also gone up by 100 000, far more than is necessary to meet the cash requirement, and leaving the bank with spare cash. Thus the money supply has risen, and, even more important, the banking system is in a position to expand its lending.

Now if the money is used to buy imports, or otherwise transferred back into foreign exchange and out of the country, then a reverse process takes place. The African importer uses his local currency to buy foreign exchange. Barclays buys the dollars for him, debits his account and debits Barclays' account at the central bank to pay for the dollars. The foreign exchange reserves, the money supply and bankers' cash all go down. So clearly the monetary impact of foreign exchange transactions occurs only when there is a *net* change. A rise in exports offset by a rise in imports has no direct monetary impact, since bankers' cash is not affected.[14] Similarly a rise in imports financed by the receipt of a foreign loan (or aid, for example), or a rise in imports by a multinational company out of its own foreign sources of credit, have no direct impact on bankers' cash.

(b) *Changes in the government's budget deficit*
Consider a decision by the government of Zambia to spend an extra K1 mn, without any offsetting extra taxation. The ministry involved writes a cheque for K1 mn on its account at the Bank of Zambia. This cheque is given to a member of the public, say a building contractor who has built a school. He pays it into his account at a commercial bank. The bank pays it into *its* account at the Bank of Zambia. The ministry has no money, so the Bank of Zambia has to 'lend' the government K1 mn in order to be able to debit the cheque to the ministry's account. The government now 'owes' K1 mn to the Bank of Zambia. But the government owns 100% of the Bank of Zambia, so the 'debt' is just a paper transaction creating no real obligation. It is of no significance that the government owes money to itself. Bankers' cash has been created simply by writing figures in a ledger, as a result of the unfinanced budget spending.

Changes in balance sheets are shown below.

Commercial Bank

Liabilities	*K mn*	*Assets*	*K mn*
Deposits of customers	+ 1	Current a/c at the central bank	+ 1

Bank of Zambia

Liabilities	*K mn*	*Assets*	*K mn*
Commercial bank deposits	+ 1	Loan to the Government	+ 1

If the government spending is financed by taxation or by borrowing from the general public, the direct monetary effect does not occur. If, for example, the government spends K1 mn on nationalising a private sector firm and the owners use the money to buy government stocks or development bonds, there is no change in bankers' cash.

In a modern economy governments can always 'finance' their spending even if they do not increase taxation and even if nobody wants to lend them money, since central banks can simply create money. This process not only creates additional *demand* and the income multiplier effects that follow, but it also creates additional bankers' cash and the possibility of an expansion in the money supply as well. Modern governments do not, therefore, have to use the printing press in order to spend money they do not have: they simply 'borrow' from the central bank, an even simpler process than printing notes and the purest form of money creation. Notes and coin in circulation may increase later, as a result; see section 3.

(c) *Central bank purchases and sales of government debt*
As part of its financing, the government sells debt to the general public. Most of this government debt is sold to financial institutions. For example, the National Provident Funds and insurance companies buy government debt so that most wage-earners are indirectly lending money to the government. Other buyers of government debt include the commercial banks and building societies. Government debt is of two main forms: Local Registered Stock and Treasury Bills. In the colonial period, some African countries issued stock in London; since independence African governments have continued to borrow abroad, but not by issuing stock to be bought in foreign markets.

If the central bank *does* buy some government debt from a financial institution then new bankers' cash is created. The central bank pays with a cheque drawn on itself. The seller pays the cheque into his bank account at a commercial bank. The commercial bank pays the cheque into *its* account at the central bank. As a result, therefore, the money supply and bankers' cash have risen.

Exactly the same process occurs when a government loan matures. That is, when the due date for repayment arrives, the central bank pays out cash on behalf of the government in exactly the way described above, and with the same result. For this reason, the central bank normally hopes that it will be able to sell a new stock to replace the old maturing one so that no new bankers' cash is created. The process of selling new loans to replace old maturing ones is sometimes known as 'funding'.

Clearly, the reverse process takes place when the central bank *sells* government debt. Payment is made by cheque, which is given to the central bank. The cheque is paid into the government's account, thus reducing a deficit or adding to a surplus. The commercial bank on which the cheque is drawn has its account at the central bank debited, and in turn debits the customer's account. Bankers' cash and the money supply go down by the amount of the cheque.

If the central bank buys government debt from a commercial bank the process is even simpler. The central bank pays with a cheque drawn on itself which the commercial bank credits to its account at the central bank. Bankers' cash increases by the amount of the cheque. Alternatively, the central bank may lend directly to the commercial bank, with the same effect on bankers' cash.[15]

The process of buying and selling government debt by the central bank has traditionally been known in industrialised countries (more precisely, in the textbooks written for students in industrialised countries) as 'open-market operations'. This is because the central bank in an industrialised country operates through a well-established stock exchange, with an active market in government debt. Even in such a market, the central bank cannot necessarily buy or sell as much government debt as it would like, certainly not without causing large movements in the prices of government stocks, and thus in interest rates.[16]

In an underdeveloped country, with an underdeveloped market in government debt, central bank buying and selling is even more constrained. Basically, the central bank reacts to *demand* for government stock by making stock available when required. There is a fairly steady demand from institutions that invest other people's savings such as the savings banks (including Post Office Savings Banks) and National Provident Funds. When these institutions require cash and wish to sell stock, the central bank acts as residual buyer in the absence of other buyers. If the central bank did *not* act as residual buyer, the financial institution might have real difficulty in meeting its obligations, which would be to nobody's advantage. Furthermore, it would be impossible to sell government debt in future if it was not 'marketable' in this sense.

Where the commercial banks are concerned, the central bank sells government debt on demand. If the commercial banks want to sell, and cannot find private sector buyers (as is very likely), then the central bank will buy. But because the central bank is the residual buyer, it can decide the price paid. If the central bank wants the commercial banks to reduce their lending to customers, then it can inflict *losses* on the commercial banks by paying a low price for their liquid assets. Alternatively the central bank can offer to lend to the commercial banks at such a high rate of interest that they prefer to reduce their lending to customers in order to repay the central bank loan. These possibilities, of inflicting financial penalties on the commercial banks, greatly add to the central bank's ability to control bank lending and the money supply, *but only when* the commercial banks have no spare cash.

Central banks do not normally lend money to commercial banks to allow or encourage an expansion of bank lending, although in theory it is possible. Lending is normally temporary, and at a high rate of interest in order to encourage early repayment. In other words, central banks' lending is normally a signal that bank lending should grow more slowly or be reduced. If a central bank wants commercial bank lending to grow, it would be more likely to buy government debt, from commercial banks or from non-bank holders, or to reduce cash and liquidity requirements.

5 *The multiplier effects of a change in bankers' cash*

The practical importance of an increase in bankers' cash, whatever the reason for it, is that it allows a *multiple* increase in the money supply.

Suppose that demand deposits are K200 mn and that commercial bank deposits at the central bank are K24 mn; and suppose that the required cash ratio is 12% so that the banks have no spare cash. Ignore time and savings deposits for the moment—they complicate the analysis, but do not really alter it.

Now suppose the government spends K1 mn, for which it has no tax revenue, and which it is unable to borrow. The government has to 'borrow' from the central bank, that is, the central bank credits the government account with K1 mn. The money supply rises by K1 mn and so does bankers' cash. Demand deposits are now K201 mn, bankers' cash is K25 mn. The commercial banks only need K24.12 mn in cash (12% of K201 mn), so they have spare cash.

If there is a demand for new credit, which is quite likely since additional unfinanced spending by the government is expansionary and has *income* multiplier effects, then the money supply can expand. The question is by how much.

As bank advances and bank deposits expand, the public's demand for notes and coin will rise. This has to be met out of bankers' cash. So the additional K1 mn in bankers' cash is needed for two purposes: to pay for the rise in notes and coin held by the public (and by the commercial banks as till money, but this is very small) and to meet the 12% cash ratio requirement of the rise in demand deposits.

Notes and coin in circulation in African economies are something of the order of 50% of demand deposits: actual percentages in 1980 ranged from 37% in Botswana and 42% in Kenya and Zambia, to 72% in Nigeria and 80% in Sierra Leone. The figure for Ghana was very much higher, at 168%, perhaps partly because successive governments have confiscated large bank balances in the belief that they represented illegal profiteering, but also because cocoa farmers are paid in cash, not with cheques.

Using a figure of 50% for the increase in notes and coin in circulation as a proportion of an increase in demand deposits, any increase in bankers' cash would have to be used:

(a) to meet the 12% cash ratio requirement of the increase in demand deposits

(b) to supply the increased demand of the general public for notes and coin (as notes and coin are withdrawn from commercial banks they have to be replaced in bank tills by new supplies from the central bank and paid for by drawing down commercial bank deposits at the central bank).

So if demand deposits were to rise by the maximum amount possible, writing D for demand deposits and ΔD for the increment, then 50% of ΔD plus 12% of ΔD must equal K1 mn. This gives

$$62\% \text{ of } \Delta D = \text{K1 mn}$$

or

$$\Delta D = \text{K1.6 mn (approximately)}.$$

The total change in the money supply equals the change in deposits, K1.6 mn, plus the change in note circulation, K0.8 mn; so the money supply rises by K2.4 mn approximately if the banks lend as much as the increase in bankers' cash makes possible. In other words the money supply can expand by nearly $2\frac{1}{2}$ times the original expansion of bankers' cash, assuming that the banks take maximum advantage of the situation–and assuming that nothing else occurs in the meantime to affect the level of bankers' cash.[17]

Generalising this, if

c = bankers' cash ratio
c' = ratio of public's cash to public's bank deposits
ΔB = change in bankers' cash
ΔD = maximum change in demand deposits
Δ Ms = change in the total money supply

then

$$c\Delta D + c'\Delta D = \Delta B$$

or

$$\Delta D = \Delta B/(c + c') \qquad (1)$$

The total change in the money supply is equal to the change in demand deposits *plus* the change in the public's note holdings, so

$$\begin{aligned} \Delta \text{Ms} &= \Delta D + c'\Delta D = \Delta D(1 + c') \\ &= \Delta B(1 + c')/(c + c') \qquad (2) \end{aligned}$$

substituting for ΔD from equation (1).

These two formulae, (1) and (2), are general in the sense that they hold for a decrease in bankers' cash as well as for an increase. But of course the commercial banks would only be forced to reduce their lending (and thus the money supply) by a reduction in their cash if they had no spare cash in the first place. If bankers' cash *is reduced* below the amount required by the cash ratio, then formula (1) shows the *minimum* by which demand deposits must be reduced in order to restore the cash ratio. When bankers' cash is *increased*, in a situation where the banks have no spare cash, formula (1) shows the *maximum* by which demand deposits can increase—whether it actually occurs or not depends on the reaction of the banks and their customers. In *both* cases, of a reduction or an increase in bankers' cash, it clearly makes no difference if the banks already have spare cash; the change merely alters the *amount* of spare cash.

However, the cause of a change in bankers' cash makes a difference. An unfinanced budget deficit stimulates demand without any compensating reduction in demand through taxation, so that one would expect (other things being equal) that bank lending would also increase in response to the increase in demand and its multiplier effects. In contrast, a purely monetary transaction, such as the purchase (in the 'market') of government debt by the central bank, does not of itself stimulate demand; lending will only increase in this situation if there was already an unsatisfied demand for credit which the banks were unable to meet because of a shortage of cash.

If, in the situation already described, the commercial banks had no spare *liquidity*, that is, their liquidity ratio was at the legal minimum, then some of the new bankers' cash would be needed to buy additional liquid assets. This would reduce the possible expansionary effect of an increase in bankers' cash. An expansion of deposits could reduce their liquidity ratio below their 'target'. The banks would expand their lending (and the money supply) by less than would otherwise be the case.

If the cash ratio is 12% and the liquidity ratio is 30% (say), then 18% of ΔD would have to be applied to buying new liquid assets if the banks had no spare liquid assets and adhered strictly to their target. This also assumes that the commercial banks are unable to buy liquid assets from anyone except the central bank. In other words, there is a *ceteris paribus* assumption about the demand for liquid assets from other financial institutions. If the banks could buy, say, Treasury Bills from the Provident Fund, then the latter would deposit the cheque with a bank and bankers' cash would not be affected. On the figures quoted above, deposits could only rise by K1.25 mn rather than the K1.6 mn derived earlier when it was assumed that no cash was needed for buying liquid assets. Similarly the money supply would rise by only about K1.85 mn[18] rather than K2.4 mn. So a tight liquidity situation added to a tight cash situation greatly reduces the expansionary effect of an increase in bankers' cash.

6 *Bank lending: the impact of imports and taxation*

The formulae derived in the previous section take no account of the extreme 'openness' of most African economies, that is, the importance of foreign trade, nor of the effect of changing tax revenues.

Suppose bankers' cash increases because of a budget deficit and that bank lending also increases–because of the stimulus to demand and the existence of additional bank liquidity. Because of the high propensity to import, bankers' cash will be *reduced* by paying for the additional imports. Indeed, a great deal of bank lending is actually used to finance imports. Banking was originally developed in Africa in order to finance foreign trade and only gradually extended to other sectors. Even where banks lend to domestic producers, the money is used indirectly to finance imports because so many inputs into, say, industry and agriculture are imported.[19]

The propensity to import is therefore a sort of leakage from bankers' cash, reducing the multiplier effects of an increase. Similarly, taxation acts as another leakage. As the economy expands, tax receipts increase, thus reducing the budget deficit or increasing the surplus. If the improved budget position is used to reduce the amount of government 'borrowing' from the central bank, that is, to reduce the amount of pure money creation caused by an unfinanced budget deficit, then bankers' cash is reduced and bank liquidity is reduced with it. In most African countries the bulk of taxation comes from foreign trade. Economic expansion leads to high imports, which in turn increase tax receipts from import tariffs.

As an extreme case, consider an increase in the price of diamonds. When the proceeds are sold to the Bank of Botswana, bankers' cash increases. But more than 70% of the increase is due to the government in taxation; some of the remainder will be paid out in dividends to foreign shareholders. Only the retained profits remain within the banking system. There are, of course, time-lags in this process since taxation is not immediately payable and dividends are even further delayed. But the commercial banks are unlikely to expand their lending on the basis of an increase in bankers' cash which they know to be temporary. In short, an economy which taxes any increase in export proceeds at a very high rate is protected to a very great extent from the *monetary* effects of fluctuations in export prices. Some effect remains, however, so that if for some reason the government wishes to prevent a monetary expansion, the excess bank liquidity will have to be neutralised in some way–for example by increasing the statutory cash ratio or by persuading the exporters to buy government debt rather than leaving their money with the banks. On occasion, the Bank of Zambia has simply required the Zambian copper companies to deposit their surplus cash at the Bank of Zambia, in the form of 'Special Deposits'.[20]

Suppose then that the government spends an additional amount of money, ΔG, and 'borrows' from the central bank in order to do so. It is assumed here that the government has the same marginal propensity to import as the rest of the economy; and it is also assumed that government spending generates the same amount of tax revenue as other forms of spending. Both the initial spending by the government, and the further spending out of the income created, will increase imports and tax revenues, both of which reduce bankers' cash. In other words, the normal income multiplier effects described in chapters 4, 5 and 6, and their impact on imports and tax revenues, must be taken into account. The same is true of the multiplier effects of increased spending financed by increased lending by the banks.

From the point of view of the commercial banks, then, an increase in government spending, ΔG, financed by the central bank and so creating bankers' cash, is needed,

(a) to meet the cash ratio requirement of any increase in demand deposits
(b) to supply the increased demand of the public for notes and coin
(c) to pay for the foreign exchange needed to buy the increased imports resulting from the multiplier effects of increased government spending and lending by the commercial banks
(d) to meet the transfer to government of increased tax revenues resulting from the same increases in spending as in (c).

Let ΔD be the maximum possible increase in demand deposits. The change in the commercial banks' balance sheets at a new equilibrium would then be:

Commercial banks

Liabilities		*Assets*	
Change in demand deposits	$+ \Delta D$	Change in deposits at the central bank (bankers' cash)	$+ c\Delta D$
		Change in loans	$+ \Delta D - c\Delta D$
Total liabilities	$+ \Delta D$	Total assets	$+ \Delta D$

The total increase in spending in the economy is therefore ΔG (the original increase in government spending) plus $\Delta D - c\Delta D$ (the increase in bank lending, arrived at from the banks' balance sheet, above). Each of these increases in spending has multiplier effects, causing an increase in both imports and tax receipts, both of which have to come out of the increase in bankers' cash. The increase in imports is km times the increase in spending[21] and the increase in tax receipts is kt times the increase in spending,[22] using the notation of chapter 6. So:

$$\begin{aligned}\Delta G = {} & \text{increase in cash requirement } (c\Delta D) \\ & + \text{increase in notes in circulation } (c'\Delta D) \\ & + km \times \text{(increase in spending)} \\ & + kt \times \text{(increase in spending)}\end{aligned}$$

$$\text{So } \Delta G = c\Delta D + c'\Delta D + km(\Delta G + \Delta D - c\Delta D) + kt(\Delta G + \Delta D - c\Delta D)$$

$$\text{or } \Delta D = \frac{\Delta G\ (1 - km - kt)}{(c + c') + (1 - c)\ (km + kt)} \qquad (3)$$

Comparing formula (3) with formula (1) from the previous section, it is clear that introducing the impact of imports and taxation reduces the possible increase in bank deposits. The terms *km* and *kt* appear as negative items on the top line, and as positive items on the bottom line, both of which tend to reduce ΔD. Supposing that an African economy has the following:

$$b = 0.8 \quad t = 0.2 \quad m = 0.5$$

then the income multiplier $k = 1.16$.

Suppose also that (as before) $c = 0.12$ and $c' = 0.5$, then ΔD, instead of being 1.6 as in the previous section where imports and taxation were ignored, becomes only 0.14, so that bank deposits could only increase by K0.14 mn following an increase of K1 mn in government spending, while the money supply would increase by K0.21 mn (compared with K2.4 mn). This demonstrates the very great impact on the order of magnitude of monetary expansion of the taxation and import propensities.

A country with a lower marginal propensity to import, or a country simply unable to increase imports because of a shortage of foreign exchange, would of course have a much larger money supply multiplier. Similarly, if increases in government revenue are immediately spent by the government, perhaps because spending had previously been held down by a shortage of revenue, then increases in tax revenue would not be a drain on bankers' cash. Recalculating the money supply increase, using a marginal propensity to import of 0.1, leaving the other parameters unchanged, gives maximum possible increases in deposits of K0.7 mn and in the money supply of K1.05 mn. These big differences are not really very surprising: after all, with a marginal propensity to import of 0.5, only half of an increase in government spending would find its way to bankers' balances in the first instance, the other half leaving the country immediately to pay for imports. Indeed, in this example, the main impact of an increase in government spending of K1 mn financed by the central bank, is not on the money supply, which rises by only K0.21 mn, but on imports, which rise by *km* times the increase in spending (by government and borrowers from the banks), which comes to K0.65 mn.

The close links between money-creation and imports mean that the government has to coordinate monetary management very closely with management of the balance of payments. For this reason the central bank is normally given responsibility for both.

7 *Time and savings deposits*

If a bank customer converts his spare cash from a demand deposit to a time deposit it presumably means that he is not planning to spend that money in the short term. It releases a small amount of bankers' cash when the official requirement is that a smaller percentage of time (and savings) deposits must be kept in bankers' cash, compared with the demand deposit requirement.[23]

Suppose that an unfinanced budget deficit of K1m, as discussed in Section 5 where the effect of imports and taxation were ignored, results in equal increases in demand deposits on the one hand, and in time and in savings deposits on the other hand.

Writing demand deposits as *Dd* and savings deposits *Ds*, *t* then the bankers' cash required to meet cash ratios is

$$12\% \text{ of } \Delta Dd + 8\% \text{ of } \Delta Ds, t$$

In addition, currency in circulation will increase by 50% of ΔDd. If *Dd* and *Ds*, *t* are roughly equal, then

$$12\% \text{ of } \Delta Dd + 8\% \text{ of } \Delta Ds, t + 50\% \text{ of } \Delta Dd = \text{K1 mn}$$

$$\text{so } \Delta Dd = \text{K1.43 mn}$$

In total, therefore, demand deposits can rise by a maximum of K1.4 mn, currency by K0.7 mn, and time and savings deposits by another K1.4 mn. So the money supply defined as currency and demand deposits only can rise by about twice the original budget deficit; and money supply defined as currency plus both sorts of deposit can rise by about three and a half times the original budget deficit.

These multipliers would be greatly reduced if account is taken of the money that would be spent on imports and taxation in an economy still able to buy additional imports and capable of taxing increases in income. The multipliers would also be slightly reduced if the banks had to use some of the additional bankers' cash to buy extra liquid assets.

8 *Alternative sources of bank liquidity*

Commercial banks do not rely entirely on their cash for liquidity. As already discussed, they also invest in Treasury Bills and short-dated government stock. These assets are attractive to commercial banks because they carry some interest but can be converted into cash at short notice and at relatively little risk of loss.[24]

Banks also invest in bills of exchange. Essentially these are ways of lending money in a way that yields a marketable asset. If a bank lends money to customers in the form of an overdraft it cannot sell the overdraft to another bank or to the central bank.[25] A bill of exchange is a promise to pay in the future. The borrower instructs his bank on a piece of paper to pay a debt some months in the future. If the borrower is regarded as creditworthy he can sell the piece of paper or bill of exchange to someone who has spare cash. The bill sells at a 'discount' or less than the amount promised in the future, so that the investor makes a profit equivalent to the interest rate. In this way the borrower gets cash now and banks, for example, acquire a liquid investment on which they earn some income.

Bills of exchange were devised to finance foreign trade and are still used almost exclusively in that field. Thus an importer in Africa wishing to buy something in, say, Germany does not wish to pay for it until it arrives. The German exporter, however, wants cash when the product leaves his factory. If he is paid by bill of exchange he can sell the bill to a bank and get his cash straight away, while the importer does not have to pay until the due date on the bill, by which time (he hopes) the goods will have arrived.

Bills of exchange are thus a way of financing the time-lags caused by international transport. Shipping is usually the cheapest sort of transport, especially for heavy bulky goods, but it is slow and so requires financing. The Treasury Bill is a special sort of bill of exchange, used by governments to finance the gap between spending and receipt of tax revenue.

If a commercial bank discounts (buys) a bill of exchange, it pays a cheque to a customer. The customer's account increases and the bank's account at the central bank is not affected. The commercial bank thus acquires a liquid asset and the money supply has increased. If the bill is bought from someone with an account at another bank there is a change in the relative cash and liquid asset position of the two banks, but overall the banking system again acquires a liquid asset and the money supply has risen by the amount of the bill.

Buying bills of exchange is thus a way for commercial banks to lend more while adding to their liquid assets. Because deposits (and probably the public's demand for currency) rise, such lending puts the same strain on *cash* resources as lending by way of granting overdrafts, but clearly it is attractive to banks in need of more liquid assets.[26]

On the other hand, the central bank can control the *type* of bills of exchange bought by commercial banks. Since bills of exchange are only really liquid if the central bank is willing to buy them, the central bank can announce which bills it will buy—for example, bills to finance imports of agricultural inputs but not bills to finance imports of luxury consumer goods. Alternatively, the central bank can discriminate by offering a better price for favoured bills (that is, discounting them at a lower rate of interest).

The final source of liquidity for a commercial bank is borrowing from the central bank. Sometimes it is simply convenient for the central bank to provide cash to the banking system in this way; or the central bank may impose conditions on its lending in order to try and get the commercial banks to comply with official policy. For example the central bank may impose a high interest rate and short repayment date, in order to get the banks to slow down their lending.

In addition, however, the central bank stands ready to lend in a real crisis. Banking depends very much on confidence. If all depositors asked for their money at once, no bank would be able to pay, since a proportion of deposits has been advanced to customers who cannot all repay at once. If, then, a bank is basically sound (that is, it has not been lending money foolishly to people who cannot repay) the central bank will lend it cash until confidence is restored. The very existence of a central bank makes a crisis of confidence, a 'run' on a bank when all depositors try and get their money out at once, less likely. But it could still happen.[27]

In most parts of Africa the banks are either subsidiaries of large international banks or government-owned, so that a crisis of confidence is unlikely. The foreign head offices would probably provide short-term finance to the expatriate banks if it were needed, as would the government to the parastatal commercial banks. But in Nigeria, for example, where a large number of small private banks were founded in the early 1950s, a great many bank failures occurred, with consequent losses for their depositors. There was also a loss of public confidence in indigenous banks which 'caused many Nigerians to decide to keep their savings in expatriate banks'.[28]

There is a slight paradox, then, in the functioning of a central bank as 'lender of last resort'. Banks which are basically sound do not usually need such support, although they may borrow from the central bank sometimes as an alternative to selling (to the central bank) some of their marketable assets. Banks which are basically unsound should not have access to central bank lending. Nevertheless, the soundness of the 'good' banks depends partly on the willingness of the central bank to lend to them, even if that willingness is seldom seriously tested.

9 *Alternative methods of controlling bank credit*[29]

African central banks have tried all sorts of ways of controlling bank credit–other, that is, than by altering cash and liquid asset ratios. The methods used fall roughly into three categories: action to change the amount of cash and liquidity of the banks, action to affect the demand for credit of bank customers, and direct controls of various sorts.

Central banks in developed countries with fully-fledged markets in government debt can operate on the cash and liquidity position of commercial banks by buying and selling government debt in the stock market. Such actions are called 'open-market operations' and have received a great deal of attention from economic theorists and writers of textbooks. It is obviously not possible for African central banks to operate in the same way. Even those countries with stock exchanges (Kenya, Nigeria, Zimbabwe) have relatively 'thin' markets in government debt, that is, there are relatively few transactions each day making it impossible in most circumstances for the central bank to buy or sell enough government debt to have a significant effect on bank cash and liquid assets. In all the other African countries, open market operations are not possible at all. From the point of view of central banks wishing to control the amount of bank lending and manage the balance of payments, it is fortunate that there are plenty of alternatives to open market operations.

Possible actions to change the level of bank cash and liquid assets include the following:

(a) The commercial banks can be required to hold 'special deposits' at the central bank. For example, the banks could be required to hold 2% of all their deposits in accounts at the central bank, such special deposits *not* to count as cash or as liquid assets. This has exactly the same effect as an increase in the cash and liquid assets ratio requirements. Releasing some or all of 'special deposits' has the opposite effect.

(b) Non-bank depositors can be required to hold deposits at the central bank. This removes cash from the commercial banks in exactly the same way as an additional tax payment or a sale of government debt to non-bank holders. Non-bank institutions may be required to hold deposits at the central bank for reasons other than control of bank credit; nevertheless, such action has the effect of reducing bank liquidity and therefore banks' ability to increase their lending.

(c) Institutions (commercial banks and others) can be forced by law to buy government debt. This may be done in order to finance the government's spending but it has the effect of reducing the banks' cash, and liquidity. An exception is when commercial banks buy government debt which falls within the current definition of liquid assets, in which case commercial bank purchases reduce their cash but not their liquid assets.

(d) Central banks can change the official definition of liquid assets. For example, in order to *reduce* bank liquidity, certain types of government debt, or bills of exchange may be *excluded* from what has previously been allowed to count as liquid assets. In the past, some countries have chosen to exclude foreign assets from official definitions of liquid assets; but this was intended to force commercial banks to sell most or all of their foreign assets, and to transfer the proceeds to the central bank in exchange for local currency deposits. This had the effect of increasing the official foreign exchange reserves but not of reducing commercial banks' cash and liquidity. In order to *increase* liquidity, central banks can of course change the definitions to *include* some commercial bank assets. Interestingly, certain categories of loans have on occasion been deemed to be liquid assets, for example loans to the agricultural sector. This has the double effect of increasing liquidity and of encouraging bank lending to agriculture. Central banks may also offer to discount (that is, to buy) agricultural loans, thus enabling commercial banks actually to acquire additional cash, or at least to be able to do so on demand.

(e) Central banks can require foreign-controlled companies, usually but not always defined as those with more than 50% foreign shareholders, to restrict their local borrowing. Such powers are usually granted to central banks as part of Exchange Control regulations, on the grounds that lending to foreign-controlled companies (even though operating locally) is rather like lending money abroad. The motives for such regulations include a desire to force foreign-controlled companies to seek more finance from abroad, a desire to make more bank credit available to locally-controlled companies,[30] or simply a desire to reduce the total of bank lending in situations where foreign-controlled companies have a large share of the total. The rules can be imposed in various ways, for example by allowing foreign-controlled companies to borrow locally only some proportion of their cash brought in from abroad, or by requiring all foreign-controlled companies to apply to the central bank for permission to borrow locally.

(f) Central banks can also place limits on the amount of local borrowing allowed by *local* companies, for example as a proportion of equity (shareholder) finance. Again, this could be done in order to improve debt-equity ratios or in order to control the total of credit in the economy.

(g) Central banks can simply impose direct limits on the amount of lending by the commercial banks. Some countries have given their central banks power to do this; in other cases the central banks can merely request the banks to comply, knowing that the request can be enforced if necessary (see below, section 11, on 'moral suasion').

The above measures all act on the supply of bank credit; that is, they affect the ability of banks to lend, rather than the *demand* of their customers to borrow. All actions to affect the supply of bank credit may have one of two effects: total activity in the economy may be reduced or borrowers may switch to foreign finance if they cannot get local finance. Of course, if the banks have enough spare cash and liquid assets to meet new official requirements (for example for special deposits) *and* the demands of their customers, there is no effect at all. Assuming that the measures *do* have an effect on bank lending, both results are likely to occur in some combination, namely a reduction in the level of economic activity and an inflow of capital from abroad. *Within* the group of bank borrowers, large or foreign companies are in general more likely to be able to obtain foreign finance than small or local ones; so a general credit squeeze is likely to be harmful to the interests of small or local companies. That is why central banks in Africa, anxious to help in developing locally-owned and controlled businesses, often choose to impose a credit squeeze in a way that discriminates against foreign companies. However, this still leaves a problem if the main objective is more to reduce the overall level of economic activity than to force more of it to be financed from abroad. It is no good imposing a credit squeeze if *local* companies are to be protected from its effects, and if *foreign* companies can borrow abroad, when the main intention is to reduce the pressure of demand on local prices, say, or when the level of overseas indebtedness is already considered to be too high. For this reason, it is often necessary for the authorities to reduce the demand for credit at the same time as they reduce the supply.

Any official action which reduces income, such as a tax increase or a reduction in government spending, also tends to reduce the demand for credit for investment purposes. Reductions, or slower growth, in income also tend to reduce borrowers' creditworthiness and so to make banks less willing to lend. In addition, the monetary authorities can try to reduce the demand for credit by making it more expensive. Higher interest rates, however, do not necessarily have much effect on investment demand (as is argued in chapter 7); higher interest rates also make it relatively more attractive to borrow abroad unless foreign interest rates rise at the same time. As with other measures, therefore, the authorities do not know whether higher interest rates will cause a reduction in the level of economic activity or an inflow of capital from abroad. Furthermore, businesses unable to borrow abroad may be more seriously affected than those who can, and in Africa that often means hardship for local businesses.

African countries continue to experiment with combinations of direct controls over bank credit, measures to affect banks' cash and liquidity situation, and measures to affect the demand for credit. The right combination is obviously very difficult to find, given that governments and central banks often have multiple objectives which may not all be reachable at once, and given that there is no way of knowing beforehand whether a given set of measures will have the desired mix of effects on the level of domestic activity and the balance of payments. When the authorities also want to discriminate between large and small borrowers, or between local and foreign-owned firms, the task is even more difficult. It is undoubtedly true, though, that monetary policy works much better if it is supported rather than opposed by fiscal policy. Put slightly differently, it is hard to make a credit squeeze effective if the government's budget deficit is increasing rapidly; and direct controls over bank credit probably need the support of a tight liquidity situation in order to be effective.[31]

In the situation of most African countries, there is a case for acting on liquidity and the demand for credit rather than using direct controls, since high-level administrators are scarce. Direct involvement in lending decisions should be confined, therefore, to cases involving very large companies which have a major impact on the entire economy: Exchange Control regulations usually ensure that cases involving large foreign companies are taken to the central bank, and regulations concerning the amount of a commercial bank's capital that may be lent to any one borrower will have the same effect for both foreign and locally controlled companies.[32] A second point is that the greater the financial importance of administrative decisions, the greater is the risk of corruption.[33] Thirdly, central bankers are not really the right people to make large numbers of decisions on individual loan applications; that is what bank managers are for and taking the decision out of their hands is in a way a waste of their expertise. It can only be done effectively if an alternative source of expertise is available, and this is not usually the case in Africa. There may be a case for controlling the total amount of credit, and directing credit to priority sectors, but that is different in principle from controlling each individual loan.[34]

10 Summary of central bank functions

The discussion so far has, in passing, already covered a large part of the most important central bank functions. Thus the central bank acts as banker to the government and to the commercial banks, and holds the country's foreign exchange. As a result changes in the government's cash position, the commercial bankers' cash position and the balance of payments are all reflected immediately and directly in accounts at the central bank—with the effects on bank liquidity and the money supply that have been discussed. The central bank thus has the opportunity to try and control bank lending by buying and selling bank liquid assets or by changing the rules—altering cash and liquidity ratios or altering what the banks can count towards those ratios.

In most African countries it is illegal for anyone to hold foreign exchange without permission from the central bank, whether in the form of foreign currency or as bank accounts abroad. If exporters keep their earnings overseas rather than selling to the central bank in exchange for local currency, they can pay for imports, dividends, foreign loan interest and repayments, etc., without the knowledge of the central bank. Fluctuations in export proceeds result, in such circumstances, in fluctuations in foreign exchange holdings of private companies without any impact, monetary or otherwise, on the domestic economy. Most governments prefer to perform the reserve-holding role themselves, through their central banks, and exercise equal control over the foreign payments of exporters and others. Having to deal with the domestic monetary impact is considered a minor price to pay for this control.[35]

The central bank handles the note issue, ordering (or performing, as in the case of the Bank of England which has its own printing works) the printing of notes, and distributing them to the commercial banks on request, either in exchange for a reduction in their accounts, or in exchange for old, dirty notes. Increases in the note issue are a theoretical liability of the central bank, against which it holds government debt. But the central bank can always meet its liability by printing more notes.

Central bank holdings of government debt against the note issue are thus a formality—the government pays the central bank interest on its holdings of debt, and the central bank, being owned by the government, pays this straight back to the government (after deduction of expenses) as its profit—or lends it back as part of its 'reserves'. What this all amounts to, therefore, is that increases in the note issue are effectively interest-free loans to the government, the only expense being the relatively very minor one of printing the notes and administering their issue. Increases in the note issue to meet the normal increasing demand for them by the public as the economy grows (and becomes monetised, in the case of underdeveloped countries) are a useful and cheap form of finance, which every government should plan for, and use gratefully.

The central bank also acts as lender of last resort to the banking system; and it provides finance to the government if nobody else will, by what is called lending but is in fact money-creation. The central bank also exercises some influence over interest rates, but other factors are also important in this, as will be explained in the next chapter.

There remain two other functions which are rather more vague, but nonetheless important. Central banks act as advisers to government on the management of the economy. A great deal of information passes through central banks simply as a result of their acting as bankers to the government and the commercial banks, and as managers of the national debt and foreign exchange. Central banks are therefore in a particularly strong position to gather and analyse up-to-date information, and this in turn should make them an important source of financial and economic advice.

The remaining function of central banks, especially in African countries, is to try and stimulate the development of financial markets and institutions, and, where appropriate, to encourage existing financial institutions to do more of what they are already doing and to do new things. The logic of this is to make more efficient the flow of savings into investment. The argument is that financial intermediation (transmitting the surplus funds of savers to borrowers for investment through financial markets or financial institutions) leads to the most efficient use of savings. Where existing banks do not make long-term loans, or do not lend enough to small-scale business or to agriculture, a central bank should, the argument runs, seek ways of stimulating or even forcing banks to make new types of loan; and if this is not possible, then new institutions should be created such as development banks and agricultural lending institutions. Alternative strategies include creation of new, usually government-owned, commercial banks[36] and takeover of existing foreign-owned commercial banks by the government.[37] It can be argued, though, that *ownership* is not so important as *localisation of staff*, especially those who make lending decisions.

Government-owned banks which are forced to use expatriate managers may not behave very diferently from foreign-owned banks with expatriate managers. Local managers, speaking local languages and being more a part of the local business community, are more likely to be able to pick out, from among those excluded in the past from access to credit, those applicants for loans most likely to make productive use of them and therefore to be able to repay them in due course.

Development of the financial sector is rather peculiar in some African countries because of the very rapid growth of the parastatal sector, both by government takeover of industrial and commercial companies and by governments creating new state-owned (or partly state-owned) companies. The logic of creating parastatal corporations is that they should buy, sell and borrow on their own account, as opposed to the Ministries of Education or Health, for example, which are funded by the government budget for both recurrent and capital expenditures. Where the modern sector of the economy is dominated by parastatal corporations, as in Tanzania or Zambia for example, it is not the logic of the market and profit-maximising that decide which companies get credit, because parastatal companies can run at a loss, and frequently do. In fact in all African countries governments themselves are also significant lenders, mainly to parastatal corporations but also to cooperatives, housing associations and other favoured institutions. In some cases, the central bank has actually lent directly to companies other than commercial banks; for example, the Bank of Zambia has lent large amounts to the copper-mining companies which are majority-owned by the Zambian government. Such activity is a long way from the idea of financial markets allocating credit according to market criteria; governments presumably allocate credit according to political criteria and the economic planning priorities they may have.

There is actually a strong case for governments to act as financial intermediaries to an increasing extent. African countries have chosen, or in some cases have been forced, to borrow extensively abroad. Such borrowing exposes the borrower to a number of risks: variable interest rates, variation in exchange rates of currencies borrowed, and fixed debt service obligations for projects with highly variable income. Governments are in a better position than domestic institutions to carry these risks, so that there is a case for governments to borrow in the first place and to lend to final borrowers on more suitable terms—for example in local currency, with fixed instead of variable interest rates or on conditions that allow debt service to be paid according to the money available each year.[38]

Despite these qualifications and reservations, financial markets and institutions continue to grow and to be encouraged by central banks. The logic is presumably that management of parastatals is more efficient if separated from direct civil service control, and in particular if borrowing is made subject to the scrutiny of bank managers, and of those in governments responsible for making loans. Even if bank managers do not apply the same criteria of creditworthiness to parastatal companies, because of their implied government support, it could be argued that banks are able to offer some useful advice, and applications to increase borrowing force somebody, whether it is in a commercial or a central bank, or in a government, to review the situation.

11 Conclusion

Even in an open economy, with commercial banks foreign-owned, the central bank can exercise considerable monetary control. But the large fluctuations in export earnings plus the importance of the public sector mean that the central bank can be presented with much bigger changes in the liquidity of the banking system than it is likely to be able to deal with by buying and selling government debt. Nevertheless, the central bank can also alter liquidity requirements and has other weapons to hand, notably exchange control, or alter liquidity (for example by calling for special deposits), or use other weapons for controlling borrowing, notably exchange controls for controlling borrowing by foreign companies and other forms of direct control over borrowing by local companies.

Central banks are also supposed to be able to influence the banking system by 'moral suasion'—which is supposed to mean by simple request. There is some scope for pointing out to the commercial banks that their interests and the national interest coincide. But the real power behind any central bank request derives from the fact that the central bank has very considerable powers. Apart from all the powers to control bank liquidity and lending which have already been described, it can inflict losses on the commercial banks—by squeezing their liquidity in such a way that they have to either sell liquid assets to the central bank (at a price chosen by the central bank) or borrow from the central bank (at an interest rate chosen by the central bank). Ability to borrow from abroad slows down but does not eliminate the central bank's powers, since head offices will lend for short but not for long periods, and can in any case be prevented if necessary. The central bank also affects commercial bank profits when it requires larger holdings of deposits with itself, or larger holdings of other liquid assets since these assets earn a lower yield then loans to customers.

Fortunately heavy taxes on exports mean that export price fluctuations produce offsetting effects on liquidity. Thus a rise in export prices increases bankers' cash but the resulting budget surplus reduces it. This offset is not complete however; nor is it immediate.

A large budget deficit is more difficult for the central bank to manage; but here again the openness of the typical African economy reduces the monetary impact. A high propensity to import drains away some of the cash created by a budget deficit, as imports rise in response to the income multiplier effects of the deficit. Of course if import and exchange controls are used to prevent imports rising then the monetary expansion must be controlled in some other way—for example by raising cash or liquidity ratios, or by finding some other way of forcing the banks to buy government debt.[39]

There remains the possibility that the economy has unemployed resources to the extent that a rise in demand will lead to a rise in domestic output without any pressure on prices. In these circumstances, it is highly unlikely that increasing bank liquidity will lead to an expansion of lending. The banks will probably have spare liquidity already, and in any case there is not likely to be an excess demand for credit (from bankable borrowers) in a slump. The correct policy measure is thus a budget deficit financed by money creation; domestic borrowing would reduce spending power and bank liquidity. These circumstances are, however, rare in modern Africa–and assume that the balance of payments can stand the strain, which is even rarer.

Appendix: definitions

1 *Government stock*

One of the ways in which the government borrows money is by issuing 'stock'. Essentially, members of the general public, and institutions, are invited to lend money (on certain terms) to the government. The government promises to pay a stated rate of interest on the loan, for a stated number of years. For example if the government announces a new stock in 1975 called '5% Local Registered Stock 1985' the investor can buy say K1000 of this stock; he will receive 5% (K50 on K1000) annually for 10 years; in 1985 he will receive back his K1000.

If the investor wants his money back *before* 1985 he can try to sell his stock to someone else. The price he gets will *not* necessarily be K1000. If the 'market' interest rate has risen in the meantime to 10%, an investor wishing to get 10% on his money will pay less than K1000 for the stock which yields only 5% at a price of K1000. Suppose the year is 1984 and the stock has just one year to 'maturity' (that is, the date on which the government has promised to repay the money). The buyer will pay roughly K955 for the 'nominal' K1000 of stock. He will then receive K50 in interest (that is fixed by the 5% 'coupon' or interest promised at issue by the government) and on maturity he will make another K45 'profit' since he will receive K1000 for stock for which he paid only K955. Altogether he will therefore receive K95, which is roughly 10% of his original investment of K955.

This example illustrates three very important principles: firstly, that the value of a fixed-interest stock changes in the *opposite* direction to changes in the rate of interest. Thus if the interest rate goes up, the market value of fixed-interest government stock goes down; and if the interest rate falls, the market value of fixed-interest stock rises.

Secondly, if there are very few buyers of government stock and the central bank acts as the residual buyer of stock it can have a very big influence on the price of stock. By offering a low price, thus lowering the value of stock, it can effectively push up the interest rate. By offering a good price, it can keep interest rates down.

Thirdly, the nearer to maturity a stock is, the nearer the market price will be to its repayment (or nominal) value and the less is the variation in its market price. That is why banks prefer short-dated stock.

2 *Treasury Bills*

Treasury Bills are simply very short-dated government debt. In Africa as elsewhere they are usually a way of borrowing money for three months. Thus if a company buys a Treasury Bill, it is lending money to the government for three months. Because Treasury Bills have a short life, the government does not 'pay' interest on them: instead it sells them at a discount, that is at less than their 'face' or nominal value.

For example, a K50 000 Treasury Bill is offered for sale on 1 March for K49 500. On 1 June the government will pay out K50 000 to the owner. The investor thus invests K49 500 and earns K500 in three months, which is roughly 1% on his money. The rate of interest is therefore roughly 4% calculated at an annual rate, as is usual.

3 *Marketability*

An investment is marketable if you can sell it. Thus a deposit in the Post Office Savings Bank is not marketable; to get your money back you *withdraw* your money, you do not sell the deposit to a friend. Government stock and Treasury Bills are marketable; the investor is issued with a piece of paper which entitles him to receive a fixed annual payment of interest (in the case of stock) and repayment of the full nominal amount (in the case of stock and Bills) on the due date (at maturity).

An investment is *more* or *less* marketable according to how easy or difficult it is to sell it. In turn this depends on how many buyers and sellers are active in the market and how well-organised the market is in bringing them together. In the case of government debt, marketability is of course greatly increased if the central bank acts as a residual buyer and seller. As already noted, the central bank has great control over the price of government debt because it acts as residual buyer and seller. The central bank has an interest, however, in maintaining a steady price for government debt in order to make it easier to sell government debt in future. If big fluctuations occur, and in particular if big and sudden rises in the interest rate (equal to falls in the price of government debt) occur, investors will be less willing to put their money into government debt in future.

Marketability of government debt, and a fairly steady price, are not just useful because they enable governments to spend more money without levying higher taxes. Some financial institutions have a real need for marketable long-term securities. For example, insurance companies and provident funds have future liabilities to pay pensions, etc. But in the meantime they have *unknown* short-term liabilities: people have accidents, die, lose their jobs and so make claims. As a result the institutions need 'liquid' investments, which give an income in the form of interest but which can be sold quickly if short-term liabilities suddenly increase. Marketability thus has an important social function.

In an economy where the major financial institutions are publicly-owned, it would clearly be possible for the government simply to make money available when needed, rather than to issue stock and then make it marketable in a rather artificial way by means of the central bank. The reason why the latter method is still used in some African countries is partly historical–that is the way it was done when financial institutions were privately-owned and the full adjustment to nationalisation has not yet been made–and partly because not all financial institutions are owned by the government; and possibly partly because it is believed to be more efficient to give parastatals considerable independence in day-to-day management and control them indirectly through the 'market'.

4 *Liquidity*

Money is perfectly liquid. Thus cash in the form of notes and coin is 100% liquid by definition–it can be spent at will. Some bank deposits are to all intents and purposes liquid if they can be converted into cash on demand–hence the term 'demand deposits'.

Investment in, say, a house is very illiquid since it takes considerable time to sell a house and thus convert it into cash. Furthermore, the price to be obtained on selling a house is uncertain, especially when the sale is made in a hurry (a 'forced sale').

Liquidity is thus made up of two elements

(a) the *speed* with which an investment can be converted into cash
(b) the degree of certainty about the *amount* of cash that will be received.

Marketable securities, for example government stocks and Treasury Bills, are very liquid in the first sense, since they can be sold for cash in the market (if there is one, or to the central bank in the absence of an active market). They are less liquid in the second sense, since their prices vary with variations in interest rates. Treasury Bills are more liquid than government stocks, in the second sense, because their price varies less. In general, the shorter-dated a stock, the less risk is there of variations in its price.

Illiquid investments can be used as security for borrowing. Thus a business with its money tied up in machinery and stocks of raw materials can usually borrow money—unless it is regarded as inefficient and on the verge of bankruptcy. One of the functions of banks is to provide liquidity for individuals and firms who do not wish to sell their longer-term investments just because they temporarily have no cash.

5 *Financing a budget deficit by borrowing from commercial banks*
It has already been explained that financing a budget deficit by 'borrowing' from the central bank is in fact money-creation and enables commercial banks to expand their lending. Financing a deficit by taxation or by borrowing from the 'non-bank' public creates no new money nor any new bankers' cash. Finance from the commercial banks is somewhere between these two extremes.

Suppose the government has an unfinanced deficit of K10 mn. Bank deposits rise by K10 mn; so does bankers' cash. Now suppose the commercial banks buy government debt—stock and Treasury Bills. Presumably they will keep K1.2 mn (12% of K10 mn) in bankers' cash, and buy K8.8 mn of government debt, unless they already have K1.2 mn of 'spare' cash. The result is then that the money supply has risen by K10 mn, but the commercial banks have no additional spare cash.

If the central bank actually succeeds in selling the full K10 mn's worth of debt to the commercial banks, then this will absorb K1.2 mn of their spare cash. The money supply will have risen by K10 mn and the capacity of the banks to expand their lending will have been reduced.

In both cases, the commercial banks' holdings of liquid assets will have risen if the increased government debt held by the banks is treated as an addition to their liquid assets. Treasury Bills are invariably treated as liquid assets; holdings of government stock are usually treated as liquid assets only if they have less than a certain period to maturity, although long-dated government stock has on occasion been included in official definitions of liquid assets in order to encourage its sale to the banks.

Suppose that the required cash ratio is 12% and the required liquid assets ratio is 30%. Suppose initially that demand deposits are K200 mn, bankers' cash K24 mn (12% of demand deposits) and liquid assets K60 mn (30% of demand deposits)—in this case the banks have no spare cash or liquid assets. Now suppose the government has an unfinanced deficit of K10 mn, the commercial banks buy K8.8 mn of government debt officially counted as liquid, and bankers' cash rises by K1.2 mn. The liquidity ratio then becomes 32.8% (K68.8 of liquid assets divided by K210 mn of demand deposits). The banks now have rather more liquid assets than officially required and can expand their lending if they can sell some of these 'spare' liquid assets. The definition of liquidity implies that it ought to be possible to sell liquid assets at a reasonable price, but in Africa official definitions do not always coincide with what can in fact be easily sold, especially if the central bank is unwilling to buy or will buy only at a low price.

In practice, the expansionary effect of the budget deficit would probably cause a rise in non-bank note holding, requiring the banks to use their liquid assets to get cash to supply notes to their customers. The central bank might also try to prevent advances from rising by use of direct controls—this would be consistent with a policy of trying to sell government debt to the commercial banks.

It is quite usual for commercial banks in Africa to try to maintain a margin of liquid assets above the official requirement. The central bank will normally be aware of this and knows therefore that it can affect bank lending by reducing liquid asset holdings below the target level. The additional safety margin gives more flexibility which has some advantages for all concerned. It would be disruptive and damaging in most circumstances if very sudden changes had to be made in bank lending.

By preventing bank lending through direct controls, by raising the liquidity ratio, or by changing the definition of the liquidity ratio, the authorities (the central bank and the government) can reduce the monetary effects of a budget deficit unfinanced by other sources. By forcing the commercial banks to buy government debt with additions to their cash, the authorities ensure that only the money supply goes up, not bank lending to the private sector.

NOTES

1 This is the most common definition of the money supply, also known as M1. Time and savings deposits, and other forms of financial asset which can quickly be converted into cash are sometimes known as 'money substitutes' or 'quasi-money'.

2 K, for Kwacha, is used here to indicate domestic currency—the currencies of both Zambia and Malawi are called Kwacha. It is necessary to use a *domestic* unit here in order to distinguish it from *foreign* currency later in the chapter. For foreign currency the US dollar is used, as the main international currency. Confusingly, two countries in Africa use the name dollar for their currency, so that there is a Zimbabwean dollar and a Liberian dollar. The Zimbabwean dollar is an independent currency; the Liberian dollar is identical to the US dollar—Liberia simply uses United States bank notes, but issues its own coins.

3 Traditionally, banks used to write overdrafts on bank statements in red figures—hence the expression 'in the red' for being in debt.

4 This practice of 'clearing' cheques with each other is the origin of the name 'clearing banks' for the biggest English banks.

5 Currency means bank notes and coin. Notes are much more important than coin. Some recent figures for coin as a proportion of notes and coin in circulation are: Botswana and Zambia both 5%, Sierra Leone 8%, Malawi 10%.

6 The coin manufacturer in the UK is called the Mint, hence the expression 'minting money'.

7 In some countries, the cash ratio *includes* notes and coin held in commercial bank tills ('till money'). In Zambia till money is excluded from the calculation of cash ratios. This detail makes no essential difference to the analysis. The Zambian cash ratio has been changed subsequently.

8 To bankers, 'cash' is what they can count towards their cash ratio, and use to meet customer withdrawals. In common speech, 'cash' means money (notes and coin) in one's pocket. For this reason, when discussing the banking system, the reader should be careful to note the specialised meaning of 'bankers' cash'. Other names for bankers' cash are 'primary reserves' and 'high-powered money'.

9 The full mechanism is as follows. Suppose that K1000 of the K2000 received by the car dealer is spent on imports. Bank S must buy the necessary foreign exchange from the central bank. The car dealer's deposit is reduced by K1000. The account of Bank S at the central bank falls by K1000. The foreign exchange reserves, part of the central bank's assets, also fall by K1000 worth of foreign currency. Using the Malawian rate for exchanging Malawian Kwacha into US dollars, the foreign exchange reserves would fall by MK1000 or US$1117, the rate in effect at the end of 1981.

10 For example, the banks in Botswana hardly increased their lending to customers at all for a period of three years or so, from March 1976 to September 1979, during which time they had bankers' cash greatly in excess of the amount required by law. *Statistical Bulletin*, various issues.

11 The 'liquidity' position is also important, as explained below.

12 For definitions of Treasury Bills, government stock, marketability and liquidity see Appendix at the end of this chapter, sections 1 to 4. Some commercial banks in Africa also have interest-bearing deposits at the central bank which count as liquid assets, but not as bankers' cash.

13 Bills of exchange and promissory notes are also liquid assets and are a form of lending to the private sector rather than to the government. This refinement is of relatively minor importance: it is dealt with in section 8 of this chapter.

14 In practice, the rising level of economic activity caused by equal rises in exports and imports would probably lead to a rising demand for notes and coin—the banks would have to pay for this by drawing *down* their central bank balances.

15 Central bank lending to commercial banks is further discussed in section 8.

16 As the market price of a government stock rises or falls, the interest that can be earned by buying some of that stock moves in the opposite direction. For a detailed explanation see section 1 of the Appendix to this chapter.

17 This is a rather unrealistic assumption: the effect of relaxing it is discussed below, later in this section and in section 6.

18 Currency would increase by half of K1.25 mn, namely K0.6 mn approximately, giving a rise in the money supply of K1.25 mn + K0.6 mn = K1.85 mn.

19 But bank lending has penetrated ever more deeply into the domestic economy. For example, between 1965 and 1978 bank lending increased 2.4 times faster than imports in Malawi. Similar figures for some other countries were Kenya 1.5, Ghana 2.3, Zambia 3.8, Tanzania 1.6. Only in Nigeria did imports increase at almost the same rate as bank lending, no doubt because of Nigeria's hugely increased revenues from oil.

20 At times, the diamond-mining company in Botswana has also shifted its deposits from the commercial banks to the Bank of Botswana, but not in this case to prevent an increase in bank lending. The reason was that the banks, having no profitable use for the money and being required to increase their reserves in line with increases in their deposits, were actually refusing to accept deposits; the Bank of Botswana offered to accept the deposits instead. See Bank of Botswana, *Annual Report 1978*, p. 20.

21 If m is the marginal propensity to import, then an increase in imports ΔM caused by a rise in income ΔY, is $m\ \Delta Y$. The multiplier formula of Chapter 6 shows that if government spending increases by ΔG, then $\Delta Y = k\Delta G$. So $\Delta M = km\ \Delta G$.

22 The increase in tax receipts is $t\Delta Y$, which equals $kt\ \Delta G$.

23 Changes in official requirements are normally reported in central bank annual reports. The reason for having a lower cash requirement for time and savings deposits was originally that banks needed a smaller amount of cash in hand for deposits that could not be withdrawn on demand. In practice, savings deposits are indeed fairly stable in aggregate, being used by large numbers of depositors each with a fairly small sum saved in this way. Time deposits, on the other hand, being used mainly by a relatively small number of large depositors, can be extremely unstable in aggregate. Demand deposits are, in aggregate, remarkably stable a great deal of the time, no doubt because, together with notes and coin, they are the money that people use for everyday transactions.

24 See Appendix to this chapter, section 4, for a discussion of liquidity.

25 In some countries loans made to certain favoured industries, for example agriculture, may be discounted, i.e. sold, to the central bank. This occurs in Jamaica, see A. Ally in P. Selwyn (ed.), *Development in Small Countries*, London, Croom Helm, 1975.

26 For this reason restrictions on the use of bills of exchange as liquid assets may be introduced–see below, section 9.

27 It happened in Britain in 1973, to one of the smaller banks, and the threat of a world trade recession in 1974 caused many rumours of bank failures in Europe; one bank (Herstatt) did fail.

28 See C.V. Brown, *The Nigerian Banking System*, London, Allen and Unwin, 1966, especially pp. 25–6.

29 For an account of the various ways in which bank credit was controlled in Zambia until 1972 see my article 'The Control of Credit in Zambia' *Journal of Modern African Studies*, 1973.

30 But this only works if (a) there is an overall shortage of credit and (b) if local companies are considered creditworthy by bankers. Restricting credit for foreign companies has no effect if banks are unwilling to lend to local companies or if they already have spare cash.

31 For a case study which supports this argument see my article 'The Control of Credit in Zambia', *Journal of Modern African Studies*, September 1973; the reverse argument, that monetary policy is relatively ineffective in encouraging increased bank lending at a time of slack demand in the economy is illustrated by the case of Botswana in the period 1976–79, see my article 'Botswana's monetary independence: real or imagined?' *IDS Bulletin*, September 1980.

32 In order to protect the public from the risk of a commercial bank failing and being unable to repay depositors, regulations usually insist that not more than (say) 10% of a bank's capital (the money invested by share holders originally) and reserves accumulated out of indistributed profits (money which is also owned by share holders as opposed to depositors) may be lent to any one borrower. The regulations may be more complicated, making a distinction for example between unsecured loans and loans backed by the assets of the borrower, but the idea is the same, namely to ensure that bad debts (failure of borrowers to repay the bank) cause reductions in profits or in shareholders' assets but not in the money available to depositors. Such regulations have the effect of restricting lending to very large companies in small economies, and, if the central bank has the power to allow exceptions to the rules, they ensure that lending to companies (local or foreign) big enough to have a macroeconomic impact is brought to the central bank's attention.

33 One might almost say, the greater is the certainty of corruption.

34 Achieving sectoral targets may come back to controlling individual loans if a sector is dominated by one institution, as can occur in Africa, especially in smaller economies.

35 Sometimes a government's priorities for allocating scarce foreign exchange may be unpopular: for example a government may choose to allow imports of military equipment when a more popular choice would be fertiliser or consumer goods. Channelling all foreign exchange through government hands is obviously only desirable if the government is genuinely doing its best to pursue the national interest.

36 For example the Ghana Commercial Bank in Ghana, the National Commercial Bank in Zambia, and the Commercial Bank of Malawi in Malawi.

37 For example the National Bank of Commerce in Tanzania (100% government owned) and the National Bank of Malawi (80% owned by parastatal holding companies). Both were created by merger and takeover of existing foreign-owned commercial banks.

38 For elaboration of these points see my book *Analysis of Project Finance in Developing Countries* (London, Heinemann, 1983) especially Chapters 4, 8 and 9.

39 See Appendix to this chapter, section 5, for an analysis of the impact on the money supply of a budget deficit financed by the commercial banks.

9 *Theories of Money and Monetary Policy*

1 Introduction

The last chapter stuck as closely as possible to the *mechanics* of money-creation, although in discussing the role of the central bank some policy issues inevitably appeared. Thus money is created by banks granting credit, by unfinanced government budget deficits and by balance of payments surpluses. The two last *also* create bankers' cash so that multiple expansions of the money supply may ensue. The 'natural' limitations upon multiple expansions of credit and money supply are the public's desire to increase their currency holdings and the need for banks to maintain stocks of cash and liquid assets. Furthermore, increases in payments of tax to the government (after a delay) and increases in imports (if they are not prevented) also reduce bankers' cash and thus restrain monetary expansion. The central bank can impose additional restrictions, for example by changing the official rules regarding cash and liquid asset ratios, by direct controls on bank lending, or by limiting the amount that foreign companies may borrow.

Implied in all this were some theories about the demand for money and the supply of money. The next task, therefore, is to make these theories explicit and to see whether they throw any further light on how the macroeconomy works and how governments can and ought to react.

2 The demand for money

There are three main motives for holding money. The first is called the 'transactions demand' and is partly implicit in assuming that the public's demand for currency increases with income. In fact, as national income increases, all types of money-owners increase their demand for both currency and bank deposits, the split between them being decided entirely by convenience. As it happens, historical evidence tends to show that the demand for money increases *faster* than income—as people become richer they can afford to maintain higher money balances as a proportion of their income. When people are very poor their average money balances tend to be very low in proportion to their incomes since they spend most of their income soon after receiving it.

Closely allied to the transactions demand for money is the precautionary motive for holding money. Essentially this reflects the desire to be prepared for abnormal spending. Like the transactions demand, the precautionary demand for money tends to rise with income. It can also be satisfied, however, by holdings of liquid assets and by the ability to borrow. In the rural areas of Africa the precautionary motive is partly or wholly satisfied by ownership of cattle, goats, chickens, maize stocks and the like, which provide against crop failures, visits from relatives, the need to reward work-parties, and so on. As the rural economy comes increasingly in contact with the use of money, and the supply of goods for money, there is a tendency for the precautionary motive to be satisfied by holding money rather than goods,[1] just as transactions increasingly use money rather than barter.

These general propositions tend to be borne out by the figures for African countries in the 1970s, as shown in Table 9.1. That is, the money supply has grown faster than GDP at current prices. This is true whether money is defined as currency plus demand deposits, or includes other bank deposits as well. The two main exceptions appear to be Malawi and Kenya: but in both cases, money increased faster than GDP at current prices if different years are chosen for the comparison.[2] In the case of the Gambia, for geographical reasons Senegalese money circulates widely but is not recorded officially in the Gambian money supply, which is understated therefore in the Table.

It may be that people also hold money for 'speculative' reasons. If there is a choice between money and some alternative asset, then it is logical to hold money if the value of the alternative asset is expected to fall. Equally, if alternatives to money are expected to increase in value then people should prefer to spend their 'asset' money and gain from the rise in price—always assuming that enough money is retained for other needs, that is, for transactions and precautionary purposes.

The possibility of a speculative demand for money has played an important part in macroeconomic theory as it has been developed in industrialised countries. If money is regarded as an alternative asset to government stock (and other fixed interest debt, also known as bonds) then expectations of interest rate changes will affect the demand for money. The argument depends on the fact that if interest rates *rise*, then the price of bonds in the market will fall; and if interest rates *fall*

Table 9.1 Increases in money and GDP at current prices in some African countries, 1970–80[a]

	Money supply (narrow definition)	*Money supply (wider definition)*	*GDP at current prices*
Botswana[b]	2.1	2.8	1.5
Ethiopia	3.6	3.5	1.9[c]
Gambia	3.7	4.7	4.9
Ghana[d]	7.8	7.1	4.9
Kenya	4.1	4.6	4.6
Malawi	3.0	4.1	4.7
Nigeria[e]	8.2	8.0	5.1
Sierra Leone	5.3	6.0	3.2
Tanzania	8.0	7.9	4.4
Zambia	2.7	2.6	2.1

NOTES

a Numbers are multiples. For example GDP at current prices in Kenya increased 4.6 times from 1970 to 1980.

b 1976–80, because Botswana used South African currency previously.

c Figure for GNP, not GDP.

d 1970–77.

e 1970–78.

Source: *International Financial Statistics*.

then the price of bonds in the market will rise. The details of this mechanism were explained in the first Appendix to chapter 8. Logically, therefore, people who expect interest rates to rise will sell their bonds and hold money instead; and people who expect interest rates to fall will hold less money, using it to buy bonds.[3]

This particular piece of theory is almost wholly irrelevant in African conditions; in African countries there is either no market at all in bonds, or a very minor market with a very small number of investors holding bonds, and very little trading. There can be no question, therefore, of there being a speculative demand for money of the type just decribed.

However, there is some possibility that the demand for money as an asset will be affected by rates of interest, even in African economies. A high rate of interest may induce some people to hold interest-bearing bank accounts rather than cattle or banknotes. Some people with demand deposit bank accounts, which normally pay no interest, may be induced to manage their financial affairs more carefully, so as to keep less money on demand deposit and more on an interest-bearing account. The effect of switching from banknotes or demand deposits, on the one hand, to interest-bearing deposits on the other hand, is very small. It reduces the amount of money according to the narrow-definition (normally called M_1) but makes no difference to the amount of money according to the wider definition (called M_2 or something similar, the nomenclature varying according to local practice). If banks have to keep fewer reserves against savings and time deposits than against demand deposits, as is quite common, then banks' capacity to lend is increased slightly; if banknotes are deposited in banks, their cash position and ability to lend again increases. If money is switched from demand deposits in banks or from banknotes to other savings institutions, such as building societies, then the latter's capacity to lend increases at the expense of the banks' capacity to lend, leaving total lending little changed.

None of these effects is likely to be very large: many rural people hold cattle or food stocks rather than bank deposits because the nearest bank branch is too far away to be convenient, or because food stocks are a more certain precaution against harvest failure than money (whose capacity to buy food varies with food prices). In other words, interest rates may affect the demand for money, but other factors are also relevant, and may in fact be more important.

The dependence of the demand for money on interest rates can be shown in a diagram.

The LL curve in Figure 9.1 expresses the theory that the demand for money is relatively low at high rates of interest, and relatively high at low rates of interest. The curve is usually labelled *L* for 'Liquidity preference'. The very weak influence of interest rates on the demand for money in Africa would, if correct, result in a very steeply sloping curve. Changes in income would cause the curve to shift. An increase in income, for example, would cause the *LL* curve to move to L^1L^1.

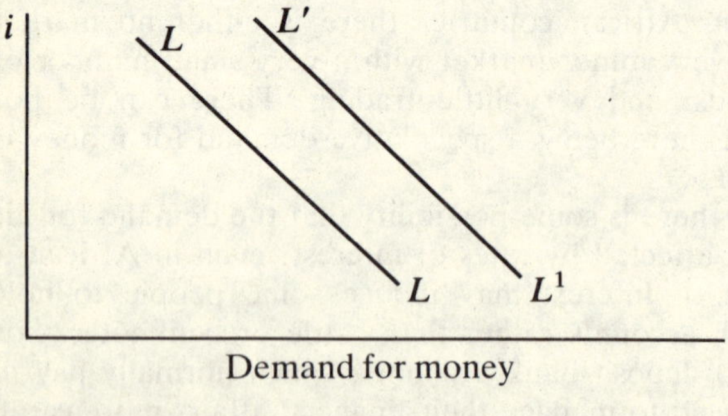

Figure 9.1 Demand for money

One of the theoretical implications of the speculative demand for money is that, in certain circumstances, increases in the supply of money may have no effect on the economy. The argument runs that if interest rates are very low, so low that everyone believes they can only go up in the future, then any addition to the money supply which has no effect on expenditure or incomes (for example, a purchase of government debt by the central bank) will be added to speculative balances rather than being spent. This sort of situation was thought to exist during prolonged economic depressions: additions to the money supply were not spent, interest rates could not be driven any lower, banks could not or would not lend money in spite of increasing excess liquidity, so monetary policy was more or less helpless to have any significant effect.

Although the speculative demand for money instead of bonds has almost no relevance in Africa, it *is* possible that in certain circumstances additions to the supply of money may have little or no impact on the level of economic activity. As expalined in the previous chapter, most of the ways in which the money supply can expand—budget deficits, increased bank lending, export surpluses—are themselves a stimulus to demand. In expansionary conditions, prices of goods are unlikely to be falling so additions to the money supply are unlikely to be added to speculative balances. If, on the other hand, the money supply increases because the central bank or the government buys an asset, at a time of depressed business conditions and falling prices, then there is a possibility that the new money will not be spent, and that banks will not want to increase their lending.

Even an export surplus may not result in increased spending. In Africa, the effect of an export price rise, as explained in chapter 6, depends on the structure of the export sector and on who actually receives the benefits. If the price of a mineral export such as copper, gold or diamonds increases, then the only beneficiaries in the short run are the mining company, or companies, and the government. If both expect prices to come down again soon, they may simply add the increased income to their reserves. Bank deposits and foreign exchange reserves rise. If the banks are unable or unwilling to increase their lending, then there is no effect on the level of economic activity.

There may also be circumstances in which governments are *unable* to spend increased income, or to increase spending more rapidly, because of a lack of matching resources such as port capacity, or skilled labour. In such circumstances money supply and foreign exchange reserves will rise even though the export price increase may *not* be thought to be temporary. A number of African economies have enjoyed such mineral export booms, for example Botswana (diamonds), Nigeria (oil) and Zambia (copper). Of course if a mineral export price boom occurs after a period of economic restraint, when all concerned have been prevented from spending by shortage of income or of foreign exchange, then the increased income will almost certainly *not* be held as unspent money balances.

A particular and rather peculiar example of the non-spending of increased money holdings occurred in Zambia in 1968 and 1969, when the copper companies were forced by new Exchange Control rules to keep half their after-tax profits in the country. Despite high copper prices, relatively little investment was taking place, probably because of uncertainties over the political future. Essentially the companies preferred not to commit themselves to more investment than they needed until they knew whether and on what terms they would be nationalised. Put another way, they preferred to hold money rather than investing in assets whose future value was highly uncertain.[4]

In contrast, price increases for agricultural exports produced by small farmers are much more likely to be spent, provided that they reach the farmer. Marketing boards in Africa have sometimes failed to pass on price increases to farmers, adding to reserves instead.

3 *The quantity theory of money*

Some of these ideas can be expressed in terms of the quantity theory of money. This theory, one of the oldest ideas in economics, is based on the 'equation of exchange':

$$MV = PT$$

where M = the average quantity of money
V = its velocity of circulation, i.e. the speed with which it gets spent on average
P = the average price of each monetary transaction
T = the number of transactions
all the symbols referring to a period of time.

The equation is in fact an *identity*, that is, it is always true with the definitions given. The quantity *theory* is that variations in M *cause* variations in P, so that V and T are assumed not to vary (or to vary in ways that cancel each other out).

In its crudest form, the quantity theory states that P varies directly with changes in M so that a 10% increase in the money supply, for example, causes prices to rise by 10%. Essentially this assumes that output (as represented by the number of transactions) is unaffected by changes in the money supply. It also assumes that the velocity of circulation of money does not change. Put differently, this last assumption is that people spend increases in their holdings of money in much the same way as before, that is, they *do not* increase (more than proportionately) their holdings of money as an asset.

An alternative version of the quantity theory is rather more flexible in its assumptions. This version is based on the equation

$$M = kP^1O$$

where M = the average quantity of money

k = the proportion of their income that people choose to hold as money

P^1 = the average price of transactions included in the measurement of national income

O = output of 'final products', i.e. those included in national income.

Changes in M can then cause changes in k (which roughly represents the speculative demand for money), in prices or in output.

It is possible for both *output* and *prices*, O and P' in the revised quantity theory equation, to rise following increases in the supply of money, M. Output will rise to the extent that unused capacity exists in the domestic economy and prices will rise where excess demand develops and imports cannot supply the difference or are prevented from doing so (for example, by import controls). But it is not necessarily correct that these changes in output and prices are *caused* by an increase in the money supply.

The main ways in which the money supply can increase are by budget deficits, increased bank lending in a situation of spare liquidity and export surpluses. All of these are themselves the result of increases in demand and spending, so that any consequent rise in output or prices can just as plausibly be put down to the increase in demand, which in turn causes *both* the increase in money *and* the increase in output, prices or both. Any *multiple* increase in the money supply that occurs because, say, a budget deficit is financed by pure money-creation, only occurs because bank customers demand credit. Bank customers do not demand credit simply because it is available but because they have unsatisfied demand which they are willing to satisfy by borrowing–and paying interest on that borrowing.

It is also possible for the money supply to increase as a result of a central bank purchase of government debt (from banks or other holders). This is not of itself an increase in demand, and it does increase the money supply. But if the seller wants cash in order to increase spending (or lending in the case of a bank) then any increase in output or prices can be attributed to demand. Similarly, a reduction in officially-required reserve ratios *permits* an increase in bank lending, but only has this result if there is excess demand for credit. It seems reasonable to say, then, that monetary policy can result in an increase in output or prices (or both) if it is in the form of taking the brakes off at a time of excess demand.

In the case of a *fall* in the money supply the sequence of events is somewhat different. The money supply can be deliberately reduced, for example by raising cash and liquidity ratios, or by sales of government debt by the central bank.[5] In these two cases the central bank is not directly affecting demand but is reducing part of the means of satisfying demand, by reducing the money supply and at the same time reducing bankers' cash. If, then, prices or output fall, one can say that it is the reduction in money supply that is the cause. If on the other hand the money supply falls because of reduced demand for bank credit, leaving the banks with excess liquidity, or because of a reduction in the export surplus, or because of a reduced budget deficit: then it is a reduction in demand which is causing a reduction in the money supply and also any fall in output or prices.

The point really is that the impact on prices and output of changes in the money supply can only usefully be analysed by looking at what caused them. It is usually unhelpful to try and explain events by looking at the money supply alone.

In the equation $M = kP'O$ only the possibility of changes in P' and O (as a result of changes in M) has so far been discussed in this section. The possibility of changes in k was discussed in the previous section: a rise in k could theoretically occur if most people expected interest rates to rise and if people regarded money as an alternative asset to bonds (whose prices would fall if interest rates rose). It is therefore theoretically possible that a rise in the money supply could be added to money holdings rather than causing an increase in prices or output, especially if the increase in money supply caused a lowering of interest rates, which in turn created expectations of a further downward moverment in interest rates.

It is also theoretically possible that the reverse could happen, namely that a fall in the money supply could be accompanied by a fall in people's desire to hold money as an asset, so that 'speculative' holdings of money would become available to meet the transactions and precautionary demand for money, leaving no impact on prices or output. As already explained in the previous section, this whole set of arguments depends on the existence of large financial markets, which do *not* exist in Africa.

There is no theoretical reason, in African conditions, to expect an increase in money of itself to cause an increase in peoples' desire to hold money, or for a decrease in the money supply to coincide with or cause a reduction in peoples' desire to hold money. Nevertheless, it is possible for an increase in the money supply to have no further impact on the economy, as was explained in section 2. So it is important to investigate a little further just what does happen to these unspent increases in money.

The holder of the increase in money will either leave it on a demand deposit account, or more likely deposit it in some fixed interest savings account, at a bank or some other financial institution. Other possibilities are buying Treasury Bills or government stock, and the holding of notes; the latter is quite likely among small businessmen, especially farmers.

If the money remains with a commercial bank, then if no additional spending is to occur, it must be assumed that the banks have no unsatisfied demand for credit. The same argument applies to other financial institutions that lend to the private sector such as building societies. If the money is lent to the government by buying government debt, for there to be no spending as a result one must assume that government spending is not affected by this additional inflow of finance. Buying of government debt may also drive down the rate of interest on that debt, or prevent it from rising.

If an increase in the money supply is held in the form of currency, it is a form of interest-free loan to the government. Suppose, for example, that a rising price for agricultural exports produced by small farmers is partly saved in the form of notes buried in boxes in the countryside. The government buys the foreign exchange from the domestic marketing board (or other intermediary). The farmer receives cash in the form of notes from the marketing board, which drew notes from its bank, which in turn obtained them from the central bank by drawing down its balance there. The government has therefore acquired foreign exchange (which it can invest in money markets overseas) in exchange for notes which it simply has printed. The commercial banks have no additional liquidity as a result of these transactions, so they cannot increase their lending. So there is no additional spending to offset the non-spending of income by the farmers, *unless* the government decides to spend.

There is thus an argument that government can or should spend to offset saving in the form of notes, since such saving is not 'matched' by spending elsewhere in the economy—as is, for example, saving in a building society which makes available money to be spent on houses. In reality, though, governments should match their spending to conditions in the economy as a whole, rather than thinking in terms of one or other type of saving. It *is* valid to argue that increases in the note issue are *not* an inflationary form of financing a budget deficit.[6]

4 The determination of interest rates: industrial economies

Where there is an active market in some form of debt, then changes in price imply changes in the interest rate of that debt. So the interest rates on Treasury Bills, or government stock, or bonds issued by large companies, where there is a large and active market in such debts, are determined by demand and supply. For example, if the government of an industrialised economy, such as Britain or the USA, is running a large budget deficit and tries to finance it by selling stock in the market, the interest rate on government stock will tend to increase. The *supply* of government stock increases, which drives down the price of such stock, which in turn implies an increase in the rate of interest. Put differently, if the government wants to persuade more people to put more of their savings into government stock, it has to offer a higher rate of interest than before.

If, in contrast, there is an increase in the number of foreigners wishing to buy government stock in one of the major industrial economies (it would be rather unlikely to occur in one of the minor ones) then this addition to demand for the stock would tend to drive up the price of the stock, which in turn implies a fall in the rate of interest.

An alternative way of expressing this is to say that the interest rate is determined by the supply of money and the demand for money. Assuming that people choose between bonds and money, an increase in the demand for bonds is the same thing as a decrease in the demand for money. So a decrease in the *demand* for money, by driving up the price of bonds, causes a fall in the 'price' of money, namely a fall in the rate of interest. Similarly, an increase in the *supply* of money, say by a purchase of bonds in the market by the central bank, causes a fall in the interest rate by driving up the price of bonds. So the market determination of interest rates can be thought of in terms of demand and supply, as for other commodities. The *mechanism* by which this takes place is the price of fixed interest bonds in a market.

The conventional way of demonstrating this in a diagram is shown opposite in Figure 9.2. In that diagram, the supply of money is assumed to be fixed by the monetary authorities, initially at M_o. The demand for money is represented by *LL* (*L* stands for liquidity preference). It slopes downwards from left to right because

(a) as interest rates rise, people try to economise on holding money, which carries no interest,

(b) as interest rates rise, bond prices fall and increasing numbers of people believe that stock prices will rise in future, buy bonds, and so reduce their demand for money.

If, for example, the central bank increases the money supply by buying bonds in the market (open market operations), increasing the supply

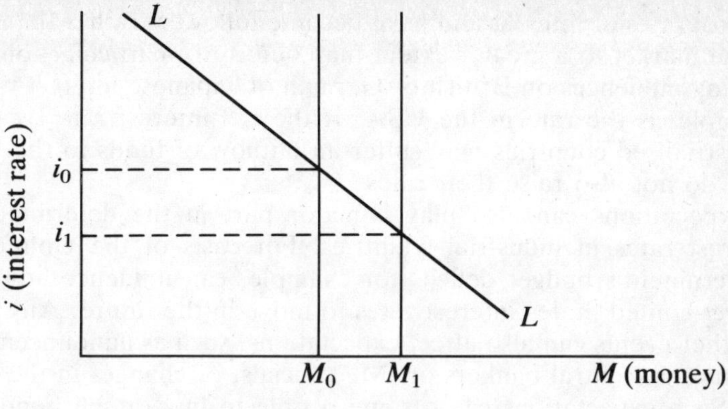

Figure 9.2 Market determination of interest rate

of money from M_o to M_1, this will drive down the rate of interest from i_o to i_1, as shown in Figure 9.2.

Even in industrial economies, interest rates are not determined entirely by market forces. Governments, usually through their central banks, intervene in the financial markets, and may thereby have a major influence on the price of their own debt, and therefore on interest rates. However, purchases and sales by the central bank also have a direct influence on the supply of money, both directly and by affecting bank liquidity. So a central bank which wishes to prevent the rate of interest from *rising*, for example, by buying stock and so preventing stock prices from *falling*, can only do so by increasing the money supply and bank liquidity. In other words, a central bank, operating in the market, cannot normally control both interest rates and the money supply.

It is possible, although much disputed, that a central bank can control, or perhaps influence, market interest rates simply by announcing a change in its own lending rate (variously called Bank Rate, Minimum Lending Rate, Central Bank Discount Rate and many other names). Such an announcement is effective in moving market interest rates in the same direction if participants in the market *believe* that the central bank can enforce its will. If market participants do *not* believe that the central bank's announcement can be enforced, then it will have little or no effect.

With the gradual integration of international financial markets, and especially with the abolition of exchange controls in the major industrial countries, so that money can flow freely from one major financial market to another, central banks have lost much of their power to control rates of interest and have become followers rather than leaders of the market to a greater extent than before. In particular, one of the leading influences on British or German or Japanese interest rates, for example, is the rate in the USA. If the US interest rate rises, other industrialised countries may suffer an outflow of funds to the USA, if they do not also raise their rates.

Expectations can also play a major part in the determination of interest rates in industrial countries. Forecasts of the United States Government's budget deficit, for example, can influence how people *expect* United States interest rates to move in the future. Any number of other events can also affect expectations, such as announcements by politicians, central bankers or IMF officials, or changes in the price of oil. Such expectations cause some people to buy or sell bonds in the market, which in turn causes changes in rates of interest. Expectations can be wrong, however, since they are only one factor acting on market-determined interest rates.

5 *Impact of industrial country interest rates on African economies*

Interest rates in the major industrial economies are also of considerable importance to African countries. African countries hold most of their foreign exchange reserves in the major currencies, borrow extensively from abroad in foreign currencies, and must at times take account of the influence of foreign interest rates on their domestic interest rates.

In deciding on how to invest the foreign exchange reserves, African central bank officials have to take account of what interest can be earned on different currencies, and also of expected future changes in interest rates. If the interest rate on US dollars is expected to rise, for example, foreign exchange reserves should be in short-term investments, to enable them to be reinvested at a higher rate in the future and to avoid losses on longer-dated marketable investments.

In addition, a rise in US interest rates may cause a change in the value of the US dollar. These problems are relatively new ones. Before and for some years after independence, African countries kept most of their reserves in the currency of the former colonial power. French-speaking African countries still invest most of their foreign exchange reserves in French francs; but the anglophone countries have diversified their investments precisely because of the greatly increased uncertainties of exchange rate movements, and the great risk of having a large proportion of the foreign exchange reserves in any one currency.

African countries also borrow extensively from abroad. These loans are nearly all denominated in the currency of the lender or in some other foreign currency or mixture of foreign currencies. Interest rates payable vary from being highly subsidised, and fixed for the life of the loan, to being at market-determined levels and variable. Variable interest rate loans require the borrower to decide whether the risk of a higher rate of interest can be safely undertaken. With fixed interest rate loans, a different interest rate is only payable when *new* loans are negotiated.

In particular, African countries have borrowed increasingly from international banks in the 'euro-currency markets', mainly in US dollars, but also in other currencies and the SDR.[7] As deposit rates change, so does the cost of these loans, since international banks borrow from short-term depositors (including African central banks), in order to on-lend to international borrowers (including African governments and parastatals). Each time the deposits have to be renewed at a different rate of interest, the banks change the rate of interest being paid on the loan.[8]

There is one possible reverse influence on international interest rates, from the borrowing of developing countries themselves. By the early 1980s, some developing countries had borrowed so much from the international banks that their growing inability to repay, or even to meet interest payments, threatened the whole international banking system. Most of the biggest borrowers were in Latin America, led by Mexico and Brazil. But there was a fear that other borrowers, including those in Africa, might default as well. This may have restrained American, and other industrial country governments, from raising their interest rates, because of the additional strain this would put on developing country borrowers, which in turn would increase the danger of a world banking crisis.

The impact of international interest rates on domestic rates of interest within African economies is discussed below, in section 6.

6 *The determination of interest rates: African economies*

In contrast with the situation in industrial economies, domestic market forces have very little influence on interest rates in African economies. Government decisions mainly decide the level of interest rates, directly by means of the rates charged by government on its own lending and on lending by official institutions, and indirectly through government influence on commercial bank and other private sector interest rates. Other, less important, factors are interest rates in other countries and decisions made within financial institutions.

A lot of lending is done directly by African governments themselves. This is true both of governments pursuing a socialist development path and of governments which rely more on the price mechanism. For example, the Botswana government had lent an estimated P148 million in March 1983, up from P115 million a year earlier. Commercial bank lending in Botswana was P149 million in March 1983, up from P143 million a year earlier.[9] Several things are important about these figures: firstly, Botswana government lending was as large as commercial bank lending; secondly, government lending can, and does sometimes, increase by a larger amount than commercial bank lending over a period of time; thirdly, the interest rate at which the government lends is both lower and less volatile than commercial bank lending rates. Interest rates in Botswana, then, depend as much on what is decided by the Botswana government on the cost of its own lending, as on commercial bank lending rates and whether or not the government controls them.

The structure of lending in each African country is different, but the importance of government lending, or of lending by wholly-owned government institutions such as development banks and marketing boards, is fairly widespread. For example, in Malawi a lot of lending was undertaken in the 1970s by ADMARC, the official agricultural marketing board, out of surpluses generated by paying below export parity prices to farmers.[10] In Ghana, the Cocoa Marketing Board made large surpluses in the 1950s and early 1960s, and on-lent the money to the government for development purposes. This also occurred in Nigeria, at the same period.[11] To the extent that the government itself then lent the money, the government was itself acting as a financial intermediary; that is, it was borrowing money to lend to others. Again, this has become an increasingly common practice in Africa, and in other developing countries.

Not only do governments control the interest rate on their own lending directly, they do *not* always change the rate when other rates change. The same is also true of many parastatal financial institutions. Governments, and many parastatal lenders, do not have to compete in the market for deposits, and so are able to maintain their lending rates when commercial bank rates go up; and do not necessarily lower their lending rates when other rates fall. In addition, some deposit rates do not change when other deposit rates change: for example, Post Office Savings Bank deposit rates for savers tend to be more stable than other rates, presumably because people who save with the Post Office are either less sophisticated than other savers and so do not move their savings in search of higher rates, or are unable to switch because they have access to the Post Office but not to a bank. Many small towns in Africa have a Post Ofice but not a bank. These points are demonstrated for Botswana in Table 9.2.

Table 9.2 Changes in selected interest rates: Botswana 1976–83

End of	*1976*	*1977*	*1978*	*1979/80*	*July 1981*	*Dec. 1981*	*Feb. 1982*	*May 1982*	*Feb. 1983*
Cost of borrowing									
Commercial banks' prime lending rate[a]	11.5	11.0	10.0	9.0	10.5	11.0	13.0	14.5	13.0
Government's lending rate	10.0	8.0	8.0	8.0/6.0	8.0	8.0	8.0	10.0	10.0
Yield on savings									
Commercial banks': 3 months deposit	7.5	7.0	6.0	5.0	8.0	9.0	11.0	12.5	11.0
Building society: shares[b]	7.5	7.5	6.5	6.0	6.0	6.0	8.0	8.0	8.0
Post Office Savings Bank	3.5	2.5	2.5	2.0	2.0	2.0	2.0	2.0	2.0

NOTES:

a Prime lending rate is the rate charged to the banks' most creditworthy customers; other borrowers pay an agreed margin above prime.

b The rate shown is for 'subscription shares' which, together with 'indefinite period paid-up shares' whose interest rate moved roughly in parallel for most of the period, accounted for about two-thirds of Building Society liabilities.

Source: Bank of Botswana, *Annual Report*, 1982.

As can be seen from Table 9.2, the Botswana government only changed its lending rate twice during a period when commercial banks' prime lending rate changed eight times. Similarly the Building society changed its deposit rate only three times and the Post Office Savings Bank only twice, while commercial bank deposit rates were changed eight times. The rates charged on loans by Botswana's National Development Bank are just as stable as those on the Government's own lending.

What, then, determines the rates at which African governments and government-owned financial institutions lend money? Clearly these rates are more stable than commercial rates, Botswana being fairly typical. No doubt this stability occurs simply because public officials do not *have* to change interest rates just because commercial rates have changed, and so prefer to avoid controversy by doing nothing. It is also clear, however, that official lending rates tend to be *below* commercial rates. The arguments for lending at sub-commercial rates are usually as follows.

(a) Parastatals and other main recipients of official credit are performing some sort of social service; this would apply to local authorities or housing corporations.

(b) Small-scale farmers, small-scale urban businessmen and other private-sector recipients of official credit should be favoured because they are a dynamic element in national development. Indeed, the argument runs, there is little point in supplying official credit, in order to encourage development, if that credit is then made expensive.

(c) Governments and national development banks are often the recipients of subsidised credit, for example loans from foreign aid donors. It is thought wrong, particularly by the final borrowers, if that cheap finance is on-lent at high commercial interest rates, providing the government or the development bank with a windfall profit.

The counter-arguments include the following.

(a) Many parastatal borrowers supply services mainly or exclusively to the higher income groups, for example, electricity and water corporations, because the poor do not have access to electricity and piped water.

(b) Making capital cheap is the wrong way to subsidise development activity, because it encourages capital-intensive methods of production. If capital is scarce, then borrowers should pay its full opportunity cost, and be subsidised if at all, by some other method.

(c) Providing cheap loans is a form of subsidy which escapes the scrutiny applied to other subsidies which have to be paid for out of the budget, and is therefore a weakness in the control of public expenditure.

Generally speaking the arguments for public sector lending at sub-commercial rates of interest nearly always prevail.

Governments in Africa also have a major influence on interest rates in non-government financial institutions. Changes in the central bank lending rate (Bank Rate) tend to be followed by changes in commercial banks' rates; or else the central bank simply 'requests' the banks to change their rates. The official request or signal is followed because of the powers of central banks: they can reduce commercial bank profits by requiring additional liquidity at low yield, or by lowering the yield on Treasury Bills; and behind every central bank request is the implied threat of nationalisation or non-renewal of a banking licence. Where there are financial markets, central banks can intervene to achieve their objective. In some countries, the authorities have legal powers to dictate interest rates, and could always pass new legislation if necessary. In short, commercial banks usually change their interest rates as required, because in the end it is in their interests to do what the authorities want them to do. In the situation where financial institutions are foreign-owned, they may be especially anxious to oblige the authorities, to avoid nationalisation or restrictions on the remission abroad of their profits.

As was mentioned in the notes to Table 9.2, not all commercial bank customers are able to borrow at the banks' prime lending rate. Less creditworthy customers, or those whose loans are more expensive to administer (for example, because they are small, or the borrower is in a remote area), pay a margin above prime. Generally speaking, such rates vary with prime, so that a borrower paying 14% when prime is 12%, will have to pay 15% if prime rises to 13%. However, it is often the case that the margin above prime varies according to market conditions. For example, when the banks can easily lend up to their legal limits, they are able to charge higher margins above prime to customers who would get better treatment when banks have spare cash and are actively seeking additional business. So the actual interest paid by borrowers from commercial banks tends to be a mixture of administrative decisions made within the banks, and financial market conditions.

There is also, in certain conditions, some influence from foreign rates of interest on rates within African economies. Some borrowers have a choice of where to borrow, and some holders of liquid assets have a choice of where to invest.

Before the introduction of exchange controls in most African countries, some individuals and some companies deposited spare cash abroad. This was partly because it appeared safer or more convenient for the finance of foreign transactions, and partly because they obtained higher rates of interest abroad. In a few African countries—Liberia, Swaziland and Lesotho—it is still perfectly legal to transfer money abroad, so that local interest rates must be kept at or above the level of the competing foreign ones, to prevent an outflow of funds.

Of rather wider importance is the choice of where to borrow. Larger companies, and especially foreign-owned ones, can often choose whether to seek foreign or local finance. Other factors may also be important. As was explained in chapter 7, foreign companies may choose to borrow locally in order to avoid committing their own funds; or they may borrow from affiliated companies abroad as a way of transferring profits out of the host country. Such decisions are also affected by the *availability* of funds: some very large companies, for example mining companies, may have to borrow abroad because local finance is not available in large enough amounts.

Relative interest rates also have an impact on how foreign trade is financed. Importers, for example, can often choose whether to borrow from a local bank or to seek credit from their suppliers. The cost of such trade credit may not always be expressed in the form of a rate of interest but in the form of a discount for early payment, or simply in the prices charged for goods supplied. Nevertheless the supplier must somehow finance the credit given when cash is not paid with an order, and the cost of that finance is usually passed on in one way or another to the buyer. If foreign credit is more expensive than local borrowing, importers may choose to borrow locally and pay earlier for imports, in order to avoid the higher cost of foreign credit. This increase in the demand for local credit may drive up its cost, as banks find that increased competition for loans enables them to charge more. More probably, in African conditions, the authorities will raise local interest rates (or put limits on local credit creation) in order to protect the foreign exchange reserves. An importer who chooses to borrow $100 worth of local currency in order to pay for imports three months earlier than was his or her custom previously, has to buy that foreign exchange out of the foreign exchange reserves. So long as the importer continues to borrow locally, the foreign exchange reserves continue to be lower than they would otherwise be. Put differently, there has been a short-term capital outflow as the importer borrows locally to repay short-term foreign credit.

The influence of foreign rates of interest is less to the extent that exchange controls reduce the ability of borrowers to make a choice. When the balance of payments problem is very severe, as in many African economies in the 1970s and 1980s, importers cease to have any choice as to when to pay for imports, and exporters are forced to sell all earnings of foreign exchange as soon as they are received. In extreme cases, importers have not been *allowed* to pay for imports for long periods: for example, Zambia built up arrears of import payments of more than two years, starting in 1975.[12] In such circumstances, relative interest rates are irrelevant. On the other hand, countries with relatively comfortable balance of payments positions do not have to close off their financial systems from the rest of the world, so that relative interest rates continue to have an influence.

Interest rate differentials are not the only consideration, even for borrowers concerned only about the cost of borrowing. The risks of exchange rate changes have also to be taken into account. If a company borrows in US dollars, say, to finance production for local markets in an African country, a local devaluation would increase the cost of repayment, in terms of local currency. The company might therefore prefer to borrow locally to avoid that risk. The risk is much less for short-term borrowing, mainly to finance foreign trade; so relative interest rates are more likely to influence short-term capital flows than long-term ones, where the exchange rate risk exists.

In summary, it seems as though interest rates in Africa are mainly determined by the government and its central bank, with minor influence from market forces where debt is marketable and some discretion in the hands of institutional lenders; at the same time the authorities must pay some attention to interest rates overseas if their controls over foreign transactions are not very complete or not very effective.

7 *Money, interest rates and national income: the IS-LM Model*

The standard macroeconomic theory, as developed and taught in industrial countries is based on the following assumptions:

(a) The money supply is assumed to be controlled by the monetary authorities; so it is fixed until they decide to change it.

(b) The demand for money depends positively on income (the transactions and precautionary motives) and negatively on interest rates (the higher the interest rate the lower the demand for money because people economise on the use of money when interest rates are high, and because at high rates of interest people buy bonds in the expectation that interest rates will fall, causing bond prices to rise and yielding a speculative capital gain).

(c) Investment depends on the rate of interest, so that as interest rates fall more investment takes place because the comparison between the rate of return on marginal investments and the cost of borrowing money becomes favourable.

(d) Savings depend on income.

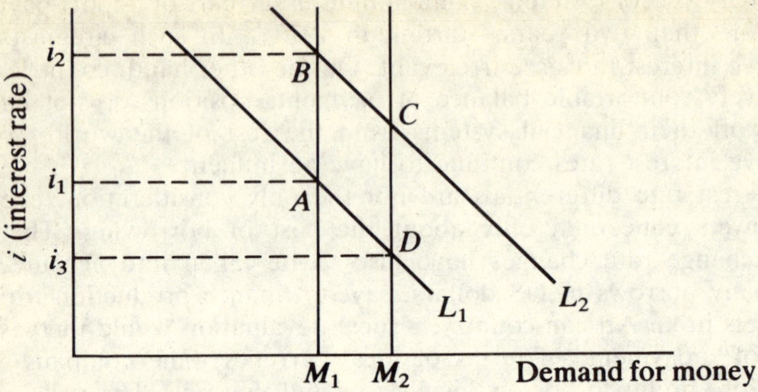

Figure 9.3 Income and interest rates

These assumptions can be shown in a series of diagrams.

In Figure 9.3, equilibrium occurs when the supply of money, M_1, equals the demand for money, L_1, shown as varying inversely with the rate of interest. Equilibrium is therefore at A. If income increases, L_1 shifts to L_2, because at any particular rate of interest, people demand more money. If the money supply remains fixed at M_1, then the new equilibrium will be at *B* and the interest rate rises from i_1 to i_2. If the supply of money increases and income remains the same, the new equilibrium will be at *D*, and the interest rate will fall from i_1 to i_3. It can be seen therefore that with a given amount of money M_1, there are a set of equilibrium points where the demand for money equals the supply of money, such that the higher the level of income, the higher the equilibrium rate of interest. This can be shown as in Figure 9.4.

The *LM* curves in Figure 9.4 show a series of points of equilibrium in the money markets, with a positive relationship between income and the rate of interest. With money supply equal to M_1, the curve is at LM_1. If money supply increases to M_2, the curve shifts to the right at LM_2, because at any particular level of income, Y_1, the equilibrium interest rate will be lower at i_2 rather than i_1. This can be derived from Figure 9.3, where at the level of income represented by L_1, equilibrium occurs at *D* instead of *A*, at a lower rate of interest.

In Figure 9.5, investment is shown as increasing as the interest rate falls. And savings are shown as increasing as income increases.

At equilibrium, investment must equal saving, so investment and saving are shown together on the horizontal axis. At interest rate i_1, investment I_1, equals saving, S_1, which must occur at a level of income Y_1. If the interest rate falls to i_2, investment rises to I_2, saving must be

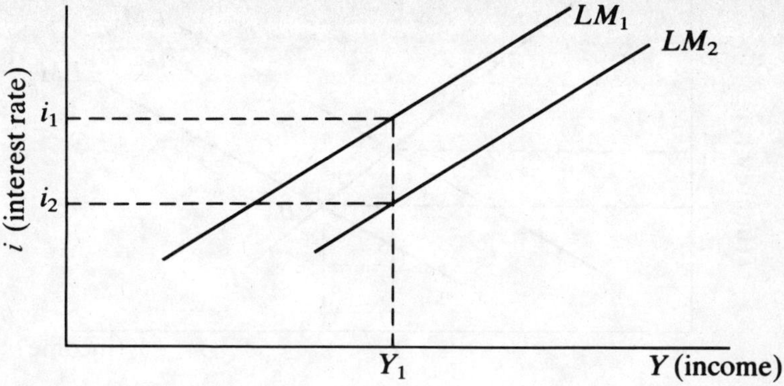

Figure 9.4 LM curves

higher at S_2, and income must be higher at Y_2. So a low interest rate occurs at a high level of income and vice versa. This can be expressed as in Figure 9.6, where the *IS* curve represents all the equilibrium points in the market for goods, at different levels of the interest rate and of income. This *IS* curve is superimposed on Figure 9.4, so that a simultaneous equilibrium in money and goods markets occurs where *LM* and *IS* curves meet.

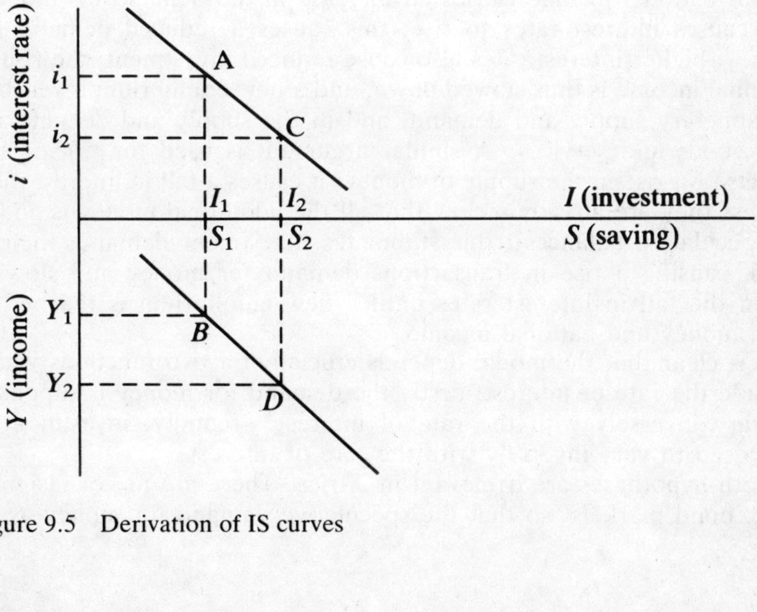

Figure 9.5 Derivation of IS curves

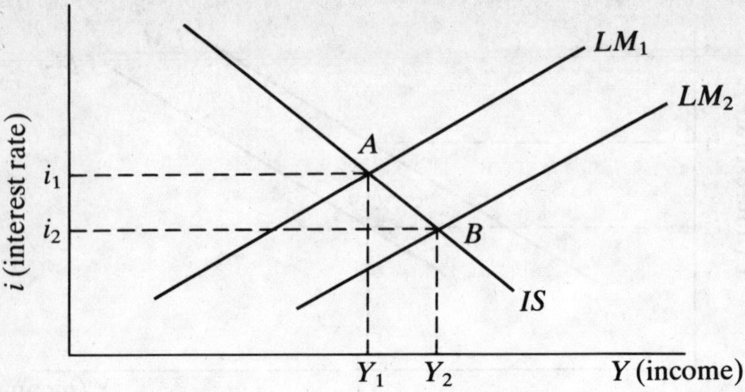

Figure 9.6 IS and LM curves

The *LM* curve is sometimes shown as having a horizontal position to the left, representing the point where additions to the supply of money are all added to speculative balances, because bond prices are so high that everybody expects them to come down in the future, and so prefers to hold money instead of bonds.

Interest rates play a key role in this macroeconomic theory, as it has been developed in industrialised countries. In particular the link between monetary theory and national income analysis depends very heavily on the part played by interest rates. The argument runs thus: a rise in national income causes an increase in the demand for money; this causes interest rates to rise; this causes a reduced demand for money; higher interest rates also cause reduced investment; the rise in national income is thus slowed down, and a new equilibrium is reached in monetary supply and demand, and in the supply and demand for real goods and services. A similar argument is used for tracing the effects of a rise in the supply of money: it causes a fall in interest rates (unless they are already so low that all the additional money is added to speculative balances); this stimulates investment demand; income rises, causing a rise in transactions demand for money and slowing down the fall in interest rates until a new equilibrium is reached in both money and national income.

It is clear that the model depends crucially on two functions which include the rate of interest: firstly the demand for money is supposed to vary inversely with the rate of interest; secondly, investment is supposed to vary inversely with the rate of interest.

Both hypotheses are irrelevant in Africa. There are no, or insignificant, bond markets, so that the speculative demand for money as an alternative asset to bonds, and dependent on the rate of interest, can be ignored. To the extent that people economise on money balances which earn no interest, when interest rates are high, they merely hold interest-bearing bank deposits instead. This has negligible effects on the banks, as has been argued earlier in this chapter.

The whole of chapter 7 was devoted to arguing that investment in Africa depends very little, if at all, on local rates of interest. Most investment takes place for reasons other than the cost of local finance: because of the discovery of a profitable mineral, or the granting of protection to a manufacturer, or the availability of foreign or local funds. It is even possible that a rise in the local rate of interest might cause some companies to borrow abroad, releasing funds for local borrowers, to whom it would be more profitable to lend at higher rates of interest. This would imply that investment might *increase* at higher rates of interest. It is unlikely to happen in practice, though, because higher interest rates are usually associated with a credit squeeze, aimed at reducing the level of lending. The evidence available suggests that there is no discernible connection between local interest rates and investment, either way.

There is a further weakness in the *IS-LM* model in an African context. The model assumes that money supply is controlled by the central bank, presumably through buying and selling in the bond market. Whatever the usefulness of this assumption in industrial economies, even as a first approximation, it is extremely unrealistic in Africa. The money supply in African economies changes mainly as a result of government deficits, export price changes and external capital flows. Central banks have very limited weapons for offsetting these movements. Certainly there can be no question of using open-market operations to offset unwanted money supply changes. Central banks do have powers to offset changes in bank liquidity–by changing liquidity ratios or special deposit requirements–but these powers tend only to be used occasionally. They are very much less flexible than the capacity to operate on a large scale in financial markets.

It would seem, therefore, that the *IS-LM* model cannot be used in African conditions. Some alternative ways of analysing the effect of changes in the supply of money, in African conditions, are discussed in the next section.

8 Money and national income determination in Africa

Although models depending on a key role for interest rates seem inapplicable to African conditions, the working of the monetary system does have some influence on changes in national income. Most of the points have already been made: this section will bring them all together.

Consider a change in income which is stimulated by something which does not *of itself* alter the money supply or bank liquidity. For example, national income might be increased by an upsurge in business confidence, causing in turn an increase in investment demand. If spending takes place and is financed by local sources (as opposed to an inflow of foreign finance, which would increase bankers' cash) then income will increase, with the usual multiplier effects. As income increases, so will the public's holdings of currency, reducing bankers' cash. Banks will face an increased demand for credit as income grows. In addition, increasing imports and tax receipts will further reduce bankers' cash, although after some delay. The banks will thus have an increasing *need* for liquid assets, while at the same time having a diminishing supply of cash to satisfy that need. If the banks do not have enough spare cash they will be unable to satisfy the increasing demand for bank credit.

Putting this slightly differently, increasing income will increase the demand for money. If the supply of money is not able to increase then the expansion will be slowed down—*not* because of a rise in interest rates and the supposed effect on the demand for money and investment demand, but because of the commercial banks' inability to expand credit (and therefore the money supply) if they do not have enough cash. If the banks *do* have enough cash, the expansion can continue unhindered, if the banks are willing to lend to those who need credit.

The reverse situation does not produce a symmetrical argument. If national income is reduced by a falling-away of investment demand, this reduces the demand for money, the banks have spare cash and thus have the financial strength to increase their lending. This is added to after a time by reduced demand for imports and reduced tax receipts. But in a situation of falling demand and income, there are unlikely to be many borrowers wanting to take advantage of spare bank liquidity; and there is a strong possibility that the banks, far from wanting to increase their lending, will want to reduce it even further because of fears about their customers' ability to repay. It is possible therefore that the monetary factor will *reinforce* the fall in income rather than offset it, as in the case of an increase.

It is possible, however, that if investment demand simply increases rather less fast in a situation of continuing expansion, then some bank lending capacity will be released to borrowers who were previously unable to get credit. The monetary factor would in these circumstances be an offset to the reduction in demand. Both arguments depend, as always, on the banks having no spare cash—when they have plenty of spare cash they can lend as they want, regardless of changes in their cash position.

Now consider a change in national income stimulated by something which of itself *does* change the money supply and bank liquidity—for example an unfinanced increase in goverment spending or an increase in investment financed from abroad. In this case the demand for money will increase with national income, but the banks' ability to increase the supply of credit (and therefore the money supply) will also have been increased. If the demand for money created by rising national income increases faster than credit can be supplied, then the monetary factor will slow the increase down a little; if the demand for money increases more slowly than credit can be increased then the monetary factor makes no difference.

In the reverse situation, for example where a reduction in government spending is not matched by a reduction in taxation, bankers' cash will be reduced, thus forcing the banks to slow down their lending if they have no spare cash. At the same time falling demand will reduce the demand for credit. If the banks are forced into reducing their lending faster than the demand for it is falling, it may reinforce the fall in income. In this case the monetary factor *reinforces* falling demand; otherwise the monetary factor makes no difference.

Although other possible variations could be explored, the essential point should be clear by now. The *availability* of finance is an important factor, even if its cost is not. It is also important to remember that the banks are not always *willing* to lend, even when they have spare liquidity and there is unsatisfied demand for credit; if the potential borrowers do not normally have access to bank credit, or are considered uncreditworthy because of general business conditions, or want long-term credit when only short-term credit is available, then a potential rise in income may be frustrated even though it looks as though the monetary factor should be no obstacle.

The above analysis assumes no reaction from the authorities; it is of course always possible that the authorities will intervene to prevent an expansion being slowed down by a lack of bank liquidity.

The monetary constraint on expansion is also less likely to operate if domestic borrowers can get foreign finance when domestic finance is scarce. If, on the other hand, foreign finance is not obtainable, perhaps because of exchange control regulations or an unwillingness by foreign lenders to supply credit, then shortage of domestic finance will more rapidly slow down an expansion. In practice, countries can usually get some additional credit from suppliers, by delaying payment. So a country tends to find it *gradually* more difficult to get foreign credit, rather than being cut off suddenly. The effect is the same, but only after a time-lag.

9 An alternative monetary model (The Polak Model)

An alternative model has been suggested for explaining the impact on African and other developing economies of changes in the money supply.[13] The model assumes that k, the demand for money *as an asset* in the quantity theory (section 3 above) is constant. So the demand for money (MO) is a function of income (Y) and is given by

$$MO = kY \qquad (1)$$

Imports (M) are a function of income, roughly as in chapter 6

$$M = mY \qquad (2)$$

where m is the marginal propensity to import. Changes in the money supply come from changes in the foreign exchange reserves (ΔFR) and from domestic credit expansion (DCE). Domestic credit expansion comes from increases in commercial bank lending to the public, and from increases in commercial bank and central bank lending to the government.

$$\Delta MO = \Delta FR + DCE \qquad (3)$$

Changes in foreign exchange reserves come from the difference between exports (X) and imports, and from any capital inflows (F). It is possible of course for F to be negative.

$$FR = X - M + F \qquad (4)$$

Finally, income is the sum of expenditures, as in the model developed in chapters 3, 4 and 5. In this model, however, consumption and investment are lumped together as domestic 'absorption' (A).

$$Y = A + X - M \qquad (5)$$

This model of the economy has a number of implications. The equilibrium level of income[14] is

$$Y = \frac{X + F + DCE}{m}$$

This equation says that income is dependent only on exports, capital inflows and credit, with the only leakage being by means of imports. The demand for money as an asset (k) does not feature because at equilibrium the demand for money is also at equilibrium.

The balance of payments, represented by changes in foreign exchange reserves (ΔFR)is defined as

$$\Delta FR = \Delta MO - DCE$$

Since ΔMO tends to zero as income approaches equilibrium, the balance of payments is mainly determined by changes in credit granted to the private sector and the government by the banking system. Since this model underlies the way that the International Monetary Fund looks at African and other underdeveloped economies, it is possible to see why such great emphasis is placed by the IMF on control of domestic credit creation–not just bank lending to the private sector, but finance of a budget deficit by the banking system. Since it is usually very difficult, in an African country, to finance an increasing budget deficit *other than* by borrowing from the banking system, control of domestic credit expansion (*DCE*) requires not just tough credit policies, but reduced budget deficits. In turn, the bulk of African tax revenue comes from exports and imports. In a balance of payments crisis, by definition exports are decreasing, or imports must be restrained, or both; the budget deficit can therefore only be reduced by cutting back on government spending. And indeed many IMF programmes, which must be agreed to as a condition for receiving an IMF loan, require cutbacks in government spending as part of the need to cut back on bank credit.

The advantage of the Polak model is that it uses variables which are usually very up to date: the money supply, bank lending (including central bank lending), exports and imports. And the policy implications of the model concern variables which the government can in principle, control to some degree.

However, it was argued in chapter 5 that government expenditure is not *in practice* at all easy to control, and it is often difficult for governments in Africa to increase tax revenues (especially in the short term). So budget deficits are in practice difficult to reduce, and financing a budget deficit by selling additional debt to the non-bank public is also difficult, in a situation of limited or non-existent financial markets. Governments, through their central banks, do have some control over commercial bank lending to the *private* sector, but that is only one part of domestic credit expansion. There is always a danger, therefore, that the impact of an attempted cutback in *DCE* will fall heavily on the private sector's main source of credit. Both public and private sector *may* be able to avoid some of the reduction in their economic activity by borrowing abroad (an increase in *F* in the model).

The disadvantage of the model is that it leaves out the choice between consumption and saving, the marginal propensity for income to be acquired by government through taxation, and the reasons why investment takes place. It does not attempt to look at what happens as money circulates *within* the economy, as does the Keynesian circular flow of income model of chapter 6. One way of comparing the two models would be to note that the Polak model assumes that any new money creation or new inflow of money from abroad flows straight out again, with the exception of any small increase in people's willingness to hold money as income increases. The Keynesian model, in contrast, examines the circular flow of income within the economy, while allowing for the leakage abroad through the marginal propensity to import.

10 Monetary policy

So far it has mostly been assumed that the central bank takes no positive action, but merely allows events to take their natural course. 'Monetary policy' is a general term for central bank action to affect monetary variables, of which no action at all (a 'neutral' policy) is only one example. Most of the possible forms of central bank action have already been discussed: the following is again a summary.

If the central bank does not want to see excess liquidity used for additional lending, it can

(a) increase the official reserve ratios, cash or liquid assets or both;
(b) alter the definition of liquid assets in such a way that some assets previously counted as liquid can no longer be included in the official ratio;
(c) require 'special deposits' from the banks, that is, require them to deposit a certain sum, or percentage of liabilities, at the central bank, such special deposits *not* to be counted as liquid;
(d) require deposits at the central bank from other institutions–this has the same effect as (c) since the deposits have to be switched from commercial banks to the central bank;
(e) move government balances from commercial banks to the central bank–obviously only possible when the government has such balances, which is rare but does sometimes happen;[15]
(f) force government debt onto non-bank holders, or onto bank holders provided that it does not then count as liquid assets;
(g) impose direct controls, for example aggregate or sectoral ceilings on lending.

If the commercial banks do not have enough liquidity to meet the demand for credit, then the central bank, if it does not wish expansion to be slowed down, can

(a) lend money to the banks
(b) lend money to non-bank institutions
(c) buy assets from the commercial banks (assuming the banks' problem is lack of cash and not lack of marketable assets)
(d) encourage the private sector, bank or non-bank, to borrow abroad (or borrow abroad on their behalf)
(e) release special deposits or move the deposits of non-bank

depositors or governments (if there are any) from the central bank to the commercial banks
(f) reduce cash reserve and liquid assets requirements
(g) remove direct controls.

In an economy with an active market in government debt the central bank can enter the market as a seller in order to reduce bank liquidity, but at the risk of lowering the price of stock and thus raising interest rates, or enter the market as a buyer in order to increase bank liquidity, but at the risk of increasing prices and reducing interest rates. The point is that in order to sell or buy significant amounts the central bank may have to influence prices by enough to encourage buyers or sellers to come forward. More often in practice the central bank finds itself buying and selling stock in order to maintain an orderly market, when nobody else will do so–regardless of the needs of monetary policy. In economies like those in Africa with very inactive markets, the central bank is very seldom in a position to pursue monetary policy by open-market operations; it simply has to act as residual buyer and seller and use other methods (of which there are plenty) to achieve the objectives of monetary policy.

So far only central bank reactions to an existing situation have been discussed. It is also possible to 'remove the brakes' in a situation of excess demand for credit; but where there is no demand for credit or the banks already have spare liquidity, purely monetary action will not succeed in expanding the economy. Similarly, action to reduce liquidity will succeed in restraining demand if the banks have no spare liquidity and there is excess demand for credit. Altering interest rates probably has little direct effect on investment demand or the demand for money, but it may influence where depositors choose to invest their spare cash and where borrowers choose to borrow. Thus a rise in interest rates should in theory cause an inflow of cash from abroad and a reduction in local borrowing in favour of foreign borrowing. So many other factors are at work, however, especially fears of exchange controls and devaluation, that interest rates are unlikely to be a major factor in this sort of way, in most African economies. In those economies in which exchange controls are still relatively liberal, interest rates do have some effect on capital flows, especially on where companies choose to borrow.

Interest rates also affect the distribution of credit within the economy. For example, suppose a government decides to impose a credit squeeze. As a result, not every potential borrower will be able to get credit. In these circumstances, large borrowers, including large foreign-owned companies, will tend to be favoured by the banks, both because large borrowers tend to have better security and so to appear less risky, and because large loans are less expensive to administer per unit of currency borrowed. In addition, with relatively low interest rates on domestic loans, large borrowers will prefer to borrow locally, even though they are in the best position to borrow abroad. So a credit squeeze with unchanged interest rates may well achieve its objective, namely a reduction in local borrowing and an inflow of capital from abroad to the extent that firms borrow abroad instead.[16] But a likely side-effect is that small-scale, local borrowers tend to be squeezed out much more than other borrowers, if interest rates are not increased. This is a difficult argument to put across to the public, since at first sight higher interest rates seem unlikely to favour the interests of small-scale borrowers; but the latter will gain nothing from low interest rates if they are unable to borrow at all.[17]

It remains to compare monetary policy with other ways of controlling demand. In a situation of excess demand, which is when monetary policy can most often be effective, there is a danger of cutting off finance to industry for increases in working capital, and thus preventing increases in output that could take place very quickly. Clearly, if large amounts of money have been spent on the fixed capital for a new factory or mine or railway, it would be very damaging to starve the new enterprise of finance for working capital. Spending on fixed capital creates demand with no matching supply so that there is a particular need to avoid any delay in the start of production.

On the other hand, monetary policy does not demand the large numbers of skilled administrators required by a new tax, nor is it as politically unpopular as a tax increase or a cut in government spending. Monetary and fiscal policy both cause distortions and disincentives, although of different kinds.

So the choice between monetary and fiscal weapons is a matter of judgement. Normally they must be used together. Certainly it makes no sense to have the budget pushing one way and monetary policy another way because of a lack of coordination in government policy. Although central banks are government agencies, it is not as rare as it should be for the Ministry of Finance and the central bank to be pushing in opposite directions, or for the one type of policy to be left to try and mitigate the damage caused by the other. It could be sensible to increase taxation and allow bank lending to expand, if it is thought that taxation will reduce consumption and increased borrowing will be spent on investment; but it would not be sensible if the objective was simply an overall reduction in aggregate demand rather than a shift of resources from one use to another.

11 Exchange rate policy

During the 1950s and 1960s, most exchange rates remained fairly stable against each other and against the official value of gold. The US dollar was pegged at $35 = 1 ounce of gold, and nearly all other currencies were pegged to the US dollar at rates which only changed very occasionally.

In the 1970s and 1980s the situation has become rather different. The US dollar is no longer pegged to gold at a fixed price; and the other major currencies move constantly in value, in terms of the US dollar and in terms of each other. This current system is called 'floating': the value of each major currency is determined from day to day, and indeed from minute to minute throughout the day, by market forces.

Exporters *sell* some or all of the foreign currency they have earned for local currency to pay for local inputs, wages, dividends, etc. Importers *buy* foreign currency to pay foreigners who do not want to be paid in local currency. People travelling abroad *buy* foreign currency. Foreigners *sell* foreign currency to buy local currency when they arrive as tourists or businessmen. Firms which borrow abroad *sell* the foreign currency in order to buy local goods and services. Firms investing abroad *buy* foreign currency in order to do so.

All these transactions take place, mainly via banks, in the market. There is no market *place*, since most transactions are done on the telephone or telex.[18] The central banks of industrialised countries are also sometimes active in this market, either simply to prevent sudden large changes in exchange rates ('smoothing operations') or to maintain a different exchange rate from the one that would prevail in a free market situation. This last type of intervention is called 'managed floating' (or sometimes 'dirty floating') to distinguish it from a purely free market determination of exchange rates, known as 'clean' floating.

The main determinants of the external value of floating currencies are

(a) interest rates
(b) balance of payments
(c) relative rates of inflation
(d) expectations.

If the interest rate on seven-day US dollar deposits is 10%, and on German Deutschemarks (DM) is 5%, then *ceteris paribus* those with spare cash would tend to hold it in US dollars, and borrowers would tend to borrow DM rather than dollars. Both these actions would tend to push *up* the value of the US dollar in terms of the DM.

If Britain, say, has a balance of payments surplus, that means that there is a tendency for operators in foreign exchange markets to want to buy more British pounds (to buy British exports or to invest in British companies) than are being offered for sale (to pay for imports into Britain or to pay for foreign investment by British firms). There will be a tendency, therefore, for the British pound to rise in value, unless the Bank of England supplies additional pounds to the market to satisfy the demand.[19]

If France has a higher rate of inflation than Germany, for example, there will be a tendency for the French to choose cheap imports from Germany rather than expensive French products. In addition, French exporters will have costs rising faster than costs in Germany, and will find it increasingly difficult to sell in international markets, unless increasing efficiency offsets rising costs. A relatively high rate of inflation would tend to worsen the French balance of payments and depress the international value of the French franc, unless the Bank of France was able to supply foreign currency to those wishing to sell French francs. Clearly, no country has enough foreign exchange reserves to finance an increasing balance of payments deficit indefinitely.

Any of the above factors, and a large number of other factors, may affect expectations of the likely future value of floating currencies. If people expect a currency to rise in value, they will buy it as an asset; they will also avoid borrowing it so as to avoid having to repay more than they borrowed. Both these actions will tend to push up the currency's value. The reverse is true if people expect a currency to fall in value, giving yet another example of self-fulfilling expectations.

The behaviour of major currencies affects African countries in a number of ways. Central banks must hold the foreign exchange reserves in foreign currencies. Like any investor, central banks must therefore try and choose those currencies which are likely to give the best return, taking both the rate of interest and the likely change of value into account. It is of course impossible to forecast currency movements without a strong possibility of being wrong, so anglophone African central banks diversified their foreign currency holdings in the 1970s, in order to spread the risk.[20] This was a major change from holding all or nearly all foreign exchange reserves in the currency of the former colonial power, a policy which was very risky. It involved African countries in large losses when, for example, the British pound was devalued in 1967. Most francophone African countries still hold their foreign exchange reserves in French Francs.

Secondly, African countries borrow abroad. Such loans are nearly all denominated in foreign currencies. Again, to avoid excessive risk, foreign debt should ideally be denominated in a mix of currencies. However, this is much harder to achieve than a balanced portfolio of currencies in the foreign exchange reserves. It is difficult, and even impossible at times, to borrow in one currency simply in order to repay a loan in another currency so as to improve the currency mix of foreign debt. Instead, each country has an existing debt portfolio at any one time, and can only change its composition gradually, as old loans are repaid and new ones negotiated. Moreover, for many loans there is no choice of currency, and the need for new capital inflows is so great that currency risk is ignored. Nevertheless, debt service tends to be dominated by the relatively high cost of shorter-term commercial loans, where there *is* often a choice of currency, so that there is *some* scope for diversification of currency risk over time.

African countries must also choose how to set the international value of their currency. There can be no question of a purely market-determined (clean) float. There are not enough transactions each day for a reasonably stable market to exist. On the export side particularly, foreign exchange earnings tend to be received in large amounts from time to time, rather than in a continuous flow: for example, agricultural export crops generate foreign exchange at particular times of year, and diamonds are sold at ten annual 'sights'. So most African countries have chosen to 'peg' their currencies to one of the major currencies, to the SDR or to some other basket of currencies chosen by the particular country to suit its circumstances. The situation in mid-1983 is shown in Table 9.3. Most of the francophone countries have retained their link to the French franc; but only the Gambia has retained its link with the British pound. Baskets other than the SDR are usually not announced publicly. Botswana, however, did reveal, when it changed from pegging to the US dollar in 1980, that the new basket was composed of the rand and the SDR; but the relative weights of the two were not given.[21] The choice of a currency or currencies against which to peg is not final; indeed most African countries apart from those in the French franc area have changed pegs at least once.

Those countries which have had a permanent peg to a single major currency–those in the French franc area, Lesotho and Swaziland (the rand) and Liberia (the US dollar)–have also had to manage their economies without a number of policies, which are available to those countries with more independent monetary systems. For example, money can flow freely from Swaziland to South Africa, or from Senegal to France, so that the smaller economy cannot have independent interest rates, and has little control over domestic bank liquidity. In addition, the larger country is liable to change its exchange control rules, its interest rates or the external value of its currency, with little or no reference to the interests of the smaller members of its currency zone, and with little or no consultation with member governments. On the other hand, member countries have access to the foreign exchange reserves of the wider system, and cannot 'borrow' more than is prudent from their central banks. Countries cannot necessarily avoid foreign debt problems as a result, however; Liberia, for example, had to reschedule foreign debts in 1980, 1981 and 1982.

Table 9.3 Choice of currency peg at June 1983 (selected African countries)

French franc	*SDR*	*Peseta*	*Rand*
Benin	Guinea	Equatorial Guinea	Lesotho
Cameroon	Guinea-Bissau		Swaziland
Central African Rep.	Kenya	*U.K. pound*	
Chad	Malawi	The Gambia	*Other*
Comoros	Sao Tome and Principe		Ghana
Congo		*Basket*	Sierra Leone
Gabon	Seychelles	Botswana	
Ivory Coast	Somalia	Madagascar	
Mali	Zaire	Mauretania	
Niger	Zambia	Mauritius	
Senegal		Tanzania	
Togo	*U.S. dollar*	Zimbabwe	
Upper Volta	Burundi		
	Djibouti		
	Ethiopia		
	Liberia		
	Rwanda		
	Sudan		

NOTES:
(1) Uganda and Nigeria are omitted because the source says 'exchange rate data not available'.
(2) The official currency of Liberia *is* the US dollar, although Liberia issues its own coins.
(3) Lesotho and Swaziland use their own currencies, but the rand also circulates and exchanges one for one with the Maloti and the Lilangeni respectively.

Source: *IMF Survey*, 25 July 1983.

The choice of a peg is mainly a matter of convenience. African countries need reasonable stability in the rate at which their currencies exchange for foreign currencies, for day-to-day transactions, and over periods of several months. Clearly, the main foreign currencies used in trade and financial transactions are the most important. So if a country does most of its foreign exchange dealing, for imports and exports and borrowing, in US dollars and British pounds, for example, then a reasonably stable rate of exchange against these two currencies is required. Unfortunately, the rates of exchange between the US dollar and other currencies (including the pound) have themselves changed, by large amounts, in recent years, making it impossible to achieve the objective of a stable exchange rate against both currencies.[22]

The best that African countries can do in these difficult circumstances is to peg to some mix of the major currencies. At least this provides greater stability than pegging to any one currency, unless trade and financial flows are overwhelmingly denominated in that currency. That may explain why several countries now peg to the SDR, which is itself a weighted average of five major currencies.[23] Such a peg is not very different, in its effects, from pegging to a basket of currencies based on a country's foreign trade;[24] the SDR is also more convenient because its value is freely available in the press and from the IMF, and because some other countries also peg to it.

The *rate* at which a domestic currency is pegged, to its chosen currency or currencies, can also be changed. The choice of a peg should not commit the domestic currency to long periods of pegging at the same rate, since the peg itself may move in an unexpected way. For example, a country that chose to peg to the US dollar would have been dragged *down* against most other major currencies in the late 1970s, and *up* in the early 1980s, by quite large amounts—unless the rate was changed from time to time. So the rate normally needs changing periodically, simply to avoid large changes against currencies not in the chosen basket.

In addition, countries may wish to change the exchange rates of their currencies because of changes in their own economic circumstances, including changes originating abroad. Discussion of devaluation (and of revaluations upwards, which also occasionally occur), the reasons for devaluation and its possible economic results, are postponed until the next chapter. Although exchange rate policy is very much a part of monetary policy in Africa, because of the great importance of the foreign sector and the balance of payments, the role of inflation is crucial. So it is better to analyse devaluation and revaluation as part of the chapter on inflation.

NOTES

1 But the tendency is a weak one: for example, holding cattle can be profitable (because they breed) whereas cash earns no interest; food stocks are better protection against physical shortages than cash. Households may also seek security by sending some of their members to town to seek cash-paying jobs; in many African countries people also migrate to neighbouring countries for work. This strategy is also risky, however: for example, in the 1970s the proportion of South Africans working on the South African gold mines rose from about 10% to about 50%, thus reducing the job chances of migrant workers; and in 1983, Nigeria suddenly decided to expel nearly all foreign migrant workers.

2 For example, from 1969 to 1979 Kenya's money supply increased 5.52 or 5.97 times depending on the definition of money supply, whereas GDP at current prices increased 4.34 times. In Malawi, the choice of different years does show money increasing faster than GDP at current prices, but only just, and only if the broader definition of money is used. It would be interesting to know why Malawi is so different from the other countries shown: it could be because although GDP increased steadily in real as well as money terms, and wage employment rose steadily too, real wages and smallholder cash incomes fell through the 1970s. For a discussion of Malawi's growth pattern, see Jonathan Kydd and Robert Christiansen 'Structural change in Malawi since independence: consequences of a development strategy based on large-scale agriculture', *World Development*, Vol. 10, No. 5, May 1982.

3 In this case, as quite often occurs in economics, expectations would tend to be self-fulfilling: if people expect interest rates to rise they sell bonds, this causes bond prices to fall, which causes the interest rates obtainable on bonds to be higher, fulfilling the original expectations. Note also that if people expect interest rates to rise, they will not only sell bonds in order to hold cash, but will also sell longer-dated bonds and buy shorter-dated bonds. The reason is that the potential fall in price of a short-dated bond is smaller than for a long-dated bond – in other words a short-dated bond is more liquid because its price in the market is more certain. What is more, the full nominal value of a short-dated bond can be obtained by holding it until maturity, which is by definition only a short period in the future.

4 Some of their unspent and undistributed income was in fact invested in Treasury Bills, which are sometimes described as 'near-money' but not usually included in money supply statistics. The increased demand for Treasury Bills drove down the rate of interest on them from over 4% in 1968 to a low of 1.2% in 1970. Other interest rates, being fixed by the authorities or by custom, remained unchanged. Zambian *Monthly Digest of Statistics*.

5 Where there is an active market in government debt the central bank may be able to sell additional debt by lowering the price, which in turn implies an increased rate of interest. Where there is not an active market, as in most African countries, additional sales of government debt can probably only be made by making it compulsory in some way, although raising the interest rate might attract some saving from other savings institutions.

6 It would, of course, be inflationary if a government were to run a deficit and literally print more notes as a way of financing some of its spending. But that is not how it actually happens in the modern world: governments pay for spending, which they cannot finance in any other way, by borrowing from the central bank, not by despatching vanloads of bank notes to pay large bills. The real point is that if people are willing to hold more bank notes, having earned them by supplying goods and services, then those people's addition to supply is greater than their addition to demand; this makes it possible for someone else (the government) to increase spending instead.

7 The SDR is the 'Special Drawing Right' of the International Monetary Fund (the IMF). The SDR is composed of five major currencies (US $ 42%, DM 19%, UK £, French franc and Japanese yen 13% each). It is possible to make deposits and to borrow in SDR's, thus having investments and loans denominated in a basket of the five constituent currencies. This avoids the problem of violent fluctuations in currency values, because the SDR, being a weighted average of the five currencies, has a relatively stable value in relation to any one of them and in relation to other currencies. Relatively few countries have so far (at the time of writing) taken advantage of this possibility, although the Ivory Coast was one of the first countries to borrow internationally in SDR's from commercial banks, in 1981. All borrowing from the IMF is denominated in SDR's.

8 For further analysis of the cost of variable interest rate loans, and some strategies for avoiding or reducing the risks of such borrowing, see below, chapter 10, and my book *Analysis of Project Finance in Developing Countries* (London, Heinemann, 1983), especially chapter 9.

9 Bank of Botswana *Annual Report* 1982, pp. 47 and 62.

10 For details, see ADMARC Annual Reports, various years. 'Export parity' is the price that a farmer would receive, if the marketing agency deducted only its expenses from the export price received, that is, if it made no profit.

11 For Ghana, see Andrzej Krassowski, *Development and the Debt Trap* (London, Croom Helm, 1974), pp. 19–20, 41, 45; for Nigeria see World Bank, 'Taxes on foreign trade in Nigeria' in R.M. Bird and O. Oldman *Readings on Taxation in Developing Countries*, (revised edition, Baltimore, Johns Hopkins, 1967) and G.K. Helleiner 'The fiscal role of the marketing boards in Nigerian economic development 1947–61', *Economic Journal*, September 1964, reprinted in M.C. Taylor (ed.) *Taxation for African Development* (London, Hutchinson, 1970).

12 During the period 1975–82, 44 countries incurred foreign payments arrears, of which only 8 countries had managed to eliminate them by the end of 1982. African countries in the list included The Gambia, Ghana, Liberia, Nigeria, Sierra Leone, Tanzania and Uganda, as well as Zambia. *IMF Survey*, 8 August 1983, p. 231.

13 Originally developed by J.J. Polak 'Monetary analysis of income formation and payments problems', *IMF Staff Papers*, Vol. 6, November 1957; reprinted in IMF, *The Monetary Approach to the Balance of Payments* (IMF, Washington DC, 1977). For an extensive discussion of the model in comparison with the Keynesian model in an African context, and their application to Kenya, see J.R. King, *Stabilization Policy in an African Setting: Kenya 1963–73* (London, Heinemann, 1979).

14 The derivation of this equation requires the solution of a first-order difference equation.

15 Botswana was in this position in 1976 and 1977; and the Swaziland government also had large deposits with the Monetary Authority (now the Central Bank) from 1974 to 1983 which could if required have been moved in and out of the commercial banks to affect liquidity. The much more common situation is for governments to be net borrowers from the banking system.

16 In Polak model terms: ΔFR increases if F increases (from equation 4); and ΔFR increases if DCE decreases ($\Delta FR = \Delta MO - DCE$ from equation 3).

17 It is also worth noting that high interest rates increase commercial bank profits, even if interest rates on time and savings deposits go up as much as lending rates. So long as the commercial banks pay no interest on demand deposits (current accounts), their profits rise when interest rates rise. It is possible simply to regard this as an offset to bad years (for profits) when interest rates are low; if, however, interest rates remain high, and if this means excessively high commercial bank profits as a return on capital and reserves, the authorities may wish to take countervailing action–for example a special tax, a reduction in other sources of bank profit such as margins on foreign exchange dealings, or a disproportionately large increase in the interest rates paid on savings and time deposits.

18 The telex is like a telephone except that the operator types rather than speaks a message into the machine, and the same message is typed out on the receiving machine–in another town or another country. There is thus a record of the 'conversation'.

19 This would result in British official foreign exchange reserves rising, since the Bank of England would be *selling* pounds in order to *buy* foreign currency.

20 *IMF Survey*, various issues, documents the changing proportions of different currencies in developing countries' foreign exchange reserves. Figures for individual countries are not publicly available.

21 Bank of Botswana, *Annual Report*, 1981, p. 5.

22 The US $/UK £ rate went from a pound being worth $1.65 to $2.40 and back to $1.55 within six years from 1977 to 1983, with many fluctuations in between.
23 See footnote 7 above for the definition of the SDR.
24 See A.D. Crockett and S.M. Nsouli 'Exchange rate policies for developing countries', *Journal of Development Studies*, Vol. 13, No. 2, January 1977.

10 *Inflation*

1 Some definitions

In a very general sort of way, inflation simply means rising prices. Although prices do not always change together, the interdependence of different parts of the economy does tend to push up all prices together. This can be seen in the behaviour of official statistics: many African countries publish different consumer price indices for high and low income groups, because of their very different consumption habits. Malawi does this, and also gives the weights given to different types of consumption spending for the two groups: the weight for food is 0.48 for low-income people and 0.23 for high-income people, and the weights for transport are 0.02 and 0.26 respectively. Within these broad spending categories, the two groups' spending habits are also different, with poor people spending on bus fares while rich people buy cars and garage services. Despite these huge differences in spending habits, the two indices often move very closely together, as they did in Malawi in 1971, 1972 and 1973.[1]

However, it is also possible for large changes in relative prices to occur: in 1973/4, for example, the oil price quadrupled, and then doubled in 1979/80. Although oil prices affect the cost of a wide range of goods and services, for example through the cost of transport, the big changes in oil prices affected rich people more than poor people (and industrialised countries which use a lot of oil more than African countries which use relatively little). So by the end of 1980, the high-income consumer price index in Malawi was 352 (on a base of 1970 = 100) compared with only 244 for the low-income index.

It can be ambiguous, therefore, to treat inflation as though it affected everyone in the same way. Unless all prices are changing together in the same way, it is necessary to ask 'inflation for whom?' There is no one ideal measure of inflation; each measure answers a particular question. In most peoples' minds, the consumer price index most nearly applicable to their own spending pattern is what they understand best by inflation. But economists generally prefer the

'GDP deflator', which is derived by dividing GDP at current market prices by GDP at constant prices. This index is more broadly based since it includes the cost of investment and government services as well as the cost of consumption. However, even this inflation indicator can be very confusing: if export prices fall at a time when all other prices are rising, as has happened to most African economies in the 1970s and 1980s, the fall in export prices can be large enough as a component of GDP to offset the increase in the prices of the other components of domestic production, giving a measure of inflation that most people would regard as misleading[2].

2 Demand and monetary inflation

The main purpose of this chapter is to examine some of the theories of inflation and to see if they are applicable in an African situation. In earlier chapters two causes of inflation have already been considered implicitly. Firstly, an excess of aggregate demand over aggregate supply, when output cannot increase, will cause a rise in prices—provided the excess demand cannot be satisfied by running down stocks, increasing imports, postponing demand or diverting supplies from the export market. This sort of inflation is called 'demand inflation' (sometimes also 'demand-pull') for obvious reasons. In practice, in a situation of excess demand it is not usually a case of 'either-or' since some or all of the possible effects will occur simultaneously, of which inflation is only one. But the scope for running down stocks and postponement of demand is limited; and few countries can allow imports to increase and exports to decrease for very long. Even in those countries fortunate enough to have, for the time being, adequate supplies of foreign exchange, the physical capacity to increase imports and make use of them is limited. For these reasons, inflation is an important element in an excess demand situation.

The second type of inflation already considered is what might be called 'monetary' inflation, that is, rising prices caused by increases in the money supply. As was argued at length in the previous chapter, however, the conditions in which an increase in the money supply can be said to cause prices to rise must be carefully identified. If the money supply rises because of a budget deficit or an export surplus, then excess demand is combined with additional liquidity in the banks. If output cannot increase, then prices probably will, with the inflation made worse by additional bank lending if (as is likely) there is excess demand for credit. This is not a 'pure' case of monetary inflation. If bank liquidity is increased independently of demand (by reducing reserve ratios, for example) then in a situation of excess demand for credit, prices will probably rise. This may reasonably be called monetary inflation—although since it depends on the existence of unsatisfied demand for credit there is an element of excess demand as well as of monetary factors in its causes.

It is an oversimplification to distinguish too nearly between situations where output can or cannot increase. There is a genuine difference between the two extremes, and between the effects of changes in demand and changes in the money supply when, for example, there is widespread spare capacity in domestic industry. But intermediate situations are more common. As spare capacity in the economy begins to be eliminated there will be increases in prices and increases in output. Some industries will reach capacity production first, while other industries are still capable of increased output. Some goods, for example radios, can easily be imported when domestic production is at full stretch, but others, for example houses, cannot.

Moreover, the ability of different producers to increase output depends very often, in Africa, on whether or not they can obtain foreign exchange to pay for imported inputs. When an African economy is suffering from a severe shortage of foreign exchange, producers who are relatively independent of imported inputs (for example farmers who use oxen rather than tractors for draught power), and producers who are favoured by the authorities in the allocation of foreign exchange, will be able to continue or increase production when other producers cannot do so. At any one time, therefore, some goods and services are likely to be in short supply, with upward pressure on prices, while others are freely available at a constant price.

It is important to remember that pressure on the price of goods in short supply is not always by way of market forces. For example, most African governments control the price of maize (and other staple foods) to the farmer, and of maize meal to the consumer. If the price to the farmers is 'too low' so that supply is less than demand, then the government may be persuaded to raise the price for the next agricultural year, in order to try and get increased supplies. In addition, many African governments have preferred to subsidise the cost of basic foods, rather than pass on cost increases in consumer prices. The pricing of very important commodities is often, therefore, primarily a political and bureaucratic process, which in turn is influenced by market conditions.

3 *Cost inflation*

There is a third theory of inflation called 'cost inflation'. The theory of cost inflation runs roughly as follows: first there is some autonomous increase in costs, such as a trade union demanding and getting an increase in wages, or a rise in import prices. Second, the rise in cost is passed on by producers in the form of higher prices. Third, the higher prices increase the cost of living, and this causes wages and incomes to rise again, because of trade union pressure, or because of clauses in wage-contracts which tie wages to the cost of living. The whole process then repeats itself.

Now this argument depends on a whole series of assumptions. Firstly, in order for unions to be able to demand wage rises successfully, without causing unemployment of their members, there must be a fairly high level of demand for labour, or the union must be of fairly highly skilled workers who cannot be replaced. In other words, unions, especially unions of the unskilled, are less likely to be able to get wage increases at a time of high unemployment, because at such a time their bargaining power is reduced. In addition, employers are less likely to grant wage increases at a time of low demand for their products, because their profits will be low and they will be less confident of their ability to pass on higher costs in the form of higher prices.

Secondly, wages are not the whole of industrial costs. Firms must also buy raw materials and semi-manufactured goods from other firms; pay rent, rates and fuel costs; set aside profits to pay for existing capital goods (depreciation) and new capital goods (investment); and meet interest and repayment costs on their borrowing. So even if wages do rise, the proportion firms must add to the prices they charge for their own products is less than the proportion by which wages have risen—unless all other costs rise simultaneously, which is only likely to occur in a situation of general excess demand. Where wages are very low initially, a wage increase may cause increased productivity—by reduced labour turnover, better management, better health of the workers—so that wage costs may not go up when wage rates rise. At the early stages of mining or industrialisation in Africa this situation is quite common, a wage-rise resulting among other things in a longer average period of employment of migrant labour, with some workers committing themselves to permanent employment. This greatly increases productivity.

Thirdly, in order to be able to pass on increased costs in higher prices, firms must have some control over their prices; or there must be excess demand for their products; or they must be confident that rival firms will also increase their prices so that a competitive position is not ruined. These possibilities are not mutually exclusive; some combination of them is clearly possible.

Fourthly, a high proportion of wage employment in many African economies is in sectors where wage increases cannot be passed on in higher prices. Mining companies and agricultural estates which produce mainly for export are price-takers, in that they cannot influence their selling prices in any way. A wage increase therefore has the effect of reducing their profits (unless the wage increase is offset by increased productivity) rather than of causing domestic inflation. Wage increases in that part of the agricultural sector which produces for local consumption may also not be passed on immediately in higher prices, if those prices are market-determined; in the longer run, reduced profitability may reduce supply and so push up prices. Where local agricultural prices are government-controlled, often the case in Africa for important foods such as maize and cooking oil, wage increases may or may not result in administered prices being raised as a result of political and administrative action.

In addition to mining companies and agriculture, government itself is also a major employer in African countries, and most government services, such as education and health services, roads, the police and so on, are not sold but are provided free. So wage increases in government service cannot be passed on in higher prices. Between them, the export sector and government services can account for a high proportion of total formal sector employment in many African economies, and an even higher proportion if agriculture is included.[3] So the possibility of wage increases being passed on in higher prices is limited to the remaining sectors. It is quite possible for a wage increase in one sector to be followed by wage increases in other sectors, and indeed both mining and government have acted as 'leading sectors' in this way. This mechanism for the transmission of inflation is different, though, from the one postulated in the theory of cost inflation.

Finally, the link between price rises and subsequent wage increases is not clear-cut. Certainly there are often delays, especially in the government sector. Civil service and teachers' salaries tend to be the subject of lengthy commissions of enquiry so that salaries are increased months and even years after price rises have occurred. Secondly, there are many types of incomes which are not well protected against rises in the cost of living: for example, people on fixed contracts, people in non-unionised jobs, and so on. Thirdly, workers may not be able to get wage increases (as a result of price rises) if overall demand for their sort of labour is low, and unemployed workers with equivalent skills are available—as already explained.

It would appear, then, that for cost inflation to occur, as in the theory described at the beginning of this section, there must also be some element of excess demand as well. Yet wage increases *can* occur in Africa independently of the level of aggregate demand, as explained in the next section. It is also important to note that the transmission process, from cost increase to prices to wages, is undoubtedly the way in which inflation continues, regardless of how it actually started. And the longer it continues, the harder it is to stop it, since the process becomes institutionalised. Wages and prices are raised regularly, sometimes according to an agreed formula, so that inflation becomes increasingly a normal and expected state of affairs. The whole continuous process is known as the 'inflationary spiral'.

4 *Cost inflation: wage increases*

It was argued, in the analysis of cost inflation, that the various steps in the process from cost rises to other price rises to wage rises, depend to some extent on there being at the same time a degree of excess demand. Thus it was argued that workers are unlikely to get wage increases unless excess demand exists for labour; employers are unlikely to grant wage increases or be able to pass them on in higher prices unless excess demand exists for their products; finally, workers may not be able to compensate for higher prices unless excess demand exists for their labour.

On the other hand, the structure of African economies is such that wage increases *can* occur independently of the aggregate demand and supply situation; in particular wage increases can occur in the modern sector despite there being more people willing to work than there are modern sector jobs.

Firstly, export industries can increase wages when export commodity prices are high—which can occur quite independently of the domestic economic situation. Secondly, import substitution industries can increase wages in the expectation of being granted increased protection by the government. Thirdly, much of industry (expecially foreign-owned industry) tends to be very capital-intensive so that higher wages have a relatively small impact on costs. Fourthly, parastatal firms often expect the government to pay if they make a loss and expect the government to lend for investment if they cannot borrow commercially. Fifthly, African governments do not pay unemployment benefit to those out of work, which reduces the government's awareness of unemployment. Sixthly, formal sector wages enable the unemployed to live relatively comfortably off their relatives with jobs,[4] thus reducing political agitation for more jobs. Seventhly, the lack of skills of the unemployed prevents them from competing directly with those in jobs.

In countries which depend very heavily on expatriates, the structure of wages is affected by their salaries which in turn are partly decided by international salaries. For example, the Zambian mineworkers demanded and got a substantial wage increase in 1966 in order to 'narrow the gap' between themselves and the expatriate mineworkers. This wage increase was granted without reference to domestic conditions or needs—except the need to buy industrial peace. In 1967, Zambian civil servants got a substantial wage increase and in due course, so did workers in other sectors.[5] This example demonstrates how international salaries can affect wage levels throughout an economy, even among those groups of lower-skilled workers who are not competitive with expatriates.

In a more general sense the level of expatriate salaries creates a target for local workers, and their consumption habits have a demonstration effect. So even when expatriates are replaced by locals, the structure of salaries will remain for a time. In addition, the infrastructure of high expatriate salaries, for example large houses in scattered suburbs requiring a car (or even two cars), will remain.

It is thus possible for high wages to exist, and for wage increases to occur, in the formal sector, at the same time as there are more people wanting jobs than can be employed. Those who cannot get formal sector jobs are not usually unemployed in the sense of having nothing to do, but work in the informal sector, where the full impact of an excess supply of labour is felt in the form of low incomes. In the informal sector, workers are not protected by unions nor by government rules (such as minimum wage laws) and there is excessive competition in the provision of services and in small-scale manufacturing (such as the making of buckets and pots and baskets). As a result incomes are very low despite long working hours; these workers have been described as the working poor.[6]

Even in industrial economies there is considerable doubt as to how much effect the level of unemployment has on the rate of increase of wages. At one time it was thought that there was a fairly close and stable link, expressed in the 'Phillips curve' of the type shown in Figure 10.1.

There is no need to discuss the Phillips curve here except to point out that in recent years the curve has not been a good representation of the relationship between unemployment and the rate of increase in wages, even in industrial countries. It is possible that as the rate of inflation has increased in industrial countries the curve AA has shifted to the right, that is, a higher rate of unemployment is necessary to reduce wage increases to a given level.

In African countries the absence of unemployment statistics makes it impossible anyway to test the Phillips curve relationship. But if the above arguments are correct, then it is not relevant to African conditions, where rapid wage rises can occur at the same time as rising urban unemployment. When income prospects for most farmers are poor, high urban wages tend to attract more people to town than there

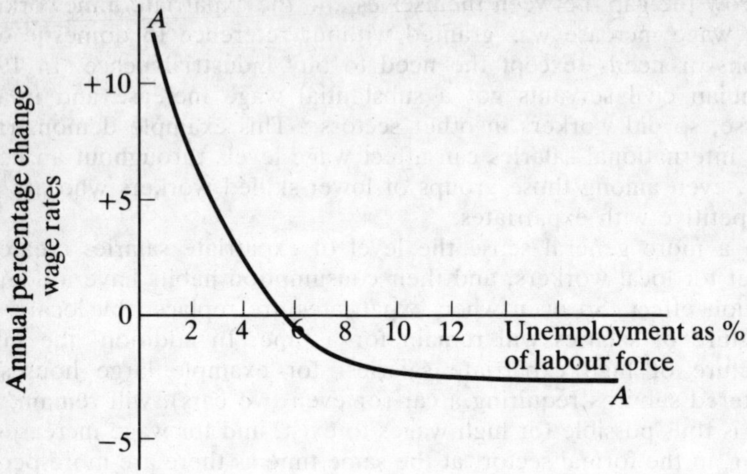

Figure 10.1 The 'Phillips curve'

are formal sector jobs, even when farming land is available (as it is in some African countries). The education system also produces more people seeking formal sector (especially office) jobs than are available. At the same time the political influence of those in jobs is fairly effective in preventing the dismissal of workers. So the existence of unemployed workers or low earnings in the informal sector does not necessarily prevent wage increases in the formal sector.

5 *Imported inflation*

All countries depend to some extent on imports, but small, underdeveloped ones are more import-dependent than large, developed ones. At a time when prices are rising all over the world it becomes very difficult for an import-dependent (or 'open') economy to avoid importing other countries' inflation in the form of higher prices for imports.

Even in a very open economy, imports are only a part of total supply, so rising import prices will not necessarily result in inflation at the same rate. If the country can avoid wages being raised to compensate for the increased cost of imported consumer goods, and if it can prevent producers from passing on in higher prices the increased cost of imported inputs, then the impact of imported inflation might be limited to its direct impact on the prices of imported goods themselves. However, it is clearly very difficult to achieve this result, especially at a time of generally rising prices. The more likely effect is for rises in import prices to give an additional impetus to the inflationary process.

In small and open African economies, domestic inflation tends to be very little different from the rate of inflation of import prices, unless the economy is cut off in some way from imports. For example in economies such as Botswana, the Gambia, Lesotho and Swaziland, a high proportion of what is consumed is imported.[7] Even in rather larger economies, local production is heavily dependent on imported inputs. If any price is prevented from increasing as fast as the price of imports, the income of the group selling those goods or services tends to fall behind the income of other groups in the country. For example, if the cost of imports including that of imported petrol (or of local petrol refined using imported oil) goes up, but transport operators are not allowed to raise their prices, then their income falls because of the higher cost of imports, and because of the higher cost of goods and services produced by those who have been able to raise their prices. Sooner or later, pressure from the transport operators on the government (in the case of controlled prices) or a reduction in the supply of transport services, will tend to push their prices up in line with other prices.

Nevertheless, a country may wish to avoid the unattractive effects of inflation–on the incentive to save, on income distribution, on the type of investment that is encouraged, and so on. Is there any way a country can insulate itself from other countries' inflation?

If a country has enough foreign exchange then it can indeed avoid importing inflation, but few countries are so fortunate. For example, if a country is receiving very high prices for exports, it can revalue the external value of the local currency upwards, thus offsetting the domestic effect of higher import prices. Thus if import prices rise by 10 per cent in dollar terms, an increase by 10 per cent of the dollar value of the local currency will mean that the prices of imports expressed in local currency will remain constant. If, on the other hand export prices are low at a time of world inflation, revaluing the local currency upwards can only go on as long as foreign exchange reserves last. In an industrial economy, the avoidance of domestic inflation should enable exporters to offer very competitive prices in world markets; as a result increased export volume may compensate for reduced export prices. But commodity exporters do not have this opportunity–supply is usually fixed in the short term and will if anything be reduced as a result of lower export prices in domestic currency.

It is relatively rare for an African country to feel able to revalue its currency upwards against foreign currencies; and it is even rarer for such a revaluation to be carried out, because of the reluctance of most governments to alter their nominal exchange rates. However, Botswana increased its exchange rate on three occasions in the late 1970s, specifically in order to reduce the amount of imported inflation. The side effects were carefully analysed at the time, and research was conducted which showed that the benefits of cheaper imports (in Pula terms) were passed on to consumers rather than being pocketed by traders.[8] The disadvantages of revaluation are, firstly, that it makes exporting less profitable and, secondly, that by making imports cheaper (which is of course the main intention) it makes it more difficult for local producers to sell in competition with imports. Revaluation is really only feasible, therefore, firstly if an economy has exports which are receiving high world prices so that exporting remains profitable even after revaluation, and secondly if import-competing industry is exceptionally low-cost, or highly protected, or simply non-existent. At times of low export prices, the revaluation option is not open; and as import-competing industry develops, revaluation becomes less and less feasible unless such industry is exceptionally efficient and low cost (which is highly unlikely) or unless it operates behind very high levels of protection (which tends to lead to inefficiency).

The above analysis suggests that African countries are unlikely to be able to avoid importing inflation at the level of their main suppliers. So long as African countries continue to be able to pay for imports, however, domestic inflation should not be much higher than imported inflation. The availability of imports and the ability to pay for them, make a crucial contribution to supply at times of excess demand. So as long as an economy *remains* open, the effectively unlimited supply of imports has an important *deflationary* effect, at least as far as internationally tradeable goods are concerned. Excess domestic demand can push up prices of *non-tradeables* (mainly services such as construction and transport), even in an open economy. Generally speaking though, inflation at rates significantly higher than imported inflation results from the closing off of the economy from imports, by means of tariffs, import controls, exchange controls and other methods. Once a higher rate of inflation has been established, the reopening of the economy may not bring inflation back down to international levels, at least not for a long time, because of the way that high rates of inflation become built into the economy, or institutionalised, as already described.

One of the ways in which inflation becomes built in, at the time that the economy is reopened to imports, is that such a reopening usually has to be accompanied by a devaluation of the domestic currency, to enable import-competing local industry to survive. The devaluation of itself raises prices by increasing the local cost of imports, and this in turn may reinforce or accelerate the rate of inflation—leading to the need to devalue again at a later date. There has been relatively little experience of this in Africa, except perhaps in Uganda; but it is quite common, for example, in South America. Devaluation is further analysed below, in section 9.

There is another way in which foreign price increases can be transmitted. If *export prices* rise, exporters may increase their domestic spending and so cause increases in domestic prices. Clearly, this effect depends on the increase in export prices actually reaching domestic spenders, rather than being cut off by taxation or by marketing boards, or remaining unspent in the hands of governments or mining companies. A second possibility is that high export prices may result in exporters paying higher wages. For example, mining companies enjoying high profits may be very willing to buy industrial peace by giving wage increases, especially if wages are a low proportion of total costs in a capital-intensive operation. While such a wage increase would of itself have only a small direct impact on local prices through the increased spending power of the mineworkers, it could have a much greater effect if other groups of workers successfully demand wage increases because of the increase granted to the miners. The danger of this happening is one reason why governments in Africa have incomes policies, one of whose objectives is to prevent rich sectors from starting off a damaging round of wage increases. Although this way of transmitting inflation originates with foreign price increases, it is not what is usually meant by 'imported inflation'; that phrase is normally reserved for increases in the prices of imports.

6 *The effects of inflation*

At first sight it might appear that it does not make much difference whether prices go up or not. After all, if all prices doubled, and so did the value of all assets and liabilities, then nothing would apparently change. In a certain very trivial sense that is what happened in those African countries where the currency was decimalised: everything became worth twice as many Kwacha, Leones or Cedi as it had previously been worth in pounds. The point is that inflation does not take place in this way.

Some prices increase faster than others; this means that those people selling goods or services whose prices rise faster than average have more rapidly rising incomes than those who have to buy such goods, and whose incomes rise slower than the average. For example, if the prices of agricultural goods increase faster than the prices of manufactured goods, then commercial farmers as a group will tend to gain at the expense of urban workers.

Some groups in society with a strong bargaining position can protect themselves against inflation by negotiating wage and salary increases. Others cannot. For example workers in well-organised unions of skilled (and thus irreplaceable) workers are more likely to be able to get wage increases to compensate for inflation than workers without unions and without skills.

Most loans are designated in money terms. As a result, lenders are repaid the amounts of money originally lent, which are worth less in real terms if prices have increased in the meantime. For the same reason, borrowers tend to do very well out of inflation because they repay less in real terms than they borrowed. Only if the rate of interest is high enough to compensate for the rate of inflation do borrowers fail to gain at the expense of lenders during an inflation.

In the mid-1970s, inflation was higher than interest rates all over the world, including the industrialised countries. Africa was no exception, with single-figure interest rates and double-digit inflation in many countries. Although there was a tendency to increase real rates of interest in the 1980s, the cost of borrowing still remained below the rate of inflation in many countries.[9] In addition, it is common for borrowers to be able to claim interest payments as an expense against profits tax or income tax, so that the true cost of borrowing is lower than indicated by the rate of interest. Similarly, depositors have to pay tax on many types of deposit, so that the actual rate of interest received is again less than that indicated by the published rate.

So using the figures for May 1982 in Botswana, from Table 9.2 in chapter 9, and a 1982 inflation figure for Botswana of about 12 per cent, commercial bank borrowers paid 13 per cent nominal, or approximately 1 per cent real.[10] But if the payment of 13 per cent reduced liability to profits tax at 35 per cent, then the real cost of such bank borrowing was only 8.45 per cent after tax, and the real rate of interest after allowing for inflation was negative, roughly −3.5 per cent. Meanwhile parastatals were able to borrow from the government at 10 per cent, also less than the rate of inflation even without allowing for tax. Savers got 11 per cent on three-month commercial bank deposits, which was only just below the rate of inflation before paying tax, but more substantially negative in real terms if tax at 30 per cent or so had to be paid. Anyone leaving money on a demand deposit account carrying no interest, or holding savings in the form of notes, saw their money lose value without any compensation at all. This applied to most people, since nearly everyone normally has some money for transaction purposes; only those with large borrowings gained more than they lost.

In general, anyone whose income and assets are fixed in money terms (or whose income and assets increase in money value by less than the rate of inflation) loses as a result of inflation. As a result there tends to be a redistribution of income from the weak to the strong. The economically and politically powerful are not only able to get increases in income to compensate for rising prices, they also have better access to credit and so tend to be net borrowers. In particular, the business sector tends to do well out of inflation: most firms have some costs which are fixed in money terms (rates, local taxes on property), are net borrowers and do well when demand is strong, so that profits tend to rise faster than prices. The wealthy, who own businesses, thus gain over the rest of the community.[11]

Another extremely important effect of inflation is on the balance of payments. If the exchange rate is held constant and domestic inflation is faster than in the countries which supply imports, then imported goods become cheaper than domestic goods, thus increasing the demand for imports. The prices of commodity exports are not affected by domestic inflation, but are made less profitable by higher domestic costs and so will be discouraged in the long term. Manufactured exports are rare in Africa–to the extent that they do exist they will be less competitive if higher production costs are passed on in prices and less profitable if prices are maintained. Rather more important is tourism: foreign tourists are discouraged from coming to a country by rising domestic prices, and local residents find that holidays abroad become cheaper relative to holidays at home. On the capital account, negative real interest rates encourage borrowers to borrow from local sources rather than from abroad, and depositors try to invest their money abroad if they are able to do so.[12] For all these reasons the balance of payments suffers.

A deterioration in the balance of payments caused by a relatively high rate of inflation *can* be self-correcting. A balance of payments deficit drains money out of the banking system and so may cause a reduction in bank lending; falling exports reduce the income and spending of exporters; and relatively cheap imports reduce the demand for import-competing goods, also reducing the income and spending of producers. All these factors reduce aggregate demand and therefore have a tendency to correct the inflation.

However, other factors may affect the self-correcting tendency. If wages are able to increase, in response to rising prices, then income and spending by wage-earners will increase. Government spending may be, and usually is, maintained; it may even be increasing rapidly, since this is frequently the original cause of a relatively high rate of inflation. A high or rising level of government spending, added to declining revenue from exports and import-competing businesses, tends not only to increase demand directly, but also to supply the commercial banks with increased liquidity.

It is common, when there is a large and increasing balance of payments deficit, for governments to try to reduce imports by various forms of controls. But such controls reduce aggregate supply and so tend to make the inflation worse. Controls on imports also make it possible for those who *are* allowed to import to make large profits: either they can resell the imports at high prices, or they can make large profits by using the imports in production. A situation where officials can decide who makes large profits, by making purely administrative decisions, is one with great potential for corruption. Even if there is no corruption, it uses up a lot of scarce administrative resources. An alternative reaction to controls is to increase tariffs on imports; this also has the effect of directly increasing prices, but has the advantage of allocating imports by means of prices rather than by administrative decisions.[13]

It is also possible, where the balance of payments is in deficit, for the currency to depreciate. In industrial countries this may occur through the operation of market forces on a floating exchange rate (although other forces may prevent it). In African countries, governments have the choice of devaluing the currency rather than using controls, as a way of correcting the situation. This option is both important and complicated, so it is discussed separately, in section 8 below.

A few fortunate African countries have avoided a balance of payments deficit despite having a relatively high rate of inflation. This can occur if at the same time the value of exports is rising rapidly, or if the country has large capital inflows, for example from aid or from foreign commercial borrowing.

Broadly, this is what happened to Zambia in the five years after independence, and in Nigeria after the development of oil exports in the 1970s. In Zambia, the price of copper fluctuated a lot, but about a rising trend. For a long time, therefore, the country was able to have rapidly increasing imports without having to worry about the balance of payments. Indeed, the price of copper rose so much that in spite of the fact that imports doubled, the foreign exchange reserves also increased. The trouble with this sequence of events, however, was that Zambia became a very high-cost economy. Domestic prices rose much more rapidly than those in, say, Kenya, yet the exchange rate between the Kenyan shilling and the Zambian Kwacha was unchanged. As a result, diversification away from dependence on copper for earning foreign exchange, by developing other export industries, was effectively discouraged; and domestic producers had to compete with relatively cheap imports. As it happened, import substitution in industry was greatly encouraged by UDI and the large increases in transport costs–but it would have been encouraged even more if inflation had been less, or if the rate of exchange of the Kwacha had reflected Zambia's higher rate of inflation. The main damage was probably in agriculture where an 'overvalued' currency discouraged existing export crops and the development of new export crops, and discouraged the use of labour (as opposed to capital). Exchange rate policy was thus a contributory factor to the decline of Virginia tobacco and groundnut exports.

It is perhaps necessary to elaborate a little further: in what sense can a country with a balance of payments surplus be said to have an overvalued currency? International trade theory suggests that such a combination is simply not possible. A balance of payments surplus would suggest that the country derives more benefit from investing in existing exports than in the alternatives. The point is that high export prices may be temporary, overdependence on one export commodity is risky, and mineral exports are an exhaustible resource so that alternative exports must be developed. Non-copper exports (in the case of Zambia) and non-oil exports (in the case of Nigeria) are so small that it is essential that their development be begun a long time before the main mineral export is exhausted. Additional reasons for developing alternative agricultural exports are the desire for a better balance between rural and urban development and the need for better income distribution.

7 *The effects of continuing inflation: divergent and convergent inflation*

Because rising prices create additional income, inflation creates a feedback effect which adds further to demand. So if there is an excess of demand over supply, rising prices do not remove this 'inflationary gap'. There are factors which tend to reduce the gap as inflation continues, thus making it a 'convergent' inflation; and factors tending to increase the gap so that the rate of inflation increases, making it a 'divergent' inflation.

Factors making for a convergent inflation are as follows.

(1) Investment should eventually result in more output, so that if excess demand is caused by increases in investment this should in time result in increases in output and so remove the supply-demand imbalance. Even investment in apparently non-productive items such as primary schools and hospitals should add to national product in the long run, by producing a better-educated and healthier population. Clearly, those investments which produce a large and rapid increase in output are much less inflationary, since supply is more rapidly in-

creased to fill the inflationary gap. One of the most fundamental problems facing underdeveloped countries in drawing up their development plans is the need for improved infrastructure: roads, railways, electricity, government offices, schools and so on. Typically, such investments have a very long life and a yield, in terms of increased output, that is spread over a very long period. The investment spending adds to demand at once, the yield adds to supply only over a long time. Development plans should therefore include a reasonable amount of investment with a low capital/output ratio, in order to mitigate the inflationary pressure of large investments in infrastructure with high capital/ouput ratios. Of course, some infrastructural investments may break supply bottlenecks and permit rapid increases in output–for example training of some key types of skilled manpower, or the building of transport routes which allow farmers to reach new markets.

(2) As has been pointed out already, inflation probably increases profits faster than other types of income. Profit-earners usually save a higher proportion of income than wage-earners and receivers of rent, so this factor should induce higher savings. In so far as profits are paid out as dividends and saved, this is a genuinely disinflationary factor. But most of the higher savings out of profits come from retained profits, which are retained for investment purposes. This type of saving is only disinflationary therefore if there is some delay between earning of profits and spending of them on investment. Such a delay is quite likely, since there is often a time-lag between the earning of profits and firms making up their accounts and knowing what their profits are; on the other hand they may not wait for this, but make informed guesses, or simply invest on the evidence of high sales. The other thing that may cause delay is shortage of capacity in the construction industry, and the capital goods sector if there is one. Investment spending on imported capital goods creates no new domestic income in itself, but has to be matched by transport capacity on import routes and construction capacity in the domestic economy–which may cause further delays. If profits are earned by foreign companies and remitted abroad then a shift in income distribution in favour of profits will be disinflationary (although bad for the balance of payments and for national income).

(3) Some incomes are temporarily fixed in money terms, and some are not able to increase as fast as prices, as already pointed out in the discussion of cost inflation. When prices rise, therefore, these incomes fall in real terms. The people involved may try to maintain consumption in real terms by reducing their savings or by borrowing; but in so far as they do not, or cannot do so, excess demand is reduced. In practice many wage increases are subject to delay, while unions

negotiate with employers or salaries commissions report to government, so that in the short term this is an important convergent factor, especially when prices first start to rise and workers' reaction is relatively slow. The lower the rate of inflation the less urgent is workers' reaction likely to be.

(4) If the taxation system is income-elastic then (by definition) inflation will cause taxation receipts to increase faster than the increase in money incomes, reducing real incomes and thus spending in real terms. Clearly this factor gains in importance the more people are affected by the tax system. In Africa, only a small proportion even of the wage- and salary-earning population pays any income tax; the progressive element in the tax system for non-income tax payers is thus confined to the higher taxation of luxury commodities. The other condition that is important here is that government spending should increase more slowly than tax revenue. In that a lot of government spending is fixed in the short term (salaries, rents) or immune from domestic inflation (imports) this condition is usually met.

(5) As money income increases, the transactions demand for money also increases. More precisely, as money income increases, bank customers draw currency from their banks, causing reduced liquidity in the banking system. In addition, as already noted, inflation tends to cause a balance of payments deficit, which also reduces bank liquidity. Under certain conditions there will be an offsetting increase in bank liquidity—for example, if a contributory cause of the inflation is an unfinanced budget deficit. Suppose, however, that inflation is occurring with no offsetting increase in bank liquidity, for example because of a rise in import prices or in government-administered prices, then unless the central bank takes steps to restore bank liquidity, the banks may be forced to reduce their lending, or at least to reduce the rate of increase over what it would otherwise have been, if they do not have enough spare liquidity. This will reduce spending, consumption or investment, that would have been financed by bank credit, and this is thus apparently a convergent factor. However, to the extent that bank credit would have been used to finance imports it may reduce short-term supply; and, as was argued in chapter 8, bank credit often provides the working capital that enables fixed capital to be used, so that credit restraint may reduce domestic supply as well. In general, however, constraints on bank credit tend to dampen demand. It is also possible that if the demand for money increases faster than supply then interest rates will rise. But in Africa this effect is limited, since interest rates are mostly determined by government policy, and very slow to react to changed monetary conditions; and in any case it was argued in chapter 7 that the cost of borrowing has little or no impact on spending. In an economy with widespread foreign ownership of industry

there is also a possibility that firms will borrow abroad if they are unable to borrow at home. Indeed, even domestically-owned firms may do so, but it is less likely and more easily controlled. Borrowing abroad enables firms to avoid credit shortages at home.

(6) Balance of payments effects, increasing imports and the increased profitability of selling export goods at home rather than abroad, have the effect of increasing aggregate supply, and thus of damping the inflation; but only so long as foreign exchange reserves last. As already pointed out, one of the likeliest reactions of government to this situation is to impose import restrictions or import taxes, both of which have the effect of increasing inflationary pressure. Another likely reaction, devaluation, also makes inflation worse.

(7) The real balance (or Pigou) effect, such as it is, by reducing the real value of liquid assets expressed in money terms, should reduce consumption. Since by definition the people who have such money balances are able to maintain consumption in real terms by spending their balances, and are also the best placed to get credit for the same purpose, the convergent effect on inflation of the Pigou effect (which is small anyway) is probably negligible.

Most of the factors making for a *divergent* inflation depend on people adjusting their behaviour to take account of expected future inflation. This occurs when inflation is continuous over a long period of time and when price rises are quite large. Both these conditions are rather vaguely stated since it is impossible to be precise about expectations. But clearly an inflation of $\frac{1}{2}$ per cent a year, even if continuous over many years, will not cause many people to adjust their behaviour in order to allow for expected future inflation. Equally, if prices sometimes fall or are stationary then expectations of future inflation will be less certain and so less likely to affect people's bahaviour. On the other hand, a doubling of prices every month would very quickly cause people to react in any way that would reduce the impact. Divergent factors include the following.

(a) If inflation does in fact produce a shift into profits from other forms of income then high, and rising, profits can be expected to encourage investment. In addition, since changes in dividend payments usually lag behind changes in profits, retained profits will rise even faster, thereby providing part of the finance for this investment. As pointed out in (2) above, this is not necessarily a factor making for a divergent inflation if there is a delay between the earning and spending of profits. One would expect there to be such a delay in the early stages of inflation; but if inflation continues businessmen will be encouraged to spend money as it accrues, in fact to anticipate future increases in prices as far as possible.

(b) Inflation is bad for most forms of personal saving, since these are mainly fixed in money terms, and thus eroded in real terms by rising prices. When inflation begins people do not realise what is happening; and while interest rates are still greater than the rate of inflation, capital values are maintained. But as an inflation continues and accelerates people observe that earlier savings have lost value, and are encouraged to buy goods rather than financial assets, either for consumption, or for a sort of speculative saving. For example, people will try to buy property during an inflation, since they normally expect property prices to keep pace with other prices, and thus to be a 'hedge' against inflation. In addition people will try and borrow as much as possible and invest in real assets, since their borrowings will have to be repaid in money terms, while their assets maintain or increase their real value. These shifts out of money into physical assets add greatly to inflationary pressure; and tend to divert savings from productive investment to speculative investment.

(c) If an inflation continues and the rate of inflation becomes very high, nobody will hold money for longer than they need. The velocity of circulation of money increases as people try to get rid of money balances as soon as they accrue. Thus the same absolute amount of money can be made to do more 'work', and a tight money policy by the central bank may be frustrated. It has been suggested that this reaction does not begin to occur until the rate of inflation is more than 10 per cent a month. That may be too precise a statement, but certainly people do not feel they need to rush out and spend their wages at the beginning rather than the end of the week or month–because of inflation–when prices are increasing at, say, only 1 per cent a month.

(d) If inflation is at a faster rate than the rate of interest then not only are savings discouraged, but borrowing becomes very cheap. Thus if prices rise by 20 per cent a year and the interest rate is only 10 per cent, then the cost of borrowing money is actually negative.[14] Even if investment is not sensitive to interest rates, negative real interest rates make it more likely that people will try to use borrowed money to buy physical assets, the money value of which is expected to keep pace with inflation. This effect only occurs though if people expect the rate of inflation to *continue* higher than the interest rate, since otherwise the nominal rate of interest may appear very high.

(e) If inflation continues and accelerates, unions are likely to realise what is happening. They then demand wage increases which not only compensate for past price increases, but anticipate expected future price increases. If firms are making high profits, and have every reason to expect that they can pass on higher wage costs in higher prices, they will have little incentive to resist wage demands.

*

In summary, divergent factors all depend on what has been called 'inflation psychology', namely, the building of inflationary expectations into economic behaviour. On the other hand, convergent factors tend to dominate when an inflation begins and when it is not very rapid. So, minor inflations which arrive unexpectedly, or which are expected to be brief and even followed by price falls, are not likely to continue or to get worse. Divergent forces, depending as they do on expectations, can only be modified if expectations can somehow be changed towards lower anticipated rates of inflation. Unless there is reason to believe that external forces will reduce inflation, shifting inflationary expectations downwards, without drastic changes in economic policy and in peoples' lives, depends ultimately on an act of collective faith. If unions, government and private sector employers all agree to co-operate in reducing inflation, they may all believe that it is possible. In these circumstances divergent forces may indeed be reduced. But it is a difficult thing to achieve and much more difficult if the first attempt fails. Alternatively, very large reductions in demand creating very large increases in unemployment can have the effect of reducing wage increases below the rate of inflation and of forcing producers to compete by means of low prices for shrinking markets.

8 Devaluation

From the arguments so far it should be clear that when inflation is more rapid than in other countries and so causes a deterioration in the balance of payments, then devaluation of the currency is a possible policy. Devaluation is also a possible policy if the balance of payments deficit becomes unmanageably large for some other reason: most commonly a fall in export prices, but also such events as an export-crop failure or food-crop failure, making it necessary to pay for extra imports, or a loss of creditworthiness resulting in reduced capital inflows, or a loss of aid for, say, political reasons. Devaluation is also invariably demanded by the IMF when countries seek to borrow from it in order to finance a balance of payments deficit. Some borrowing from the IMF is unconditional: for example the first 25% of a country's quota can be borrowed without the IMF imposing any policy conditions, as can borrowing from the Compensatory Finance Facility (CFF) when export prices fall. But countries frequently have to seek additional IMF loans, in which case one of the conditions is always a devaluation.

The immediate effect of a devaluation is to make imports more expensive (unless foreign suppliers choose to reduce their prices); and to increase the profits of exporters. Exporters of primary products cannot normally control their export prices as expressed in foreign currency. Thus whether an African country devalues or not, the number of pounds or dollars or yen earned by exports is unchanged. If the local currency is devalued, that means that when the foreign earnings are sold (to the central bank) the exporter receives more local currency than before.

Of course the exporter must pay more, in local currency, for his imported inputs, but his profits increase nevertheless, unless the cost of imported inputs is greater than the value of exports. In most cases, African exporters export all or nearly all of their output, in which case they are always better off as a result of a devaluation. In a minority of cases, the bulk of output is sold on the domestic market with a relatively small proportion exported; in such a case, the additional cost of imported inputs could exceed the gains from a higher local currency price for exports–some agricultural exporters, for whom there is also a substantial home market, could be in this position. Even in such a case, devaluation makes exporting relatively more attractive than supplying the home market, if domestic prices increase less than the price received for exporting, so that producers may be encouraged to try and increase production for export. In general, therefore, a longer-run effect for *all* exporters should be to encourage increased production for export, as a result of it having become more profitable.

In particular, agricultural producers will be encouraged to increase output of export products such as coffee and tobacco, either at the expense of commodities sold mainly on the home market such as maize and vegetables, or in addition to existing output for the home market. This response does depend on a number of assumptions: that the infrastructure exists to handle increased export sales; that farmers can obtain the necessary inputs; that the increased value in domestic currency of export sales is actually passed on to producers; and that the *domestic* prices of commodities sold mainly on the home market are not also raised at the time of a devaluation.

Because the prices of imports increase, devaluation adds directly to inflation. If local industry is in a position to increase output in the short term, devaluation may shift demand from imports to domestic output and result in an output increase which is counter-inflationary. Where devaluation is in response to inflation, domestic output may not be able to increase; inflationary conditions usually imply that the economy has very little spare capacity. In Africa, there is the additional problem that shortage of foreign exchange may mean that producers cannot obtain essential inputs which have to be imported. Inflation itself may have created a large balance of payments deficit; or the reason for devaluation may be a fall in export prices or some other factor making foreign exchange scarce and inducing governments to put severe controls on imports.

In theory, devaluation itself, especially if undertaken as part of an agreement with the IMF (as is very often the case) can make foreign credit available, including IMF credit. It is often pointed out that reaching agreement with the IMF is sufficient to encourage other foreign lenders to make new credits available, so that even if the amount of foreign exchange lent by the IMF itself is inadequate, it is worthwhile going through the difficult process of reaching agreement. A relatively small IMF loan is supposed, according to this argument, to unleash much larger amounts of money, because of the gain in credit-worthiness from having an IMF 'seal of approval'. But many African countries remain unattractive to foreign lenders, even *after* reaching agreement with the IMF. So there is a real danger that the main effect of a devaluation will be a cost inflation. In many African economies, which produce a relatively narrow range of goods at home, devaluation causes price increases in a wide range of goods including some necessities, so wage-earners are particularly likely to try and seek higher incomes to compensate. In addition much of local industry depends heavily on imports of intermediate goods, so production costs also rise. Price increases are then likely to spread to locally-produced goods, further increasing the probability of wage demands.

A major question in any devaluation is thus the reaction of the labour force to the resulting higher prices. In particular the more powerful groups of workers, such as civil servants or unions of mine-workers or railway workers, would be likely to seek a wage rise; if it were successful there would be a danger of this spreading to other sectors of the economy. On the demand side, the biggest single question would be whether the increase in government revenue from the export sector is spent or not.[15] On the assumption that most forms of government spending cannot be increased at once, it should be relatively easy for the inflationary impact of a devaluation to be contained. However, the government would be likely to face demands for an increase in civil service wages to compensate for higher import prices, and it *is* possible for them to be increased very quickly—so again the importance of controlling wages is fundamental if devaluation is not to create further inflationary pressure.

A third question relates to credit. A devaluation is unlikely to be successful if commercial banks and other lenders are allowed to increase their lending rapidly, because of the effect on the balance of payments and on prices. Part of any Domestic Credit Expansion (DCE as in the Polak model) relates to the funding of the government—either by the commercial banks or by the central bank. The other part relates to bank lending to the rest of the economy. Control over DCE and control over government spending are thus closely related. IMF programmes usually include limits on both. An important criticism of limits on DCE is that producers may need credit to increase production, whether of exports or of import-competing output for the local market. If credit is severely constrained, output increases may also be prevented. In that case, the IMF programme following a devaluation becomes simply a reduction in demand in order to reduce imports, rather than a way of encouraging additional output in order to correct the balance of payments and the imbalance between supply and demand. Again, if producers are able to obtain additional *foreign* credit, output can increase without domestic credit expansion and without reducing foreign exchange reserves. An increase in output financed from abroad must clearly go mainly to exports and to substituting for imports, not to net increases in consumption out of higher domestic incomes, if the resulting increase in foreign indebtedness is to be manageable. As already mentioned, import substitution industries based on the local processing of imported inputs, a category which includes a large part of manufacturing industry in Africa, face increased costs as a result of devaluation. All industries use *some* imported inputs, of course, but in Africa as in most developing countries many new industries are very heavily dependent on imported inputs, with relatively low local value added. The effect of devaluation on such industries is to reduce their profits quite sharply unless they are able (or allowed by the government where prices are controlled) to raise their selling prices. Local industries do, on the other hand, gain a competitive advantage over imports, where competing imports are still allowed into the country.

Essentially what a devaluation does in domestic industry is to increase import costs in relation to local costs (including labour). So industries which use relatively *large* amounts of local raw materials and labour (especially local labour since expatriate labour may be in a better position to get compensating wage rises) and relatively *small* amounts of imported raw materials, intermediate goods and capital equipment, gain an advantage over other industries.

Devaluation should therefore encourage the growth of production which is relatively independent of imports, both by making it immediately more competitive, and in the longer run by making it clear that import-dependent industry is much more vulnerable at times of crisis.

A relatively minor aspect of devaluation, in countries heavily dependent on expatriates, is that it reduces the foreign exchange cost of expatriate remittances. Expatriate workers also have to pay more for imports and so have lower savings to send out of the country. In the longer-run, expatriates can probably obtain higher salaries successfully, because of the need for employers to be internationally competitive when recruiting and renewing contracts.

Devaluation also affects those with foreign assets and liabilities. In most African economies, only the central bank is legally permitted to hold significant amounts of foreign exchange (although in Sierra Leone, for example, both the marketing board and the commercial banks held foreign financial assets greater than working balance requirements in the late 1970s). Devaluation *increases* the local currency equivalent of such foreign assets, although it makes no difference at all to their value in foreign currency terms. So the central bank's profits, which are published in local currency, show a windfall gain after a devaluation, even though the foreign exchange reserves are unchanged when expressed in US dollars. Since central banks are owned by governments, which normally have large foreign debts, the net effect depends on the relative size of foreign debts and foreign reserves.

All net foreign borrowers face increased costs of interest and capital repayments after a devaluation, in local currency terms. If, however, relatively high domestic inflation has increased producers' profits, such increased costs need not necessarily create any problem. For the country as a whole, devaluation makes no immediate difference to the flow of foreign currency, in which foreign debt service is expressed. Individual borrowers, though, for example parastatal corporations, may have to be helped by the government (or allowed to increase their prices) because of the increased cost of foreign debt service payments in local currency terms.

In summary, devaluation makes exporting more profitable; makes import substitution industries more competitive but at the same time makes them less profitable unless they are able to offset the increased cost of imports by increasing prices; favours industries with a high proportion of local costs (including especially labour) over industries with a high proportion of import costs (including imported capital goods); reduces the volume and foreign exchange costs of expatriate remittances provided expatriate workers are not compensated by higher pay; increases the cost of living because of the increased cost of imports; may increase government revenue where there is a high marginal tax rate on export profits; puts pressure on the government to increase its spending (and borrowing) to pay for more expensive imports and higher wages; and also puts pressure on the government to allow parastatal industries (such as electricity and water supply) to raise their prices. There is a considerable danger that a devaluation will set off further inflationary forces unless wage demands are restrained (especially in export industries and in government), and unless home demand is also restrained (especially government expenditure and bank lending).

If domestic output is able to increase, to meet both the shift in demand from more expensive imports and the increased profitability of exporting, then the danger of further inflation following a devaluation is reduced. If domestic output is not able to increase, then further inflation would eventually create a need for further devaluation, and so on in a worsening and continuous cycle of inflation and devaluation. So while devaluation may frequently be *necessary* as a way of discouraging imports and encouraging exports by bringing local prices more nearly into line with foreign prices, it is not a *sufficient* policy on its own to achieve those objectives. It must be accompanied by other measures, of an unpopular type, to ensure that it does not simply make matters worse by accelerating the existing inflation.

Put slightly differently, a balance of payments deficit means that a country is using more foreign resources (imports) than the rest of the world wants to buy from it (exports); or at any rate the difference (the balance of payments current account deficit) is larger than can be financed from available and continuing foreign credits (sustainable foreign capital inflows). Without some hugely fortunate windfall, such as the discovery of oil or diamonds, such a situation requires that the country reduce its demand for imports in some way, and preferably also increase its export earnings. The choice of policies is limited. The government can:

(a) reduce income and expenditure, by taxation, reduced government spending, reductions in bank lending, wage restraint, etc;
(b) make imports more expensive by increased tariffs and exports more profitable by subsidising them;
(c) use controls to reduce imports (and conceivably also to increase exports for example by compulsory purchase and sale abroad of some part of local output);
(d) devalue.

For various reasons, devaluation is seldom a first choice. In addition to any obvious reluctance to devalue because of the bad side effects described already, governments apparently choose not to devalue from a belief that devaluation is in some sense dishonourable, or damaging to national pride. Whatever the reason, there is evidence that a majority of African countries have overvalued currencies, some of them by huge percentages, when local prices are compared with international prices:

The most striking similarity in the trade and exchange rate policies of African governments has been the tendency to let real official exchange rates become overvalued because of higher inflation at home than abroad. According to a study by the African Centre for Monetary studies, exchange rates rose in all but one (Sierra Leone) of 19 Sub-Saharan African countries between 1963 and 1977–78. Another study showed that they rose in 19 of the 27 countries examined. In four countries (Ghana, Mali, Uganda and Zaire), the exchange rate appreciatd by over 100%.[16]

The problem about *delay* in adjusting the exchange rate is that the greater the gap is between local and international prices, the greater is the devaluation needed. But it is very much harder to contain the inflationary (and political) impact of a large devaluation than a small one. So reluctance to devalue increases as the need becomes greater; this must be a major explanation as to why so many African economies become subject to increasingly strict controls, with all the consequences of corruption, black markets, smuggling and large numbers of scarce administrative resources employed in implementing the controls.

This line of argument also explains why African governments, like other developing-country governments, find it so hard to reach agreement with the IMF. Indeed, the unwillingness of governments to have to negotiate over national policy with the IMF, frequently delays a borrowing request. In turn, this is yet another reason for delay in devaluation. Unwillingness to agree to very large devaluation can then lead to even further delay. Very roughly, that is what happened in Tanzania in the early 1980s, when the IMF was demanding a much larger devaluation than the Tanzanian government was willing to implement, with the result that the currency was not devalued at all, despite the government's recognition that the currency was indeed overvalued to some extent.

9 *Using inflation as a tax*

By spending money which is not covered by taxation receipts or non-bank borrowing, governments can cause a shift of resources away from the private sector towards the public sector. The government action causes prices to rise if output cannot increase in the short term, some people's real incomes and wealth fall, and the government is able to spend money and command real resources at their expense.

There has been a great deal of discussion in economic writing on development as to whether in fact the governments of underdeveloped countries should use this method of 'taxation' to finance their development plans. The argument runs that because of shortage of administrative staff, and political realities, increased taxation may not be possible. Therefore inflation is the only way of transferring additional resources to the government. In using this argument, one must be careful to emphasise that such an inflation should be short, and be followed by a period of relative price stability, in order that divergent forces do not become established in the economy. Ideally, government spending financed by money creation should be on investments with a very high and rapid return, in the form of additional output. The inflationary addition to demand from the deficit spending would then be quickly matched by the addition to supply from new output, which would thus ensure that the inflation was temporary and short-lived.

The alternative view on this is that any country attempting development is going to experience *some* inflation, because of the inflexibility of the economy, inelasticities of supply in many sectors, shortages of key goods and skills, etc. Furthermore, even a comparatively mild inflation causes some inequities, for example against those on fixed money incomes, or those too weak to protect their real incomes, and against those who have saved, and perhaps invested in government loans. If, *on top of this*, the government attempts to use inflation as a tax, the rate of inflation will very quickly reach the point where divergent forces could take hold; the government might then find it was no longer able to control the inflation, with the usual serious effects on incentives, allocation of investment, and so on. In short, inflation is a very dangerous weapon, which can easily do more harm than good. At most the government may not wish to try and reduce a 'modest' rate of inflation.

The case for using inflation as a tax is based on a number of assumptions that are frequently incorrect, especially in African conditions. Firstly, it assumes that the government will make better use of the resources it 'captures' from the private sector than the latter would have done. It also assumes that the greater value of government's use of these resources is enough to offset the distortions caused by inflation. This is true of all forms of taxation, but in using conventional taxes the government has to make a more positive political decision, pass legislation and face up to the political and economic consequences in a more direct way. The costs of inflation are less obvious, being indirect and delayed, so that the danger of excessive use of inflation as a tax are very great.

Finally, it assumes that domestic finance is the dominant constraint acting on new investment. But it is likely that other constraints are also operating in Africa, most notably skilled labour and foreign exchange. Attempts to increase investment are likely to be frustrated, therefore, by inability to implement projects and by balance of payments crisis. In practice, it is far more common for African governments to be seeking ways of cutting back on government spending, in order to reduce balance of payments deficits and ease the pressure of excess demand on scarce domestic resources, than it is for them to be considering additional unfinanced spending with the deliberate intention of increasing inflation.

10 Controls on prices and incomes

For obvious reasons governments often try to control inflation by direct attack on prices themselves, and on wages when these are believed to be the main cause of inflation. There is also a case for controlling wages on grounds of equity, to prevent strongly organised groups of workers from gaining at the expense of other workers, and to prevent workers in general from gaining at the expense of farmers and the unemployed. To complete the circle of argument, if wages are controlled then it seems fair to control prices in order to prevent profits from rising as a result of wage controls.

Most governments try to keep wages and prices down, at first, by talking. Ministers make speeches about the public interest, the government as a whole lays down 'norms' for price and wage increases which people are asked not to exceed, on a voluntary basis. The trouble with this strategy is that, being difficult to police, it is unlikely to be universally observed. Those who obey the government's requests then lose out to those who do not—and any system that makes the 'good guys' look foolish is unlikely to last long.

Compulsory wage and price control is also difficult to enforce, especially when administrative staff are scarce and expensive. Furthermore, it prevents the price mechanism from allocating resources according to scarcity. For example, if the government obeys its own rules and restrains civil service pay, and if other employers disobey the rules or find ways round them, then over time the government will find it difficult to recruit and keep able people who can find better-paid employment elsewhere. The same argument applies within the private sector. In the very long run, if pay is not allowed to respond to shifts in the demand and supply of different types of skill, in the different parts of the country and the economy, the government will be forced into *directing* people to jobs. To a small extent this is already done, when those given an expensive university education at government expense are 'bonded' to work where they are placed for a number of years. But it is quite a big step from that to the direction of all workers. So leadership codes, salary reductions for cabinet ministers and the like are essentially political gestures in the context of making wage restraint acceptable and of altering inflationary expectations, rather than ways of effecting a lasting reduction in the differentials between top salaries and average incomes. The latter is only likely to be achieved at all effectively where the government is in direct control of nearly all top salaries, by ownership or participation in the majority of big employers, and where dependence on expatriates does not drive up all top salaries.

Similar arguments apply to trying to control prices. For example, if the government uses its power over agricultural prices to keep down the price of food, farmers have less incentive to produce more, consumers buy more because the price is low, and scarcities or expensive imports are the result. Or else the government is led into using expensive subsidies to keep down the price of food while offering farmers a good price. Another likely result is the creation of unofficial ('black') markets where the price is higher than the official price. All these results of price controls tend to induce yet more controls, more administrators and greater opportunities for administrative delay, mismanagement and corruption.

A further problem with price control is that governments tend to find it difficult to raise prices once they have introduced controls. Precisely because a controlled price has become the direct responsibility of a government, any increase is blamed directly on that government. As a result, controlled prices tend to be held down for long periods and diverge increasingly from the general level of uncontrolled prices, during an inflationary time. As the gap grows, between a controlled price and the cost of imports or the price that would be needed to generate an adequate domestic supply, it becomes increasingly expensive to provide the necessary subsidy while at the same time the difficulty of decontrolling the price also increases. There is a parallel in fact with the control of the foreign exchange rate (which is simply the price of foreign currency); it too can become harder to adjust as it diverges further from what it would be, if foreign exchange were not rationed.

In addition, if a government tries to control a wide range of prices, it will find it very difficult to obtain and analyse correctly the information needed to adjust prices as economic circumstances change; and the information itself will be incomplete and biased, since some producers will be more effective than others in providing the information needed to justify price increases, while consumers' interests may be less well represented than those of producers. These arguments do not necessarily add up to a case against control of prices (and incomes). The alternative of leaving price determination to markets may be worse, because markets often work imperfectly. But it is the case that a prices and incomes policy is difficult to implement effectively over long periods of time, and often more difficult to implement than is realised at the start.

There is much more to the proper analysis of prices and incomes policies than there is space for here. The main point to make in the context of a chapter on inflation is that a prices and incomes policy may be essential for breaking the vicious circle of divergent forces acting in an inflationary situation. If inflationary expectations create more inflation, which makes people expect yet more inflation with greater certainty, then the government may have to intervene. The government may also have to control prices of key commodities like maize and cooking oil at times of temporary shortage (or temporary excess supply) in order to prevent excessive profits at the expense of the poor.[17] The point is that the case for intervention is essentially one for temporary intervention, not for permanent controls, unless the government wishes to move towards a controlled economy, and has the administrative capacity to do so.

NOTES

1 Figures for Malawi from *Monthly Statistical Bulletin* (National Statistical Office, Zomba).

2 This happened in Botswana in 1981, for example.

3 Employment in government, agriculture and mining combined is over 50% of total wage employment in Zambia and Malawi, and just under 50% for Botswana.

4 'Living off' the employed consists not only of direct help, but also making some sort of a living in the 'informal' urban sector, by providing services such as car-washing, petty retailing, cycle repair, etc.

5 See J.B. Knight, 'Wages and Zambia's economic development' in Charles Elliott, *Constraints on the Economic Development of Zambia* (Nairobi, OUP, 1971).

6 See, for example, the definition in ILO, '*Employment, Incomes and Equality: a strategy for increasing productive employment in Kenya* (Geneva, 1972), p. 9.

7 See E.O. Ochieng', 'Botswana's trade structure compared with those of other small countries', in Charles Harvey (ed.), *Papers on the Economy of Botswana* (London, Heinemann, 1981), p. 127, for the changing import-dependency of these and other small economies.

8 See Bank of Botswana, *Annual Report 1977*, pp. 13–16. From a comparison with the movement in prices in neighbouring parts of South Africa, from which 85% or more of imports came, it was clear that prices of imported goods in Botswana had risen by roughly 5 percentage points less than equivalent prices in South Africa, as a result of the 5% revaluation of the Botswana Pula in 1977.

9 For example, interest rates adjusted for inflation in Ghana and Kenya were

	1978/79	*1979/80*	*1980/81*
Ghana	−36.4	−19.6	−48.2
Kenya	− 1.7	− 7.1	− 4.9

whereas interest rates in the major industrialised countries went from negative to positive over the same period. Figures taken from A. Lanyi and R. Saracoglu, 'The importance of interest rates in developing economies', *Finance and Development*, Vol. 20, no. 2, June 1983. In calculating the real rate of interest the authors used the current rate of inflation, as is customary, because there is no way of calculating the *expected* rate of inflation.

10 A quick way of calculating the real rate of interest is simply to deduct the rate of inflation from the appropriate rate of interest. This always gives the right sign, but gives slightly too big a number (more negative than it should be when the real rate of interest is negative, and larger than it should be when the real rate is positive). The correct formula is

$$\text{real rate of interest} = \frac{(1+i)}{(1+p)} - 1$$

where i is the rate of interest and p the rate of inflation expressed in decimal form.

11 There are, of course, exceptions to this: not all firms are selling goods the prices of which rise faster than costs, and, as is explained below, importers do better than exporters.

12 As already noted, most African countries do not allow residents to hold foreign bank balances. But some countries do; and in those that do not allow it, there are many illegal ways of moving money abroad. Exchange controls are seldom fully effective in preventing money from flowing abroad, although they can have a temporary effect, and they can make it more expensive to move money out of the country.

13 In extreme conditions, import controls are almost certainly necessary despite their disadvantages. If a country is really desperately short of foreign exchange, as many were in the early 1980s for example, then it becomes necessary *politically* to prevent the import of obvious luxuries, and *economically* prudent to decide which of many competing uses of scarce foreign exchange are most urgent.

14 This statement assumes that the income of the borrower rises in line with the general rate of inflation.

15 Most African governments derive a large part of their revenue from the export sector, and this revenue increases as a result of a devaluation, provided that the tax system produces increased tax revenue when profits increase. However, some governments are such major buyers of imports, that devaluation does not necessarily improve the budget position, the higher cost of imports offsetting the gain in revenue from exports. This would have been the case in Botswana in 1977, where the calculation was done in reverse, for a revaluation; and in Zambia, for example, revenue from the copper mines fell from more than 60% of revenue in the early 1970s, to zero by 1977.

16 World Bank, *Accelerated Development in Sub-Saharan Africa: an agenda for action* (Washington DC, 1981, p. 24) referring to African Centre for Monetary Studies, *Balance of Payments Problems of African Countries and their Effects on Development Objectives* (Dakar, August 1979, p. 69) and to another unnamed study.

17 Agricultural products are a special case because of the variations in supply caused by the weather, disease, etc. Even so, the possibility of imports and exports even out the effect of these fluctuations for many products.

11 *Theory of Public Finance*

1 *Introduction*

The theory of public finance is the theory of the economic functions of government: why they are undertaken, how many should be undertaken, who should perform them and how the resources should be provided. The classic work on this subject[1] identifies three main economic functions of government: the *allocation* of resources between private and public sectors; the *distribution* of income, and the *stabilisation* of national income, that is the management of aggregate demand so as to avoid severe depressions and excessive inflation. To these three functions most people would now add a fourth, which is the active promotion by government of economic development; and, although economic development can be defined to include almost anything, most African governments would probably single out the promotion of economic independence as a separate objective.

2 *Allocation: collective goods and merit goods*

The most basic reason for governments to interfere in the allocation of resources is the need for collective goods (also known as social wants) which the market economy cannot provide. The classic collective good is defence. Defence services are indivisible; that is, they are provided to the community as a whole, so nobody can be *excluded* from the benefits.[2] Indeed everyone must 'consume' collective goods in equal amounts. In addition, they must be paid for collectively. Because collective goods are indivisible and so cannot be sold individually, the community must find the necessary resources as a community. No individual will volunteer to pay for collective goods, since he or she cannot be excluded and so will enjoy the benefits whether he or she pays for them or not. So collective goods must be paid for by taxation or by some other compulsory method. Therefore the government intervenes to reduce the demand for private goods, for example by reducing people's incomes through taxation and using the tax revenue to pay for collective goods.

Governments also seek to provide some goods, known as merit goods, free or at less than the market price. Examples are education and health services or, for example milk, which was at one time supplied at half-price to low-income families in Zambia. Essentially, the government decides that some goods would not be demanded, or not demanded in adequate quantities, or not demanded by those who need them, if the full cost had to be paid by individuals. The reason is that people are thought not to appreciate the benefits fully. It may also be that people do not have sufficient income, in which case the provision of merit goods is to some extent part of the distribution function.

An interesting distinction between collective goods and merit wants is that one might expect people to vote for collective goods, provided they are sufficiently well informed to identify their collective needs. Thus although one cannot rationally expect people to volunteer to pay for collective goods, because they cannot be excluded from enjoying them, one could expect them to want them; so government could respond to the people's wishes in supplying things like defence, police services, flood protection, law courts, and so on.

Almost by definition, however, people do not identify their needs for merit wants, since if they did they would buy enough of them, without having to be taxed and have them supplied or subsidised by the government. It may be that some merit goods are desired by people all right, but they are too poor to afford them. In this case government is acting to redistribute income in supplying the goods free, or more cheaply than the market. It might be thought that the same redistribution effect could be achieved by a transfer from tax revenues to the incomes of the poor, thus allowing them to satisfy their needs. This assumes, however, that everyone has in fact successfully identified his needs. Governments tend not to make this assumption, but to be afraid that income transfers will be spent on beer or betting; so increased consumption of merit goods is usually attempted by direct supply or by direct subsidy.

In principle, the government should only decide to increase its own share of total spending if the additional benefits are greater than the loss of goods and services available in the private sector. This assumes full employment of resources; if the stabilisation function of government is being properly performed, then resources should be as fully employed as possible; if not, then the government can increase its own demands on the resources of the economy without reducing the resources available for satisfying private sector demands.

Within the government's budget, the marginal benefits from the spending of the last dollar or shilling on each service should be equal; for example, if more benefit accrues from spending an extra dollar on health than accrues from the last dollar spent on education, then less should be spent on education, and more on health—at least from the economic point of view. Such rules are, however, easy to express on paper, but difficult to put into practice, mainly because the marginal benefits from most types of government spending are difficult if not impossible to evaluate.

In the long run, the total resources used by government tend to be determined to a large extent by available financial resources—mainly taxation, but including borrowing, foreign exchange reserves, money creation and foreign aid. In principle a government has the power to tax people more heavily if it believes that a bigger proportion of total resources should be used to provide government services. However, people do not like paying taxes, so governments need an 'excuse' for imposing heavier taxation. The result seems to be that only in times of crisis, such as a war, are governments able to make big increases in the proportion of income that people pay in taxes.

In more normal times, people tend to regard the existing level of taxation as the maximum tolerable. Research in the UK has shown that after wars the proportion of income paid in taxation falls, but does not fall to the pre-war level. The reason suggested is that people quite quickly get used to a higher level of taxation, once it has successfully been imposed, so that governments are not forced to return to the pre-war position.[3] If, on the other hand, taxes are sharply increased without adequate political justification, the result is likely to be tax riots, the fall of the government or ignominious removal of the offending taxes. If the country is heavily dependent on internationally-recruited labour, heavy increases in income tax may have to be reversed, or compensated by higher wages, because of expatriate workers' ability to leave the country.[4]

The permanent upward shift in the proportion of income which people will pay in taxes has been called the 'displacement effect'. Associated with it is an 'inspection effect'. In times of crisis existing ideas of what needs to be done by government are shaken up and changed. Governments 'inspect' their activities and the people's needs, and discover new spending requirements.

There was a sharp increase in the level of spending by many African governments after independence. In this instance, however, it was not so much the new governments being forced by some crisis to discover new needs. The needs were well enough known to the new governments; it was simply that they had been badly neglected before independence. The same sort of thing can occur when a new government takes office as a result of an election or of a revolution. If the desire to spend more is not matched by increased government revenue, a new government is very likely to run into severe financial difficulties. This happened, for example, after independence in Ghana, when the reserves accumulated in the 1950s were quickly run down and more foreign borrowing was undertaken than could be repaid.[5]

3 *Distribution*

Governments interfere in the distribution of income because communities seldom believe that market forces distribute income justly. In addition the community may wish to discriminate against certain types of income, such as rent or profits, or against income earned by foreigners.

In a market economy people earn incomes which roughly reflect the scarcity of their skills on the one hand, and their economic and political bargaining powers (usually in groups) on the other. The difficulty lies in distinguishing a high income which results from hard work and enterprise, virtues which most societies accept as deserving economic rewards, from a high income which results from luck, or the use of monopoly power or from some other circumstance which the community feels gives 'excessive' rewards. In practice it is not possible to make such a distinction, so high incomes are taxed at higher rates than low incomes, regardless of the source of income – at the risk of creating a disincentive to effort and enterprise. And those who receive rent or profit income may be taxed more heavily, *either* from a belief that such income does *not* represent hard work and enterprise, *or* from a belief that such income is only received by the rich. Both beliefs may of course be incorrect.

Taxation is discussed at some length in the next chapter. The point to make here is that African governments tend to find it very difficult in practice to redistribute income by means of the tax system – in spite of high marginal rates of tax on high incomes, and heavy taxation of luxury goods. Mainly for practical reasons, governments also rely rather heavily on other forms of taxation which bear disproportionately on the poor. Income tax, also for practical reasons, tends to be very difficult to administer so that it does not have the effect it should have in taxing high incomes heavily. The overall result is therefore that tax systems do not succeed in being progressive (by which is meant that the proportion of each person's income paid in tax does not rise as income rises). In Kenya, for example, a study found that the overall effect of the tax system on income distribution was more or less negligible.

Table 11.1 Combined incidence of direct and indirect taxes in Kenya

Monthly income (in shillings)	*Tax incidence as a percentage of income*	*Monthly income (in shillings)*	*Tax incidence as a percentage of income*
0–199	11.5	700–999	10.5
200–299	11.3	1,000–1,399	9.3
300–399	8.5	1,400–1,999	9.6
400–499	8.3	2,000 and over	12.7
500–699	8.0		

Source: Report of ILO employment mission to Kenya, *Employment, Incomes and Inequality: a strategy for increasing productive employment in Kenya*, ILO, Geneva, 1972, p. 272, quoting M.J. Westlake, 'Tax evasion, tax incidence and the distribution of income in Kenya', University of Nairobi, Institute of Development Studies, 1971, mimeo.

The distributive effects of mineral taxes depend on who, in principle, is really entitled to the profits. This is obviously very important in major mineral-exporting countries where mineral taxes are a large proportion of government revenue. If oil or copper is being exploited by foreign companies, from rich countries and (probably) owned by rich people in those countries, then heavy taxation of the profits is arguably a redistribution of income, via government spending in the country where the minerals are. It is surely much more reasonable to argue, however, that the most the foreign companies are entitled to is a 'reasonable' payment for their capital and skills and the risks taken (if any). Any remaining profit on copper or oil or diamonds, say, legitimately belongs to all of the people of Zambia or Nigeria or Botswana. If the government spending out of mineral revenues benefits all the people equally then the overall effect is merely neutral; and if the benefits of government spending out of mineral revenues fails to reach the poorer groups such as remote subsistence farmers, then the overall effect is actually to make income distribution worse.

If tax systems tend to be ineffective in redistributing income, then it remains to ask whether government spending can be more effective, since clearly it is the overall impact of the fiscal system that really matters.

Many government services are provided free, or at less than cost, in order that they shall be equally available to all. One problem of this form of redistribution is that services provided free may be 'over-consumed'—that is, people may demand more than they need of a service because it is free or cheap. For example, people may use health services which they do not really need because no payment is required and they having nothing to lose. In the case of health, it may be better to risk some over-consumption than to risk a sick person being denied health services because he cannot afford to pay–but this assumes an adequate overall supply.

A much more important problem in providing free services arises when there is not enough for everybody, as is common in poor countries. Not everyone who needs it can gain access to clinics, doctors, schools, subsidised credit, etc. In these circumstances, distribution must be decided by some administrative process. The result is often that the richer people succeed in gaining access. When some services are of better quality than others, it is again the already-privileged who tend to succeed in gaining access to the better services. The reasons are many: rich people are better at filling in forms, are better-informed, are better-placed (they live in towns, near to good schools and hospitals), or they simply have influence with which to gain access. Furthermore, richer people tend to carry greater political weight when it comes to deciding what new services shall be provided, and where. That is why urban people are better served by public services than rural people.

If richer people do succeed in getting access to government services provided free, then the result is in one sense the same as if the government charged a fee, since under either system poor people are excluded. The difference is that rich people are subsidised if services are free. In these circumstances it might be better to charge a fee, which if spent on increasing the services available, would result in more people being able to gain access. Alternatively, administrative methods can be changed in order to achieve more egalitarian distribution–but this is extremely difficult.

A special case of a government service provided free (or very heavily subsidised) is education. On the one hand the community needs highly trained manpower and needs to select as efficiently as possible those who can benefit from each level of education above primary (everyone is assumed to need primary schooling). On the other hand this process means selecting the brightest students, who would be most likely to succeed in earning high incomes anyway, and then spending large sums of government money on further increasing this earning power. Some sacrifice is required of students in that often they have a lower income while studying than they could earn in a job, but the student life is itself often quite pleasant, and the subsequent financial rewards very high in countries where educated people are very scarce, and top salaries are heavily influenced by international salary levels.[6] In addition, the children of richer parents have advantages, not only in gaining access to the better schools, but in passing exams. Children coming from better-off families are well known to have enormous advantages in conventional education, because of parental encouragement, a literate home background, etc. The result is again that an apparently egalitarian policy, the provision of free education, is likely to give great additional advantages to the already privileged—who could afford to pay.[7]

A distinction needs to be made, therefore, between the effect on income distribution of collective goods which are indivisible and have to be consumed equally,[8] and the effect on income distribution of government services which are divisible but subsidised. It is the latter which are liable to reinforce unequal income distribution, even when governments have the opposite intentions.

Most government policies have some impact, intentional or not, on income distribution. The most important intentional distribution policy, apart from taxation and the provision of government services, is a prices and incomes policy. This has already been discussed in the context of inflation (chapter 10, section 10) where it was also mentioned that equity and fairness were involved. It is a reasonable generalisation that economic and political power are often cumulative. Thus, those who have scarce skills are in a strong position to bargain for even higher incomes than they already receive; those with high and stable incomes are able to borrow and invest in farms and businesses which increase their incomes even further. The rich tend to have influence on the political and administrative process by which their own incomes are decided—whether it be by keeping down urban prices, by influencing the nature of taxation or by deciding their own salaries. So governments try to intervene directly in the determining of prices and incomes, and by legislating to prevent the privileged from having several sources of income (for example, Zambia's Leadership Code) not only in order to control inflation, but in order to redistribute income.

In the context of income distribution, the really important point to make about an incomes policy is that many policies intended to introduce greater equity are not as simple in their impact as they seem. For example, increasing the price of maize has been discussed as a way of redistributing income from town to country—but its effect may be to redistribute income from the urban poor (who are the majority of urban consumers and must spend a high proportion of their income on basic food) to the rural rich (who produce the bulk of marketed maize). Similarly, a leadership code may have the effect of redistributing income from those to whom it applies (civil servants) to those who are left out of its provisions (in the private sector). In general, income distribution must be looked at in its entirety, including possession of assets with which to earn income (physical assets, human capital and access to key resources such as credit). It may be that egalitarian asset distribution, especially of land in predominantly rural countries, is a much more powerful way of redistributing income than the whole of fiscal and incomes policy.

4 *Stabilisation*

A large part of this book has been about the stabilisation function of government, namely the need to prevent the under-utilisation of resources on the one hand, and excess demand on the other. Ideally the government should try and use tax, expenditure and monetary policy in such a way that income is as stable as possible around an ideal level.[9] Although that is very difficult, governments should normally be able to prevent extremes of surplus unused capacity and very high levels of excess demand.

The realisation that governments can control aggregate demand (more precisely, the balance between aggregate demand and supply) was of great benefit after 1945 in preventing excessive waste of productive capacity, as occurred in the depression of the 1930s. There was a tendency for governments of industrial countries to pay more attention to the risk of unemployment (whether of people or of other resources) than to the risk of inflation. The result was steadily rising prices which led, as explained in chapter 10, to inflationary expectations and to the institutionalising of a constant process of inflation. These make inflation worse, or at least make it very difficult to stop inflation from continuing for long periods.

Reductions in demand then had progressively less and less impact on prices. Even those countries which managed their affairs differently had to 'import' to some extent other countries' inflation. The stabilisation function of government has thus tended to shift in emphasis from the prevention of too little aggregate demand to the control of inflation.

It would be ironic if the ability to 'manage' the economy (that is, the stabilisation function), resulted in either the destabilising effect of accelerating inflation or the need for much larger reductions in demand (in order to control inflation) than would otherwise have been necessary. In Africa, the stabilisation function has become increasingly a matter of managing crises in the balance of payments rather than of correcting internal imbalance between aggregate demand and aggregate supply. The latter may indeed be one of the causes of a balance of payments deficit; but deficits can also be caused by adverse shifts in the terms of trade (falls in export prices or increases in import prices or both at the same time) or by such internal factors as a fall in food production.[10]

In the short run, an African government faced with an external imbalance must decide to what extent it should reduce aggregate demand and therefore imports, and to what extent it is both advisable and possible to finance the deficit by running down the foreign exchange reserves or by borrowing abroad. The choice depends on whether the deficit is thought to be temporary, in which case it is reasonable to avoid adjustment by financing it, or permanent, in which case an adjustment must be made in the long run, with perhaps some financing to enable the adjustment to be less abrupt (than would otherwise be the case).

In practice, it is never possible to be sure whether a deficit is temporary or permanent, so that some *combination* of adjustment and finance is prudent.[11] A government does not want to reduce demand, which reduces income and slows growth, if the balance of payments is going to recover quite quickly. On the other hand, if a deficit turns out not to be temporary, adjustment is more difficult. The country may have already run down its reserves and used up much of its capacity to get foreign finance so that aggregate demand may have to be reduced by more, and more abruptly, with greater damage to the people's welfare and to the process of development. Even if some adjustment sometimes turns out to be unnecessary, that may be a small price to pay for avoiding the risk of a much more severe balance of payments and debt crisis, arising out of failure to begin the process of adjustment soon enough. Long run adjustment should, of course, include measures to increase export production, by making it more profitable or by shifting additional resources to export production by some other means.

5 *Automatic stabilisation*

In chapter 5 (section 5) it was explained that receipts from most taxes tend to vary with income and spending, and that this reduces the multiplier effect of changes in demand. Thus the formula for the multiplier without government spending and taxation was

$$k = \frac{1}{1 - b}$$

and when G and T were introduced the formula was

$$\frac{1}{1 - b + bt}$$

So income fluctuations tend to be smaller as a result of a tax function which depends on income. The major qualification of this formulation is that some income and tax changes have little or no feedback effect on spending. This is allowed for by having a tax function of the form

$$T = \bar{t} + ty$$

where $\bar{t}$ is that part of tax receipts which is independent of income in the short term. Where taxes on exports are large, as in many African economies, changes in income caused by *internal* events, such as an increase in government spending, have no short-term effect on receipts from export taxes. In such a case $\bar{t}$ would be relatively large. Where changes in income arise from changes in export earnings, tax receipts also change and $\bar{t}$ would be relatively small.

Automatic stabilisation, that is the reduction in income fluctuations as a result of the nature of the tax system and government spending, is greater as t is greater. It is thus open to governments to choose taxes for their automatic stabilising effects.

In effect, West African marketing boards did this, in an extreme way, by paying a fixed price to farmers producing export crops such as cocoa, and allowing the entire impact of export price fluctuations to be reflected in marketing board surpluses and deficits. Strictly speaking, this amounts to a stabilisation scheme and not taxation. Indeed the original intention was purely stabilisation with no taxation element, but the price to farmers turned out to be consistently below the world price so that *de facto* the farmers were being taxed—and to add insult to injury, the marketing board surpluses were not, by and large, used for investment in agriculture but were spent on industrial development, much of which was not successful.[12]

At the other extreme, the income tax in many African countries only applies to a very small proportion of the population so that it has relatively minor automatic stabilising effects. Other taxes on individual income, such as payroll taxes, personal levies and provident fund contributions, also tend to be relatively minor in their impact. Thus few of the Sub-Saharan African countries raise as much as 20% of central government revenue from taxes on individual income, and several raise less than 10%.

In industrial economies, on the other hand, income tax tends to be very much more important: the equivalent figures to those in Table 11.2 for the USA and Britain were 45% and 32% respectively. In addition, industrial countries tend to raise a lot of revenue from social security contributions, paid in varying combinations by employers and employees. Thus Switzerland, for example, raised only 10% of revenue from income taxation, but raised a further 49% of revenue from social security contributions. Such contributions are very small in Africa.

Table 11.2 Proportion of central government revenue from taxes on individual incomes (percentages)

Ethiopia	7	Malawi	12
The Gambia	5	Mauritius	13
Ghana	8	Sierra Leone	6
Lesotho	6	Swaziland	12
Liberia	17	Zambia	19

Source: International Monetary Fund, *Government Finance Statistics Yearbook, 1981*, summary table, p. 19.

As a result, almost all of an increase in wages in Africa becomes disposable income and is available to be spent. The same applies to the increase in income from an increase in numbers employed. In reverse, spending is likely to fall by almost the full amount of a fall in wage income.

The main contribution to tax revenue of African wage earners and self-employed people is in the form of indirect taxes, that is, taxes on expenditure. These include taxes on domestically-produced goods (and sometimes services such as airport taxes and hotel taxes) and import duties, usually with a very much higher rate of taxation on alcoholic drinks and cigarettes (sometimes called *demerit goods*). Relatively high expenditure taxes, with increasing coverage, result in marginal propensities for tax revenue to increase with increases in income (t) that are quite high in Africa, despite the lack of coverage of taxes on personal income.

Just as important as tax in providing automatic stabilisation is government spending. In African countries there tends to be little or no automatic increase in government spending as income falls (there being no payment to the unemployed as in industrialised countries) but government spending is much more stable than private consumption and investment. Basically, as discussed at length in chapter 5, government spending is independent of short-term changes in income. So the larger is G as a proportion of total spending, the smaller do fluctuations tend to be. Since this proportion has tended to increase over time, there has been a tendency towards greater automatic stabilisation.

All the above analysis applies almost exclusively to the monetary economy. The subsistence sector's income fluctuates mainly as a result of the weather and other natural causes. The existence of the public sector affects this sector directly only in extreme circumstances, by providing famine relief, although if a comparison is made with the distant past, the existence of strong government has also reduced cattle and slave-raiding and other violent disruptions in supply.

6 Growth and development

This book is about short-term changes in macroeconomics aggregates, not about growth and development which involves the longer term. The points to be made here are why governments have become involved in promoting development and just what this additional function implies.

Governments in industrial countries became interested in promoting growth because the elimination of widespread unemployment by demand management enabled them to look to other ways of increasing income. In the rest of the world, contact with richer countries awakened governments to the possibilities of growth, as did the gaining of independence in many countries in recent years.

By actively promoting growth, governments are interfering with individual choice in a new way. Firstly, they are deciding that change in social habits, in social relations, in physical surroundings, in traditional values, in the ways in which people work, is worthwhile for the rewards of growth. Secondly, government is deciding, very often, that present sacrifice is worthwhile for future benefit. For example, if government imposes additional taxation to finance some project whose benefit is spread over 25 years starting after 5 years, it is effectively interfering with people's time preferences, by reducing their consumption in the present for the sake of increased consumption later.

To the extent that governments represent people's wishes in promoting growth, time preference is merely being expressed collectively rather than individually. But it is part of the nature of development that changes are made which are outside the range of understanding and imagination of many people; and in any case the amount of interference with time preference, that is the amount of present sacrifice for the sake of future income growth, cannot normally be expressed collectively. It is a new type of decision which did not have to be made when governments were concerned only with allocation, distribution and stabilisation. People's own private savings, and therefore investment, determined the nation's time preferences between present and future consumption; any government savings were determined by the stabilisation function.

Although at one time it was believed that growth was determined by investment, it is now thought that investment as conventionally defined only creates part of economic growth, the remainder coming as a result of improvements in productivity whose causes are much in dispute. Statistical analysis shows typically that less than half of growth can be attributed to physical investment; the remainder is attributed to education, research, better health or nutrition, improved management or any number of other causes according to the prejudices of different writers. The point to make here is that some spending conventionally classified as consumption undoubtedly contributes to income growth: this means that governments must interfere not only with time preferences in the pursuit of income growth but also in the choice of consumption items, both individual and collective.

7 *Economic independence*

The most important variables which African countries perceive as affecting their economic independence include (not necessarily in order of importance)

(a) the ratio of foreign trade to GNP;
(b) the proportion of imports that are supplied by one or a few countries;
(c) the proportion of certain strategically important products that have to be imported (such as oil, food, armaments) especially if supplied by one or a few countries;
(d) the amount of foreign ownership and control of domestic production, particularly export production;
(e) the degree of dependence on foreign skilled manpower[13] especially if supplied by one or a few countries;
(f) the degree of dependence on other countries for employment of the national workforce as migrant workers;
(g) the degree of dependence on one or a few export products, especially if sold in unstable markets;[14]
(h) the size of the current account deficit of the balance of payments, implying dependence on capital inflows to maintain external balance, especially if from a few sources;
(i) the size of the foreign debt, and in particular the ratio of current foreign debt service to current foreign exchange earnings (the debt service ratio).

In the case of land-locked countries, of which there are fourteen in Africa, nearly all foreign trade is dependent on the continuing cooperation of neighbouring transit states. There are in fact degrees of 'landlockedness', depending, for example, on how many alternative routes to the sea exist and on how many transit countries are involved in each route.[15]

The importance attached to different types of economic dependence varies from country to country, and with different circumstances. Not every form of dependence has been listed above; and some form of dependence may seem unimportant at any particular time. For example, being dependent on imported oil mattered very little when oil was both cheap and freely available; and dependence on one country for a high proportion of imports is unimportant if supply is unlikely to be cut off, or if alternative sources could easily and cheaply be found.

Not all forms of dependence are necessarily wholly bad. It may be unfortunate to depend heavily on oil or diamonds for export revenue, but countries without oil wells or diamond mines would almost certainly like to have some. Countries with large amounts of foreign investment in their economies probably prefer to have the problems of negotiating with foreign investors to reduce their bad effects, to being without the assets, output, tax revenue, skills and other benefits created by their investments. Rapidly growing exports may create increasing dependence on foreign trade, but they also create increased income, with which it is much easier to tackle development problems, including those of economic dependence. A large and growing foreign debt *may* be a sign of success, in attracting foreign capital and investing it successfully in productive assets, as well as a form of dependence. In short, some problems are nice ones to have.

A second point is that, even where economic dependence seems most extreme, the dependent country usually has *some* bargaining power. Thus transit states earn income from the transit trade of land-locked countries and so have something to lose from halting transit traffic. Some potential foreign investors have markets to lose if they do not invest (see chapter 7, especially section 4); and all *actual* foreign investors have committed capital to the creation of fixed assets, and so have the investment and the profits on it to lose. Even aid donors have some self-interest in their aid programme, as can be seen from the fact that aid *negotiations* take place.

Thirdly there is much that can be done, to reduce at least some forms of dependence. All African countries have, for example, greatly diversified their sources of foreign aid and private capital inflows since the 1960s. Botswana built oil-storage capacity to give the country time to organise alternative supplies in the event of a cut-off of supply from South Africa. Zambia and Tanzania built the Tazara railway to Dar-es-Salaam to add to the railways that go from Zambia to the sea via Zaire and Zimbabwe. Every African country has enormously expanded education and training in order to reduce dependence on foreign skills. Many foreign firms have been nationalised or partially nationalised, and many new foreign investments have been undertaken with local participation from the start (this is discussed more fully in the next section). Most African countries have sharply diversified their import sources from their dependence on a few countries in colonial times.

It is often extremely difficult to decide to what extent such expenditures are justified. Decisions to expand education tend to be *relatively* easy, since there is a positive economic return to training people, especially if they are to replace expensive expatriates, *as well as* a gain in independence. Decisions to spend money in order to guard against a disaster that may never occur, are much more difficult. The risk of drought or flood can (in principle) be calculated, if historical records exist. The cost of food storage can then be compared with the cost of imports, or the cost of flood control can be compared with the possible losses from floods. But the political risk, of such things as a cut-off in oil supplies or of transit routes, is impossible to calculate in such a way as to be able to compare it with the cost of oil storage or new trade routes.[16]

8 *Publicly-produced goods*

Should collective goods and merit goods be supplied by governments or supplied by the private sector and paid for by government? What other goods should be produced within the public sector?

In extreme cases the answer is fairly obvious. Hiring out defence services to private contractors is not done very often and is seldom successful when it is done (for example, African experience with mercenaries). Defence and police services, law courts and government administration are too vital to be run by anybody but the government itself (although some internal security services are provided by private sector security companies and by individual watchmen).

It is also common for governments to own the providers of such public services as telephones, electricity and water. The argument for public ownership in these cases is that 'utilities' are 'natural monopolies'. That is, it is more efficient (cheaper) to have one monopolistic corporation supplying electricity, for example, because of the waste of resources if two rival suppliers had to lay electricity cables all over the country. Public ownership of so-called natural monopolies is not universal, however: for example, telephone services are provided by a private sector corporation in the USA.[17] There are a number of other services which are publicly owned in some countries but not in others, or which are provided by public and private suppliers in various combinations: for example, bus services and agricultural marketing.

The underlying point is that ownership is only one way of safeguarding the public interest. Parastatal companies can act in much the same way as private companies, giving rise to the phrase 'state capitalism'. The managers of large corporations, whether publicly or privately-owned, tend to control corporation policy unless the owners take a lot of trouble to exert control. So *all* corporations are capable of acting against the public interest, for example by using their monopoly power to set prices higher than is thought proper (however defined), and need to be controlled by other means.

If the government of an African country owns some or all of the shares in a company, whether the company is providing a service such as electricity or producing mineral exports, ownership in itself simply entitles the government to appoint some or all of the board of directors. The government directors are usually senior civil servants or prominent local lawyers or businessmen. Inevitably, being busy people, they come to board meetings poorly briefed, and the directors who represent management and control the flow of information to the board, and who have the technical expertise concerning the actual running of the corporation, are in a very strong position to get their way at board meetings. Public ownership is not enough, therefore, and the government must continue to enforce public policy by all the usual methods: taxation, wage policy, pricing policy, localisation policy, employment and residence permits for expatriates, control of pollution, etc. Indeed there is a serious risk that governments, having established public ownership, may relax the implementation of public policy by other means, in the belief that public ownership is sufficient, which it is not.[18]

In Africa there is a further aspect of public ownership. The primary motive in most of the many African nationalisations has been to lessen foreign ownership and control rather than to achieve public ownership itself. Thus where private-sector institutions and private individuals have been available to take over from foreigners, they have been used–examples are retailers and small-scale building contractors. Where no private-sector institutions were able to take over the foreign concerns, the government did so–as in the case of some foreign mining companies. Similarly, where governments want new foreign investment to be undertaken in collaboration with local people, the sheer size of some operations often dictates that the government itself is the only possible partner.

Criticisms of the parastatal sector, even when valid in themselves, often neglect the point that the choice in Africa is not between public ownership and private ownership, in the same way as the choice exists in Western Europe or North America.[19] The choice is often between ownership by the African government and private *foreign* ownership. Foreign companies present some quite different conflicts of interest between themselves and governments, from the conflicts that arise between purely local private-sector companies and their governments.

Transnational companies (TNCs) wish to maximise their *global* profits, which means they may

— expand production capacity in some other country
— prefer to buy inputs from their own factories abroad rather than from local sources.
— use transfer-pricing to avoid local taxation and exchange controls
— be unwilling to transfer technology and skills because that would reduce their bargaining power
— choose technology unsuited to local conditions because managers are more familiar with it.

If, for example a *local* company pays less tax than the government would like, at least it is likely that the additional post-tax profits will be distributed or invested within the domestic economy; in the case of a foreign company, such an assumption cannot be made. In short, the working of the price mechanism cannot be assumed to work in the interests of any one economy in the case of companies that operate in a global context. So special measures, including but not only public ownership, are necessary.

Public ownership is also a way of securing for the public sector the profits of the industries concerned. Again, taxation is a clear alternative method, although it can be objected that discriminatory taxation against particular firms or industries is wrong. In practice, public ownership seldom increases government revenue: either profits are all reinvested or, as is frequently the case, the industry is run at a loss and the government has to cover the cost.

The strongest arguments against public ownership are that governments and their civil servants are less efficient at running productive industry than private firms, and that governments never allow inefficient firms to fail, thus perpetuating inefficiency and the need for subsidy. These arguments are about matters of fact, however, and should be based on pragmatic appraisal of each situation. There is no *a priori* reason why either private or public management should be more efficient. In Africa, where most countries are rather small and remote and thus at a disadvantage when dealing with large foreign companies, public-sector participation is often the only way of finding out enough about the way companies are run to exercise effective control in the national interest—but even this is not true in every case.

9 *Conclusion*

Although the problem of paying for government services is very much a part of the theory of public finance, it is such a big subject in itself that it is covered in the next chapter.

NOTES

1 R.A. Musgrave, *The Theory of Public Finance*, New York, McGraw-Hill, 1959.

2 The fact that people can be *excluded* from consuming most goods and services, so that it becomes possible to produce and sell them for profit, is sometimes referred to as the 'exclusion principle'.

3 See A.T. Peacock and J. Wiseman, *The Growth of Public Expenditure in the United Kingdom*, Oxford University Press, 1961, Introduction and chapter 1.

4 This roughly explains what happened in Zambia's 1974 budget when the previous year's income tax increase was reversed, officially instead of wage increases, unofficially because of increasing expatriate labour turnover on the mines. See 1974 Budget Speech.

5 See Tony Killick, *Development Economics in Action* (London, Heinemann 1978). A similar but slightly different point, that new socialist governments tend to neglect the financial implications of their spending and structural reform programmes, is made in Stephany Griffith-Jones, *The Role of Finance in the Transition to Socialism* (London, Frances Pinter, 1981).

6 Graduate unemployment was already apparent in some African countries in the 1980s, for example in Ghana and Uganda, and would have appeared elsewhere without government guarantees of graduate employment, as for example in the Sudan.

7 Education systems also have the effect of removing the most able from the rural areas by giving them a taste for town life, and because the bulk of jobs requiring education are in towns.

8 Although it has been argued that rich people, having more to lose, gain more from defence and police services than poor people.

9 It would be more accurate to say that stabilisation should be around a high level of utilisation of a growing production capacity—however, the additional complication of growth over time is ignored here.

10 An external crisis might also occur because external capital inflows suddenly slow down, perhaps because foreign lenders change their opinion as to the country's creditworthiness.

11 The same point was made in the context of government expenditure policy, chapter 5, section 4.

12 See G.K. Helleiner, 'The fiscal role of the Marketing Broads in Nigerian economic development, 1947–61', *Economic Journal*, September 1964, reprinted in Milton C. Taylor, *Taxation for African Economic Development*, London, Hutchinson, 1970; and G.K. Helleiner 'Marketing Boards and domestic stabilisation in Nigeria', *Review of Economics and Statistics*, February, 1966.

13 Some countries are concerned about dependence on foreign *unskilled* manpower: for example, South Africa deliberately reduced the proportion of foreign unskilled workers on the gold mines from 90% or so to 50% or less in the 1970s.

14 Selling exports to only a few countries is sometimes considered as a form of economic dependence. Most African exports are primary commodities sold at prices determined by world markets, so that it does not normally matter which country actually buys them. However, there are some important exceptions. The fact that diamonds are mostly marketed in London, and paid for in US dollars is not very important. The fact that the market for rough diamonds is controlled very closely most of the time, by De Beers through its Central Selling Organisation, matters very much indeed to diamond producers, whose freedom of action is enormously reduced by the De Beers marketing monopoly. The sale of beef to the EEC at privileged prices by Botswana and Swaziland is another example.

15 See Zdenek Cervenka (ed.), *Land-locked Countries of Africa*, Uppsala, Scandinavian Institute of African Studies, 1973, especially the paper by Douglas Anglin in

which he lists no fewer than 29 routes to the sea from Zambia, of which 21 have actually been used – pp. 122–3.

16 See D.P. Ghai (ed.) *Economic Independence in Africa* (East African Literature Bureau, 1973) which contains essays on Egypt, Kenya, Sudan and Zambia, as well as several more general discussions of the subject.

17 The British Government was planning to 'privatise' part of the public telephone service at the time of writing, so that Britain could also be an exception by the time this book is published.

18 For a detailed description of the way the former management retained control of the copper mining companies after the 1969 takeover, see M. Bostock and C. Harvey (eds), *Economic Independence and Zambian Copper*, New York, Praeger, 1972, chapter 7.

19 See World Bank, *Accelerated Development in Sub-Saharan Africa: an agenda for action* (Washington DC, 1981) and various critiques, including *Institute of Development Studies Bulletin*, January 1983, Vol. 14 No. 1 'Accelerated development in Sub-Saharan Africa: what agendas for action?' and Charles Harvey, 'The Economy of Sub-Saharan Africa: a critique of the World Bank's report', *African Contemporary Record, 1981–82* (London, Holmes and Muir, 1982).

12 *Paying for Government Spending*

1 Introduction

There are many ways of meeting the cost of government services—most of them require a degree of compulsion. As already explained, it is irrational to volunteer to pay one's share of the cost of collective goods. Ideally, the community should make a collective decision on how to pay—by taxation, by borrowing from itself or from others, by providing free labour, and so on—but in the end that decision must be enforced since few people are willing to contribute their share unless everyone else does so too. Thus even if a small village community decides to provide itself with a dam or a road or a school building by communal labour, it is necessary that everyone contribute (and be seen to contribute). It may be hard to exclude shirkers once the new facility is built and available and it would be unjust to exclude their children.

In a modern economy, taxation is normally by far the most important way of providing resources to the government, but other methods do exist. This chapter will deal mainly with the principles of taxation, but it is important to remember that governments can choose not only between different types of tax but also between tax and other ways of allocating resources from the private to the public sector. Governments can also choose to get resources for the public sector without reducing the resources available to the private sector, by foreign borrowing.

2 Basic principles of taxation

Probably the most basic principles of taxation are those of horizontal and vertical equity. Horizontal equity requires that all those with an equal ability to pay should pay the same amount of tax; vertical equity requires that those with a greater ability to pay should pay more. These principles are easy enough to express on paper but extraordinarily difficult to put into practice. What is more, they may conflict with various other criteria. Thus tax systems should be cheap to administer; should be good at controlling private sector expenditure (economic efficiency); should encourage, or discourage as little as possible, saving, investment, production and the supply of effort (incentive effects); should not distort the allocation of resources within the private sector, except where this is a deliberate policy (neutrality); should maintain or even increase the government's share of income as income increases (income elasticity); should provide revenue that is easy to forecast accurately, so as to make planning easier (fiscal marksmanship); should make groups pay for benefits, such as local services, from which they benefit more than others (the benefit principle); and should have a high marginal tax rate with respect to short-term changes in income (automatic stabilisation).

No tax system can be ideal in the sense of fulfilling all these criteria perfectly. African tax systems, however, are particularly imperfect. Partly this is because African tax systems still reflect the political realities of the colonial period; partly it is because of the structure of African economies; partly it is because tax systems have been heavily influenced by taxes used in industrialised economies. Some examples should make this clear.

One of the first taxes used in Africa was the poll or hut tax. The official justification for this tax was to make Africans contribute to the cost of administering their affairs; the real reason for imposing it was to force Africans to work on European-owned farms and mines in order to earn the money to pay the tax. The poll tax took no account of differing ability to pay, nor of the effect on agricultural production of men being absent from their homes, nor of the social costs of migrant labour, nor of the injustice of making relatively very poor people pay for government services, nor of the inequitable distribution of government services, nor of the political injustice of imposing taxes on people who had no representation.

Mining company taxation has been a curious mixture of history, convenience and the distribution of bargaining power between foreign mining companies and African governments. For example, royalty on Zambian copper-mining companies was paid to a foreign company until 1964, even though that company's claim to the mining rights was very doubtful. What is more, the royalty was based on production rather than on profits, so that even after it began to be paid to the Zambian government it continued to discourage the mining of low-grade ores, and discouraged production in high-cost but basically profitable mines. The export tax introduced in Zambia in 1966 was successful in capturing a bigger proportion of the very high profits from a high copper price, but was also a disincentive to produce and invest. There were other things wrong with the system of taxing copper in Zambia before 51% government participation in 1969; the point is that the taxes were a combination of history and convenience (they were very easy to collect) but ignored incentive effects.[1]

Income taxation in English-speaking Africa reflects both political power and the influence of the British income tax system. A comparison of African income tax systems in 1968 showed that white-dominated South Africa had the least burdensome income tax.[2] This is because income tax bears more heavily on the better-off while taxes on goods and services bear more heavily on the poor, in relation to their incomes. The 'allowances' in many income tax systems are ill-adapted to African conditions. Thus deductions (allowances) are subtracted from salaries for a wife and children, before applying income tax rates. This is intended to make the income tax more equitable, by allowing for the expense of maintaining a family. But in Africa a man with a high-income job is responsible for other members of his family as well. The allowances therefore tend to make the system less rather than more equitable by reducing the tax payable by a man supporting his wife and children but not reducing the tax payable by a man supporting his brothers, sisters, nephews, nieces, parents, grandparents, etc. Furthermore, the allowances are worth more the higher is the man's income and are worth nothing at all to those whose incomes are too low to pay income tax. It would be possible to make the income tax much simpler, and thus much easier to administer, by abolishing allowances without making it less equitable– indeed a simpler income tax would be more equitable. Ghana and Tanzania, for example, have done this.

Tax systems tend to be biased against the use of labour and in favour of the use of other inputs, especially capital. Allowances in the company tax based on capital spending make capital cheaper,[3] as do low tariffs on imported goods and on other imported inputs. High tariffs on consumer goods tend to increase the cost of labour (since they are bought by wage-earners). Compulsory contributions to provident funds are effectively a tax on labour, thus raising its cost. One should add that low interest rates and overvalued exchange rates also reduce the cost of capital. The overall result is to reduce the rate of growth of employment, by violating the neutrality principle. That is, the tax system interferes in the allocation of resources in the wrong direction. Interference may be justified but it should make (plentiful) labour cheaper and (scarce, expensive, imported) capital more expensive. There are many other factors pushing African economies into using capital-intensive techniques, some of which may be outside the government's control. It may be that the tax system is not the most important factor; but it is something that the government *can* change, so that it is clearly unnecessary for it to be creating the wrong incentive effects.

The taxation effect of marketing boards, which offer a stable price to farmers, while export prices fluctuate, has already been discussed (chapter 11, section 5). It is also common for agricultural exports to be taxed, thus creating an incentive for farmers to produce other products, for the home market. Even where there are no possibilities for avoiding the tax in this way, a tax based on production is inequitable because it bears more heavily on the smaller producer and because it taxes the exporter but no other producers.[4]

These examples cover some of the major types of tax in Africa, suggesting that extensive tax reform is required. But while it is easy to be critical, it is very difficult to devise a better tax system. The next section tries to explain why.

3 *The application of theory*

Horizontal and vertical equity, or ability-to-pay, would suggest an income tax. Income, if all sources of income could be properly measured and included in the assessments, is the best single measure of individual ability to pay. People with the same income should pay the same amount of tax; and people with high incomes should pay more than people with low incomes.

In principle, an income tax should be backed by a tax on assets (for example, a wealth tax). The latter is necessary because otherwise people with assets which do not yield any (or very much) monetary income–such as owner-occupied houses, under-utilised land–would excape taxation. In addition, people spending more than their incomes by running down their capital would be making large demands on society's output, but not paying tax appropriate to that high level of consumption.[5] Alternatively the 'yield' from such assets should be estimated in some way, added to monetary income and taxed. In practice this is seldom done, mainly because of the heavy administrative task of valuing assets or estimating their yield. In Africa, the need to tax capital (wealth) is not as great as in developed economies, simply because less personal wealth has been accumulated.

There are a number of reasons, however, why it is not possible to rely heavily on an income tax, with or without a wealth tax to back it up. The idea of finding out each person's income, and then taxing it on some agreed scale, is attractively simple. But in practice it turns out to be very difficult, even in industrial economies where most people get most of their income from wages and other easily identified sources.

In the first place, if all of a government's revenue had to derive from income taxation, tax *rates* would have to be very high. The higher is the tax rate, the greater is the incentive to avoid paying tax. As a result, rich men and profitable companies find it worthwhile to devote more energy to reducing the amount of tax they pay, than to earning more income. The government is then forced to counter with more highly paid lawyers, policemen, etc. The end result is that a significant proportion of the country's most able and highly-trained people are occupied in the tax fight: lawyers, legislators amending the law, accountants, judges hearing tax cases, and so on. This is very wasteful.

Secondly, the first problem is made much worse by the complications that are introduced into income tax systems in an attempt to make them more equitable. It is true that people with the same income may have different tax-paying capacity. As already noted in the previous section, one complication introduced in industrial economies is to reduce people's liability to income tax according to whether they are supporting a spouse and children. Other income tax deductions have been introduced at one time or another in order to encourage something that seems desirable, or in response to energetic political lobbying: for example for life insurance premiums, educational or health expenditures, the cost of borrowing money for buying a house, and many others. While it is relatively easy to persuade governments to make such concessions, it is much harder for government to remove them. So income tax systems tend to get more complicated over time. The same is true of taxation of company profits. The more complicated is the tax system, the greater is the scope for dispute over how much each company should pay.

Thirdly, it is much cheaper to collect income tax from a person who earns income in the form of wages, than from the self-employed. One main reason is that the self-employed person is, quite rightly, allowed to deduct the expenses incurred in earning income before arriving at the amount of income liable to income or profits tax. So the farmer must be allowed to deduct the cost of seed, fuel, fertiliser and farm workers' wages from the revenue he receives from selling his farm products; the trader must be allowed to deduct the cost of goods bought (and other expenses) from the cost of goods sold; and so on. The problem arises from the fact that the self-employed person can sometimes claim that personal expenses are business expenses, thus reducing his tax bill. For example a farmer or trader can claim that the cost of running a vehicle is a business expense, while using it partially for private purposes. An employed person normally has no such opportunity. Furthermore, the employed person usually has tax deducted from wages before they are paid to him or her; the self-employed person, on the other hand, often receives income from a variety of sources, much of it in cash, that is very much more difficult for the tax authorities to trace.

As a result, income taxation tends to be unequal in its impact as between employed and self-employed people. This unfairness is greatly increased in Africa, where relatively few people are employed, and a relatively large number of people are self-employed.

A fourth problem in Africa is that income taxation requires an adequate supply of literate and numerate administrators, and literate and numerate taxpayers. Yet both are in short supply in Africa. Tax departments tend to be seriously undermanned; and many small-scale but prosperous businessmen keep no books – some are even illiterate. For example 'Nswima kept the store open from 6.00 am. to 8 pm. and half a day on Sunday. He could neither read nor write, nor did he use any method of book-keeping. He simply remembered prices and quantities. . . We found that Nswima netted K680 a month profit from his business, a figure much higher than any observer in Zambia thought possible'.[6] The source does not specify, but he probably paid no income tax. Certainly it would have been very difficult for the income tax department to find out his income, since such a man would have tremendous scope for concealing his income and for treating personal expenses as business costs and so reducing his tax.

Some improvements can be suggested. If the personal income tax were simplified, getting rid of the rich-country complications, more administrative time could be devoted to the really difficult task of taxing businesses. Even small businesses without accounts can be taxed by quite simple methods – high rule-of-thumb estimates (based on spot checks of stocks, for example) can be used for assessing tax, throwing the burden on the taxpaper to prove his tax liability is less. But the higher are tax rates (because of heavy reliance on income taxation) the more the system will not be fair, nor be seen to be fair. Furthermore, the incentive to corrupt and the scope for corruption increases the higher are taxes and the more flexible are the rules (the greater the discretion given to the tax officer, the easier it is for him to bend the rules in response to a bribe without being found out).

Nor surprisingly then, in view of this analysis, African governments have relied on ease of collection more than on abstract principles of equity. Poll taxes apart (where the cost and difficulty of collection was considered worthwhile in order to increase the supply of labour) exports and imports are the obvious candidates for taxation. Most countries have only a few ports, border-crossing points and international airports so that it is quite easy to 'catch' the goods for taxation.[7] Furthermore, international trade tends to be in the hands of a relatively small number of large-scale businesses – as opposed to internal trade with its multitude of small-scale operators. International trade was in fact the way in which monetary transactions first penetrated African economies on a large scale, so it was the obvious candidate for taxation.

Export taxes on commodities are very certain in their 'incidence', that is, they cannot normally be 'shifted'.[8] Almost all African commodity exports (except oil and possibly cashew nuts and cloves from Zanzibar) are sold at a world price over which individual countries have no influence; so there is no question of forcing prices up to uncompetitive levels, although there is a danger that high rates of tax may encourage some producers to switch to other products. Most export producers have little choice but to accept lower incomes because of taxation, in the short run. In the long run, the value to the economy of export taxes depends on whether governments or exporters invest more out of the proceeds and how productive such investments are.

Import duties serve the double purpose of raising revenue for governments and protecting local industry from competition. Their incidence is partly on importers because demand is reduced, and partly on consumers who pay higher prices. As African economies develop import-substituting industry, the structure of imports shifts away from consumer goods to intermediate and investment goods which are taxed less. Governments have tended to be slow to tax most domestic products, however, precisely because these products need protection from overseas competition. Favourite candidates for taxation are 'demerit' goods–mainly alcohol and tobacco. These have the advantage of fairly inelastic demand–people go on buying when the price is increased by taxation–but the disadvantage of being regressive (they bear disproportionately on poor people) and encouraging illegal production (shebeens). Ministers of finance can also find themselves in the dilemma of wishing to discourage drinking and smoking but being very dependent for revenue on alcohol and tobacco taxes.

4 *Taxation of foreign firms*

There are a number of special problems relating to the taxation of foreign firms. Firstly, they have opportunities for shifting their profits to other countries and so avoiding taxation. For example, if a firm is assembling locally intermediate goods supplied by the same firm in another country, it can pay artificially high prices for the inputs, thus reducing its local profits and increasing its profits overseas. This practice, known as transfer pricing, can also occur where firms are not associated, if they agree to collude. Exporters can also undercharge for goods supplied to firms overseas, with the same effect. Transfer pricing can also be used to avoid local exchange control rules on the remission abroad of profits. High rates of profits tax increase the incentive to use transfer pricing as do severe constraints on profit remission.

As far as tax is concerned, African countries can do three things about transfer pricing. Firstly, if local tax rates are no higher than rates in the foreign investors' countries of origin then there is no incentive to avoid local taxation. Secondly, governments can negotiate double taxation agreements, whereby they agree that taxes paid in Africa are offset against, say, British tax liability, so that again the firm has no incentive to avoid local taxation.[9] Thirdly, governments can try to secure better information on what international trading prices ought to be, in order to prevent transfer pricing. This is extremely difficult, time-consuming and expensive to do (and sometimes impossible) but nevertheless worth trying. It is almost certainly a situation in which African governments could usefully combine.

Some companies have much fewer opportunities to use transfer pricing than others. For example most mining companies sell their output at a published world price; and generally are horizontally rather than vertically integrated. That is, they have mining enterprises in other parts of the world but are not in general in the business of supplying mining inputs. Firms assembling imported inputs are at the other extreme. Clearly there is an added reason here for encouraging the development of local supplies of inputs as fast as possible.

Another way in which foreign firms can avoid local taxation is by borrowing money from abroad rather than using equity capital (direct investment in the firm). Under 'normal' (that is, foreign-type) tax laws, interest on loans counts as a cost and is deducted from profits before tax is paid. Interest on foreign loans may thus leave the country free of tax. The return to direct investment is in the form of profits, which are taxed. For this reason many African governments have introduced a withholding tax on interest payments on foreign borrowing. This is an imperfect solution, since withholding taxes are at a lower rate than profits taxes and the rate of interest may simply be increased on future loans to offset the tax. Nevertheless, a withholding tax is a step in the right direction. Similar measures are necessary for management fees, licensing payments and other ways of getting money out of the country labelled as costs when they are partly disguised profits.

A second problem is that new foreign investors, that is firms looking to invest in a country for the first time, are frequently offered tax concessions. The commonest of these is a tax holiday–by which is meant that no tax need be paid on profits for the period of the holiday. As explained in chapter 7, section 3, this type of concession is based on a mistaken theory of investment. Most foreign investors are not simply looking for opportunities to make a profit on their local production.

Moreover African countries tend to compete in offering tax concessions to international investors. This reduces taxation all round, without in the end inducing much additional investment.

Thus if an investor is trying to protect or increase his market share by setting up locally, or to make a profit on the sale of machinery or inputs, then tax concessions will add to his profits but not affect his investment decision very much. Furthermore, if profit on local production is determined by such factors as the degree of protection, price control, monopoly powers granted, etc., then tax concessions become merely a part of the bargaining between the investor and the government, and not necessarily the most important part. So the investor who actually needs to make a profit on his local operation (as opposed to making a profit out of some other part of the operation) is primarily concerned to secure guarantees of profitability and permission to remit. At the extreme, if tax concessions are not granted he will simply try to rearrange other concessions to compensate. Most fundamentally of all, many foreign investors are not going to be interested in investing in what they see as small, remote, unstable countries, liable to expropriate investments and prevent remission of profits at any moment, unless they have some other motive than simply a 'normal' rate of return on local production. The only possible exception to this in Africa is Nigeria which is large and, since the oil boom, relatively rich.

A third problem is that mining companies, which have accounted historically for the bulk of foreign investment in Africa, can make exceptionally high profits. This happens, for example, if an orebody turns out to be much richer than originally expected, or if mineral prices rise much faster than mining costs. Such profit bonanzas tend in the long run to result in renegotiation of mining taxation agreements, but not before the mining company has enjoyed a period of very high after-tax profits. Increasingly, therefore, African governments try to build into mining taxation agreements, from the beginning, high marginal tax rates on higher-than-expected profits.[10]

Another way of taxing multinational companies has recently been tried, mainly by individual states in the USA, led by California. In order to tax a reasonable share of the profits of multinational companies, 'unitary taxation' simply declares that a proportion of the company's world-wide profits shall be deemed to have arisen locally, for taxation purposes, the proportion being calculated on the basis of the local share of assets, or employment, or sales, or some other measure. Developing countries could do the same. The risk, however, would be that companies would choose not to invest in countries imposing unitary taxation, so that short-term gains in tax revenue could be offset by long-term losses of international investment.

5 Rural taxation

Most direct taxes reduce income and so give people an incentive to work more and restore their income: this is the 'income effect'. Income taxes also reduce the marginal return to extra work, and so give people an incentive to work less, by substituting leisure for work: the 'substitution effect'. The substitution effect can also be described by saying that an income tax cuts the cost of leisure (by reducing the amount of income forgone in not working) and so induces people to 'consume' more leisure. The poll tax had an income effect, inducing people to work in order to earn income and pay the tax; but had no substitution effect because additional work and income-earning did not attract additional income tax.

The Uganda tax on rural income had a similar effect in a rather more sophisticated way.[11] Essentially it assessed the income-earning *potential* of a farmer's assets—acres of various crops, coffee trees, stores, cattle, etc.—and levied a tax on that basis. This sort of tax reduces income and thus has an income effect; there is no substitution effect because tax liability does not rise with income. A tax based on land value is similar in effect if land value (and thus tax payable) is not affected by short-term changes in yield. Land taxes are impractical in much of Africa, because land is not easily valued. Either there is no market in land at all, or the administrative task of valuation is too much for local resources. Furthermore, if such a tax is to give an increasing yield as productivity grows (that is, if it is to be income-elastic), then revaluations must be fairly frequent. An interesting variation has been proposed in India where tax liability would be based on the average value of crops grown in the previous ten years. This proposal has the advantage of continuous upward revision of tax liability in response to growth at the same time as not penalising success in the short term; that is, an income effect and some income elasticity but no substitution effect.[12]

Clearly the Uganda type of tax can (and should) also adapt to rising income. It is quite likely to do so if it is raised and spent within a localised level of government. There is a strong case anyway for devolving some tax-raising responsibility onto local authorities: taxpayers, especially rather unsophisticated taxpayers, are more likely to pay up if the proceeds are spent locally, and can be seen and appreciated. There is thus a case for locally-based agricultural taxation even in countries with adequate central revenues, in order to encourage production and local participation in development. It is difficult to involve people in development except as individual producers if both money and decisions are perceived to come ultimately from the centre. Although the urban wealth of some African countries, such as

Botswana and Zambia, makes it impossible to think of raising as much from a local tax as from the central 'Western' type of income tax (as was at one time the case in Uganda), enough money could be raised to make a significant contribution at the local level.[13]

It is also argued that locally-provided benefits should be paid for locally rather than by taxpayers generally. For example, local street lighting mainly benefits local people and so should be paid for by them—the benefit principle. If carried too far, however, this principle would perpetuate and make worse existing inequalities between different parts of a country.

6 *Economic efficiency*

Economic efficiency refers to the effect of taxes on aggregate demand. A tax is 'efficient' if it reduces private sector spending by the full amount of the tax collected: it is inefficient if a large part of the tax is paid out of money that would not have been spent domestically. For example, a tax on low-wage earners is likely to reduce consumption by the full amount of the tax since such people have little or nothing in the way of savings; a tax on high-income salary earners is likely to be paid partly out of savings with only a relatively small impact on consumption. Of course if a government wishes to run a surplus and pay off its debts without reducing aggregate demand very much, it may choose an 'inefficient' tax.

In general, the economic efficiency of a tax depends on the propensity to spend locally of the person or institution which actually bears the burden of the tax. At one extreme, increases in the rate of tax on a foreign-owned mine have almost no short-term impact on demand within the local economy. The company cannot shift the tax onto international mineral exports, because Africa's mineral export prices are determined in international markets. The incidence of the tax is thus on mining profits. The short-term effect is to alter one or more of government revenues, profits remitted abroad and profits retained in the African economy, with almost no effect on demand. Any long-term effect will be on the propensity to invest because of the reduced after-tax profitability of the industry.[14]

At the other extreme, increases in income tax on medium-income taxpayers (who save very little) or increases in the tax on beer which is bought by urban wage-earners (who save very little and tend to reduce their consumption of other items if the beer price goes up) are extremely efficient in reducing domestic demand.

Somewhere in between is an increase in income tax on high-income salary earners, who are able to maintain part of their consumption out of savings. If a lot of them are foreigners, they may manage to secure salary increases, thus shifting the tax on to their employers and offsetting the immediate impact of the tax on demand. Another intermediate tax increase would be one on luxury consumption items for which demand is sensitive to price. Thus if the tax on luxury consumer durables is increased this will reduce demand for them (thus shifting the incidence onto producers and their employees) and will also be paid partly out of the savings of the high-income buyers of luxuries. Insofar as many luxuries are imported, reduction in demand for them will bear partly on distributors and partly on overseas producers.

A second consideration in choosing between types of tax to change is the political impact on the one hand and the dangers of cost inflation on the other. If people are more aware of direct taxes on their incomes then they are more likely to object to an increase, but indirect taxes are usually added directly to prices (although they can sometimes be absorbed by, that is shifted on to, producers) and so may start off a cost inflation.

The dangers of political reaction and cost inflation are both reduced if tax increases are small. People, whether as voters or as wage-earners, are much more likely to react to big increases in tax. This suggests a strategy of tax reform, namely that even when major tax reforms are very desirable, the government should move only gradually towards the ideal system unless a major crisis offers an opportunity for a major shift. This is important even if the government does not wish to alter the total amount of tax, but merely wishes to shift the burden between groups. It is also politically important to combine tax increases with well-publicised increases in relatively popular forms of government spending (education, health, housing) rather than relatively unpopular ones (defence, central administration). It is thus vital that even quite small tax changes be made as part of a long-term strategy of tax reform, rather than being made hastily and without thought, in response to immediate needs and opportunities.

7 *Tax expectations*

The effects of a tax change which is expected to be permanent and of one which is expected to be temporary can be quite different. For example, if the government announced a temporary sales tax for one year, people would postpone as many purchases as they comfortably could in order to be able to buy at lower prices once the tax was removed. As a result even quite a small tax increase could have a very large effect on consumption. This way of reducing consumption is clearly particularly useful in a temporary crisis, where resources have to be diverted to output of non-consumption goods, such as armaments or new transport routes in a landlocked country. A government using this technique must expect to be able to produce additional consumption goods at some time in the near future since demand is only postponed.

In contrast, an increase in income tax that was believed to be temporary would be less effective than one that was believed to be permanent, since people would not bother to readjust their normal consumption patterns for a short period only. A tax surcharge will increasingly appear to taxpayers to be permanent the longer it is continued, so consumption will be reduced over time both for this reason and because people begin to run out of savings and credit out of which to maintain consumption.

Expectations also affect the speed with which tax changes can be implemented. Delays can be considerable because tax changes often take time to legislate for and introduce administratively. Many taxes are also paid in arrears. However, indirect taxes can usually be increased instantly, so that even if the increased revenues do not immediately flow to the government, consumers face higher prices with only a small time-lag. Furthermore, even those tax changes, such as in the income tax, which take a lot of time to implement can have an immediate impact on spending if taxpayers start saving for future tax liabilities.

8 *Financing a deficit–domestic sources*

If government spends more than it collects in tax, it has a budget deficit which must be financed. Some money simply accrues to the government as the economy expands. Thus the public's holdings of currency increase and this amounts to a loan to the government.[15] Furthermore as the economy expands, banks and other financial institutions need liquid assets–that is, somewhere to invest their money where it can be quickly recovered when needed. The need of commercial banks for such assets has already been discussed; in their case, the government actually enforces the holding of government debt by legislating for liquidity ratios which exclude other types of investment (except bills of exchange).

Other financial institutions, such as insurance companies, provident funds and so on, also require liquid investments–in Africa, government debt is very often the only possibility within the country. In colonial times financial institutions (including banks) invested in liquid assets in places like London, but independent governments have tried to end this practice in two main ways: firstly by providing government debt in which to invest, secondly by legislating that local institutions must have some or all of their investments in local assets.

There is thus a fairly steady flow of lending to the government as the monetary economy expands. Typically, however, there is very little domestic borrowing by African governments from individuals, who hold almost no stock or Treasury Bills.[16] Individual investment is indirect, via financial institutions. Deposits in government savings banks (such as Post Office Savings Banks) are virtually all invested in government debt[17]; deposits in building societies and commercial banks, compulsory savings with pension funds, are partly lent or invested in the private sector and partly lent to the government.

Governments do try to encourage individuals to lend money to the public sector. At times quite a lot of money, political energy and administrative time is devoted to 'savings campaigns'. The official justification is twofold: to restrain consumption and to 'put people's savings to work'.

There is very little evidence that savings campaigns have any impact on aggregate consumption, which is largely determined by income (as discussed at length in chapter 4). Some savings may be switched from other savings media (for example from commercial bank savings deposit accounts and building societies) but this does not add to aggregate savings.

If savings are switched from notes and coin buried in the ground or hidden under the bed, to savings accounts, then the individual gains by receiving interest (although he loses liquidity) but again aggregate savings are unaffected. Meanwhile the government pays interest on its debt instead of receiving an interest-free loan, which is what the hoarding of currency amounts to in practice. Governments also press commercial banks to open more branches, especially in the rural areas, to encourage saving and to 'put idle money to work'. If in fact people switch their savings from currency to bank deposits, command over resources is shifted from the government to those who borrow from banks. This only helps the economy to the extent that banks make better use of resources than the government.[18]

In practice, savings campaigns are usually used as an excuse for not cutting expenditure or raising taxes, both of which are unpopular. Their true justification should not be as a short-term policy of restraining consumption, but as a long-term policy of educating people in self-reliance. The amount actually available to African governments from Post Office Savings Banks and similar institutions is normally very small anyway.

There are thus two ways in which an African government can try to finance more of its deficit by domestic borrowing: firstly by offering a higher rate of interest on government debt than is available from competing private-sector financial institutions, secondly by forcing financial institutions to hold more government debt. If the commercial banks are forced to hold more government debt this tends to be inflationary, as explained in section 5 of the Appendix to chapter 8. If the deficit is financed by the central bank, it is money-creation, not borrowing, and is highly inflationary unless the domestic economy has spare capacity.[19] If the commercial banks can be prevented from using the additional liquidity created, then the inflationary impact is reduced; this really comes back to forcing the commercial banks to hold government debt instead of lending to the private sector. Forcing insurance companies, say, to hold more government debt transfers resources from the private or parastatal sector to the government.

Financing a deficit by money creation via the central bank need not be inflationary if the excess demand created can be satisfied by allowing imports to increase. But this requires either that the government has adequate foreign exchange reserves and is prepared to use them, or that the government has other sources of foreign exchange. These are dealt with in the next section.

9 *Financing a deficit–foreign sources*

Governments can borrow from abroad, thus using savings from some other economy, or they can use up foreign reserves. There is also aid. Most aid is in fact borrowing on concessionary terms ('soft loans'), the difference between concessionary and commercial terms being the aid element. A small amount of aid is in the form of grants, with no interest or repayment obligations.

Both soft loans and grants tend to have conditions attached, both political and economic. These conditions (or 'strings') can make the aid much less valuable than it at first appears: for example, if a loan is 'tied' to purchases from the lending country whose prices are higher than those of other countries, then the borrowing country could be better off with a commercial loan and freedom to buy at cheaper prices. In addition, both bilateral and multilateral aid donors[20] tend to interfere in local decision-making, by deciding which projects they will finance, and by demanding changes in their chosen projects. Such interference can lead to long delays in negotiating loans[21].

African countries also borrowed rapidly-increasing amounts of money in the 1970s from suppliers and private banks. These 'hard' loans were very much more expensive in terms of interest, short or non-existent grace periods (the number of years before capital repayments have to begin), and relatively short repayment periods. For example, the annual debt service (the cost of interest and capital repayments) on a 25-year loan of $10 million at 3% interest, repayable in equal annual instalments of interest and capital combined, is £0.6 million a year. The cost of debt service on a 7-year loan of $10 million from a consortium of banks operating in the eurodollar market[22], with an effective rate of interest of 12%, is $2.2 million a year, more than three-and-a-half times as much as the soft loan of the same amount. Furthermore, the interest rate on most eurodollar loans can vary during the life of the loan, so that the borrower does not know in advance how much debt service will have to be paid. Interest rates varied enormously in the 1970s and early 1980s, from 7% or 8% to over 20%. The main advantages of commercial loans are that they are not tied to purchases in any one country, the degree of interference by lenders is usually much less than for soft loans, and commercial loans can usually be arranged very quickly, provided that the borrower is considered creditworthy by the banks.

Table 12.1 External debt outstanding in Sub-Saharan Africa

	1970	*1979*	*$ billion*
Bilateral	2.3	8.5	
Official export credits[a]	0.3	2.2	
Multilateral	0.8	6.6	
Private	2.2	14.5	
	5.6	31.8	

NOTE:
a Official export credits are provided mainly by the industrial countries for purchase of their exports, at rates of interest and periods of repayment slightly softer than commercial credits.

Source: World Bank, *Accelerated Development in Sub-Saharan Africa: an agenda for action* (Washington DC, 1981).

As can be seen from Table 12.1, African countries were forced to rely increasingly on more expensive commercial debt in the 1970s, greatly increasing the cost of debt service. With the exception of countries lucky enough to export oil (Angola, Congo, Nigeria, Gabon), debt service as a percentage of export earnings (the debt service ratio) doubled from 1970 to 1979 in African countries. The situation worsened further after 1979, as a result of the second big oil price increase and the prolonged world recession that followed. Many countries were forced to seek 'rescheduling' of their external debts, that is to ask their creditors for longer to pay.[23] While rescheduling does give some relief to the balance of payments, it also tends to make the borrowing country appear less creditworthy. As a result, the flow of new commercial credit may cease.[24]

Table 12.2 shows the big increase in African current account deficits after 1979, when the oil price rose sharply for the second time, and a prolonged world recession began which damaged African export earnings. Grants and long-term borrowing from official sources (aid) did not increase at all, even in money terms, and fell therefore in real terms as a result of inflation. So African oil-importers were forced into short-term borrowing from the IMF and from private sources, and into running down their foreign exchange reserves. There are obvious limits to running down reserves; and short-term private borrowing tended merely to postpone but not to prevent painful cutbacks in imports. Meanwhile, borrowing from the IMF also results in having to cut back demand in order to reduce the demand for imports. In these circumstances, many African countries were suffering from extreme shortages of imports, with factories working at low levels of capacity-utilisation and rising unemployment as a result.

Table 12.2 African oil-importers: current account financing, 1979–82 ($ billions)

	1979	*1980*	*1981*	*1982*
Current account deficit	6.5	9.4	18.6	16.3
Grants, etc.	3.8	4.6	4.9	4.5
Borrowing: Official sources	5.1	4.2	5.3	4.5
Private long-term	– 0.5	1.3	0.9	3.1
IMF, etc.	0.2	0.3	1.8	2.1
Other short-term	– 1.7	– 1.0	4.2	1.6
Use of reserves	– 0.4	—	1.5	0.5
Total financing	6.5	9.4	18.6	16.3

Source: IMF *World Economic Outlook*, 1983.

From the point of view of short-term management of the economy, foreign sources of finance do add to the resources available to government–but only by providing foreign exchange. They do not add to domestic resources. So if shortage of foreign exchange is preventing the government from spending, while at the same time there is spare capacity in the domestic economy so that domestic output can increase rapidly, then foreign finance does enable the government to spend more without creating excess demand. If, however, there is no spare capacity at home, foreign finance will not enable the government to spend more unless all the additional spending is on imports. In practice, most imports require matching domestic resources—skilled labour, transport, construction capacity, etc.

The distinction between government borrowing internally and externally is therefore as follows. Internal borrowing from non-bank sources means that resources are not available for use in the private sector. If private consumption is reduced as a result, then people are worse off, but this may be compensated by future increases in consumption (provided that the government invests successfully) or by increases in collective consumption through the provision of current government services. If private sector investment is reduced then people will be better off in the future if the government makes better use of the money than the private sector—and vice versa.

External borrowing enables additional consumption and investment to take place without any reduction in domestic consumption or investment. There is a risk, however, namely that in the future the payment of interest and repayment of the loan will have to be made out of resources that were not increased by the borrowing. Furthermore, repayment has to be made in foreign currency which may be scarce—for example if export prices are low.[25]

In other words, countries which borrow abroad run the risk of an external debt crisis, either through mismanagement of the funds borrowed, or because external circumstances make it difficult to maintain debt service. Such a crisis is likely to be worsened if expected capital inflows decrease suddenly by a large amount, *as a result of* the crisis itself. African countries find it hard enough to cope with increased import costs, or the need to increase import volumes (of food for example), or falls in export earnings; a sudden fall in capital inflows can make matters very much worse.

Debt crises seldom occur as a result of borrowing on concessional terms (soft loans). The big risks arise from expensive, short-term, commercial borrowing. Countries may be 'forced' into such dangerous borrowing, by the impossibility of reducing imports quickly enough to cope with a fall in export prices, for example; but several African countries have borrowed large amounts of expensive short-term, commercial money to fund long-term development projects, or projects with little prospect of increasing output by significant amounts (airports, for example), or have simply borrowed so much, so quickly, that the country's capacity to invest the money productively was inadequate. Ghana in the early 1960s and Zaire in the early 1970s are examples of the latter. On the other hand, Zambia, for example, managed to finance a large part of its balance of payments deficit in the period after 1975 by running up large 'payments arrears', that is, by simply delaying payment for imports. Even though the delay in paying for imports increased steadily in every year except one from 1975 to 1981, Zambia managed to avoid defaulting and debt rescheduling during that period. Suppliers continue to export to countries with payments arrears so long as payments continue to be made eventually, in order not to lose a useful market. However, willingness to continue supplying must put the suppliers in a position where they can easily charge high prices.[26]

It is sometimes argued that even internal borrowing imposes a burden on people in the future because of the interest payments (repayment of principal is usually out of new borrowing). The counter-argument is that interest on the internal debt is merely a transfer from one section of the community (taxpayers) to another (holders of the national debt). This argument is correct, but the process of payment is not costless–the collecting of taxes and paying of interest requires real resources and the additional taxes needed for this purpose may have additional distorting and disincentive effects of the sort already discussed. But these costs are typically very small; most of the real costs of domestic borrowing are met at the time when the borrowing takes place, when private-sector consumption and investment are reduced. The real costs of *foreign* borrowing are pushed forward to the time of interest-payment and repayment of principal (if this is not met from new borrowing). If national income has been increased by the spending of the foreign borrowing then this cost should be easily met. In practice, as mentioned already, foreign exchange may be scarce when payments have to be made.

Is there a real burden arising from foreign borrowing if it is never actually repaid, but continues to increase indefinitely? There *is* a real burden to the extent that interest payments are higher than the rate of inflation of export prices; and there is a hidden cost, in that the borrower must meet whatever conditions are imposed by lenders on an increasing amount of gross borrowing. Suppose, for example, that a borrowing country has $100 million of foreign debt to be repaid in a given year; it must borrow $110 in that year in order to get a net inflow of foreign capital of $10 million. So it must satisfy the lenders of $110 million of new loans, for the relatively small gain of $10 million new money. In any case, as already argued, African countries are not in the position of really big international borrowers like Brazil and Mexico, of being able to assume that their foreign debt can always be 'rolled over' in that way.

It has been argued that using foreign finance (loans, aid and foreign investment) reduces domestic saving. Statistical analysis has not on the whole clarified the debate on this point. It is not clear whether some countries borrow because they save very little, or save very little because they borrow abroad. One would expect some foreign finance to be used for current consumption since the objective is to optimise consumption patterns over time—and this includes current consumption. On the one hand it might seem reasonable in very poor countries, whose poverty makes it difficult to save, for them to borrow foreign savings in order to avoid the very painful effort to reduce domestic consumption and so increase domestic savings. On the other hand, relying on foreign finance creates economic and political dependence, which reduces future freedom of manoeuvre. Yet it is precisely the poorer countries that most need to use foreign finance. There is no way out of this dilemma.

10 Other ways of 'paying' for collective goods

Governments can commandeer resources—for example by making it compulsory for all young men (and women in a few countries) to serve in the armed forces or for all university students to do work in rural development. Although conscripts are paid, their income is less than would be required to get the same people to volunteer. The difference between the cost of volunteers and conscripts is the money value of the resources commandeered. Other examples are compulsory labour on public works and the use of prisoners as cheap labour.

Governments can confiscate assets (usually of foreigners) or take over assets with very little compensation, using their political power to pay less than the market price would be under 'free' conditions. Some governments even use the threat of force to induce 'gifts' from the rich—this method was used by English kings in the Middle Ages.

The surpluses (profits) of publicly-owned corporations are rather neglected as a source of revenue—the tendency is to hold their prices (and profits) down, because of the political unpopularity of high prices and profits in the public sector. Yet electricity supply to private houses, for example, is a luxury that can and perhaps ought to be 'taxed' as such in poor countries. It may be that politically it is more sensible to impose a tax rather than to impose a high price and make a big profit even if the financial result (a transfer from the private to the public sector) is the same.

Inflation can provide resources to the government by reducing the real value of privately-held money balances—as explained in chapter 9.

It has been argued that unemployed or under-employed labour is a resource that can be used to create more collective goods. For example, farmers with little to do at certain times of year can get together to improve roads and drainage systems, to build dams and clinics. However there is a limit to what can be produced with labour alone; if other resources are needed as well, then there is a problem of financing their purchase—whether they be skilled labour or tools.

If the government wants to employ surplus labour to produce collective goods, and pays cash wages, then the income of the workers will create demand for private consumption goods, which again must somehow be taxed away from others. It is thus quite difficult to use the resource available in the form of surplus labour unless the government has matching resources. It is clear, however, that the government's financial resources can be made to produce more if they are combined with surplus labour using labour-intensive methods to produce collective goods, than if this resource is neglected.

NOTES

1 For a more detailed analysis see chapter 6, 'Tax reform in the mining industry' in M. Bostock and C. Harvey, (eds,) *Economic Independence and Zambian Copper* New York, Praeger, 1972, or 'The system' in Charles Elliott, *Constraints on the Economic Development of Zambia* (Nairobi, OUP, 1971). The latter contains a description and critique of most of the tax system in Zambia in 1968.

2 Elliott, *op.cit.*, pp. 175–7.

3 Strictly speaking, there is only a bias if allowances over the life of an asset are greater than its cost or if allowances are especially generous in the early years. Both are very common, out of a desire to encourage investment.

4 An export tax is not inequitable if it merely recovers the extra money spent by government on services to exporters. In Botswana, for example, the government subsidises veterinary and other services to cattle farmers who sell mainly for export, so that a tax on beef exports is justified in order to recover these costs, quite apart from any case for taxing the richer cattle farmers on grounds of vertical equity. See Derek J. Hudson, 'The taxation of income from cattle farming', in Charles Harvey (ed.), *Papers on the Economy of Botswana* (London, Heinemann, 1981.)

5 For this reason, it has been suggested that taxation should be based on an individual's total expenditure rather than on his or her total income. See N. Kaldor, *An Expenditure Tax* (London, Allen and Unwin, 1955).

6 A.A. Beveridge and A.R. Oberschall, *African Businessmen and Development in Zambia* (Princeton University Press, 1979, pp. 92–93). K680 a month was about twice a university senior lecturer's salary at the time of the research in 1969.

7 This is not always true. Quite a lot of smuggling to avoid taxation occurs between some West African states. For example, some 12% of the Ghanaian cocoa crop was estimated to have been smuggled to neighbouring countries in 1970; see A. Kumar, 'Smuggling in Ghana', *Nigerian Journal of Economic and Social Studies*, July 1973.

8 Incidence refers to who actually bears the burden of a tax. Some taxpayers can shift the burden on to someone else, by raising the selling price, or in the case of an income tax by securing higher income from their employers.

9 In the case of ex-British colonies, double taxation agreements have frequently offered less advantage to African countries than provisions which already existed in British law. See *Tax Treaties Between Developed and Developing Countries* (UN

publication, Sales No. E69XV12), 5, 1969. The same argument applies to USA, Germany, Italy and France. For the Scandinavian countries a double taxation agreement is necessary.

10 Such a tax, originally called a 'resource rents tax', was proposed in R. Garnaut and A. Clunies Ross 'Uncertainty, risk aversion and the taxation of natural resources', *Economic Journal*, June 1975. It was actually adopted by, among others, the Papua New Guinea government, under the name of 'Additional Profits Tax (APT)', see C. Emerson, 'Mining enclaves and taxation', *World Development*, July 1982.

11 For a lengthier description see J.F. Due, *Taxation and Economic Development in East Africa*, Cambridge, Mass., MIT Press, 1963, chapter 5. This tax has now been abandoned in Uganda, but the same method is used in Tanzania.

12 See my paper, 'Agricultural taxation policy in Africa and the Raj report for India', IDS Discussion Paper No. 20, 1973.

13 It is possible though, that the theoretical incentive benefits would be less than the collection costs. It is also possible to localise decision-making without localising taxation.

14 If shortage of foreign exchange had been causing the government to restrain demand, then an increase in mining taxation might release that constraint, allowing demand to increase in the short term.

15 See chapter 9, section 3.

16 For example, the Bank of Zambia's *Quarterly Statistical Review* for June 1974 shows the results of an issue of stock in May 1974. The issue was of K10 mn. The commercial banks bought K3 mn, other financial institutions K2 mn and the 'household sector' a mere K24,000 (0.2%). The Bank of Zambia was left holding the remainder (just under K5 mn).

17 Although Botswana's Post Office Savings Bank lent (at least up to 1983) most of its depositors' money to the National Development Bank, which in turn lent it to the commercial banks. This unusual arrangement was no doubt a result of the Botswana government not needing to borrow locally at the time.

18 See R.C. Porter, 'The promotion of the "banking habit" and economic development', *Journal of Development Studies*, July 1966, Vol. 2, No. 4.

19 A small increase in borrowing from the central bank, roughly proportionate to income growth, is not inflationary, because of the need of commercial banks for additional balances at the central bank as deposits grow.

20 'Bilateral donors' are individual countries, such as the USA and France; 'multilateral donors' are such agencies as the World Bank, which accounts for more than half of all multilateral aid, the African Development Bank and the European Investment Bank.

21 For a detailed description of how to calculate the costs of 'soft' and 'hard' loans, how to compare them, and how to decide which type of loan is best suited to which type of project, see Charles Harvey, *Analysis of Project Finance in Developing Countries* (London, Heinemann, 1983).

22 Eurodollars are simply US dollar deposits with banks operating outside the USA, mainly in London, but also in an increasing number of other centres. These banks combine in syndicates to make loans to borrowers who include multinational companies and developing country governments. The market also operates in other currencies but more than 90% of loans to developing countries have been in US dollars.

23 See Chandra S. Hardy, *Rescheduling Developing Country Debts, 1956–81: lessons and recommendations* (Overseas Development Council, Washington DC, 1982). Sub-Saharan African countries to reschedule up to 1981 were Ghana (1966, 1968, 1970, 1974), Zaire (1976, 1977, 1979, 1981), Sierra Leone (1977, 1980), Gabon (1978), Sudan (1979), Togo (1979, 1981), Liberia (1980, 1981), Central African

Republic (1981), Madagascar (1981), Senegal (1981), Uganda (1981).

24 Some very large borrowers, notably Mexico and Brazil, were able to obtain new credits in 1982 and 1983, despite being unable to meet debt service on old credits. Mexico and Brazil were such large borrowers from international banks that their default would have threatened the world's banking system. So the IMF and major central banks brought pressure on the banks to increase their lending. African countries had not borrowed nearly as much and so were not in a position to demand similar treatment.

25 An additional risk of foreign borrowing is that it is virtually all *denominated* in foreign currency, so that if the currency borrowed *appreciates* against other currencies, the cost of repayment will be higher than it would otherwise be. It is also possible for the currency borrowed to *depreciate*, in which case debt service costs less than anticipated. It is impossible to predict which currencies will be strong and which will be weak, over the repayment period of a foreign loan, so the only policy possible to borrowing countries is to diversify as far as possible the currencies borrowed.

26 Other African countries to have used payment arrears as a way of financing a balance of payments deficit as of end 1981 included Ghana, Sierra Leone, Tanzania and Uganda; see *International Financial Statistics*.

Index